Java By Dissection

Java By Dissection

Ira Pohl

Charlie McDowell

University of California, Santa Cruz

 **ADDISON-WESLEY**

**Addison-Wesley is an imprint
of Addison Wesley Longman, Inc.**

Reading, Massachusetts ▪ Harlow, England
Menlo Park, California ▪ Berkeley, California
Don Mills, Ontario ▪ Sydney ▪ Bonn ▪ Amsterdam
Tokyo ▪ Mexico City

Acquisitions Editor: Maite Suarez-Rivas
Senior Acquisitions Editor: Susan Hartman
Senior Production Editor: Amy Rose
Editorial Assistant: Lisa Kalner
Composition: Northeast Compositors, Inc.
Project Management: Diane Freed Publishing Services, Inc.
Copyeditor: Jerry Moore
Proofreader: Karen Cakebread
Art source: Marita Froimson
Cover Designer: Diana Coe

Access the latest information about Addison-Wesley books from our World Wide Web site: http://www.awlonline.com

Many of the designations used by manufacturers and sellers to distinguish their products are claimed as trademarks. Where those designations appear in this book, and Addison Wesley Longman Inc. was aware of a trademark claim, the designations have been printed with initial capital letters or in all capitals.

The programs and applications presented in this book have been included for their instructional value. They have been tested with care, but are not guaranteed for any particular purpose. The publisher does not offer any warranties or representations, nor does it accept any liabilities with respect tot he programs or applications.

Library of Congress Cataloging-in-Publication Data

Pohl, Ira.
   Java by dissection : the essentials of Java programming / Ira
Pohl, Charlie McDowell.
     p.   cm.
   Includes bibliographical references.
   ISBN 0-201-61248-8
    1. Java (Computer program language)   I. McDowell, Charlie.
  II. Title.
  QA76.73.J38P66   2000
  005.7'2—DC21   99-33159
                                             CIP

ISBN 0-201-61248-8
1 2 3 4 5 6 7 8 9 10-MA-0302010099
First printing, October 1999

Contents

Preface

Java By Dissection is an introduction to programming in Java that assumes no prior programming experience. As such it thoroughly teaches modern programming techniques using Java. It shows how all the basic data types and control statements are used traditionally. It then progresses to the object-oriented features of the language and their importance to program design.

The second half of the book explains in detail much that is sophisticated about Java, such as its threading, graphical user interface (GUI), and file manipulation capabilities. The book is suitable as the primary text in an advanced programming course, or as a supplementary text in a course on data structures, software methodology, comparative languages, or other course in which the instructor wants Java to be the language of choice.

Java, invented at Sun Microsystems in the mid-1990s, is a powerful modern successor language to C and C++. Java, like C++, adds to C the object-oriented programming concepts of *class, inheritance,* and *run-time type binding.* The class mechanism provides user-defined types also called *abstract data types.* While sharing many syntactic features with C and C++, Java adds a number of improvements, including automatic memory reclamation called *garbage collection,* bounds checking on arrays, and strong typing. In addition, the standard Java libraries, called *packages* in Java, provide platform independent support for distributed programming, multi-threading, and graphical user interfaces.

Although Java shares many syntactic similarities to C, unlike C++, Java is not a superset of C. This has allowed the creators of Java to make a number of syntactic improvements that make Java a much safer programming language than C. As a result, Java is much better as a first programming language.

Java By Dissection begins with a classical programming style starting with programs as a simple sequence of instructions, then adding in control flow and functional abstraction.

After that comes arrays and data abstraction using classes, which can be covered in either order—arrays first, or data abstraction with classes first. Then comes the material on inheritance and graphical user interfaces. Again, the chapter on inheritance can be covered before or after the first chapter on graphical user interfaces. Finally come the advanced chapters. The following figure illustrates the flexibility in the order in which the material can be covered.

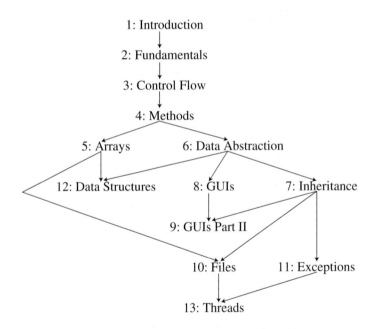

The book emphasizes working code. One or more programs particularly illustrative of the chapter's themes is analyzed by dissection, which is similar to a structured walk-through of the code. Dissection explains to the reader newly encountered programming elements and idioms.

Because Java includes a relatively easy-to-use, standard package for creating graphical user interfaces, it is possible to introduce the use of GUIs in a beginning programming book. Creating programs with GUIs is as fundamental today as being able to create nicely formatted text output. To fully understand the GUI packages in Java, it is necessary to have some understanding of OOP and inheritance. The main chapters on GUI building immediately follow the chapters on objects and inheritance. For those students interested in getting an early exposure to some of the graphical aspects of Java, we have provided a series of extended exercises at the end of the early chapters, which introduce GUIs and applets. These exercises provide templates for some simple applets, without providing complete explanations of some of the language features required.

The following summarizes the primary design features that are incorporated into this book.

Teaching by Example.   The book is a tutorial that stresses examples of working code. Right from the start the student is introduced to full working programs. Exercises are integrated with the examples to encourage experimentation. Excessive detail is avoided in explaining the larger elements of writing working code. Each chapter has several important example programs. Major elements of these programs are explained by dissection.

Object-Oriented Programming (OOP).   The reader is led gradually to an understanding of the object-oriented style. Objects as data values are introduced in Chapter 2. Chapter 6 shows how the programmer can benefit in important ways from Java and object-oriented programming. Object-oriented concepts are defined, and the way in which these concepts are supported by Java is introduced. Chapter 7 develops inheritance and dynamic method dispatch, two key elements in the OOP paradigm.

Terminal Input.   For an existing, widely used language, Java continues to lack support for simple terminal input. This either forces the student to build and use GUIs immediately, or to use cumbersome constructs from the standard I/O package. Going directly to GUIs requires the student to use many language features that they do not understand yet. Likewise, using the relatively powerful and flexible standard I/O package for simple input of text and numeric data requires the use of, as yet, unexplained language features. We have addressed this shortcoming by providing a package, `tio`, that supports simple input of numeric and text data, and simple formatted output. A complete listing of the package is included in Appendix C and the source is available electronically from the Addison-Wesley Web site. The main class in this package simplifies many common input processing needs and has been used in a number of real applications.

Data Structures in Java.   The text covers many of the standard data structures from computer science. Stacks, safe arrays, dynamically allocated multidimensional arrays, lists, and strings are all discussed. Exercises extend the student's understanding of how to implement and use these structures. Implementation is consistent with an abstract data type and object-oriented approach to software.

Graphical User Interfaces.   An important part of Java is its support for platform independent creation of graphical user interfaces and the web based programs called applets. In Chapters 8 and 9 we present a basic introduction to using the standard Java package Swing, for building GUIs. These chapters provide enough information to create useful and interesting applets and GUIs. A few additional GUI components are presented briefly in Appendix D. For students anxious to begin writing applets, simple applets are introduced in a series of exercises beginning in Chapter 2. These exercises are completely optional. The coverage of applets and GUIs in Chapters 8 and 9 does not depend upon the student having done or read the earlier applet exercises.

Threads. Multi-threaded programming is not usually discussed in a beginning text. However, some understanding of threads is essential for a true understanding of the workings of event driven GUI based programs. In addition, the authors feel that thread-based programming will become increasingly important at all levels of the programming curriculum. Threading is explained in Chapter 13, and used to introduce the reader to client/server computing. This book gives a treatment suitable to the beginning programmer that has mastered the topics in the preceding chapters.

Course-Tested. This book is the basis of courses given by the authors, who have used its contents to train students in various forums since 1997. The material is course-tested, and reflects the author's considerable teaching and consulting experience.

Code Examples. All the major pieces of code were tested. A consistent and proper coding style is adopted from the beginning and is one chosen by professionals in the Java community. The code is available at the Addison Wesley Longman Web site `ftp://ftp.awl.com/cseng/authors/pohl-mcdowell`.

Exercises. The exercises test and often advance the student's knowledge of the language. Many are intended to be done interactively while reading the text, encouraging self-paced instruction.

Web site. The examples both within the book and at Addison-Wesley's Web site are intended to exhibit good programming style. The Addison-Wesley Web site for this book contains the programs in the book as well as adjunct programs that illustrate points made in the book.

Course use:

- The book can be used as a basic first programming course, similar in scope to courses that used C, Pascal, or C++. Chapters 1 through 8 cover such a curriculum.

- The book can be used as a second or advanced course covering object-oriented programming.

- Chapters 2 through 5 can be skimmed by anyone already familiar with a procedural programming language such as C or Pascal.

- A programmer already familiar with OOP concepts could also skim chapters 6 and 7.

- Chapters 8 through 13 provide a mix of interesting advanced topics, not generally covered in a beginning programming course. In a beginning course, the instructor can use `tio` and take a conventional text input/output approach, or by assigning the optional applet based exercises, beginning in Chapter 2, students can be introduced immediately to using applets.

Acknowledgments

Our special thanks go to Debra Dolsberry and Linda Werner for their encouragement and careful reading and suggestions for improvement. Debra was especially helpful with typesetting issues. Our student Sarah Berner was an important contributor to the effectiveness of the text and especially helpful in converting many examples and exercises over to SWING. Additional reviewers who provided helpful suggestions include:

Massoud Ghyam	University of Southern California
Titus Purdin	University of Arizona
Brahma Dathan	St. Cloud State University
Stan Lipson	Kean University
Arthur Chou	Clark University
Hugh McGuire	University of California at Santa Barbara
Ray Lischner	Oregon State University
Evelyn Stiller	Plymouth State College
Jennifer Sedelmeyer	Broome Community College

In addition we would like to thank our AWL editorial team Susan Hartman and Maite Suarez-Rivas for their careful attention to the production of this book.

Charlie McDowell and Ira Pohl
University of California, Santa Cruz

1

Introduction

Java is the first major programming language to be shaped by the World Wide Web (the Web). Java allows you to do traditional programming. Java also has many special features and libraries that allow you conveniently to write programs that can use the Web's resources. These include extensive support for graphical user interfaces, the ability to embed a Java program in a Web document, easy communication with other computers around the world, and the ability to write programs that run in parallel or on several computers at the same time.

In this chapter we give an overview of how to solve a problem on a computer. In this process, you must first construct a recipe for solving the problem. Then you must convert the recipe into a detailed set of steps that the computer can follow. Finally, you must use a programming language, such as Java, to express the steps in a form "understandable" by the computer. The Java form of the solution is then translated by a program called a compiler into the low-level operations that the computer hardware can follow directly.

We then discuss why Java is creating such a fuss in the computing world. In general terms, we explain the importance of computing on the Web and the character of the graphical user interfaces, or GUIs, that are partly behind the switch to Java.

Throughout this text we feature carefully described examples, many of which are complete programs. We often dissect them, allowing you to see in detail how each Java programming construct works. Topics introduced in this chapter are presented again in later chapters, with more detailed explanations. The code and examples are meant to convey the flavor of how to program. You should not be concerned about understanding the details of the examples. They are given in the spirit of providing an overview. If you are already familiar with what a program is and want to start immediately on the nitty-gritty of Java programming, you may skip or scan this chapter.

1.1 RECIPES

Computer programs are detailed lists of instructions for performing a specific task or for solving a particular type of problem. Programlike instruction lists, sometimes called *algorithms*, for problem solving and task performance are commonly found in everyday situations. Examples include detailed instructions for knitting a sweater, making a dress, cooking a favorite meal, registering for classes at a university, traveling from one destination to another, and using a vending machine. Examining one of these examples is instructive.

Consider this recipe for preparing a meat roast:

> Sprinkle the roast with salt and pepper. Insert a meat thermometer and place in oven preheated to 150 °C. Cook until the thermometer registers 80 °C–85 °C. Serve roast with gravy prepared from either meat stock or from pan drippings if there is a sufficient amount.

The recipe is typically imprecise—what does "sprinkle" mean, where is the thermometer to be inserted, and what is a "sufficient amount" of pan drippings?

However, the recipe can be formulated more precisely as a list of instructions by taking some liberties and reading "between the lines."

COOKING A ROAST

1. Sprinkle roast with 1/8 teaspoon salt and pepper.
2. Turn oven on to 150° C.
3. Insert meat thermometer into center of roast.
4. Wait a few minutes.
5. If oven does not yet register 150° C, go back to step 4.
6. Place roast in oven.
7. Wait a few minutes.
8. Check meat thermometer. If temperature is less than 80° C, go back to step 7.
9. Remove roast from oven.
10. If there is at least 1/2 cup of pan drippings, go to step 12.
11. Prepare gravy from meat stock and go to step 13.
12. Prepare gravy from pan drippings.
13. Serve roast with gravy.

These steps comprise three categories of instructions and activities—those that involve manipulating or changing the ingredients or equipment, those that just examine or test the "state" of the system, and those that transfer to the next step. Steps 1 and 6 are examples of the first category; the temperature test in step 8 and the pan dripping test in step 10 are instances of the second category; and the transfers in steps 5 and 8 ("go to step *x*") are examples of the last category.

By using suitable graphical symbols for each of these categories, a simple two-dimensional representation of our cooking algorithm can be obtained, as shown in the following illustration.

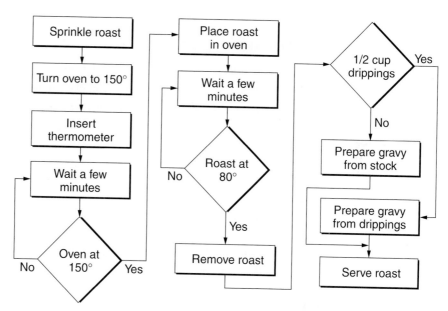

Such a figure is called a *flowchart*. To perform the program (prepare the roast), just follow the arrows and the instructions in each box. The manipulation activities are contained in rectangles, the tests are shown in diamonds, and the transfer or flow of control is determined by the arrows. Because of their visual appeal and clarity, flowcharts are often used instead of lists of instructions for informally describing programs. Some cookbook authors even employ flowcharts extensively. In this book we use flowcharts in Chapter 3 when describing the behavior of some Java language constructs.

1.2 ALGORITHMS—BEING PRECISE

Our recipe for preparing a roast can't be executed by a computer because the individual instructions are too loosely specified. Let's consider another example—one that manipulates numbers instead of food. You need to pay for some purchase with a dollar bill and get change in dimes and pennies. The problem is to determine the correct change with the fewest pennies. Most people do this simple everyday transaction unthinkingly. But how do we precisely describe this algorithm?

In solving such a problem, trying a specific case can be useful. Let's say that you need to pay 77 cents and need change for a dollar. You can easily see that one dollar minus the 77 cents leaves you with 23 cents in change. The correct change having the fewest coins in dimes and pennies would be two dimes and three pennies.

The number of dimes is the integer result of dividing 23 by 10 and discarding any fraction or remainder. The number of pennies is the remainder of dividing the 23 cents by 10. An algorithm for performing this change for a dollar is given by the following steps.

CHANGE-MAKING ALGORITHM

1. Assume that the price is written in a box labeled `price`.
2. Subtract the value of `price` from 100 and place it in a box labeled `change`.
3. Divide the value in `change` by 10, discard the remainder, and place the result in a box labeled `dimes`.
4. Take the integer remainder of `change` divided by 10 and place it in a box labeled `pennies`.
5. Print out the values in the boxes `dimes` and `pennies` with appropriate labels.
6. Halt.

This algorithm has four boxes, namely, `price`, `change`, `dimes`, and `pennies`. Let's execute this algorithm with the values given. Suppose that the price is 77 cents. Always start with the first instruction. The contents of the four boxes at various stages of execution are shown in the following table.

Box	Step 1	Step 2	Step 3	Step 4	Step 5
price	77	77	77	77	77
change		23	23	23	23
dimes			2	2	2
pennies				3	3

To execute step 1, place the first number, 77, in the box `pennies`. At the end of instruction 2, the result of subtracting 77 from 100 is 23, which is placed in the box `change`. Each step of the algorithm performs a small part of the computation. By step 5, the correct values are all in their respective boxes and are printed out. Study the example until you're convinced that this algorithm will work correctly for any price under $1.00. A good way to do so is to act the part of a computer following the recipe. Following a set of instructions in this way, formulated as a computer program, is called *hand simulation* or *bench testing*. It is a good way to find errors in an algorithm or program. In computer parlance these errors are called *bugs,* and finding and removing them is called *debugging*.

We executed the change-making algorithm by acting as an agent, mechanically following a list of instructions. The execution of a set of instructions by an agent is called a *computation*. Usually the agent is a computer; in that case, the set of instructions is a computer program. In the remainder of this book, unless explicitly stated otherwise, we use *program* to mean *computer program*.

The algorithm for making change has several important features that are characteristic of all algorithms.

- The sequence of instructions will terminate.
- The instructions are precise. Each instruction is unambiguous and subject to only one interpretation.
- The instructions are simple to perform. Each instruction is within the capabilities of the executing agent and can be carried out exactly in a finite amount of time; such instructions are called *effective*.
- There are inputs and outputs. An algorithm has one or more outputs ("answers") that depend on the particular input data. The input to the change-making algorithm is the price of the item purchased. The output is the number of dimes and pennies.

Our description of the change-making algorithm, although relatively precise, is not written in any formal programming language. Such informal notations for algorithms are called *pseudocode*, whereas real code is something suitable for a computer. Where appropriate we use pseudocode to describe algorithms. Doing so allows us to explain an algorithm or computation to you without all the necessary detail needed by a computer.

The term *algorithm* has a long, involved history, originally stemming from the name of a well-known Arabic mathematician of the ninth century, Abu Jafar Muhammed Musa Al-Khwarizmi. It later became associated with arithmetic processes and then, more particularly, with Euclid's algorithm for computing the greatest common divisor of two integers. Since the development of computers, the word has taken on a more precise meaning that defines a real or abstract computer as the ultimate executing agent—any terminating computation by a computer is an algorithm, and any algorithm can be programmed for a computer.

1.3 IMPLEMENTING OUR ALGORITHM IN JAVA

In this section we implement our change-making algorithm in the Java programming language. You need not worry about following the Java details at this point; we cover all of them fully in the next two chapters. We specifically revisit this example in Section 2.10.1. For now, simply note the similarity between the following Java program and the informal algorithm presented earlier. You not only have to be able to formulate a recipe and make it algorithmic, but you finally have to express it in a computer language.

```
// MakeChange.java - change in dimes and pennies
import tio.*; // use the package tio

class MakeChange {
  public static void main (String[] args) {
    int price, change, dimes, pennies;

    System.out.println("type price (0:100):");
    price = Console.in.readInt();
    change = 100 - price;      //how much change
    dimes = change / 10;       //number of dimes
    pennies = change % 10;     //number of pennies
    System.out.print("The change is :");
    System.out.print(dimes);
    System.out.print(" dimes ");
    System.out.print(pennies);
    System.out.print(" pennies.\n");
  }
}
```

DISSECTION OF THE MakeChange PROGRAM

■ `import tio.*; // use the package tio`

A package is a library or collection of previously written program parts that you can use. This line tells the Java compiler that the program `MakeChange` uses information from the package `tio`. We developed this package especially for this book to simplify keyboard input for you. It allows you to write `Console.in.readInt()`, which we explain shortly.

■ `int price, change, dimes, pennies;`

This program declares four integer variables. These hold the values to be manipulated.

■ `System.out.println("type price(0 to 100):");`

This line is used to *prompt* you to type the price. Whenever a program is expecting a user to do something, it should print out a prompt telling the user what to do. The part in quotes appears on the user's screen when the program is run.

■ `price = Console.in.readInt();`

The `Console.in.readInt()` is used to obtain the input from the keyboard. The value read is stored in the variable `price`. The symbol = is called the *assignment operator.* Read the first line as "`price` is *assigned the value* obtained from `Console.in.readInt.`" At this point you must type in an integer price. For example, you would type 77 and then hit Enter.

■ `change = 100 - price;      //how much change`

This line computes the amount of change.

■ `dimes = change / 10;       //number of dimes`
`pennies = change % 10;     //number of pennies`

The number of dimes is the integer or whole part of the result of dividing change by 10. The symbol /, when used with two integers, computes the whole (nonfraction) part of the division. The number of pennies is the integer remainder of change divided by 10. The symbol % is the integer remainder or modulo operator in Java. So if change is 23, the integer divide of 23/10 is 2 and the integer remainder or modulo of 23 % 10 is 3.

▪
```
System.out.print("The change is : ");
System.out.print(dimes);
System.out.print(" dimes ");
System.out.print(pennies);
System.out.print(" pennies.\n");
```

In this example the System.out.print() statements cause the values between the parentheses to be printed on the computer console. The first one just prints out the characters between the quotation marks. The second one converts the value in dimes to the sequence of digits and prints those digits. The other print statements are similar. For an input value of 77, the output would be

```
The change is : 2 dimes 3 pennies
```

The \n in the last print statement indicates that a newline should be sent to the console, ending the line of output.

1.4 WHY JAVA?

A variety of programming languages are available for expressing programs, but the most useful ones are suitable for both machine and human consumption. In this book we cover programming by using one such language—the programming language Java.

Java is a relatively new programming language, first introduced in 1995. In this book a language is needed that allows algorithms to be easily understood, designed, analyzed, and implemented as computer programs. The following is an excerpt from the original paper introducing Java to the world.

In his science-fiction novel *The Rolling Stones*, Robert A. Heinlein comments:

> Every technology goes through three stages: first a crudely simple and quite unsatisfactory gadget; second, an enormously complicated group of gadgets designed to overcome the shortcomings of the original and achieving thereby somewhat satisfactory performance through extremely complex compromise; third, a final proper design therefrom.

Heinlein's comment could well describe the evolution of many programming languages. Java presents a new viewpoint in the evolution of programming languages—creation of a small and simple language that's still sufficiently comprehensive to address a wide variety of software application development. Although Java is superficially similar to C and C++, Java gained its simplicity from the systematic removal of features from its predecessors.

We agree with its creators that Java has, to a large extent, lived up to the promise of a small, simple, yet comprehensive programming language. As such, Java is both an excellent programming language for real program development and a good first programming language.

Possibly even more important for Java's success are the features that make it appropriate for development of programs distributed over the Internet. These programs, called *applets*, execute inside Internet browsers such as Netscape and Internet Explorer.

1.5   NETWORK COMPUTING AND THE WEB

Much of modern computing is done in a connected environment. That is, computers are connected to other computers in a network. This connection allows the computers to exchange information or to "talk to each other." Java was developed with network computing as the normal environment. It has many features and libraries of parts of programs that promote networking. Earlier languages and systems viewed a computer as a lone instrument doing significant computations, the results of which would largely be output to a screen or printer. By promoting networking whereby computers are connected and pass results to each other dynamically—and cooperate on large-scale computations—Java became the principal language for computing on networks.

The largest network is the global network called the *Internet*. Using the Internet, researchers at the European Particle Physics Laboratory (CERN) developed a way to share information via a formatting language called *hyper-text markup-language*, or *HTML*. The computers exchanged HTML documents by means of a protocol called *hyper-text transfer protocol*, or *HTTP*. A *protocol* is like a language that computers use to "talk" to each other. HTML allows one electronic document to link to another electronic document on a different computer. The program used to view HTML documents and follow the links is called a *browser*. With the click of a button, a user could move from one document on one computer to another, related document, on another computer. Because of these links, the resulting web of documents was dubbed the *World Wide Web* or simply *the Web*. Today, many people equate the Web with the Internet, but the Web is only one application of the technology known as the Internet.

Java programs, called *applets*, can be written to automatically load and execute by following a link in the Web. This ability to embed Java programs in HTML documents is a primary factor in the success of Java. With Java applets, Web documents are no longer static text, images, or video segments. Web documents can provide all the interaction of any program. We discuss graphical user interfaces and applets in Chapter 8.

If you're interested in an early exposure to applets, we also provide templates for simple applets in the exercises at the end of Chapters 2 through 6.

From the World Wide Web (www) and HTTP, you can begin to make some sense of the ubiquitous Internet addresses such as *http://www.company.com*. This type of address is called a *universal resource locator*, or *URL*. These are addresses embedded in HTML documents, linking one document to another.

Client-server computing is an essential new element in computers that manage communications and computations. The server, typically a fast computer with a very large amount of hard disk storage, gives out information to clients upon request. An example would be a server giving out stock market quotes to clients that request it. The network support in Java makes implementing client–server programming solutions easy. In Chapter 13 we show you how to implement a simple Java server program that can connect and respond to requests from multiple clients on other computers.

1.6   HUMAN–COMPUTER INTERACTION AND THE GUI

In the early days of computing, most interaction between a computer and a human being was in the form of typed input to the computer and printed output to the person. Most human–computer interaction today is done with a *graphical user interface* (*GUI*—pronounced gooey). The user has a keyboard, usually similar to a standard typewriter keyboard, a pointing device, usually a mouse, and a display device capable of displaying both text and graphics.

The user's display is usually divided into viewing areas called *windows*. Associated with the windows are menus of commands relating to manipulation of the data displayed in the window. The display (screen) may also contain icons, or small graphical images, whose visual appearance is designed to signify their functions. For example, a picture of a trash can represents deleting a file, and an arrowhead is used to scroll a viewing screen. The following screen shot of a typical desktop shows several windows, icons, and a row of menus across the top of each window.

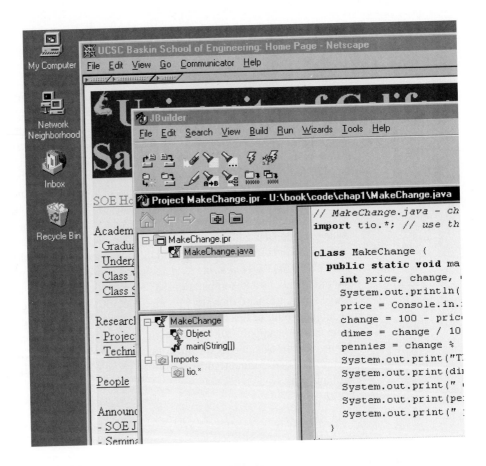

For many years, the task of creating a graphical user interface for a new application was extremely time-consuming and difficult. The programming languages and operating systems in use did not make building such interfaces easy. These interfaces were usually built from libraries of program parts that were suitable only for one particular operating system. If a company building a new program wanted to have its program run on computers with different operating systems, it would have to create multiple versions of the programs.

Java provides a solution. Software companies now sell programs that make building graphical user interfaces relatively easy. Java includes a library of program parts called *Swing* for building graphical user interfaces. The program parts in Swing can be used on any computer that can run Java programs. Thus a programmer can now write one version of a program and have it run on many different kinds of computers. Although in-depth coverage of Swing is beyond the scope of this book, Swing is simple enough to use that even beginning programmers can begin to build programs with graphical user interfaces. We discuss Swing further in Chapters 8 and 9.

By the end of this book, you will be writing your own sophisticated applets and regular Java programs with GUIs. If you've used a Java-enabled browser, such as Netscape or Explorer, you've probably unknowingly made use of an applet. If not, you can try out a simple applet that lets you draw on the screen right now by going to *www.JavaByDissection.xyz* and clicking on our `draw` applet there. This is the same applet presented in Section 8.8, on page 296.

Summary

- Informally, an algorithm is a list of instructions for performing a specific task or for solving a particular type of problem. Algorithmlike specifications for problem solving and task performance are commonly found in everyday situations. A recipe is a kind of algorithm.

- One graphical representation of an algorithm is a flow chart. To perform the algorithm, the user just follows the arrows and the instructions in each box. The manipulation activities are contained in rectangles, the tests are shown in diamonds, and the transfer or flow of control is determined by the arrows. Because of their visual appeal and clarity, flow charts are often used instead of lists of instructions for informally describing algorithms.

- Algorithms that can be executed on computers are called programs. Programs are written in special languages called programming languages, such as Java, which we use in this book.

- Modern computing is done in a connected environment. A computer is connected to other computers in a network. This connection allows the computers to exchange information or to "talk to each other." Java was developed with network computing as the normal environment. The largest network is the global network called the Internet. This network is used to exchange documents throughout the world with a common format called HTML. This format allows links to be followed across the Internet. Because of these links, the resulting web of documents was named the World Wide Web or simply the Web.

- It is possible to write Java programs called applets, that are automatically loaded and executed as the result of following a link in the Web. This ability to embed Java programs in HTML documents is a primary factor in the success of Java. With Java applets, Web documents are no longer static text, images, or video segments. Web documents can provide all the interactions of any program.

Review Questions

1. What is an algorithm?

2. A graphical description of a computation using boxes and arrows is called a
   _____.

3. Informal, but relatively precise descriptions of algorithms are called
   _____.

4. What is bench testing? Why is it important?
5. What did `tio` refer to in the `MakeChange.java` program?
6. What was `System.out.print()` used for in the Java program?
7. What is HTML? What is HTTP? What is URL?
8. What is a browser? Name a commonly used browser.
9. What are the primary components of a typical human–computer interface today?
10. The information provided by the user to a program when it executes is called the _____. The answers provided by the program are called the _____.
11. What is Swing?

Exercises

1. Write a flow chart for the following recipe for cooking baked beans (taken from *The Natural Foods Cookbook*, Nitty Gritty Productions, Concord, California, 1972).

   Bring apple juice and water to a boil and add beans so slowly that boiling doesn't stop. Reduce heat after beans are in water and simmer 2 to $2\frac{1}{2}$ hours or until beans are almost tender. Drain beans, reserving liquid, and add other ingredients to beans. Place in oiled baking dish and bake covered 2 to 3 hours in 250° oven. Uncover for the last hour of cooking. If beans become dry, add a little of the reserved bean water. About 15 minutes before removing from the oven, add the fresh diced tomato.

2. Let m and n be positive integers. Draw a flowchart for the following algorithm for computing the quotient q and remainder r of dividing m by n.

   a. Set q to 0.
   b. If $m < n$, then stop. q is the quotient and m is the remainder.
   c. Replace m by $m - n$.
   d. Increment q by *1*.
   e. Go to step b.

3. Bench test the algorithm in the previous exercise. Use $m = 4$ and $n = 2$ as values.
4. Let a rectangle that is aligned with the coordinate axes be represented by the coordinates of its lower left and upper right corners, ($xmin$, $ymin$) and ($xmax$, $ymax$), respectively, as shown in the following illustration. Given two such rectangles, $R1$ and $R2$, devise an algorithm that finds the rectangle, if any, that is common to both $R1$ and $R2$. The input data are the eight real numbers representing the coordinates of the rectangles' corners. The illustration shows two rectangles that have a common rectangle, shown in grey.

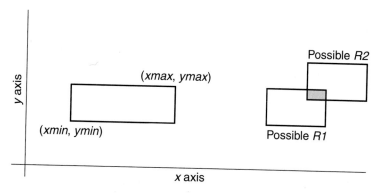

5. Suppose that a line segment is represented by its two endpoints, $PE = (xe, ye)$ and $PP = (xp, yp)$. For two line segments $L1$ and $L2$, devise an algorithm that computes the coordinates of their point of intersection, if any. (Two line segments intersect if they have only one point in common.)

6. Make a list of all the automatic interactions that you have with computers—for example, utility bills, automatic mailing lists, class scheduling, and so on.

7. Give a detailed step-by-step procedure, also called an algorithm, for

   a. traveling from your place of residence to school or work,

   b. manually dividing one number by another (long division),

   c. taking an unordered set of numbers and putting them in ascending sequence (i.e., "sorting" the numbers in ascending sequence), or

   d. playing, and never losing, the game of Tic-Tac-Toe.

2

Program Fundamentals

In this chapter we introduce programming fundamentals in Java. We write a Java program by using different elements of the Java language. The most basic elements are the *tokens* of the language. Tokens are the words that make up the sentences of the program. Programming is comparable to writing. To write an essay we write words that make up sentences, sentences that make up paragraphs, and paragraphs that make up essays. In this chapter we concentrate on how to use the "words" and combine them into the program equivalent of useful sentences and paragraphs.

2.1 "HELLO, WORLD!" IN JAVA

A simple first Java program is the classic "Hello, world!" program, so named because it prints the message Hello, world! on the computer's screen.

```
/* HelloWorld.java
 * Purpose:
 *    The classic "Hello, world!" program.
 *    It prints a message to the screen.
 * Author: Jane Programmer
 *        as derived from Kernighan and Richie
 */
class HelloWorld {
  public static void main (String[] args) {
    System.out.println("Hello, world!");
  }
}
```

DISSECTION OF THE HelloWorld PROGRAM

■
```
/* HelloWorld.java
 * Purpose:
 ...
 */
```

Everything between a `/*` and a `*/` is a comment. Comments are ignored by the Java compiler and are inserted to make the program more understandable to the human reader. Every program should begin with a comment such as the one in this example. In our examples, the name of the file appears in the comment. This example indicates that it is from the file *HelloWorld.java*. Other things to include in program comments are the function or purpose of the program, the author of the program, and a revision history with dates, indicating major modifications to the program.

■
```
class HelloWorld {
```

The word `class` is a keyword preceding the name of the *class*. A *keyword* has a predefined special purpose. A *class* is a named collection of data and instructions. The name of the class being defined in this example is `HelloWorld`. The left brace "{" begins the definition of a class. A matching right brace "}" is needed to end the class definition. Forgetting to match braces is a common error.

■
```
public static void main (String[] args) {
```

This line declares that the class `HelloWorld` contains a *method* with the name `main`. A *method* is a named group of instructions within a class. In this example, only one method, named `main`, is defined for the class `HelloWorld`. In Chapter 4 we create classes that contain several methods in a single class. When we use the name of a method, we add parentheses at the end to remind you that it is a method. This convention comes from actual Java code, wherein the name of a method is always followed by parentheses. The method defined by this line is thus referred to as `main()`.

There are two kinds of Java programs: *stand-alone applications* and *applets*. The method `main()` appears in every stand-alone Java program indicating where program execution will begin. Later we use a different line that serves a similar purpose for applets. An explanation of the words `public`, `static`, and `void` in this line is left until later.

■
```
{
    System.out.println("Hello, world!");
}
```

The entire body of the method `main()`, the real instructions to the computer, appears between the braces. In this example, just one instruction prints the desired message. You can memorize this instruction and use it as an incantation to get something printed out on your computer screen. What gets printed is between the quotation marks.

2.2 COMPILING AND RUNNING YOUR JAVA PROGRAM

You will be dealing with two different representations of your programs: the part you write and a form more suitable for the computer to use when it finally runs your program. The text you write to give the computer instructions is called the *source code* or simply the *source*. This source code will be compiled by the Java *compiler* into a form more suitable as instructions to the computer called *object code*. The source code form of the program is represented in the language Java that you will be learning. Informally, you can think of the source code as the *raw* form of the program in contrast to the object code, which is the *cooked* or compiled form. In Java, all source code file names have the suffix *.java*, such as *HelloWorld.java*. The result of correctly compiling *HelloWorld.java* is the object code *HelloWorld.class*. In some situations, the name of the file without the *.java* and the name of the class defined in the file must be the same. Although this requirement does not apply to the programs in the first part of this book, we follow that practice even when it isn't required and suggest that you do the same.

There are many names and forms for the machine representation of a program after it has been processed somewhat by the computer. A common first step in processing source code is to compile it, which means to translate it into a form more suitable for the computer. For most common programming languages, this compiled form is called the *machine code, object code,* or *binary form*. When you buy a piece of software you usually get *binaries* or an *executable image*. For Java, this form is a bit different and is called *Java Bytecode*. These bytecodes are the same whether you are running on a Macintosh, on an Intel machine with Microsoft Windows, or on a machine from Sun running Unix. This sameness is an important advantage of Java programs, as they can be written to be platform independent, which is generally not true for most other programming languages, such as C or COBOL.

In Java, all bytecode files must have a name that ends in *.class* such as *HelloWorld.class*. The word *class* is used because, in Java, programs are broken into chunks called classes, much like a chapter is broken into sections. The following diagram illustrates the compilation process and the conventions just described.

There are two principal methods for compiling and running Java programs. One method uses an Integrated Development Environment (IDE), of which there are many for Java. The actual details of compiling for each of the IDEs vary slightly but the basic steps are the same.

1. Use the editor that comes with the IDE to create the source file. These editors generally help with syntax by using special fonts or colors for keywords and helping you match braces, and so on.
2. Create some kind of project and add your source file to the project.
3. Select Run from a menu. The IDE will automatically determine that the source file needs to be compiled and compile it before trying to run the program.

The other principal method is the command line approach. In it you run the compiler yourself from the command line of either a DOS or Unix shell program. For both Unix and DOS shells the steps are the same.

1. Use your favorite text editor to create the source file.
2. Compile the program with the command `javac` followed by the source file name—for example, `javac HelloWorld.java`.
3. If the program compiles without errors, run the program with the command `java` followed by the name of the class. Do not append *.class*, as in *Hello-World.class*; use only the class name— for example, `java HelloWorld`.

The last two steps are shown as follows for the program `HelloWorld`.

```
os-prompt>javac HelloWorld.java
os-prompt>java HelloWorld
Hello, world!
os-prompt>
```

2.3 LEXICAL ELEMENTS

As with any language there are certain rules about how words in the Java programming language are formed and what constitutes a legal sentence. In addition, Java has rules about how sentences can be put together to form a complete program, somewhat like the less formal rules about how to format a formal letter with the address of the recipient and opening salutation. In this section we begin by looking at the various words and symbols, called *lexical elements*, that are used to construct Java programs.

The most fundamental element in the structure of a program is a single character that can be displayed on a computer screen or typed at a computer keyboard. Prior to Java, most programming languages, such as C and C++, used the ASCII character set. It provides for 127 different characters, which is enough to represent all the characters on the conventional English language keyboard. This set may seem like a lot, but when you consider all the human languages in the world and the various symbols they use, it is inadequate. Because Java was designed to be used throughout the world, not just in English-speaking countries, Java developers adopted the Unicode character set. It provides for more than 64,000 different characters.

When a Java compiler first begins to analyze a Java program, it groups the individual characters into larger lexical elements, usually called *tokens*. Some tokens—such as the plus sign, +, which is the Java symbol used to add two numbers—are only one character long. Other tokens—such as the keywords `class` and `public`—are many characters long. These basic tokens are then combined into larger language forms, such as expressions.

There are five types of tokens: keywords, identifiers, literals, operators, and punctuation. White space and comments are two additional lexical elements that are discarded early in the compilation process.

2.3.1 WHITE SPACE

White space in Java refers to the space character, which you get when you strike the space bar on the keyboard; the tab character, which is actually one character, although it may appear as several spaces on your screen; and the newline character which you get when you hit the Return or Enter key on the keyboard. White space is used primarily to make the program look nice and also serves to separate adjacent tokens that are not separated by any other punctuation and would otherwise be considered a single, longer token. For example, white space is used to separate the following three tokens:

```
public static void
```

in the `HelloWorld` program. In such situations, where one white space character is required, any number of white space characters can be used. For example, we could have put each of the words `public`, `static`, and `void` on separate lines or put lots of spaces between them as in

```
public        static        void        main(...
```

Except for string literals, which we discuss shortly, any number of adjacent white space characters—even mixing tab, space, and newline characters—is the same as just one white space character as far as the structure and meaning of the program are concerned. Stated another way, if you can legally put in one space, you can put in as many spaces, tabs, and newlines as you want. You can't put white space in the middle of a *keyword* or *identifier*, such as a *variable* or class name. We discuss keywords, identifiers, and variables later in this chapter.

2.3.2 COMMENTS

Comments are very important in writing good code and are too often neglected. The primary purpose of a comment is to provide additional information to the person reading a program. It serves as a concise form of program documentation. As far as the computer is concerned, the comment does not result in a token; it separates other tokens or is ignored completely when it isn't needed to separate tokens. Java has three ways to specify comments.

A *single line* comment begins with // and causes the rest of the line—all characters to the next newline—to be treated as a comment and ignored by the compiler. It is called a single line comment because the comment can't be longer than a single line. By definition, the comment ends at the end of the line containing the //.

A *multiline* comment can extend across several lines in a program. The beginning of the comment is marked with /* and the end of the comment is marked with */. Everything between the marks and the marks themselves is a comment and is ignored. Here is the multiline comment from our first Java program.

```
/* HelloWorld.java
 * Purpose:
 *    This is the classic "Hello, world!" program.
 *    It simply prints a message to the screen.
 * Author:
 *    Jane Programmer
 *       as derived from Kernighan and Richie
 */
```

The single asterisks on the intermediate lines are not required and are used merely to accent the extent of the comment. These comments are also called *block comments*.

The third style of comment is a minor variation on the multiline comment. The beginning marker has an additional asterisk; that is, the beginning of the comment is marked with /** and the end of the comment is marked with */. These comments are identical to the multiline comment except that they are recognized by a special program called *javadoc* that automatically extracts such comments and produces documentation for the program organized as an HTML document. See Section 4.13 for more about *javadoc*.

2.3.3   KEYWORDS

Keywords, also known as *reserved words*, have a predefined special purpose and can't be used for any but that purpose. Each of the 47 keywords in Java has a special meaning to the Java compiler. A keyword must be separated from other keywords or identifiers by white space, a comment, or some other punctuation symbol. The following table shows all the Java keywords.

abstract	default	if	private	throw
boolean	do	implements	protected	throws
break	double	import	public	transient
byte	else	instanceof	return	try
case	extends	int	short	void
catch	final	interface	static	volatile
char	finally	long	super	while
class	float	native	switch	
const	for	new	synchronized	
continue	goto	package	this	

The keywords `const` and `goto` have no meaning in Java. They are keywords in C++, a language that was a precursor to Java. They are included as keywords to facilitate error reporting when programmers with C++ experience accidentally use them. In addition, the words `null`, `true,` and `false` look like keywords in that they have a predefined meaning, but they are in fact literals, as discussed later.

2.3.4 IDENTIFIERS

Identifiers are the names used to specify different elements of a Java program, such as a class, method, or variable. (We discuss variables in Section 2.4.1.) An identifier in our first program was `HelloWorld`, a name we picked for the `class`. Another identifier was the library method name `println`, a name picked by the Java developers. In both cases, the name gives a clue as to the use of that element of the program. An *identifier* is any sequence of Java letters and digits, the first of which must be a *Java letter*, with two exceptions. A keyword can't be an identifier, and the special literal terms `true`, `false`, and `null` can't be used as identifiers. The Java letters and digits include the letter and digit symbols for many modern written languages. The Java letters include the English language uppercase and lowercase letters, the $, and the _ (underscore). The last two are included because of Java's close kinship to the programming language C, which included these symbols as legal characters in identifiers. The Java digits are 0 through 9. In our examples, we use only English letters and digits. The following are some examples of legal identifiers along with comments providing some explanation.

```
data                          //variable name conveying its use
HelloWorld                    //class name
youCanAlmostMakeASentence     //unlikely
readInt                       //method name from tio
x                             //simple variable usually double
__123                         //obscure name-a poor choice
```

The following are some illegal identifiers, along with comments indicating what the sequence of symbols really is.

```
3              //a digit or integer literal
x+y            //an expression where x and y are identifiers
some***name    //illegal internal characters
no Space       //intended was noSpace
1floor         //cannot start with a digit
class          //keyword - cannot be used as an identifier
```

2.3.5 LITERALS

Java has built-in *types* for numbers, characters, and booleans. Java also has a standard class type for strings. The *type* of a data value tells the computer how to interpret the data. These built-in types are called *primitive types* in Java. *Literals,* also called *constants,* are the literal program representations of values for the primitive numeric types, the primitive type `boolean`, the primitive character type `char`, and the standard class string type `String`. Without going into the details of these various types, the following are some examples of literal values.

Java Type	Explanation	Examples
int	Integers—numbers without fractional parts	`123  -999  0`
double	Double precision numbers with fractional parts	`1.23  -0.01`
String	Arbitrary strings of characters	`"Oh J" "123"`
boolean	Logical values true or false	`true  false`
char	Single characters	`'a'   '1'`

Like keywords, the symbols `true` and `false` can't be used as identifiers. They are reserved to represent the two possible boolean values. We explain later, in more detail, what constitutes an acceptable literal for each data type.

2.3.6 OPERATORS AND PUNCTUATION

In addition to keywords, identifiers, and literals, a Java program contains operators and separators or punctuation. The operators are things like "+", and the separators are things like the ";" that terminates some statements and the braces "{ }" used to group things. To fully understand operators, you need to understand type, precedence, and associativity. *Type* determines the kind of value computed, such as `int` or `double`. *Precedence* determines among operators, such as + and / used in an expression, which is done first. *Associativity* is the order in which operators of the same precedence are evaluated and is usually left-most first—for example,

```
int n = 1;
n = n * 3 + 2;     //an assignment expression
```

The variable n is an integer variable initialized to 1. Next n is multiplied by the integer literal 3. This result is added to 2, and finally this value is assigned to n. The result is 5, which is then assigned to n. Precedence of the multiplication operator * is higher than +, so the multiplication is done before the addition. Precedence of the assignment operator = is lowest, so assignment occurs as the last action in this expression. We discuss precedence and associativity of operators further in Section 2.13.

2.4 DATA TYPES AND VARIABLE DECLARATIONS

In order to do something useful, computer programs must store and manipulate data. Many programming languages, including Java, require that each data item have a declared type. That is, you must specify the kind of information represented by the data, or the data's *type*. The data's type determines how data is represented in the computer's memory and what operations can be performed on the data.

Different programming languages support different data types. A data type can be something as fundamental as a type for representing integers or as complex as a type for representing a digital movie. Some examples of data types found in Java are

- `int`—for representing integers or whole numbers;
- `double`—for representing numbers having a fraction;
- `String`—for representing text;
- `Button`—for representing a push button in a graphical user interface; and
- `Point`—for representing points in a plane.

The types of data that are created, stored, and manipulated by Java programs can be separated into two main groups: *primitive types* and class types, or simply *classes*.

There are eight primitive types:

- the numeric types `byte`, `short`, `int`, `long`, `float`, and `double` for storing numeric values;
- the character type `char` for storing a single alphabetic character, digit, or symbol; and
- the type `boolean` for storing `true` or `false`.

Primitive data values can be created by using literals such as `100`, `-10.456`, `'a'`, and `true`. Primitive values can also be operated on by using built-in operators such as + for addition and – for subtraction of two numeric values, producing a new primitive value. For example,

```
2 + 3
```

uses + (addition) to operate on the two numeric literal values, 2 and 3, to produce the new primitive value, 5.

Standard Java has more than 1500 classes. The `String`, `Button`, and `Point` types mentioned previously are standard Java classes. You will learn in Chapter 6 that you can create your own classes. Also, in Chapter 5 we discuss arrays, which are a special case of class types.

The data values that are class types are called *objects*. You can create object data values by using the special operator `new` followed by the class name and possibly some additional values needed to create the new object. For example,

```
new Button("Quit")
```

creates a new object describing a button with the label "Quit."

You can create new objects of type `String`, as a special case, by using the string literal notation that surrounds the text of the string with double quotation marks. For example, `"Hello, world!"` creates a new string object.

In most cases, the operations supported for the particular class are given a name and invoked by placing the name after the object value, separated by a dot. For example,

```
"Hello, world!".length()
```

operates on the literal string `"Hello, world!"` and evaluates to 13—the number of characters in this string, including any blanks. Operations such as `length()` defined for a particular class are called *methods*. We discuss methods in great detail in subsequent chapters.

2.4.1 VARIABLES

In all but the most trivial programs, such as `HelloWorld`, you will declare *variables* that are identifiers used to refer to data values that are stored in the computer's memory. These are called variables because a variable actually refers to a particular place in the computer's memory, and the value stored in the computer's memory can vary as the program runs. A variable declaration always begins with a type and ends with a semicolon. The *type* is used to identify the kind of data that will be stored in the memory location associated with the variable being declared. Some examples of variable declarations are

```
int i, j;
String sentence;
boolean flag1, flag2, flag3;
Button clickToExit;
```

Note that you can declare several variables of the same type by separating the names with a comma. Good choice of variable names is important to writing clearly understandable code. Stylistically, choose variable names that are meaningful. Also, variable names usually start in lowercase, and if they are multiword, the internal words start with an uppercase character, as in `clickToExit`.

2.4.2 VARIABLE INITIALIZATION

Variables can be given initial values. The preceding set of declarations given initial values for each variable becomes

```
int i = 2, j = 3;
String sentence = "I am a camera.";
boolean flag1 = true, flag2 = true, flag3 = false;
Button clickToExit = new Button("Exit");
```

Initializing variables with literals of their respective type is normal. In this example, the `int` variable `i` is initially given the value 2. The `boolean` variable `flag1` is initially `true`. The `String` variable `sentence` is initialized with a string literal.

With the exception of `String`, Java has no literals for creating object values. You initialize the `Button` variable by creating a `Button` object, using `new` as discussed briefly earlier. We discuss object creation in Chapter 6.

2.5 AN EXAMPLE: STRING CONCATENATION

The following example is a complete program that declares three variables: `word1`, `word2`, and `sentence`. Values are then assigned to the parts of the computer memory referred to by those variables.

```java
// HelloWorld2.java - simple variable declarations
class HelloWorld2 {
  public static void main (String[] args) {
    String word1;   // declare a String variable
    String word2, sentence;  // declare two more

    word1 = "Hello, ";
    word2 = "world!";
    sentence = word1.concat(word2);
    System.out.println(sentence);
  }
}
```

DISSECTION OF THE HelloWorld2 PROGRAM

- ```java
  String word1;   // declare a String variable
  String word2, sentence;  // declare two more
  ```

Whenever you introduce a new identifier you must declare it. You declare that an identifier is a variable by first writing the name of the kind of value the variable refers to, called the *type*. The type is `String` in this example. Insert the name of the new variable after the type. For variables in Java, the computer must always know the type of value to be stored in the memory location associated with that variable. As shown in the second line, you can declare more than one variable at a time by giving first the type and then a comma separated list of new identifiers.

- ```java
  word1 = "Hello, ";
  word2 = "world!";
  ```

The symbol = is called the *assignment operator* and is used to store values in variables. Read the first statement as "word1 *gets* the value `Hello, `" or "word1 is *assigned* the value `Hello, `". Here it is used to assign the `String` literals `"Hello, "` and `"world!"` to the newly declared variables `word1` and `word2`, respectively. The variable name will always be on the left and the new value to be assigned to the variable will always be on the right. Saying "assign the value `"Hello, "` to the variable `word1`" really means to store the `String` value `"Hello, "` in the computer memory location associated with the variable `word1`.

- ```java
  sentence = word1.concat(word2);
  ```

This statement contains an expression used to create a third `String` value, which is then assigned to the variable `sentence`. This expression uses the method `concat()`, which is defined for values of type `String`. Recall that operations on objects are
  ```

called methods. This particular operation requires a second `String` value placed between the parentheses. The method name `concat` is short for concatenation. The concatenation of two strings is a new string that contains the symbols from the first string followed by the symbols from the second string. Note that the first string, `word1`, contains a space at the end. Thus, when we concatenate the two strings, we get the new string `"Hello, world!"`, which is assigned to the variable `sentence`.

- `System.out.println(sentence);`

The program then prints out the string in the variable `sentence`, which now is `"Hello, world!"`.

As we showed earlier, when a variable is declared, it can be given an initial value. This approach essentially combines an assignment with the declaration. Using this notation, you can now write the body of `main()` in `HelloWorld2` as

```
String word1 = "Hello, ";
String word2 = "world!";
String sentence = word1.concat(word2);
System.out.println(sentence);
```

You could even combine two initializations in a single statement,

```
String word2 = "world!", sentence = word1.concat(word2);
```

although, as a general rule, multiple complex initializations such as this should be placed on separate lines.

2.5.1 STRINGS VERSUS IDENTIFIERS VERSUS VARIABLES

A *string* is a particular data value that a program can manipulate. A *variable* is a place in the computer's memory with an associated *identifier*. The following example uses the identifier `hello` to refer to a variable of type `String`. The identifier `stringVary` refers to a second variable of type `String`. We first assign `stringVary` the value associated with the `String` variable `hello`. Later we reassign it the string value `"hello"`.

```
//StringVsId.java - contrast strings and identifiers
class StringVsId {
  public static void main(String[] args) {
    String hello = "Hello, world!";
    String stringVary;
    stringVary = hello;
    System.out.println(stringVary);
    stringVary = "hello";
    System.out.println(stringVary);
  }
}
```

The output of this program is

```
Hello, world!
hello
```

The program demonstrates two important points. First it shows the difference between the identifier `hello`, which in fact refers to the string `"Hello, world!"`, and the string `"hello"`, which is referred to at one point by the variable `string-Vary`. This example also shows that a variable can *vary*. The variable `stringVary` first refers to the value `"Hello, world!"` but later refers to the value `"hello"`.

2.6   USER INPUT

In the programs presented so far, we have generated output only by using `System.out.println()`. Most programs input some data as well as generate output. There are lots of ways to input data in Java, but the simplest is to use a class provided in the text input–output package `tio`, as shown in the following example. This package isn't a standard Java package but is provided for use with this text. The complete source for `tio` is listed in Appendix C.

```
// SimpleInput.java - reading numbers from the keyboard
import tio.*;    // use the package tio

class SimpleInput {
  public static void main (String[] args) {
    int width, height, area;

    System.out.println("type two integers for" +
            " the width and height of a box");
    width = Console.in.readInt();
    height = Console.in.readInt();
    area = width * height;
    System.out.print("The area is ");
    System.out.println(area);
  }
}
```

DISSECTION OF THE SimpleInput PROGRAM

■   `import tio.*;       // use the package tio`

This line tells the Java compiler that the program `SimpleInput` uses some of the classes defined in the package `tio`. The `*` indicates that you might use any of the classes in the package `tio`. The class used here is `Console`, allowing you to write

`Console.in.readInt()`, which we explain shortly. Because only `Console` is used from `tio`, you could also write `import tio.Console;`, but common practice is to import the entire package.

■ `int width, height, area;`

This program declares three integer variables. The width and height must be whole numbers; fractional values are not allowed.

■ `System.out.println("type two integers for" +`
`" the width and height of a box");`

A string literal must be on one line. You can't type a newline between the quotation marks. When the string that you want to print is too long to fit on a single line, you can break it into pieces and then put them back together, using the + for string concatenation, as shown here. You can put newlines, or any amount of white space, around the + symbol.

Use `println()` to *prompt* a user to do something—here to type two numbers. Whenever a program is expecting the user to do something, it should print out a prompt telling the user what to do.

■ `width = Console.in.readInt();`
`height = Console.in.readInt();`

The statement `Console.in` is similar to `System.out`. For now just memorize `Console.in.readInt()` as an idiom for reading an integer from the keyboard. The expression `Console.in.readInt()` is replaced at execution time by the integer value corresponding to that typed by the user. That value is stored in the variable whose identifier appears on the left of the assignment operator. If the user types something other than a string of digits, then the program will print an error message and terminate.

■ `area = width * height;`

The asterisk, *, is the Java symbol for multiplication. The result of multiplying the values stored in `width` and `height` is assigned to the variable `area`.

■ `System.out.print("The area is ");`

Here `System.out.print()` is used. Note the absence of `ln` at the end. This line is just like `System.out.println()` except that it doesn't append a newline.

■ `System.out.println(area);`

Note that you can use `System.out.println()` to print both an `int` and a `String`. The same applies to `System.out.print()`. The two outputs will appear on the same line on the screen. Be sure that the last line in a series contains the `ln`. Nothing will appear on your screen until a newline is printed.

2.7 CALLING PREDEFINED METHODS

A *method* is a group of instructions having a name. In the programs introduced so far, we've defined a single method called `main()`. In addition, we've used some methods from other classes that were either standard Java classes or were part of the `tio` package provided with this book. The methods have names, which makes it possible for you to request the computer to perform the instructions that comprise the method. That's what we're doing by using the expression `System.out.println("Hello, world!")`. We're *calling* a method with the name `println` and asking that the instructions be executed. Just as two people can have the same name, two methods can have the same name. We must therefore, in general, tell Java where to look for the method. Using `System.out` tells Java that we're interested in the `println()` method associated with the object identified by `System.out`. (We must still postpone a full explanation of the meaning of `System.out`.) As we have shown, the same method can be called several times in one program. In `SimpleInput`, we called the method `println()` twice.

For many methods, we need to provide some data values in order for the method to perform its job. These values are provided to the method by placing them between parentheses following the name of the method. These values are called the *parameters* of the method, and we say that we are *passing* the parameters to the method. The `println()` method requires one parameter, which is the value to be printed. As we indicated previously, this parameter can be either a string or a numeric value. In the latter case the numeric value will be converted by the `println()` method to a string and then printed. If more than one parameter is required, we separate the parameter values by commas. For example, the predefined method `Math.min()` is used to determine the minimum of two numbers. The following program fragment will print out 3.

```
int numberOne = 10, numberTwo = 3, smallest;
smallest = Math.min(numberOne, numberTwo);
System.out.println(smallest);
```

The method `min()` is contained in the standard Java class `Math`, which includes other common mathematical functions, such as `Math.sqrt()` that is used to find the square root of a number.

Here are some of the predefined methods that we've mentioned so far.

```
System.out.print(x)        //print the value of x
System.out.println(x)      //print the value of x
                           //followed by a newline
Console.in.readInt()       //get an int from the keyboard
Math.min(x,y)              //find the smaller of x and y
Math.sqrt(x)               //find the square root of x
w1.concat(w2)              //concatenate the strings w1 and w2
word.length()              //find the length of the string word
```

Java includes a rich set of many more predefined methods. They include methods for the most common mathematical functions (see Appendix B), for creating graphical user interfaces (see Chapters 8 and 9), for reading and writing information from and to files (see Chapter 10), for communicating with programs on other computers using a network (see Chapter 13), and many more. An important aspect of Java is the ability to use parts of programs created by others.

2.8   MORE ON `print()` AND `println()`

As the program `SimpleInput` shows, methods `System.out.print()` and `System.out.println()` can print more than just strings. The `print()` and `println()` methods can print all the primitive types.

We also showed in previous examples how two or more strings can be combined by using the string concatenation operator +. Using this operator, we can print out a long line of text without having to have a long line in our program, which would make the program hard to read. We demonstrated this capability in

```
System.out.println("type two integers for" +
            " the width and height of a box");
```

Of course we could have achieved the same result by using a `print()` and then a `println()`, as in

```
System.out.print("type two integers for");
System.out.println(" the width and height of a box");
```

The earlier version would have allowed us to include even more actual text in the message to be printed. Recall, however, that you can't put a newline in the middle of a string, so the following would not be legal.

```
System.out.println("type two integers for
            the width and height of a box");
```

In the same way that you can combine two strings with the string concatenation operator you can also combine one string and one value of any other type. In this case, the nonstring operand is first converted into a new string and then the two strings are concatenated. This allows rewriting the printing of the result in `SimpleInput` from Section 2.6, on page 27, in the form

```
System.out.print("The area is " + area);
```

This version emphasizes that one message will appear on a single line of the output. The `int` value `area` is first converted to a `String` and then combined with the other string, using string concatenation.

What about the opposite? What if you wanted to have an output message that spanned several output lines but with a single `println()`? You can do so by putting the symbols \n in a string literal to represent internally newlines within the string. Such a string will print on more than one output line. Thus for

```
System.out.println("One\nword\nper\nline.");
```

The output is

```
One
word
per
line.
```

The pair of symbols \n, when used in a string literal, mean to put a newline at this point in the string. This *escape sequence* allows you to escape from the normal meaning of the symbols \ and n when used separately. You can find out more about escape sequences in Section 2.9.3, on page 35.

The method System.out.println() is a convenient variant of System.out.print(). You can always achieve the same effect by adding \n to the end of what is being printed. For example, the following two lines are equivalent.

```
System.out.println("Hello, world.");
System.out.print("Hello, world.\n");
```

Care must be taken when you're using string concatenation to combine several numbers. Sometimes, parentheses are necessary to be sure that the + is interpreted as string concatenation, not numeric addition. For

```
int x = 1, y = 2;
System.out.println("x + y = " + x + y);
```

the output is x + y = 12 because the string "x + y =" is first concatenated with the string "1", and then "2" is concatenated onto the end of the string "x + y = 1". To print x + y = 3 you should use parentheses first to force the addition of x and y as integers and then concatenate the string representation of the result with the initial string, as in

```
System.out.println("x + y = " + (x + y));
```

2.9 NUMBER TYPES

There are two basic representations for numbers in most modern programming languages: integer representations and floating point representations. The integer types are used to represent integers or whole numbers. The floating point types are used to represent numbers that contain fractional parts or for numbers whose magnitude exceeds the capacity of the integer types.

2.9.1 THE INTEGER TYPES

A *bit* is the smallest unit of information that can be stored in a computer. It can represent only two values, such as 1/0 or on/off or true/false. A sequence of bits can be used to represent a larger range of values. For the integer types, the bits are interpreted with the binary number system. The binary number system has only two digits: 0 and 1. These two digits can be combined to represent any number in the same way that the 10 digits of the normal, decimal number system can be combined to form any number. (See Appendix A).

Some mechanism is needed to represent positive and negative numbers. One simple solution would be to set aside one bit to represent the sign of the number. However, this results in two different representations of zero, +0, and –0, which causes problems for computer arithmetic. Therefore an alternative system called two's complement is used.

An 8-bit value called a *byte* can represent 256 different values. Java supports five integral numeric types. The type char, although normally used to represent symbolic characters in a 16-bit format called Unicode, can be interpreted as an integer. As discussed shortly, the result of combining a char value with another numeric value will never be of type char. The char value is first converted to one of the other numeric types. These types are summarized in the following table.

Type	Number of Bits	Range of Values
byte	8	–128 to 127
short	16	–32768 to 32767
char	16	0 to 65536
int	32	–2147483648 to 2147483647
long	64	–9223372036854775808 to 9223372036854775807

The asymmetry in the most negative value and the most positive value of the integer types results from the two's complement system used in Java to represent negative values.

Literal integer values are represented by a sequence of digits. An integer literal is either an int or long. An explicit conversion, called a *cast*, of an int literal must be used to assign them to the smaller integer types short and byte (see Section 2.10.2, on page 38). Integer literals can be expressed in base 10 (decimal), base 8 (octal), and base 16 (hexadecimal) number systems. Decimal literals begin with a digit 1-9, octal literals begin with the digit 0, and hexadecimal literals begin with the two-character sequence 0x. To specify a long literal instead of an int literal, append the letter *el*, uppercase or lowercase, to the sequence of digits.

Here are some examples:

- 217—the decimal value two hundred seventeen
- 0217—an octal number equivalent to 143 in the decimal system $((2 \times 8^2 + 1 \times 8^1 + 7))$
- 0195 would be illegal because 9 is not a valid octal digit (only 0–7 are octal digits)

- 0x217—a hexadecimal number equivalent to 535 in the decimal system ($2 \times 16^2 + 1 \times 16^1 + 7$); the hexadecimal digits include 0–9 plus $a = 10$, $b = 11$, $c = 12$, $d = 13$, $e = 14$, and $f = 15$.
- 14084591234L—a long decimal literal; without the L this would be an error because 14084591234 is too large to store in the 32 bits of an int type integer.

2.9.2   THE FLOATING POINT TYPES

Java supports two floating point numeric types. A floating point number consists of three parts: a sign, a magnitude, and an exponent. These two types are summarized in the following table.

Type	Number of Bits	Approximate Range of Values	Approximate Precision
float	32	$+/- 10^{-45}$ to $+/- 10^{+38}$	7 decimal digits
double	64	$+/- 10^{-324}$ to $+/- 10^{+308}$	15 decimal digits

To represent floating point literals, you can simply insert a decimal point into a sequence of digits, as in 3.14159. If the magnitude of the number is too large or too small to represent in this fashion, then a notation analogous to scientific notation is used. The letter e from *exponent* is used to indicate the exponent of 10 as shown in the following examples.

Java Representation	Value
2.17e-27	2.17×10^{-27}
2.17e99	2.17×10^{99}

Unless specified otherwise, a floating point literal is of type double. To specify a floating point literal of type float, append either f or F to the literal—for example, 2.17e-27f.

2.9.3   THE char TYPE

Java provides char variables to represent and manipulate characters. This type is an integer type and can be mixed with the other integer types. Each char is stored in memory in 2 bytes. This size is large enough to store the integer values 0 through

65535 as distinct character codes or nonnegative integers, and these codes are called Unicode. Unicode uses more storage per character than previous common character encodings because it was designed to represent all the world's alphabets, not just one particular alphabet.

For English, a subset of these values represents actual printing characters. These include the lowercase and uppercase letters, digits, punctuation, and special characters such as % and +. The character set also includes the white space characters blank, tab, and newline. This important subset is represented by the first 128 codes, which are also known as the ASCII codes. Earlier languages, such as C and C++, worked only with this more limited set of codes and stored them in 1 byte.

The following table illustrates the correspondence between some character literals and integer values. Character literals are written by placing a single character between single quotes, as in `'a'`.

Some Character Constants and Their Corresponding Integer Values

Character constants	`'a'`	`'b'`	`'c'`	...	`'z'`
Corresponding values	97	98	99	...	112
Character constants	`'A'`	`'B'`	`'C'`	...	`'Z'`
Corresponding values	65	66	67	...	90
Character constants	`'0'`	`'1'`	`'2'`	...	`'9'`
Corresponding values	48	49	50	...	57
Character constants	`'&'`	`'*'`	`'+'`		
Corresponding values	38	42	43		

There is no particular relationship between the value of the character constant representing a digit and the digit's intrinsic integer value. That is, the value of `'2'` is *not* 2. The property that the values for `'a'`, `'b'`, `'c'`, and so on occur in order is important. It makes the sorting of characters, words, and lines into lexicographical order convenient.

Note that character literals are different from string literals, which use double quotes, as in `"Hello"`. String literals can be only one character long, but they are still `String` values, not `char` values. For example, `"a"` is a string literal.

Some nonprinting and hard-to-print characters require an escape sequence. The horizontal tab character, for example, is written as `\t` in character constants and in strings. Even though it is being described by the two characters `\` and `t`, it represents a single character. The backslash character `\` is called the *escape character* and is used to escape the usual meaning of the character that follows it. Another way to write a character constant is by means of a hexadecimal-digit escape sequence, as in `'\u0007'`. This is the alert character, or the audible bell. These 4 hexadecimal digits are prefixed by the letter u to indicate their use as a Unicode literal. The 65,536 Unicode characters can be written in hexadecimal form from '\u0000' to '\uFFFF'.

The following table contains some nonprinting and hard-to-print characters.

Name of Character	Escape	int	hex
Backslash	\\	92	\u005C
Backspace	\b	8	\u0008
Carriage return	\r	13	\u000D
Double quote	\"	34	\u0022
Formfeed	\f	12	\u000C
Horizontal tab	\t	9	\u0009
Newline	\n	10	\u000A
Single quote	\'	39	\u0027
Null character		0	\u0000
Alert		7	\u0007

The alert character is special; it causes the bell to ring. To hear the bell, try executing a program that contains the line

```
print('\u0007');
```

Character values are small integers, and, conversely, small integer values can be characters. Consider the declaration

```
char   c = 'a';
```

The variable c can be printed either as a character or as an integer:

```
print(c);        // a is printed
print((int)c);   // 97 is printed
```

2.9.4 NUMBERS VERSUS STRINGS

The sequence of 0s and 1s inside a computer used to store the String value "1234" is different from the sequence of 0s and 1s used to store the int value 1234, which is different from the sequence of 0s and 1s used to store the double value 1234.0. The string form is more convenient for certain types of manipulation, such as printing on the screen or for combining with other strings. The int form is better for some numeric calculations, and the double form is better for others. So how does the computer know how to interpret a particular sequence of 0s and 1s?

The answer is: Look at the type of the variable used to store the value. This answer is precisely why you must specify a type for each variable. Without the type information the sequence of 0s and 1s could be misinterpreted.

We do something similar with words all the time. Just as computers interpret sequences of 0s and 1s, human beings interpret sequences of alphabetic symbols. How people interpret those symbols depends on the context in which the symbols appear. For example, at times the same word can be a noun, and at other times it can be a verb. Also, certain sequences of letters mean different things in different languages. Take the word *pie* for example. What does it mean? If it is English, it is something good to eat. If it is Spanish, it means foot.

From the context of the surrounding words we can usually figure out what the type of the word is: verb or noun, English or Spanish. Some programming languages do something similar and "figure out" the type of a variable. These programming languages are generally considered to be more error prone than languages such as Java, which require the programmer to specify the type of each variable. Languages such as Java are called *strongly typed* languages.

2.10 ARITHMETIC EXPRESSIONS

The basic arithmetic operators in Java are addition +, subtraction -, multiplication *, division /, and modulus %. You can use all arithmetic operators with all primitive numeric types: `char`, `byte`, `short`, `int`, `long`, `float`, and `double`. In addition, you can combine any two numeric types by using these operators in what is known as *mixed mode arithmetic*. Although you can use the operators with any numeric type, Java actually does arithmetic only with the types `int`, `long`, `float`, and `double`. Therefore the following rules are used first to convert both operands into one of four types.

1. If either operand is a `double`, then the other is converted to `double`.
2. Otherwise, if either operand is a `float`, then the other is converted to `float`.
3. Otherwise, if either operand is a `long`, then the other is converted to a `long`.
4. Otherwise, both are converted to `int`.

This conversion is called *binary numeric promotion* and is also used with the binary relational operators discussed in Section 3.2.1.

When both operands are integer types, the operations of addition, subtraction, and multiplication are self-evident except when the result is too large to be represented by the type of the operands.

Integer values can't represent fractions. In Java, integer division truncates toward 0. For example, `6 / 4` is `1` and `6 / (-4)` is `-1`. A common mistake is to forget that integer division of nonzero values can result in 0. To obtain fractional results you must force one of the operands to be a floating point type. In expressions involving literals you can do so by adding a decimal point, as in `6.0 / 4`, which results in the floating point value `1.5`. In addition, integer division by zero will result in an error called an `ArithmeticException`. An *exception*, as the name implies, is something unexpected. Java provides a way for you to tell the computer what to do when exceptions occur. If you don't do anything and such an error occurs, the program will print an appropriate error message and terminate. We discuss exceptions in Chapter 9.

Unlike some programming languages, Java doesn't generate an exception when integer arithmetic results in a value that is too large. Instead, the extra bits of the true result are lost, and in some cases pollute the bit used for the sign. For example, adding two very large positive numbers could generate a negative result. Likewise, subtracting a very large positive number from a negative number could generate a positive result. If values are expected to be near the limit for a particular type, you should either use a larger type or check the result to determine whether such an overflow has occurred.

When one of the operands is a floating point type, but both operands are not of the same type, one of them is converted to the other as described earlier. Unlike some programming languages, floating point arithmetic operations in Java will never generate an exception. Instead three special values can result: positive infinity, negative infinity, and "Not a Number." See Appendix A for more details.

The modulus operator `%` returns the remainder from integer division. For example, `16 % 3` is 1, because 16 divided by 3 is 5 with a remainder of 1. The modulus operator is mostly used with integer operands; however, in Java it can be used with floating point operands. For floating point values `x % y` is n, where n is the largest integer such that `y * n` is less than or equal to `x`.

2.10.1 AN INTEGER ARITHMETIC EXAMPLE: `MakeChange.java`

The computation in Section 1.3, on page 6, whereby we made change for a dollar, is a perfect illustration of the use of the two integer division operators, `/` and `%`.

```
// MakeChange.java - change in dimes and pennies
import tio.*;      // use the package tio

class MakeChange {
  public static void main (String[] args) {
    int price, change, dimes, pennies;

    System.out.println("type price (0:100):");
    price = Console.in.readInt();
    change = 100 - price;       //how much change
    dimes = change / 10;        //number of dimes
    pennies = change % 10;      //number of pennies
    System.out.print("The change is : ");
    System.out.println(dimes + " dimes " +
                    pennies + " pennies");
  }
}
```

DISSECTION OF THE MakeChange PROGRAM

- ■ `int price, change, dimes, pennies;`

This program declares four integer variables. These types determine the range of values that can be used with these variables. They also dictate that this program use integer arithmetic operations, not floating point operations.

- ■ `price = Console.in.readInt();`

The `Console.in.readInt()` is used to obtain the input from the keyboard. The `readInt()` method is found in the `tio` package. At this point we must type in an integer price. For example, we would type 77 and hit Enter.

- ■ `change = 100 - price; //how much change`

This line computes the amount of change. This is the integer subtraction operator.

- ■ `dimes = change / 10;        //number of dimes`
  `pennies = change % 10;      //number of pennies`

To compute the number of dimes, we compute the integer result of dividing change by 10 and throw away any remainder. So if `change` is 23, then the integer result of 23/10 is 2. The remainder 3 is discarded. The number of pennies is the integer remainder of `change` divided by 10. The `%` operator is the integer remainder or modulo operator in Java. So if `change` is 23, then `23 % 10` is 3. In Exercise 18, on page 51, we ask you to use `double` for the variables and to report on your results.

2.10.2 TYPE CONVERSION

You may want or need to convert from one primitive numeric type to another. As mentioned in the preceding section, Java will sometimes automatically convert the operands of a numeric operator. These automatic conversions are also called *widening primitive conversions*. These conversions always convert to a type that requires at least as many bits as the type being converted, hence the term *widening*. In most but not all cases, a widening primitive conversion doesn't result in any loss of information. An example of a widening primitive conversion that can lose some precision is the conversion of the `int` value 123456789 to a `float` value, which results in 123456792. To understand this loss of information, see Appendix A. The following are the possible widening primitive conversions:.

From	To
byte	short, int, long, float, or double
short	int, long, float, or double
char	int, long, float, or double

From	To
int	long, float, or double
long	float or double
float	double

In addition to performing widening conversions automatically as part of mixed mode arithmetic, widening primitive conversions are also used to convert automatically the right-hand side of an assignment operator to the type of the variable on the left. For example, the following assignment will automatically convert the integer result to a floating point value.

```
int x = 1, y = 2;
float z;
z = x + y;    // automatic widening from int to float
```

A *narrowing primitive conversion* is a conversion between primitive numeric types that may result in significant information loss. The following are narrowing primitive conversions.

From	To
byte	char
short	byte or char
char	byte or short
int	byte, short, or char
long	byte, short, char, or int
float	byte, short, char, int, or long
double	byte, short, char, int, long, or float

Narrowing primitive conversions generally result only from an explicit type conversion called a *cast*. A cast is written as *(type) expression*, where the expression to be converted is preceded by the new type in parentheses. A cast is an operator and, as the table in Section 2.13, on page 45, indicates, has higher precedence than the five basic arithmetic operators. For example, if you are interested only in the integer portion of the floating point variable someFloat, then you can store it in someInteger, as in

```
int someInteger;
float someFloat = 3.14159;
someInteger = (int)someFloat;
System.out.println(someInteger);
```

The output is

```
3
```

If the cast is between two integral types, the most significant bits are simply discarded in order to fit the resulting format. This discarding can cause the result to have a different sign from the original value. The following example shows how a narrowing conversion can cause a change of sign.

```
int i = 127, j = 128;
byte iAsByte = (byte)i, jAsByte = (byte)j;
System.out.println(iAsByte);
System.out.println(jAsByte);
```

The output is

```
127
-128
```

The largest positive value that can be stored in a `byte` is 127. Attempting to force a narrowing conversion on a value greater than 127 will result in the loss of significant information. In this case the sign is reversed. To understand exactly what happens in this example, see Appendix A.

COMMON PROGRAMMING ERROR

Remember that integer division truncates toward zero. For example, the value of the expression 3/4 is 0. Both the numerator and the denominator are integer literals, so this is an integer division. If what you want is the rounded result, you must first force this to be a floating point division and then use the routine `Math.round()` to round the floating point result to an integer. To force a floating point division you can either make one of the literals a floating point literal or use a cast. In the following example first recall that floating point literals of type `float` are specified by appending the letter `f`. Then for

```
int x = Math.round(3.0f/4);
```

the variable `x` will get the value 1. Forcing the division to be a floating point divide is not enough. In the following example, `z` will be 0.

```
int z = (int)3.0f/4;
```

The conversion of 0.75 to an `int` truncates any fractional part.

2.11   ASSIGNMENT OPERATORS

To change the value of a variable, we have already made use of assignment statements such as

```
a = b + c;
```

Assignment is an operator, and its precedence is lower than all the operators we've discussed so far. The associativity for the assignment operator is right to left. In this section we explain in detail its significance.

To understand = as an operator, let's first consider + for the sake of comparison. The binary operator + takes two operands, as in the expression a + b. The value of the expression is the sum of the values of a and b. By comparison, a simple assignment expression is of the form

variable = rightHandSide

where *rightHandSide* is itself an expression. A semicolon placed at the end would make this an assignment statement. The assignment operator = has the two operands *variable* and *rightHandSide*. The value of *rightHandSide* is assigned to *variable*, and that value becomes the value of the assignment expression as a whole. To illustrate, let's consider the statements

```
b = 2;
c = 3;
a = b + c;
```

where the variables are all of type int. By making use of assignment expressions, we can condense these statements to

```
a = (b = 2) + (c = 3);
```

The assignment expression b = 2 assigns the value 2 to the variable b, and the assignment expression itself takes on this value. Similarly, the assignment expression c = 3 assigns the value 3 to the variable c, and the assignment expression itself takes on this value. Finally, the values of the two assignment expressions are added, and the resulting value is assigned to a.

Although this example is artificial, in many situations assignment occurs naturally as part of an expression. A frequently occurring situation is *multiple assignment*. Consider the statement

```
a = b = c = 0;
```

Because the operator = associates from right to left, an equivalent statement is

```
a = (b = (c = 0));
```

First, c is assigned the value 0, and the expression c = 0 has value 0. Then b is assigned the value 0, and the expression b = (c = 0) has value 0. Finally, a is assigned the value 0, and the expression a = (b = (c = 0)) has value 0.

In addition to =, there are other assignment operators, such as += and -=. An expression such as

```
k = k + 2
```

will add 2 to the old value of k and assign the result to k, and the expression as a whole will have that value. The expression

```
k += 2
```

accomplishes the same task. The following list contains all the assignment operators.

Assignment Operators

=	+=	-=	*=	/=	%=	>>=	<<=	&=	^=	|=

All these operators have the same precedence, and all have right-to-left associativity. The meaning is specified by

$$variable \ op= \ expression$$

which is equivalent to

$$variable \ = \ variable \ op \ (\ expression \ )$$

with the exception that if *variable* is itself an expression, it is evaluated only once. Note carefully that an assignment expression such as

```
j *= k + 3     is equivalent to    j = j * (k + 3)
```

rather than

```
j = j * k + 3
```

The following table illustrates how assignment expressions are evaluated.

Declarations and Initializations

```
int     i = 1, j = 2, k = 3, m = 4;
```

Expression	Equivalent Expression	Equivalent Expression	Value
i += j + k	i += (j + k)	i = (i + (j + k))	6
j *= k = m + 5	j *= (k = (m + 5))	j = (j * (k = (m + 5)))	18

2.12   THE INCREMENT AND DECREMENT OPERATORS

Computers are very good at counting. As a result, many programs involve having an integer variable that takes on the values 0, 1, 2, . . . One way to add 1 to a variable is

```
i = i + 1;
```

which changes the value stored in the variable i to be 1 more than it was before this statement was executed. This procedure is called *incrementing* a variable. Because it is so common, Java, like its predecessor C, includes a shorthand notation for incrementing a variable. The following statement gives the identical result.

```
i++;
```

The operator ++ is known as the increment operator. Similarly, there is a decrement operator, --, so that the following two statements are equivalent:

```
i = i - 1;
i--;
```

Here is a simple program that demonstrates the increment operator.

```
//Increment.java - demonstrate incrementing
class Increment {
  public static void main(String[] args) {
    int i = 0;
    System.out.println("i = " + i);
    i = i + 1;
    System.out.println("i = " + i);
    i++;
    System.out.println("i = " + i);
    i++;
    System.out.println("i = " + i);
  }
}
```

The output of this program is

```
i = 0
i = 1
i = 2
i = 3
```

Note that both increment and decrement operators are placed after the variable to be incremented. When placed after its argument they are called the *postfix* increment and *postfix* decrement operators. These operators also can be used before the variable. They are then called the *prefix* increment and *prefix* decrement operators. Each of the expressions ++i *(prefix)* and i++ *(postfix)* has a value; moreover, each causes the stored value of i in memory to be incremented by 1. The expression ++i causes the stored value of i to be incremented first, with the expression then taking as its value the new stored value of i. In contrast, the expression i++ has as its value the current value of i; then the expression causes the stored value of i to be incremented. The following code illustrates the situation.

```
int    a, b, c = 0;
a = ++c;
b = c++;
System.out.println("a = " + a);    //a = 1 is printed
System.out.println("b = " + b);    //b = 1 is printed
System.out.println("c = " + ++c); //c = 3 is printed
```

Similarly, --i causes the stored value of i in memory to be decremented by 1 first, with the expression then taking this new stored value as its value. With i-- the value of the expression is the current value of i; then the expression causes the stored value of i in memory to be decremented by 1. Note that ++ and -- cause the value of a variable in memory to be changed. Other operators do not do so. For example, an expression such as a + b leaves the values of the variables a and b unchanged. These ideas are expressed by saying that the operators ++ and -- have a *side effect*; not only do these operators yield a value, but they also change the stored value of a variable in memory.

In some cases we can use ++ in either prefix or postfix position, with both uses producing equivalent results. For example, each of the two statements

```
++i;    and    i++;
```

is equivalent to

```
i = i + 1;
```

In simple situations you can consider ++ and -- as operators that provide concise notation for the incrementing and decrementing of a variable. In other situations, you must pay careful attention as to whether prefix or postfix position is used.

2.13 PRECEDENCE AND ASSOCIATIVITY OF OPERATORS

When evaluating expressions with several operators, you need to understand the order of evaluation of each operator and its arguments. *Operator precedence* gives a hierarchy that helps determine the order in which operations are evaluated. For example, precedence determines which arithmetic operations are evaluated first in

```
x = (-b + Math.sqrt(b * b - 4 * a * c))/(2 * a)
```

which you may recognize as the expression to compute one of the roots of a quadratic equation, written like this in your mathematics class:

$$x = -b + \frac{\sqrt{b^2 - 4ac}}{2a}$$

To take a simpler example, what is the value of integer variable x after the assignment x = 7 + 5 * 3? The answer is 22, not $(7 + 5) \times 3$ which is 36. The reason is that multiplication has *higher precedence* than addition; therefore 5 * 3 is evaluated before 7 is added to the result.

In addition to some operators having higher precedence than others, Java specifies the *associativity* or the order in which operators of equal precedence are to be evaluated. For example, the value of 100 / 5 * 2 is 40, not 10. This is because / and * have equal precedence and arithmetic operators of equal precedence are evaluated from left to right. If you wanted to do the multiplication before the division, you would write the expression as 100 / (5 * 2). Parentheses can be used to override the normal operator precedence rules.

This left to right ordering is important in some cases that might not appear obvious. Consider the expression x + y + z. From simple algebra, the associativity of addition tells us that (x + y) + z is the same as x + (y + z). Unfortunately, this is true only when you have numbers with infinite precision. Suppose that y is the largest positive integer that Java can represent, x is -100, and z is 50. Evaluating (y + z) first will result in integer overflow, which in Java will be equivalent to some very large negative number, clearly not the expected result. If instead, (x + y) is evaluated first, then adding z will result in an integer that is still in range and the result will be the correct value.

The precedence and associativity of all Java operators is given in Appendix B. The following table gives the rules of precedence and associativity for the operators of Java that we have used so far.

Operator Precedence and Associativity

Operator	Associativity
( ) ++ (postfix) -- (postfix)	Left to right
+ (unary) - (unary) ++ (prefix) -- (prefix)	Right to left
new (*type*)*expr*	Right to left
* / %	Left to right
+ -	Left to right
= += -= *= /= *etc.*	Right to left

All the operators on the same line, such as *, /, and %, have equal precedence with respect to each other but have higher precedence than all the operators that occur on the lines below them. The associativity rule for all the operators on each line appears in the right-hand column.

In addition to the binary +, which represents addition, there is a unary +, and both operators are represented by a plus sign. The minus sign also has binary and unary meanings. The following table gives some additional examples of precedence and associativity of operators.

Declarations and Initializations

```
int    a = 1, b = 2, c = 3, d = 4;
```

Expression	Equivalent Expression	Value
a * b / c	(a * b) / c	0
a * b % c + 1	((a * b) % c) + 1	3
++a * b - c--	((++a) * b) - (c --)	1
7 - - b * ++d	7 - ((- b) * (++d))	17

2.14 PROGRAMMING STYLE

A clear, consistent style is important to writing good code. We use a style that is largely adapted from the Java professional programming community. Having a style that is readily understandable by the rest of the programming community is important.

We've already mentioned the importance of comments for documenting a program. Anything that aids in explaining what is otherwise not clear in the program should be placed in a comment. Comments help the programmer keep track of decisions made while writing the code. Without good documentation, you may return to some code you have written, only to discover that you have forgotten why you did some particular thing. The documentation should enable someone other than the original programmer to pick up, use, and modify the code. All but the most trivial methods should have comments at the beginning, clearly stating the purpose of the method. Also, complicated blocks of statements should be preceded by comments summarizing the function of the block. Comments should add to the clarity of the code, not simply restate the program, statement by statement. Here is an example of a useless comment.

```
area = width * height;      // compute the area
```

Good documentation includes proper choice of identifiers. Identifiers should have meaningful names. Certain simple one-character names are used to indicate auxiliary variables, such as i, j, or k, as integer variables.

The code should be easy to read. Visibility is enhanced by the use of white space. In general, we present only one statement to a line and in all expressions separate operators from arguments by a space. As we progress to more complex programs, we shall present, by example or explicit mention, accepted layout rules for program elements.

SOME NAMING CONVENTIONS USED BY MANY JAVA PROGRAMMERS

- Class names start with uppercase and embedded words, as in `HelloWorld`, are capitalized.
- Methods and variables start with lowercase and embedded words, as in `readInt`, `data`, `toString`, and `loopIndex`, are capitalized.
- Although legal, the dollar sign, `$`, should not be used except in machine-generated Java programs.

Summary

- To create a Java program first define a class. Give the class a method called `main()`. Put whatever instructions you want the computer to execute inside the body of the method `main()`.
- A program stores data in variables. Each variable is given a type, such as `int` for storing integers or `String` for storing strings.
- You can use literals to embed constant values of various types in a program, such as in the constant string `"Hello, world!"` or the integer constant `123`.
- You can combine literals and variables in expressions by using operators such as `+` for addition or string concatenation and `*` for numeric multiplication.
- You can store the result of evaluating an expression in a variable by using the assignment operator `=`. The variable is always on the left, and the expression being assigned to the variable is always on the right.
- You can call a method from another class by writing the name of the class followed by a dot and the name of the method—for example, `Math.sqrt()`.
- The lexical elements of a Java program are keywords, identifiers, literals, operator symbols, punctuation, comments, and white space.
- You can print strings and numbers to the screen by using the method `System.out.print()` or `System.out.println()`. The latter appends a newline to whatever is printed. These methods are part of the standard Java classes.
- You can input integers (whole numbers) from the keyboard by using the method `Console.in.readInt()`. This method isn't a standard Java class but is provided in the package `tio`. The full text of the package appears in Appendix C.
- Java supports the primitive integer types `char`, `byte`, `short`, `int`, and `long`. It also supports two floating point types, `float` and `double`.
- Integer division truncates toward zero—it doesn't round to the nearest whole number. You can use `Math.round()` if rounding is what you want.

Review Questions

1. What line appears in every complete Java program indicating where to begin executing the program?
2. What one-line instruction would you use to have a Java program print `Goodbye`?
3. What affect do strings such as `/* what is this */` have on the execution of a Java program?
4. What is a variable?
5. What is a method?
6. Complete the following table.

Text	Legal ID	Why or Why Not
`3xyz`	No	Digit is first character.
`xy3z`		
`a = b`		
`main`		
`Count`		
`class`		

7. What does the symbol = do in Java?
8. Programmers say _____ a method when they mean go and execute the instructions for the method.
9. True or false? A multiline comment can be placed anywhere white space could be placed.
10. True or false? Keywords can also be used as variables, but then the special meaning of the keyword is overridden.
11. What convention for identifiers given in this chapter is used in `whatAmI`, `howAboutThis`, `someName`?
12. What primitive types are used to store whole numbers?
13. What is the difference between `x = 'a'` and `x = a`?
14. What is the difference between `s = "hello"` and `s = hello`?
15. Which version of the Java program `HelloWorld` is the one you can view and edit with a text editor, *HelloWorld.java* or *HelloWorld.class*? What does the other one contain? What program created the one you do not edit?
16. What is Unicode?
17. List the primitive types in Java.
18. Before it can be used, every variable must be declared and given a _____.
19. What is the value of the Java expression `"10"+"20"`? Don't ignore the quotation marks; they are crucial.
20. Write a Java statement that could be used to read an integer value from the keyboard and store it in the variable `someNumber`.

21. What is wrong with the following Java statement?

```
System.out.println("This statement is supposed
          to print a message. What is wrong?");
```

22. Every group of input statements should be preceded by what?
23. How do you write x times y in Java?
24. What is the difference between `System.out.print("message")` and `System.out.println("message")`?
25. Write a *single* Java statement that will produce the following output.

```
X
XX
XXX
```

26. Approximately, what is the largest value that can be stored in the primitive type `int`? One thousand? One million? One billion? One trillion? Even larger?
27. What primitive Java type can store the largest numbers?
28. What is the value of the following Java expressions?

```
20 / 40
6 / 4
6.4 / 2
```

Exercises

1. Write a Java program that prints "Hello *your name*." You can do this by a simple modification to the `HelloWorld` program. Compile and run this program on your computer.
2. Write a Java program that prints a favorite poem of at least eight lines. Be sure to print it out neatly aligned. At the end of the poem, print two blank lines and then the author's name.
3. Design your own signature logo, such as a sailboat icon if you like sailing, and print it followed by "yours truly—*your name*." A sailboat signature logo might look like

```
              /\

             /  \

            /    \

           /      \

           |

       =====================

      \  Yours truly  /

         Bruce McPohl
```

4. Write a Java program to read in two numbers and print the sum. Be sure to include a message to prompt the user for input and a message identifying the output. See what

happens if you type in something that is not a number when the program is run. See how large a number you can type in and still have the program work correctly.

5. The following code contains three syntax errors and produces two syntax error messages from *javac*. Fix the problems.

```
// Ch2e1.java - fixing syntax errors
Class Ch2e1 {
  public static void main(String[] args) {
    System.out.println(hello, world);
  }
```

The *javac* compiler's message reads:

```
Ch2e1.java:2: Class or interface declaration
expected.
 Class ch2e1 {
  ^
Ch2e1.java:7: Unbalanced parentheses.
 ^
2 errors
```

6. The following code produces one syntax error message from *javac*. Fix the problem.

```
// Ch2e2.java - more syntax errors
class Ch2e2 {
  public static void main(String[] args) {
    int count = 1, i = 3,
    System.out.println("count + i = ",  count + i);
  }
}
```

The *javac* compiler's message reads

```
Ch2e2.java:6: Invalid declaration.
 System.out.println("count + i = ", count + i);
                      ^
1 error
```

Here, unlike the previous exercise, the compiler doesn't as clearly point to the errors. Frequently, errors in punctuation lead to syntax error messages that are hard to decipher. After you fix the first syntax error in the code, a second error will be identified.

7. Continue with the code class Ch2e2. If you fixed just the syntax errors, you may get a running program that still has a run-time bug. Namely, the output is not the sum of count + i. Fixing run-time or semantic bugs is harder than fixing syntax bugs because something is wrong with your understanding of how to program the solution. Without introducing any other variables fix the run-time bug.

8. Write a program that draws a box like the one shown, using a *single* println() statement.

```
*********
*       *
*       *
*********
```

9. Use `Console.in.readDouble()` to read in one double precision floating point number and then print the results of calling `Math.sin()`, `Math.cos()`, `Math.asin()`, `Math.exp()`, `Math.log()`, `Math.floor()`, and `Math.round()` with the input value as a parameter. Be sure to prompt the user for input and label the output.

10. Write a program to read two double precision floating point numbers, using `Console.in.readDouble()`. Print the sum, difference, product, and quotient of the two numbers. Try two very small numbers, two very large numbers, and one very small number with one very large number. You can use the same notation used for literals to enter the numbers. For example, `0.123e-310` is a very small number.

11. Write a program to compute the area of a circle given its radius. Let `radius` be a variable of type `double` and use `Console.in.readDouble()` to read in its value. Be sure that the output is understandable. The Java class `Math` contains definitions for the constants `E` and `PI`, so you can use `Math.PI` in your program.

12. Extend the previous program to write out the circumference of a circle and the volume of a sphere given the radius as input. Recall that the volume of a sphere is

$$V = \frac{4 \times \pi r^3}{3}$$

13. Write a program that asks for a `double` and then prints it out. Then ask for a second `double`, this time printing out the sum and average of the two `doubles`. Then ask for a third double and again print out the accumulated sum and the average of the three doubles. Use variables `data1`, `data2`, `data3`, and `sum`. Later, when we discuss loops, you will see how this is easily done for an arbitrary number of input values.

14. Write a program that reads in an integer and prints it as a character. Remember that character codes can be nonprinting.

15. Write a program using `Console.inreadChar()` to read in a character and print its integer value. This `tio` method returns an integer value, so it need not be cast from a `char` to an `int`. By the way, the reason is that the end-of-file character translates to −1. This method allows you to detect when you have reached the end of the input when reading from the keyboard or from a disk file (see Section 10.7).

16. Write a program that asks for the number of quarters, dimes, nickels, and pennies you have. Then compute the total value of your change and print the number of dollars and the remaining cents. The preferred output form would be $X.YY, but this is surprisingly difficult in Java and requires techniques not yet introduced. To get a handle on the problem, try storing $2.50 as a `float` then print it. Then try storing $2.05 as two numbers, one for the dollars and one for the remaining cents. Try to print these two numbers in the preferred format.

17. Write a program capable of converting one currency to another. For example, given U.S. dollars it should print out the equivalent number of French francs. Look up the exchange rate and use it as input.

18. Change the `MakeChange` program to use variables that are `doubles`. Run the program and see what goes wrong.

```
class MakeChange {
  public static void main (String[] args) {
    double price, change, dimes, pennies;
    . . .
```

19. The following is a C program for printing "Hello, world!".

```
/* Hello World In C
 * Purpose:
 *    The classic "Hello, world!" program.
 *    It simply prints a message to the screen.
 * Author:
 *     Jane Programmer
 *        as derived from Kernighan and Richie
 */

#include <stdio.h>      /* needed for IO */
int main(void) {
    printf("Hello, world!\n");
    return 0;           /* unneeded in Java */
}
```

Note how similar this program is to the Java version. A key difference is the lack of class encapsulation of `main()`. As in Java, `main()` starts the program's execution. In C, methods are known as functions. The `printf()` function is found in the standard input–output library imported by the C compiler for use in this program. The `return 0` ends program execution and is not used in Java. Convert the following C program to Java.

```
#include <stdio.h>
int main(void) {
    printf("Hello, world!\n");
    printf("My name is George.\n");
    printf("Yada Yada Yada ...\n");
    return 0;
}
```

20. In C, the `printf()` function can also be used to print primitive values, such as integer values and floating point values as in the following program.

```
#include <stdio.h>
int main(void) {
    double side = 3.5;    /* side of a cube */
    double volume;

    printf("The side of my cube is %f feet.\n", side);
    volume = side * side * side;
    printf("The cubes volume is %f cubic feet.\n",
              volume);
    return 0;
}
```

If you have a C compiler, such as *gcc,* compile and run this program. Then write the equivalent program in Java. The `%f` is a format control that tells the `printf()` function where to place the value of the corresponding variable, such as `side` or `volume`, in the program. Getting this format wrong causes many programming errors in C. This is one of the places that Java, a type-safe language, provides better support than C.

Applet Exercise

The following program is an example of a Java applet. This program uses several features of Java that we explain later. Note that there is no method `main()`; instead there is the method `paint()`. For now just concentrate on the body of the method `paint()`, treating the surrounding code as a template to be copied verbatim. By invoking the appropriate drawing operations on the `Graphics` object g, you can draw on the applet.

```
/* To place this applet in a web page, add the
   following two lines to the html document for the
   page.
   <applet code="FirstApplet.class"
   width=500 height=200></applet>
*/
// AWT and Swing together comprise the collection of
// classes used for building graphical Java programs
import java.awt.*; //required for programs that draw
import javax.swing.*; //required for Swing applets

public class FirstApplet extends JApplet {
  public void paint(Graphics g) {
    // draw a line from the upper left corner to
    // 100 pixels below the top center of the Applet
    g.drawLine(0,0,250,100);
    // draw a line from the end of the previous line
    // up to the top center of the Applet
    g.drawLine(250,100,250,0);
    // draw an oval inscribed in an invisible
    // rectangle with its upper left corner at the
    // intersection of the two lines drawn above
    g.drawOval(250,100,200,100);
  }
}
```

The class `Graphics` is used for simple drawing, and many drawing operations are defined for it. In this example we use the method `drawLine()` to draw a line. The first two numbers in parentheses for the `drawline()` operation are the *xy* coordinates of one end of the line, and the last two numbers are the *xy* coordinates of the other end. As you can see from the output of the program, the location (0, 0) is in the upper left corner, with increasing *x* moving to the right and increasing *y* moving down. To draw an oval, give the coordinates of the upper left corner and the width and height on an invisible rectangle. The oval will be inscribed inside the rectangle. To execute an applet, first compile it like you do other Java programs. Then you can either run the program *appletviewer* or use a web browser to view the applet. To view the applet `FirstApplet` using the *appletviewer* on Unix and Windows machines, type the following at a command line prompt.

```
appletviewer FirstApplet.java
```

Notice that we are passing `FirstApplet.java`—not `FirstApplet` or `FirstApplet.class`—to the appletviewer. This procedure is different from running regular Java programs. In fact `appletviewer` just looks in the text file passed to it for an applet element. An applet element begins with `<applet` and ends with `</applet>`. Any text file containing the applet element shown in the opening comment for `FirstApplet.java` would work just as well.

To view the applet in a Web browser, create a file—for example, `FirstApplet.html`. Put the applet tag in the html file. Put the html file in the same directory as your applet and then open the html file with a Web browser.

The applet looks like the following when run with an `appletviewer`.

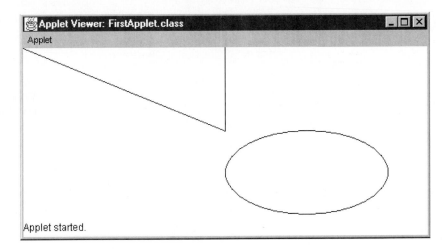

Modify this applet to draw a simple picture. Look up the documentation for `Graphics` on the Web at

```
http://java.sun.com/products/jdk/1.2/docs/api/
java.awt.Graphics.html#_top_
```

and use at least one method/operation of `Graphics` not used in `FirstApplet`.

3

Statements and Control Flow

The program examples presented until now have executed from top to bottom without making any decisions. In this chapter, we have programs select among two or more alternatives. We also demonstrate how to write programs that repeatedly execute the same sequence of instructions. Both instructions to computers and instructions in everyday life are filled with conditional and iterative statements. A conditional instruction for your microwave oven might say "*If* you wish to defrost press the defrost button; otherwise, press the full power button." An iterative instruction for baking a loaf of bread might say "Let the dough rise in a warm place *until* it has doubled in size." Conditional and iterative statements are controlled by boolean expressions. A *boolean expression* is either true or false. "If it is raining, wear your raincoat" is an instruction given by many parents and is followed if it is true that it is raining. In Java, expressions that evaluate as true or false are of type `boolean`. To direct the flow of control properly you need to learn how to write `boolean` expressions.

3.1 EXPRESSION, BLOCK, AND EMPTY STATEMENTS

Java has many kinds of *statements*. Most of the statements that we have shown have specified the evaluation of an expression. We'll soon look at statements that select between two alternatives and statements that repeat many times. Before doing that, we need to look more closely at the statements that we have been using. The normal flow of instructions in Java is to execute the statements of the program in sequential order from top to bottom.

All the statements used so far have been either *variable declaration statements* or *expression statements*. Variable declaration statements begin with a type, such as `int` or `String`, and end with a semicolon, as in

```
int width, height, area;
String hello = "Hello, world!";
double size = 1.5, x;
```

The first declares three variables of type int. The second declares one variable of type String and initializes it. The third declares and initializes the variable size, but not the variable x. Declaration statements start with a type and are followed by a comma separated by a list of variables. The variables may be initialized by using the equals sign followed typically by a literal. In Java all variables need to be declared.

Expression statements are formed by adding a semicolon to the end of an expression. Expressions are basic to performing computations. Not all expressions are valid in expression statements. The two types of expressions used so far that are valid in expression statements are assignment expressions and method call expressions. An *assignment expression* is any expression involving the assignment operator. A *method call expression* does not involve an assignment operator. The following are examples of expression statements.

```
area = width * height;   //simple assignment statement
System.out.println(...); //method call expression
```

A statement used for grouping a number of statements is a block. A *block* is a sequence of one or more statements enclosed by braces. A block is itself a statement. A simple example is

```
{
  x = 1;
  y = 2 * x + 1;
  System.out.println(y);
  System.out.println(x);
}
```

Statements inside a block can also be blocks. The inside block is called an *inner block*, which is *nested* in the *outer block*. An example is

```
{ //outer block
  x = 1;
  { //inner block
    y = 2;
    System.out.println(y);
  } //end of inner block
  System.out.println(x);
}
```

This example merely demonstrates the syntax of a block; we wouldn't normally put a block inside another block for no reason. Most nested blocks involve declaration statements that create local variables. A simple example of a block with declarations is

```
{
  int i = 5 + j;
  //i is created in this block, j is from elsewhere
  ...
} //end of block i disappears
```

In this example the `int` variable `i` is created when this block is executed. When this block is started, `i` is placed in memory with its initial value calculated as 5 plus the value of `j`. When the block is exited, the variable disappears.

Blocks are not terminated by semicolons. Rather they are terminated by a closing brace, also called the right brace. Recall that the semicolon, when used, is part of the statement, not something added to the statement. For example, the semicolon turns an expression into a statement. Understanding this will make it much easier for you to create syntactically correct programs with the new statement types that we introduce in this chapter.

3.1.1   EMPTY STATEMENT

The simplest statement is the *empty statement*, or *null statement*. It is just a semicolon all by itself and results in no action. A semicolon placed after a block is an empty statement and is irrelevant to the program's actions. The following code fragment produces exactly the same result as the nested block example in the preceding section. The string of semicolons simply create seven empty statements following the inner block.

```
{
  x = 1;
  {
    y = 2;
    System.out.println(y);
  };;;;;;;
  System.out.println(x);
}
```

3.2   BOOLEAN EXPRESSIONS

A *boolean expression* is any expression that evaluates to either true or false. Java includes a primitive type `boolean`. The two simplest boolean expressions are the boolean literals `true` and `false`. In addition to these two literals, boolean values result from expressions involving either relational operators for comparing numbers or logical operators that act on boolean values.

3.2.1   RELATIONAL AND EQUALITY OPERATORS

All conditional statements require some boolean expression to decide which execution path to follow. Java uses four *relational operators*: less than, `<` ; greater than, `>` ; less than or equal, `<=` ; and greater than or equal, `>=` . Java also contains two equality operators: equal, `==` ; and not equal, `!=` . They can be used between any two numeric values. The equality operators may also be used when comparing non-numeric types. They are listed in the following table.

Operator	Name	Example
<	Less than	`10 < 20` is true.
>	Greater than	`10 > 20` is false.
==	Equal	`10 == 20` is false.
<=	Less than or equal	`10 <= 10` is true.
>=	Greater than or equal	`11 >= 10` is true.
!=	Not equal	`10 != 20` is true.

The relational operators can be used in assignment to boolean variables, as in

```
int i = 3, j = 4;
boolean flag;
flag = 5 < 6;          //flag is now true
flag = (i == j);       //flag is now false
flag = (j + 2) <= 6;   //flag is now true
```

3.2.2 LOGICAL OPERATORS

Once you have a boolean value, either stored in a variable representing a primitive boolean value (for example, `boolean done = false;`) or as the result of an expression involving a relational operator (for example, `(x < y)`), you can combine these boolean values by using the logical operators. Java provides three logical operators, "and," "or," and "not." The meaning of these operators is given in the following table.

Operator	Name	Description	Example—Assume x is 10 and y Is 20
&&	and	The expression x `&&` y is true if both x AND y are true and false otherwise.	`(x < 20) && (y < 30)` is true.
||	or	The expression x `||` y is true if either x OR y (or both) is true and false otherwise.	`(x < 20)||(y > 30)` is true.
!	not	The expression `!`x is true if x is false and false otherwise.	`!(x < 20)` is false.

For example, if you wanted to determine whether a person in a database was an adult but not a senior citizen, you could check if their age was greater than or equal to 18 *and* their age was less than 65. The following Java code fragment will print out "full fare adult is true" if this condition is met; otherwise, it prints "full fare adult is false".

```
boolean b = (ageOfPerson >= 18 && ageOfPerson < 65);
System.out.println("full fare adult is " + b);
```

For an example of the use of "or," consider the opposite situation as above where you wanted to find out if a reduced fair was appropriate. You might write

```
b = (ageOfPerson < 18 || ageOfPerson >= 65);
System.out.println("reduced fare is " + b);
```

The logical operators `&&` and `||` use *short-circuit evaluation*. In the preceding example of a logical "and" expression, if the `ageOfPerson` were 10, then the test for `ageOfPerson < 65` would be omitted. Used partly for efficiency reasons, this approach is helpful when the second part of such an expression could lead to an undesirable result, such as program termination.

As with other operators, the relational, equality, and logical operators have rules of precedence and associativity that determine precisely how expressions involving these operators are evaluated, as shown in the following table.

Operator Precedence and Associativity

Operators					Associativity
`( )` `++` (postfix) `--` (postfix)					Left to right
`+` (unary) `-` (unary) `++` (prefix) `--` (prefix) `!`					Right to left
`*` `/` `%`					Left to right
`+` `-`					Left to right
`<` `<=` `>` `>=`					Left to right
`==` `!=`					Left to right
`&&`					Left to right
`||`					Left to right
`=` `+=` `-=` `*=` `/=` *etc.*					Right to left

Note that with the exception of the boolean unary operator negation, the relational, boolean, and equality operators have lower precedence than the arithmetic operators. Only the assignment operators have lower precedence.

3.3 THE if STATEMENT

Computers make decisions by evaluating expressions and executing different statements based on the value of the expression. The simplest type of decision is one that can have only two possible outcomes, such as go left versus go right or continue versus stop. In Java, we use *boolean expressions* to control decisions that have two possible outcomes.

The if *statement* is a conditional statement. An if statement has the general form

```
if ( BooleanExpr )
   Statement
```

If the expression *BooleanExpr* is true, then the statement, *Statement,* is executed; otherwise, *Statement* is skipped. *Statement* is called the *then statement*. In some programming languages, but not Java, then is used to signal the then statement. After the if statement has been executed, control passes to the next statement. The flow of execution can skip around *Statement* as shown in the following diagram.

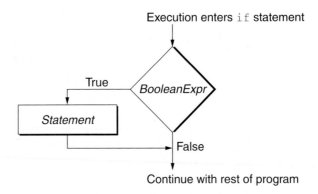

Note the absence of semicolons in the general form of the if statement. Recall that the semicolon, when required, is part of the *Statement* and is not used to separate statements, as in

```
if (temperature < 32)
   System.out.println("Warning: Below Freezing!");
System.out.println("It's " + temperature + "degrees");
```

The message `Warning: Below Freezing!` is printed only when the `temperature` is less than 32. The second print statement is always executed. This example has a semicolon at the end of the `if` statement because the statement inside the `if` statement is an expression statement that ends with a semicolon.

When the *Statement* inside an `if` statement is a block, you get `if` statements that look like

```
if (temperature < 32)
{
  System.out.println("Warning Warning Warning!");
  System.out.println("Warning: Below Freezing!");
  System.out.println("Warning Warning Warning!");
}
```

Here you can see the importance of the block as a means of grouping statements. In this example, what otherwise would be three separate statements are grouped, and all are executed when the boolean expression is true. The formatting shown of the `if` statement with a block as the *Statement* aligns vertically with the braces of the block statement. An alternative formatting—and the one that we use—places the opening brace on the same line as the keyword `if` and then aligns the closing brace with the keyword as shown here.

```
if (temperature < 32) {
  System.out.println("Warning Warning Warning!");
  System.out.println("Warning: Below Freezing!");
  System.out.println("Warning Warning Warning!");
}
```

At the end of this chapter, we discuss further which style to choose.

3.3.1 PROBLEM SOLVING WITH THE if STATEMENT

A different number is initially placed in each of three boxes, labeled *a*, *b*, and *c*, respectively. The problem is to rearrange or sort the numbers so that the final number in box *a* is less than that in box *b* and that the number in box *b* is less than that in box *c*. Initial and final states for a particular set of numbers are as follows.

	Before		After
a	17	*a*	6
b	6	*b*	11
c	11	*c*	17

Pseudocode for performing this sorting task involves the following steps.

PSEUDOCODE FOR THREE-NUMBER SORT

1. Place the first number in box a.
2. Place the second number in box b.
3. Place the third number in box c.
4. If the number in a is not larger than the number in b, go to step 6.
5. Interchange the number in a with that in b.
6. If the number in b is larger than the number in c, then go to step 7; otherwise, halt.
7. Interchange the numbers in b and c.
8. If the number in a is larger than that in b, then go to step 9; otherwise, halt.
9. Interchange the numbers in a and b.
10. Halt.

Let's execute this pseudocode with the three specific numbers previously given: 17, 6, and 11, in that order. We always start with the first instruction. The contents of the three boxes at various stages of execution are shown in the following table.

Box	Step 1	Step 2	Step 3	Step 5	Step 7
a	17	17	17	6	6
b		6	6	17	11
c			11	11	17

To execute step 1, we place the first number, 17, in box a; similarly, at the end of instruction 3, the 6 has been inserted into box b, and box c contains the 11. As 17 is larger than 6, the condition tested in step 4 is false, and we proceed to instruction 5; this step switches the values into boxes a and b so that box a now contains the 6 and box b has the 17. Step 6 has now been reached, and we compare the number in box b (17) to that in box c (11); 17 is greater than 11, so a transfer is made to step 7. The numbers in boxes b and c are then interchanged so that box b has the 11 and box c has the 17. The test in step 8 fails (6 is not larger than 11) and the computation then halts. The three numbers have been sorted in ascending sequence (i.e., $6 < 11 < 17$). You should convince yourself by bench testing this algorithm with other values of a, b, and c that the computation described by the pseudocode will work correctly for any three numbers. A flowchart of the sorting algorithm is shown in the following diagram.

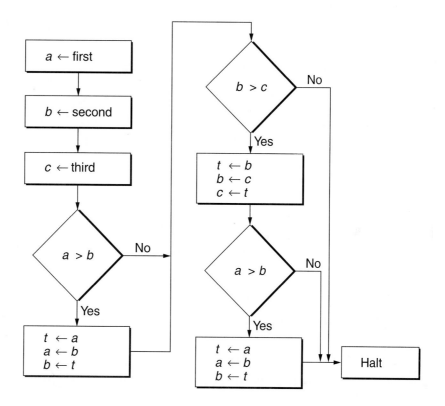

Note that we decomposed the operation of interchanging two numbers into three more primitive instructions. Box *t* is used as temporary storage to hold intermediate results. In order to interchange or switch the two numbers *a* and *b*, we first temporarily store one of the numbers, say, *a*, in *t* ($t \leftarrow a$); next the other number is stored in *a* ($a \leftarrow b$), and, last, the first number is placed in *b* ($b \leftarrow t$). Note that the instruction sequence "$a \leftarrow b$; $b \leftarrow a$" will not interchange *a* and *b* because the first instruction effectively destroys the old value in *a*. In computer terms, the labeled boxes are analogous to memory or storage areas that can contain values.

Next we code in Java the pseudocode version of our sorting program.

```
// SortInput.java - sort three numbers
import tio.*; // use the package tio

class SortInput {
  public static void main (String[] args) {
    int a, b, c, t;

    System.out.println("type three integers:");
    a = Console.in.readInt();
    b = Console.in.readInt();
    c = Console.in.readInt();
```

```
    if (a > b) {
       t = a;
       a = b;
       b = t;
    }
    if (b > c) {
       t = b;
       b = c;
       c = t;
    }
    if (a > b) {
       t = a;
       a = b;
       b = t;
    }
    System.out.print("The sorted order is : ");
    System.out.println(a + ", " + b + ", " + c);
  }
}
```

DISSECTION OF THE SortInput PROGRAM

- `int a, b, c, t;`

This program declares four integer variables. The variables a, b, and c are inputs to be sorted, and t is to be used for temporary purposes, as described in the pseudocode.

- `System.out.println("type three integers:");`

This line is used to *prompt* the user to type the three numbers to be sorted. Whenever a program is expecting the user to do something, it should print out a prompt telling the user what to do.

- `a = Console.in.readInt();`
  `b = Console.in.readInt();`
  `c = Console.in.readInt();`

The method call expression `Console.in.readInt()` is used to obtain the input from the keyboard. Three separate integers need to be typed. The values read will be stored in the three variables.

- ```
  if (a > b) {
     t = a;
     a = b;
     b = t;
  }
  if (b > c) {
     t = b;
     b = c;
     c = t;
  }
  ```
  ```

```
if (a > b) {
   t = a;
   a = b;
   b = t;
}
```

The `if` statements and resulting assignments are Java notation for the same actions described in the sort flow chart. To comprehend these actions you need to understand why the interchange or swapping of values between two variables, such as `a` and `b`, requires the use of the temporary `t`. Also note how the three assignments are grouped as a block, allowing each `if` expression to control a group of actions.

■
```
   System.out.print("The sorted order is : ");
   System.out.println(a + ", " + b + ", " + c);
}
```

If the input values were 10, 5, and 15, the output would be

```
The sorted order is : 5, 10, 15
```

3.4 THE if-else STATEMENT

Closely related to the `if` statement is the `if-else` *statement*. An `if-else` statement has the following general form:

`if (` *BooleanExpr* `)` *Statement1* `else` *Statement2*

If the expression *BooleanExpr* is true, then *Statement1* is executed and *Statement2* is skipped; if *BooleanExpr* is false, then *Statement1* is skipped and *Statement2* is executed. *Statement2* is called the `else` statement. After the `if-else` statement has been executed, control passes to the next statement. The flow of execution branches and then rejoins, as shown in the following diagram.

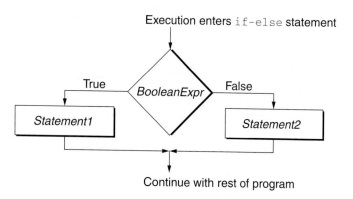

Consider the following code:

```
if (x < y)
  min = x;
else
  min = y;
System.out.println("min = " + min);
```

If $x < y$ is true, then `min` will be assigned the value of x; if it is false, then `min` will be assigned the value of y. After the `if-else` statement is executed, `min` is printed.

As with the `if` statement, either branch of an `if-else` statement can contain a block, as shown in the following example.

```
if (temperature < 32) {
  System.out.println("Warning Warning Warning!");
  System.out.println(32 - temperature + "(F) below Freezing!");
  System.out.println("Warning Warning Warning!");
}
else {
  System.out.println("It's " + temperature +
                      "degrees fahrenheit.");
}
```

COMMON PROGRAMMING ERROR

A semicolon is used to change an expression to an expression statement. All statements do not end in semicolons, and extraneous semicolons can cause subtle errors. Look carefully at the following code fragment. What is printed when it executes if x is 3 and y is 4?

```
if (x < y);
  System.out.println("The smaller is " + x);
if (y < x);
  System.out.println("The smaller is " + y);
```

The answer is

```
The smaller is 3
The smaller is 4
```

Note the extra semicolon after the close parenthesis in each `if` statement. The indentation is misleading: All four lines should be indented the same to reflect what is actually going to happen. The true branch of each `if` statement is the empty statement ";". The example code is syntactically correct but semantically incorrect.

Another common error is to be misled by indentation and to try to include two statements in one branch without using a block. Consider this example.

```
if (temperature < 32)
  System.out.print("It is now");
  System.out.print(32 - temperature);
  System.out.println(" below freezing.");
System.out.println("It's " + temperature + "degrees");
```

A user might mistakenly think that, if `temperature` is 32 or above, the code will execute only the last print statement displaying `temperature`. That is almost certainly what was intended. Unfortunately, if `temperature` is 32 or above, only the first `print()` would be skipped. If `temperature` is 45 the following confusing message would be printed:

```
-13 below freezing.
It's 45 degrees
```

To get the behavior suggested by the indentation shown, a block must be used, as in

```
if (temperature < 32) {
  System.out.print("It is now");
  System.out.print(32 - temperature);
  System.out.println(" below freezing.");
}
System.out.println("It's " + temperature + "degrees");
```

3.4.1   NESTED `if-else` STATEMENTS

The `if` statement is a full-fledged statement and can be used anywhere a statement is expected, so you could put another `if` statement in either branch of an `if` statement. For example, you could rewrite the earlier air fare checking statement as

```
if (ageOfPerson >= 18)
  if (ageOfPerson < 65)
    System.out.println("full fare adult");
```

If the expression `(ageOfPerson >= 18)` is true, then the statement

```
  if (ageOfPerson < 65)
    System.out.println("full fare adult");
```

is evaluated. The true branch for the `ageOfPerson >= 18` if statement is itself an `if` statement. In general, if the true branch of an `if` statement contains only another `if` statement, writing it as a single `if` statement is more efficient, combining the expressions with the operator `&&`, as we did in Section 3.2.2. Using `&&` in most cases is also clearer.

These nested `if` statements can't always be collapsed. Consider the following variation on our earlier example involving temperature.

```
if (temperature < 32) {
  System.out.println("Warning Warning Warning!");
  if (temperature < 0)
    System.out.println((-temperature) + "(F) below Zero!");
  else
    System.out.println(32 - temperature +
                  "(F) below Freezing!");
  System.out.println("Warning Warning Warning!");
}
else {
  System.out.println("It is " + temperature +
                  "degrees fahrenheit.");
}
```

The `then` statement for the outer `if-else` statement is a block containing another `if-else` statement.

COMMON PROGRAMMING ERROR

In algebra class you came across expressions such as $18 \le age < 65$. This expression tempts many new programmers to write

```
if (18 <= age < 65) ...
```

In evaluating the expression, Java first evaluates `(18 <= age)`—let's call it `part1`—which is either true or false. It then tries to evaluate `(part1 < 65)`, which is an error because relational operators are used to compare two numbers, not a boolean and a number. The only good thing about this type of mistake is that the compiler will catch it. Our example earlier for printing `full fare adult` showed the proper way to handle this situation.

3.4.2   if-else-if-else-if ...

In the preceding example, the nesting was all done in the `then` statement part of the `if-else` statement. Now we nest in the `else` statement part of the `if-else` statement:

```
if (ageOfPerson < 18)
  System.out.println("child fare");
else {
  if (ageOfPerson < 65)
    System.out.println("adult fare");
  else
    System.out.println("senior fare");
}
```

The braces are not needed; we added them only for clarity. This form is so common that experienced programmers usually drop the braces. In addition, the else and the following if are usually placed on the same line, as in

```
if (ageOfPerson < 18)
  System.out.println("child fare");
else if (ageOfPerson < 65)
  System.out.println("adult fare");
else
  System.out.println("senior fare");
```

Note that the second if statement is a *single* statement that constitutes the else branch of the first statement. The two forms presented are equivalent. You should be sure that you understand why they are. If you need to, look back at the general form of the if statement and recall that an entire if-else statement is a statement itself. This fact is illustrated in the following figure, wherein each statement is surrounded by a box. As you can see, there are five different statements.

Sometimes this chain of if-else-if-else-if-else... can get rather long, tedious, and inefficient. For this reason, a special construct can be used to deal with this situation when the condition being tested is of the right form. If you want to do different things based on distinct values of a *single* expression, then you can use the switch statement, which we discuss in Section 3.8.

3.4.3 THE DANGLING else PROBLEM

When you use sequences of nested if-else statements, a potential problem can arise as to what if an else goes with, as for example in

```
if (Expression1)
    if (Expression2)
        Statement1
else
    Statement2
```

The indenting suggests that *Statement2* is executed whenever *Expression1* is false; however, that isn't the case. Rather, *Statement2* is executed only when *Expression1* is true and *Expression2* is false. The proper indenting is

```
if (Expression1)
    if (Expression2)
        Statement1
    else
        Statement2
```

The rule used in Java is that an else is always matched with the nearest preceding if that doesn't have an else. To cause *Statement2* to be executed whenever *Expression1* is false, as suggested by the first indenting example, you can use braces to group the statements as shown.

```
if (Expression1) {
    if (Expression2)
        Statement1
}
else
    Statement2
```

The braces are like parentheses in arithmetic expressions that are used to override the normal precedence rules. The nested, or inner, if statement is now inside a block that prevents it from being matched with the else.

3.5 THE while STATEMENT

We have added the ability to choose among alternatives, but our programs still execute each instruction at most once and progress from the top to the bottom. The *while statement* allows us to write programs that run repeatedly.

The general form of a while statement in Java is

```
while ( BooleanExpr )
    Statement
```

Statement is executed repeatedly as long as the expression *BooleanExpr* is true, as shown in the following flowchart.

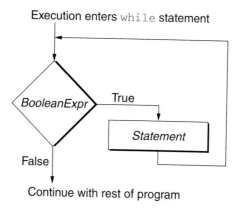

This flowchart is the same as the one for the `if` statement, with the addition of an arrow returning to the test box.

Note that *Statement* may not be executed. That will occur when *BooleanExpr* evaluates to false the first time. Note also, that like the description of the `if-else` statement, there are no semicolons in the general form of the `while` statement. The semicolon, if any, would be part of the statement that follows the parenthesized boolean expression.

A simple example for use on Valentine's Day is

```
// Valentine.java - a simple while loop
class Valentine {
  public static void main(String[] args) {
    int howMuch = 0;

    while (howMuch++ < 5)
      System.out.println("I love you.");
  }
}
```

The output is

```
I love you.
I love you.
I love you.
I love you.
I love you.
```

When the body of the loop is a block you get

```
while ( BooleanExpr ) {
    Statement1
    Statement2
    . . .
}
```

Modifying our earlier example gives

```
int howMuch = 0;
while (howMuch++ < 5) {
    System.out.print("I love you.");
    System.out.println (" @----->- my rose.");
}
```

which results in the output

```
I love you. @----->- my rose.
I love you. @----->- my rose.
I love you. @----->- my rose.
I love you. @----->- my rose.
I love you. @----->- my rose.
```

Most `while` statements are preceded by some initialization statements. Our example initialized the loop counting variable `howMuch`.

3.5.1   PROBLEM SOLVING WITH LOOPS

Suppose that you wanted to have a program that could read in an arbitrary number of nonzero values and compute the average. If you were to use pseudocode, the program might look like the following.

PSEUDOCODE FOR AVERAGE, USING `goto`

1. Get a number.
2. If the number is 0 go to step 6.
3. Add the number to the running total.
4. Increment the count of numbers read in.
5. Go back to step 1.
6. Divide the running total by the count of numbers in order to get the average.
7. Print the average.

In this pseudocode, step 5 goes back to the beginning of the instruction sequence, forming a loop. In the 1950s and 1960s many programming languages used a *goto statement* to implement step 5 for coding such a loop. These `goto` statements resulted in programs that were hard to follow because they could jump all over the place. Their use was sometimes called *spaghetti code*. In Java there is no `goto` statement. Java includes `goto` as a keyword that has no use so that the compiler can issue an error message if it is used inadvertently by a programmer familiar with C or C++. Today *structured control constructs* can do all the good things but none of the bad things that you could do with `goto` statements.

A *loop* is a sequence of statements that are to be repeated, possibly many times. The preceding pseudocode has a *loop* that begins at step 1 and ends at step 5. Modern programs require that you use a construct to indicate explicitly the beginning and the end of the loop. The structured equivalent, still in pseudocode, might look like the following.

PSEUDOCODE FOR AVERAGE, WITHOUT USING `goto`

```
get a number
while the number is not 0 do the following:
    add the number to the running total
    increment the count of numbers read in
    get a number
(when the loop exits)
divide the running total by the count of numbers to
    get the average
print the average
```

The loop initialization in this case is reading in the first number. Somewhere within a loop, typically at the end, is something that prepares the next iteration of the loop—getting a new number in our example. So, although not part of the required syntax, `while` statements generally look like the following

```
Statement_init        // initialization for the loop
while ( BooleanExpr ) {
    Statement1
    Statement2
    . . .
    Statement_next // prepare for next iteration
}
```

The `while` statement is most often used when the number of iterations isn't known in advance. This situation might occur if the program was supposed to read in values, processing them in some way until a special value called a *sentinel* was read in. Such is the case for our "compute the average" program: It reads in numbers until the sentinel value 0 is read in.

We can now directly translate into Java the pseudocode for computing an average.

```
// Average.java - compute average of input values
import tio.*;

public class Average {
  public static void main(String[] args) {
    double number;
    int count = 0;
    double runningTotal = 0;
    // initialization before first loop iteration
    System.out.println("Type some numbers, " +
        "the last one being 0");
    number = Console.in.readDouble();

    while (number != 0) {
      runningTotal = runningTotal + number;
      count = count + 1;
      // prepare for next iteration
      number = Console.in.readDouble();
    }
    System.out.print("The average of the ");
    System.out.print(count);
    System.out.print(" numbers is ");
    System.out.println(runningTotal / count);
  }
}
```

DISSECTION OF THE Average PROGRAM

■   `double number;`
     `int count = 0;`
     `double runningTotal = 0;`

The variable `number` is used to hold the floating point value typed in by the user. No initial value is given in the declaration because it gets its initial value from user input. The variable `count` is used to count the number of nonzero values read in. Counting is done efficiently and accurately with whole numbers, so the variable `count` is an `int` initialized to zero. The variable `runningTotal` is used to accumulate the sum of the numbers read in so far and is initialized to zero. Similar to assignment statements, these are declaration statements with initial values. Later we show how declaration statements can be used but assignment statements can't.

■   `System.out.println("Type some numbers, " +`
         `"the last one being 0");`
     `number = Console.in.readDouble();`

A message should always be printed to prompt the user when the user is expected to enter data. We could have initialized `number` when it was declared, but it is central to the loop so we initialized it just before entering the loop. These two statements correspond to the first line of our pseudocode. All the preceding code is supporting syntax required by Java.

■ ```
while (number != 0) {
```

The loop will continue *while* the value stored in the variable number is not 0. The value 0 is used to detect the end of the loop. It acts as a *sentinel* to keep the loop from running forever. A *sentinel* is an important technique for terminating loops correctly.

■ ```
runningTotal = runningTotal + number;
count = count + 1;
number = Console.in.readDouble();
}
```

The first statement in the loop body would look strange in a mathematics class unless number was 0. Recall that the symbol = is not an equals sign; it is the assignment operator. It means: Evaluate the expression on the right and then assign that value to the variable on the left. The result in this case is to add the value of number to the value of runningTotal and store the result in running-Total. This type of expression is common in computer programs: It computes a new value for a variable, using an expression that includes the old value of the variable. Similarly, we increment the value of count. The last statement in the body of the loop gets ready for the next iteration by reading in a new value from the user and storing it in number. This action overwrites the old value, which is no longer needed. At this point the computer will go back and evaluate the boolean expression to determine whether the loop should execute again (i.e., number isn't 0) or continue with the rest of the program.

■ ```
System.out.println(runningTotal / count);
```

When the user finally types a 0, the program prints the answer and exits. We have already used the print() and println() methods with a string and with a number. Here we show that the number can be an expression. Recall that the symbol / is the symbol for division. If the first number typed is 0, this program will terminate by printing

```
The average of the 0 numbers is NaN
```

The symbol NaN stands for *not a number* and results from dividing zero by zero. A better solution might be to test, using an if-else statement, for this special case and print a more appropriate message. We leave that for you to do as an exercise.
```

COMMON PROGRAMMING ERROR

Every programmer has probably forgotten the "prepare for next iteration" line at least once, causing a program to loop forever. When coding a `while` statement, be careful to verify that some variable changes each time around the loop. Also check to be sure that the loop condition will eventually be reached. How many times will the following loop execute?

```
int count = 13;
System.out.println("The multiples of 13 between " +
                   "1 and 100 are:");
while (count != 100){
  System.out.println(count);
  count = count + 13;
}
```

The loop will run forever because `count` will never equal 100. The problem is obvious in this small example, and such problems do occur—although they're not always so apparent. A test for less than or greater than is always preferable to a test of strict equality or inequality.

3.6   THE for STATEMENT

You can use the `while` construct to create any loop you will ever need. However, Java, like most modern programming languages, provides two alternative ways to write loops that are sometimes more convenient. The `for` *statement* is a looping statement that captures the initialization, termination test, and iteration preparation all in one place at the top of the loop. The general form of the `for` statement is

```
for ( ForInit;  BooleanExpr ;  UpdateExpr )
     Statement
```

As part of the syntax of the `for` statement, the semicolons are used to separate the three expressions. Note the absence of a semicolon between *UpdateExpr* and the closing parenthesis.

The following steps occur in the execution of a `for` statement.

1. *ForInit* is evaluated *once*—before the body of the loop.
2. *BooleanExpr* is tested *before each iteration* and, if true, the loop continues (as in the `while` statement).
3. The loop body *Statement* is executed.

4. *UpdateExpr* is evaluated at the *end of each iteration.*
5. Go to step 2.

The following diagram also shows the flow of execution.

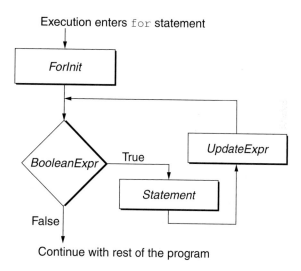

Compare this general form and the flow with that of the while statement. In the for statement, the initialization expression represented by *ForInit* and the iteration expression represented by *UpdateExpr* frequently involve the use of an assignment operator, but one is not required.

The for statement applies most naturally to situations involving going around a loop a specific number of times. For example, if you wanted to print out the square roots of the numbers 1 through 10 you could do so as follows.

```java
// SquareRoots.java - print square roots of 1 - 10
public class SquareRoots {
  public static void main(String[] args) {
    int i;
    double squareRoot;

    for (i = 1; i <= 10; i++) {
      squareRoot = Math.sqrt(i);
      System.out.println("the square root of " + i +
                         " is " + squareRoot);
    }
    System.out.println("That's All!");
  }
}
```

DISSECTION OF THE SquareRoots PROGRAM

■ `for (i = 1; i <= 10; i++) {`

The expression i = 1 is evaluated only once—before the loop body is entered. The expression i <= 10 is evaluated before *each* execution of the loop body. The expression i++ is evaluated at the *end of each* loop body evaluation. Recall that i++ is shorthand for i = i + 1.

■
```
    squareRoot = Math.sqrt(i);
    System.out.println("the square root of " + i +
                       " is " + squareRoot);
}
```

The body of the loop is one statement—in this case a block. The braces are part of the block syntax, not part of the syntax of a for statement.

■ `System.out.println("That's All!");`

When the loop exits, program execution continues with this statement.

We can redo the square root printing loop by using a while statement as follows.

```
// SquareRoots2.java - replace for with while
public class SquareRoots2 {
  public static void main(String[] args) {
    int i;
    double squareRoot;
    i = 1;                    // initialization-expr
    while (i <= 10) {
      squareRoot = Math.sqrt(i);
      System.out.println("the square root of " + i +
                         " is " + squareRoot);
      i++;                    // iteration-expr
    }
    System.out.println("That's All!");
  }
}
```

In both versions of this program, the same sequence of steps occurs.

1. The variable i is initialized to 1.
2. The boolean expression i <= 10 is tested, and if true, the loop body is executed. If the expression is false, the loop statement is completed and execution continues with the next statement in the program, the final print statement.
3. After executing the print statement within the loop, the statement incrementing the variable i is executed, in preparation for the next loop iteration.
4. Execution continues with step 2.

3.6.1   LOCAL VARIABLES IN THE for STATEMENT

The *ForInit* part of the `for` statement can be a local declaration. For example, let's write a loop that reads characters and prints them as uppercase.

```
char c;
for (int i = 1; i <= 10; i++) {
  c = (char)Console.in.readChar();
  if ( c >= 'a' && c <= 'z')
    c = (char)(c - ('a' - 'A'));
  System.out.print(c);
}
```

In this case, the `int` variable `i` declared in the `for` statement is limited to the `for` statement, including the body of the loop. The variable's existence is tied to the `for` statement code; outside the `for` statement it disappears. If you want the variable `i` to exist independently of the `for` statement you must declare it before the `for` statement. It then is available throughout the block containing the `for` statement. The variable is said to have *local scope*. We discuss scope further in Section 4.4.

    In the preceding example, we used a property of the character codes for the English alphabet. The property is that the difference between any lowercase letter and its uppercase equivalent is always the same. You compute that difference with the expression (`'a'` - `'A'`). You could just as easily use the expression (`'z'` - `'Z'`) or any other pair of matching uppercase and lowercase letters. Also, recall that when you use `Console.in.readChar()` from `tio` it returns an `int` value and hence a cast is needed. When you use (`c` - (`'a'` - `'A'`)) a cast to `char` is necessary because the resulting expression is converted to the wider `int` type.

3.7   THE break AND continue STATEMENTS

Two special statements,

`break;`   and   `continue;`

interrupt the normal flow of control. The `break` statement causes an exit from the innermost enclosing loop. The break statement also causes a `switch` statement to terminate. (We discuss the `switch` statement in Section 3.8.) In the following example, a test for a negative argument is made. If the test is true, then a `break` statement is used to pass control to the statement immediately following the loop.

```
while (true) {        //seemingly an infinite loop
  System("Enter a positive integer:")
  n = Console.in.readInt();
  if (n < 0)
    break;             // exit loop if n is negative
```

```
      System.out.print("squareroot of " + n);
      System.out.println(" = " + Math.sqrt(n));
}
```

```
// break jumps here
```

This use of the `break` statement is typical. What would otherwise be an infinite loop is made to terminate upon a given condition tested by the `if` expression.

The `continue` statement causes the current iteration of a loop to stop and causes the next iteration of the loop to begin immediately. The following code adds `continue` to the preceding program fragment in order to skip processing of negative values.

```
// BreakContinue.java - example of break and continue
import tio.*;

class BreakContinue {
  public static void main(String[] args) {
    int n;

    while (true) {          //seemingly an infinite loop
      System.out.print("Enter a positive integer ");
      System.out.print("or 0 to exit:");
      n = Console.in.readInt();
      if (n == 0)
        break;               // exit loop if n is 0
      if (n < 0)
        continue;            //wrong value
      System.out.print("squareroot of " + n);
      System.out.println(" = " + Math.sqrt(n));
      //continue lands here at end of current iteration
    }
    //break lands here
    System.out.println("a zero was entered");
  }
}
```

The output of this program, assuming that the user enters the values 4, -1, 9, and 0, is

```
os-prompt>java BreakContinue
Enter a positive integer or 0 to exit:4
squareroot of 4 = 2.0
Enter a positive integer or 0 to exit:-1
Enter a positive integer or 0 to exit:9
squareroot of 9 = 3.0
Enter a positive integer or 0 to exit:0
a zero was entered
os-prompt>
```

The continue statement may only occur inside for, while, and do loops. As the example shows, continue transfers control to the end of the current iteration, whereas break terminates the loop.

The break and continue statements can be viewed as a restricted form of a goto statement. The break is used to go to the statement following the loop and the continue is used to go to the end of the current iteration. For this reason, many programmers think that break and continue should be avoided. In fact, many uses of break and continue can be eliminated by using the other structured control constructs. For example, we can redo the BreakContinue example, but without break and continue, as follows.

```java
// NoBreakContinue.java - avoiding break and continue
import tio.*;

class NoBreakContinue {
  public static void main(String[] args) {
    int n;

    System.out.print("Enter a positive integer ");
    System.out.print("or 0 to exit:");
    n = Console.in.readInt();
    while (n != 0) {
      if (n > 0) {
        System.out.print("squareroot of " + n);
        System.out.println(" = " + Math.sqrt(n));
      }
      System.out.print("Enter a positive integer ");
      System.out.print("or 0 to exit:");
      n = Console.in.readInt();
    }

    System.out.println("a zero was entered");
  }
}
```

The loop termination condition is now explicitly stated in the while statement and not buried somewhere inside the loop. However, we did have to repeat the prompt and the input statement—once before the loop and once inside the loop. We eliminated continue by changing the if statement to test for when the square root could be computed instead of testing for when it could not be computed.

3.8 THE switch STATEMENT

The switch statement can be used in place of a long chain of if-else-if-else-if-else statements when the condition being tested evaluates to an integer numeric type. Suppose that we have an integer variable dayOfWeek that is supposed to have a value of 1 through 7 to represent the current day of the week. We could then print out the day as

```
if (dayOfWeek == 1)
  System.out.println("Sunday");
else if (dayOfWeek == 2)
  System.out.println("Monday");
else if (dayOfWeek == 3)
  System.out.println("Tuesday");
else if (dayOfWeek == 4)
  System.out.println("Wednesday");
else if (dayOfWeek == 5)
  System.out.println("Thursday");
else if (dayOfWeek == 6)
  System.out.println("Friday");
else if (dayOfWeek == 7)
  System.out.println("Saturday");
else
  println("Not a day number " + dayOfWeek);
```

An alternative is to use a `switch` statement as follows.

```
switch (dayOfWeek) {
  case 1:
    println("Sunday");
    break;
  case 2:
    println("Monday");
    break;
  case 3:
    println("Tuesday");
    break;
  case 4:
    println("Wednesday");
    break;
  case 5:
    println("Thursday");
    break;
  case 6:
    println("Friday");
    break;
  case 7:
    println("Saturday");
    break;
  default:
    println("Not a day number " + dayOfWeek);
}
```

Unlike the `if-else` and looping statements described earlier in this chapter, the braces are part of the syntax of the `switch` statement. The controlling expression in parentheses following the keyword `switch` must be of integral type. Here it is the `int` variable `dayOfWeek`. After the expression has been evaluated, control jumps to the appropriate `case` label. All the constant integral expressions following the `case` labels must be unique. Typically, the last statement before the next `case` or `default` label is a `break` statement. If there is no `break` statement, then execution "falls through" to the next statement in the succeeding case. Missing `break` statements are a frequent cause of error in `switch` statements. For example, if the `break;` was left out of just `case 1` and if `dayOfWeek` was 1, the output would be

```
Sunday
Monday
```

instead of just

```
Sunday
```

There may be at most one `default` label in a `switch` statement. Typically, it occurs last, although it can occur anywhere. The keywords `case` and `default` can't occur outside a `switch`.

Taking advantage of the behavior when `break;` is not used, you can combine several cases as shown in the following example.

```
switch (dayOfWeek) {
  case 1:
  case 7:
    System.out.println("Stay home today!");
    break;
  case 2:
  case 3:
  case 4:
  case 5:
  case 6:
    System.out.println("Go to work.");
    break;
  default:
    println("Not a day number " + dayOfWeek);
    break;
}
```

Note that the `break` statement—not anything related to the case labels—causes execution to continue after the `switch` statement. The `switch` statement is a structured `goto` statement. It allows you to go to one of several labeled statements. It is then combined with the `break` statement, which does another `goto`, in this case "go to the statement after the `switch`."

THE EFFECT OF A `switch` STATEMENT

1. Evaluate the `switch` expression.
2. Go to the `case` label having a constant value that matches the value of the expression found in step 1; or, if a match is not found, go to the `default` label; or, if there is no `default` label, terminate `switch`.

3. Continue executing statements in order until the end of `switch` is reached or a `break` is encountered.

4. Terminate `switch` when a `break` statement is encountered, or terminate `switch` by "falling off the end."

3.9 USING THE LAWS OF BOOLEAN ALGEBRA

Boolean expressions can frequently be simplified or more efficiently evaluated by converting them to logically equivalent expressions. Several rules of Boolean algebra are useful for rewriting boolean expressions.

1. Commutative law: *a or b == b or a* and a *and b == b and a.*
2. Distributive *and* law: *a and (b or c) == (a and b) or (a and c).*
3. Distributive *or* law: *a or (b and c) == (a or b) and (a or c).*
4. Double negation: *!!a == a.*
5. DeMorgan's laws: *!(a or b) == !a, and !b* and *!(a and b) == !a or !b.*

In the expression `x || y`, `y` will not be evaluated if `x` is true. The value of `y` in that case doesn't matter. For this reason, it may be more efficient to have the first argument of a boolean *or* expression be the one that most often evaluates to true. This is the basis for short-circuit evaluation of the logical *or* operator.

```
while (a < b || a == 200) {
   . . .
}
while (a == 200 || a < b) {
   . . .
}
```

For the two controlling expressions, which order is more likely to be efficient? Note that by the commutative law both `while` conditions are equivalent.

3.10 PROGRAMMING STYLE

We follow Java professional style throughout the programming examples. Statements should readily display the flow of control of the program and be easy to read and follow. Only one statement should appear on a line. Indentation should be used consistently to set off the flow of control. After a left brace, the next line should be indented, showing that it is part of that compound statement. There are two conventional brace styles in Java. The style we follow in this book is derived from the C and C++ professional programming community. In this style, an opening or left brace stays on the same line as the beginning of a selection or iteration statement.

The closing or right brace lines up under the keyword that starts the overall statement. For example,

```
if (x > y) {
  System.out.println("x is larger " + x);
  max = x;
}

while (i < 10) {
  sum = sum + i;
  i++;
}
```

An alternative acceptable style derives from the Algol60 and Pascal communities. In this style each brace is kept on a separate line. In those languages the keywords `begin` and `end` were used to set off compound statements and they were placed on their own lines. For example,

```
if ( x > y)
{
  System.out.println("x is larger " + x);
  max = x;
}
```

However, be consistent and use the same style as others in your class, group, or company. A style should be universal within a given community. A single style simplifies exchanging, maintaining, and using each others' code.

Summary

- An expression followed by a semicolon is an expression statement. Expression statements are the most common form of statement in a program. The simplest statement is the empty statement, which syntactically is just a semicolon.
- A group of statements enclosed by braces is a block. A block can be used anywhere a statement can be used. Blocks are important when you need to control several actions with the same condition. This is often the case for selection or iteration statements such as the `if-else` statement or the `for` statement, respectively.
- All statements don't end with a semicolon. The only statements covered in this chapter that end with a semicolon are expression statements and declaration statements.
- The general form of an `if` statement is

  ```
  if ( BooleanExpr )
      Statement
  ```

- The general form of an `if-else` statement is

  ```
  if ( BooleanExpr )
      Statement1
  else
      Statement2
  ```

- When nesting an `if` statement inside an `if-else` statement or vice-versa, the `else` will always be matched with the closest unmatched `if`. This precedence can be overridden with a block statement to enclose a nested `if` statement or `if-else` statement.
- The general form of the `while` statement is

  while (*BooleanExpr*)
     Statement

- The general form of the `for` statement is

  for (*ForInit* ; *BooleanExpr* ; *UpdateExpr*)
     Statement

- Java includes the usual logical operators *and*, *or*, and *not*.
- The `break` statement can be used to terminate abruptly the execution of either a `switch` statement or a looping statement. When a `break` is executed inside any of those statements, the enclosing `switch` or loop statement is immediately terminated and execution continues with the statement following the `switch` or loop.
- The `continue` statement is used only inside a looping statement. When a `continue` is executed, the remaining portion of the surrounding loop body is skipped and the next iteration of the loop is begun. In the case of the `while` statement, the loop termination expression is tested as the next operation to be performed after the continue. In the case of the `for` statement, the update expression is evaluated as the next operation, followed by the loop termination test.
- The `switch` statement is an alternative to a sequence of `if-else-if-else...` statements. The `switch` statement can be used only when the selection is based on an integer-valued expression.

Review Questions

1. True or false? An expression is a statement.
2. How do you turn an expression into a statement?
3. True or false? All statements end with a semicolon. If false, give an example to show why.
4. True or false? An `if` statement is always terminated with a semicolon. If false, give an example to show why.
5. What are the values of the following Java expressions?

   ```
   true && false
   true || false
   ```

6. Write a Java expression that is true whenever the variable x is evenly divisible by both 3 and 5. Recall that (x % y) is zero if y evenly divides x.
7. What is printed by the following program fragment?

   ```
   x = 10;
   y = 20;
   if ( x < y)
   ```

```
    System.out.println("then statement executed");
  else
    System.out.println("else statement executed");
    System.out.println("when is this exeucted?");
```

8. What is printed by the following program, if 3 and 12 are entered as x and y? Now if you change the order and enter 12 and 3, what is printed?

```
//PrintMin.java - print the smaller of two numbers
import tio.*;

class PrintMin {
  public static void main(String[] args) {
    System.out.println("Type two integers.");
    int x = Console.in.readInt();
    int y = Console.in.readInt();

    if (x < y)
      System.out.println("The smaller is " + x);
    if (y < x)
      System.out.println("The smaller is " + y);
    if (x == y)
      System.out.println("They are equal.");
  }
}
```

9. For the declarations shown, fill in the value of the expression or enter *illegal*.

```
int   a = 2, b = 5, c = 0, d = 3;
```

Expression	Value
b % a	
a < d	
(c != b) && (a > 3)	
a / b > c	
a * b > 2	

10. What is printed by the following program fragment? How should it be indented to reflect what is really going on?

```
x = 10;
y = 20;
z = 5;
if ( x < y )
if ( x < z )
System.out.println("statement1");
else
System.out.println("statement2");
System.out.println("statement3");
```

11. How many times will the following loop print testing?

```
int i = 10;
while (i > 0) {
   System.out.println("testing");
   i = i - 1;
}
```

12. How many times will the following loop print testing?

```
int i = 1;
while (i != 10) {
   System.out.println("testing");
   i = i + 2;
}
```

13. What is printed by the following loop? See Question 6, on page 86.

```
int i = 1;
while (i <= 100) {
   if (i % 13 == 0)
      System.out.println(i);
   i = i + 1;
}
```

14. Rewrite the loop in the previous question using a for statement.

15. Rewrite the following loop, using a while statement.

```
for (i = 0; i < 100; i++) {
   sum = sum + i;
}
```

16. True or false? Anything that you can do with a while statement can also be done with a for statement and vice-versa.

17. How many times will the following loop go around? This is a trick question—look at the code fragment carefully. It is an example of a common programming error.

```
int i = 0;
while (i < 100) {
   System.out.println(i*i);
}
```

18. What is printed by the following program?

```
class Problem18 {
  public static void main(String[] args) {
    int i, j = 0;

    for (i = 1; i < 6; i++)
      if (i > 4)
        break;
      else {
        j = j + i;
        System.out.println("j= " + j + " i= " + i);
      }
      System.out.println("Final j= " + j + "i= " + i);
  }
}
```

Exercises

1. Write a program that asks for the number of quarters, dimes, nickels, and pennies you have. Then compute the total value of your change and print the amount in the form $X.YY. See Exercise 16 on page 51, in Chapter 2.

2. Write a program that reads in two integers and then prints out the larger one. Use Review Question 8, on page 48, as a starting point and make the necessary changes to class PrintMin to produce class PrintMax.

3. Modify the class Average from this chapter to print a special message if the first number entered is 0.

4. Write a program that reads in four integers and then prints out yes if the numbers were entered in increasing order and prints out no otherwise.

5. Write a program that prompts for the length of three line segments as integers. If the three lines could form a triangle, the program prints "Is a triangle." Otherwise, it prints "Is not a triangle." Recall that the sum of the lengths of *any* two sides of a triangle must be greater than the length of the third side. For example, 20, 5, and 10 can't be the lengths of the sides of a triangle because 5 + 10 is not greater than 20.

6. Write a program that tests whether the formula $a^2 \times b^2 = c^2$ is true for three integers entered as input. Such a triple is a *Pythagorean triple* and forms a right-angle triangle with these numbers as the lengths of its sides.

7. An operator that is mildly exotic is the conditional operator ? :. This operator takes three arguments and has precedence just above the assignment operators, as for example in

```
s = (a < b)? a : b;
// (a < b) true then s assigned a else s assigned b
```

Rewrite the code for class PrintMin, in Review Question 8, on page 87, using this operator to eliminate the first two if statements. We chose not to use this operator because it is confusing to beginning programmers. It is unnecessary and usually can readily and transparently be replaced by an if statement.

8. Write a program that reads in integers entered at the terminal until a value of 0 is entered. A *sentinel* value is used in programming to detect a special condition. In this case the sentinel value is used to detect that no more data values are to be entered. After the sentinel is entered, the program should print out the number of numbers that were greater than 0 and the number of numbers that were less than 0.

9. Write a program that reads in integers entered at the terminal until a sentinel value of 0 is entered. After the sentinel is entered, the program should print out the smallest number, other than 0, that was entered.

10. Rewrite Exercise 8 to print the largest number entered before the sentinel value 0 is entered. If you already did that exercise, only a few changes are needed to complete this program. Now code a further program that ends up printing both the smallest or minimum value found and the largest or maximum value found.

11. Rewrite Exercise 5 to continue to test triples until the sentinel value 0 is entered.

12. Write a program that reads in characters and prints their integer values. Use the *end-of-file* value −1 as a guard value to terminate the character input. For Unix systems, the end-of-file character can be generated by hitting Ctrl+D on the keyboard. For Windows systems, the end-of-file character can be generated by hitting Ctrl+Z on

the keyboard. Note again that readChar() returns an int value. This action allows you to test the end-of-file value. If you convert this value to a char, negative numbers would not be representable. Explain why.

13. Write a program to input values as in Exercise 12. This time run it with the input taken as a file through *redirection*. If the compiled Java program is *TestChar.class,* then the command

```
java TestChar < myFile
```

will use myFile for input. Redirection is possible with Unix or the Windows console window.

14. Write a program to print every even number between 0 and 100. Modify the program to allow the user to enter a number *n* from 1 through 10 and have the program print every *n*th number from 0 through 100. For example, if the user enters 5, then 0 5 10 15 20…95 100 are printed.

15. Write a program that will print out a box drawn with asterisks, as shown.

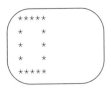

Use a loop so that you can easily draw a larger box. Modify the program to read in a number from the user specifying how many asterisks high and wide the box should be.

16. Write a program that reads in numbers until the same number is typed twice in a row. Modify it to go until three in a row are typed. Modify it so that it first asks for "how many in a row should I wait for?" and then it goes until some number is typed that many times. For example, for two in a row, if the user typed "1 2 5 3 4 5 7" the program would still be looking for two in a row. The number 5 had been typed twice, but not in a row. If the user then typed 7, that would terminate the program because two 7s were typed, one directly after the other.

17. Write a program that prints all the prime numbers in 2 through 100. A prime number is an integer that is greater than 1 and is divisible only by 1 and itself. For example, 2 is the only even prime. Why?

PSEUDOCODE FOR FINDING PRIMES

```
for n = 2 until 100
   for i = 2 until the square root of n
      if n % i == 0 the number is divisible by i
         otherwise n is prime
```

Can you explain or prove why the inner-loop test only needs to go up to the square root of *n*?

18. Write a program that prints the first 100 prime numbers. Use the same algorithm as in Exercise 17, but terminate the program upon finding the 100th prime. Assume that the search needs to go no farther than *n* = 10,000.

19. Write a program that generates all Pythagorean triples (see Exercise 6, on page 89) whose small sides are no larger than *n*. Try it with $n \leq 200$. (*Hint:* Use two `for` loops to enumerate possible values for the small sides and then test to determine whether the result is an integral square.

20. Write a program that gives you a different message each day of the week. Use a `switch` statement. Take as input an integer in the range 1 through 7. For example, if 6 means Friday, the message might say, `Today is Friday, TGIF`. If the user inputs a number other than 1 through 7, have the default issue an appropriate message.

21. Write a program that gives you a fortune based on an astrological sign. Use a `switch` statement to structure the code.

22. Write a program that generates an approximation of the real number *e*. Use the formula

$$e \approx 1 + \frac{1}{1!} + \frac{1}{2!} + \frac{1}{3!} + \dots + \frac{1}{k!} + \dots$$

where *k*! means *k* factorial $= 1 * 2 * \dots * k$. Keep track of term $1/k!$ by using a `double`. Each iteration should use the previous value of this term to compute the next term, as in

$$T_{k+1} = T_k \times \frac{1}{k+1}$$

Run the computation for 100 terms, printing the answer after each new term is computed.

23. Write your own pseudorandom number generator. A pseudorandom sequence of numbers appears to be chosen at random. Say that all the numbers you are interested in are placed in a large fishbowl and you reach in and pick out one at a time without looking where you are picking. After reading the number, you replace it and pick another. Now you want to simulate this behavior in a computation. You can do so by using the formula $X_{n+1} = (aX_n + c) \bmod m$. Let *a* be 3,141,592,621, *c* be 1, and *m* be 10,000,000,000 (see Knuth, *Seminumerical Algorithms*, Addison-Wesley 1969, p. 86). Generate and print the first 100 such numbers as `long` integers. Let $X_1 = 1$.

Applet Exercise

Redo any one of the first ten exercises in this chapter but use an applet for input and output. You are to do so by modifying the following applet. Recall that the Applet Exercises in Chapter 2 introduced a special kind of Java program called an *applet*. Among other things, an applet may be used to create graphical output such as plots or diagrams. In order to be useful, most programs, including applets, need some way to receive input. For the regular applications that we've created so far, we've used `Console.in.readInt()`, etc., to read values from the console. This exercise introduces you to the use of a `JTextField` object to get input from an applet.

For this exercise we need to introduce two more methods: `init()` and `action-Performed()`. As with the earlier applet exercise, for now you need only to concentrate on the body of the methods `init()` and `actionPerformed()`, treating the surrounding code as a template to be copied verbatim. The following applet reads two numbers and then displays their sum.

```java
/* <applet code="AppletSum.class"
    width=420 height=100></applet> */
//AppletSum.java - Text input with an applet
import java.awt.*;
import java.awt.event.*;
import javax.swing.*;

public class AppletSum extends JApplet
    implements ActionListener {
  JTextField inputOne = new JTextField(20);
  JTextField inputTwo = new JTextField(20);
  JTextField output = new JTextField(20);
  public void init() {
    Container pane = getContentPane();

    pane.setLayout(new FlowLayout());
    pane.add(new JLabel("Enter one number."));
    pane.add(inputOne);
    pane.add(
      new JLabel("Enter a number and hit return."));
    pane.add(inputTwo);
    pane.add(new JLabel("Their sum is:"));
    pane.add(output);
    inputTwo.addActionListener(this);
  }
  public void actionPerformed(ActionEvent e) {
    double first, second, sum;

    first = Double.parseDouble(inputOne.getText());
    second = Double.parseDouble(inputTwo.getText());
    sum = first + second;
    output.setText(String.valueOf(sum));
  }
}
```

DISSECTION OF THE AppletSum PROGRAM

■
```java
import java.awt.*;
import java.awt.event.*;
import javax.swing.*;

public class AppletSum extends JApplet
  implements ActionListener
```

For now this code is all part of the template for an applet. The only part that you should change is to replace `AppletSum` with the name of your applet. The `import` statements tell the Java compiler where to find the various classes used in this program, such as `JTextField` and `JApplet`. The `extends JApplet` phrase is how we indicate that this class is defining an applet instead of a regular application. The `implements ActionListener` phrase is needed if we want to have our program do something when the user has finished entering data.

■
```
JTextField inputOne = new JTextField(20);
JTextField inputTwo = new JTextField(20);
JTextField output = new JTextField(20);
```

`JTextField` is a standard Java class. A `JTextField` is a graphical user interface component in which the user can enter text and the program can then read the text entered by the user. This program will create three text fields—two for the input values and one to display the sum of the first two. Note that these variables aren't declared inside any method. These variables need to be referenced by both the methods in this applet. You should think of them as part of the applet class `AppletSum` and not part of any one method. (We discuss such declarations in Chapter 6.)

■
```
public void init() {
    Container pane = getContentPane();
    pane.setLayout(new FlowLayout());
```

The method `init()` is rather like `main()` for an applet. This method is called to initialize the applet. The first thing we do in the method is get the content pane. The *content pane* is the part of the applet used to display the various graphical components that we add to the applet. The `setLayout()` method is used to adjust the content pane so that when components are added, they are arranged in lines, like words of text in a word processor. The components are allowed to "flow" from one line to the next. For now, just always include the two statements in your `init()` method.

■
```
pane.add(new JLabel("Enter one number."));
pane.add(inputOne);
pane.add(
    new JLabel("Enter a number and hit return."));
pane.add(inputTwo);
pane.add(new JLabel("Their sum is:"));
pane.add(output);
```

The method `add()` is used to add some labels and text fields to the content pane of the applet. `JLabel` is a standard Java class that is used to place labels in graphical user interfaces. Unlike with a `JTextField`, the user can't enter text in a `JLabel` when the applet is running. The order in which we add all the components to the applet is important. The components are placed in the applet, like words in a word processor. That is, the components will be displayed from left to right across the applet until the next component won't fit, in which case a new line of components is started. Later, you'll learn more about controlling the placement of components, but for now just add them in the desired order and then adjust the width of the applet to get the desired appearance. Here is what the applet will look like.

- `inputTwo.addActionListener(this);`

The last statement in the `init()` method says that the `actionPerformed()` method in the applet referred to by `this` should be called when Return is hit in the text field, `inputTwo`.

- ```
  public void actionPerformed(ActionEvent e) {
      double first, second, sum;

      first = Double.parseDouble(inputOne.getText());
      second = Double.parseDouble(inputTwo.getText());
      sum = first + second;
      output.setText(String.valueOf(sum));
  }
  ```

This method is called each time the user hits Return with the cursor placed in the text field `inputTwo`. The method gets the text that was entered in the first two text fields by invoking their `getText()` methods. The resulting strings are then converted to floating point numbers, using the standard Java method `Double.parseDouble()`. Next the two numbers are added and stored in the variable `sum`. The floating point value stored in `sum` is converted to a `String`, using `String.valueOf()`, which can be used to convert any primitive value to a `String`. Finally the method `setText()` from the class `JTextField` is used to set the value of the text displayed in the `JTextField` object `output`.
  ```

4

Methods: Functional Abstraction

Structured programming is a problem-solving strategy and a programming method-ology that includes two guidelines.

STRUCTURED PROGRAMMING GUIDELINES

- The flow of control in a program should be as simple as possible.
- The construction of a program should embody top-down design.

Top-down design, also referred to as *stepwise refinement*, consists of repeat-edly decomposing a problem into smaller problems. Eventually, you have a collec-tion of small problems or tasks, each of which can be easily coded. Object-oriented programming strategy encompasses structured programming but has additional elements, which we explain in Chapter 6.

The *method* construct in Java is used to write code that solves the small problems that result from this decomposition. *Methods* are, in classical program-ming terms, *functions* or *procedures*. Methods are combined into further meth-ods and ultimately used to solve the original problem. Some methods, such as `System.out.println()`, are provided by the system; others are written by the programmer.

We illustrate structured programming and top-down design in this chapter, but first we describe the method mechanism in more detail.

4.1 METHOD INVOCATION

A simple program is made up of one or more methods contained in a class, one of them being `main()`. In these simple cases, program execution begins with `main()`. When program control encounters a method name followed by parentheses, the method is *called*, or *invoked*. That is, program control passes to the method. After the method does its work, program control is passed back to the calling environment, where program execution continues. As a simple example, consider the following program, which prints a message.

```
// Message.java: Simple method use
class Message {
  public static void main(String[] args) {
    System.out.println("HELLO DEBRA!");
    printMessage();                        //method call
    System.out.println("Goodbye.");
  }
  //definition of method printMessage
  static void printMessage() {
    System.out.println("A message for you:   ");
    System.out.println("Have a nice day!\n");
  }
}
```

The method definition includes the name of the method and a method body. The *method body* is a block that is executed when the method is invoked. Program execution begins in `main()`. When program control encounters `printMessage()`, the method is called, or invoked, and program control is passed to it. After the two `println()` statements in `printMessage()` have been executed, program control passes back to the calling environment, which in this example is in `main()`. In `main()`, the program finishes by printing "Goodbye."

`System.out.println("HELLO DEBRA!")` is also a method call, as are the two statements that constitute the body of the method `printMessage()`. Because `println()` isn't defined in the class `Message`, we need to tell the computer where to find `println()`; hence the `System.out` preceding the method name. We present the details of how the method names are used in Section 6.7. The complete sequence of calls for this program is as follows.

The system calls `main()` to start the program.
    `main()` calls `System.out.println()`.
      `"HELLO DEBRA!"` is printed.
      `System.out.println()` returns.
    `main()` calls `printMessage()`.

```
    printMessage() calls System.out.println().
        "A message for you:  " is printed.
        System.out.println() returns.
    printMessage() calls System.out.println() again.
        "Have a nice day!\n" is printed
        System.out.println() returns.
    printMessage() returns.
main() calls System.out.println().
    "Goodbye." is printed.
    System.out.println() returns.
main() returns to the system.
```

The program ends.

4.2   STATIC METHOD DEFINITIONS

The simplest methods are called *class methods* or *static methods*. (You will learn about a different type of method in Chapter 6.) The general form for static methods is

`public static` *ReturnType Identifier* (*ParameterList*) `block`

The *block*—also known as the *method body* of the method definition—contains variable declarations and statements that are executed when the method is called. The variables declared in the method's block are said to be within the scope of the method (see Section 4.4). The *ReturnType* of the method is the type of the value returned by the method. For example, `Math.sqrt()` returns a `double` that can be used in an expression such as `Math.sqrt(x) + y`. If nothing is returned, as in our example `printMessage()`, the keyword `void` is used. The optional *ParameterList* describes the number and types of the arguments that are passed to the method when it is invoked. If no arguments are passed, the list is empty.

The parameters in the parameter list are variables and can be used within the body of the method. Sometimes the parameters in a method definition are called *formal parameters* to emphasize their role as placeholders for actual values that are passed to the method when it is called. Upon method invocation, the value of the actual argument corresponding to a formal parameter is used to initialize the formal parameter, as shown in the next example.

The keyword `public` is optional, except with the method `main()`. This requirement for `public` with `main()` isn't part of the Java syntax; rather, it is part of the specification of how to run a Java program. We discuss `public` and other method *access modifiers* in Section 6.4.

To illustrate these ideas, we can rewrite the preceding program so that the method `printMessage()` has a formal parameter. The parameter is used to specify how many times the message is to be printed.

```
// Message2.java: method parameter use
class Message2 {
  public static void main(String[] args) {
    System.out.println("HELLO DEBRA!");
    printMessage(5);                        //actual argument is 5
    System.out.println("Goodbye.");
  }
  static void printMessage(int howManyTimes) {
  //formal parameter  is howManyTimes
    System.out.println("A message for you:  ");
      for (int i = 0; i < howManyTimes; i++)
        System.out.println("Have a nice day!\n");
  }
}
```

DISSECTION OF THE Message2 PROGRAM

■ `class Message2 {`

A simple program is a collection of methods within a class. The class `Message2` encapsulates the various method definitions. The method `main()` begins executing first.

■ `printMessage(5);`   `//actual argument is 5`

This line is the method call for `printMessage()`. The actual argument is the constant 5, which is passed to the method and used to initialize the formal parameter `howManyTimes`.

■ `static void printMessage(int howManyTimes) {`

The return type is `void`, which tells the compiler that the method doesn't return a value. In programming language terminology such a method is called a *pure procedure* as opposed to a function, which returns a value. The parameter list is `int howManyTimes`, which tells the compiler that the method takes a single argument of type `int`. The parameters specified in the definition of a method are called formal parameters. For now, methods must be declared as `static`. We discuss nonstatic methods when we introduce object-oriented programming in Chapter 6.

■ `{`
```
    System.out.println("A message for you:  ");
      for (int i = 0; i < k; i++)
        System.out.println("Have a nice day!\n");
}
```

The code between the braces constitutes the body of the method definition for `printMessage()`. If `howManyTimes` has the value 5, the message is printed five times. When program control reaches the end of the method, control is passed back to `main()`.

COMMON PROGRAMMING ERROR

A common mistake is to forget to include `static` in the definition of a method. In Chapter 6 we discuss methods that don't include `static` and how they are called. If you leave `static` out of the method definition but then try to call a method following the example in this section, then you will get an error message similar to

```
Can't make static reference to method returnType
methodName(parameterTypes) in class YourClass.
```

This message may also include some indication of where the invalid method invocation is located. This message can be confusing at first because it isn't the invocation that's at fault. The error is in the declaration of the method being invoked.

4.3 THE `return` STATEMENT

When a `return` statement is executed within a method, program control is immediately returned to the point right after the call to the method; if an expression follows the keyword `return`, the value of the expression is also returned to the calling environment. Some examples are

```
return;
return a;
return (a * b + c);
```

You can enclose the expression being returned in parentheses. If the expression is complicated, it is considered good programming practice to do so.

There can be zero or more `return` statements in a method. If there is no `return` statement, control is passed back to the calling environment when the closing brace of the body is encountered. This action is called *falling off the end* and is permitted only when the return type is `void`. To illustrate the use of `return` statements, we can write a program that computes the minimum of two integers.

```
// Min2.java: return expression in a method

class Min2 {
  public static void main(String[] args) {
    int    j = 78, k = 3 * 30, m;
```

```
        System.out.println("Minimum of two integers Test:");
        m = min(j, k);
        System.out.println("The minimum of : "
            + j + " , " + k + " is  " + m);
    }
    static int min(int a, int b) {
      if (a < b)
        return a;
      else
        return b;
    }
}
```

DISSECTION OF THE Min2 PROGRAM

■ `public static void main(String[] args) {`
    `int    j = 78, k = 3 * 30, m;`

The variables j, k, and m are declared to be of type int. The variables j and k are assigned constant expressions for test purposes. We could modify the program to request values as input using `Console.in.readInt()`.

■ `m = min(j, k);`

The values of j and k are passed as actual arguments to min(). The method min() returns a value, which is assigned to m.

■ `static int min(int a, int b)`

This line is the *header* of the method definition for min(). The return type of the method is int. The value returned from within the method will be converted, if necessary, to an int before it is returned to the calling environment. The parameter list

`int a, int b`

declares a and b to be of type int. The formal parameters are used in the body of the method definition.

■ `{`
    `if (a < b)`
      `return a;`
    `else`
      `return b;`
  `}`

The code between the braces constitutes the body of the method definition for min(). If the value of a is less than the value of b, the value of a is returned to the calling environment; otherwise, the value of b is returned.

Even small methods such as `min()` provide useful structuring to the code. In a real program, there might be several places in the code where the minimum of two numbers is needed. Without the method `min()`, we'd end up with something like

```
...
if (a < b)
  x = a;
else
  x = b;
...
if (c < d)
  y = c;
else
  y = d;
...
```

Using our method `min()` changes this code to

```
...
x = min(a, b);
...
y = min(c, d);
...
```

The latter code is both shorter and easier to read, making the overall structure of the program clearer. Another important benefit is that we need to debug only the code that finds the minimum once. In the version without the method `min()`, because we have to type the conditional statement each time we want the minimum, we are much more likely to make an error.

If we want to modify our program so that the maximum value is also computed, we can use a method `max()` to do so. We have to add its method definition to the class `Min2`. Here is the method definition.

```
static int max(int a, int b) {
  if (a > b)
    return a;
  else
    return b;
}
```

4.4 SCOPE OF VARIABLES

Variables such as `j` and `k` in `main()` for the class `Min2` are called *local variables*—they can be accessed only "locally" or "nearby." For example, you can't refer to the variable `j` declared in `main()` of `Min2`, from within `min()`.

The *scope* of a variable is the range of statements that can access the variable. The scope of a local variable extends from the point where the variable was declared (where it was first mentioned and given a type, as in `int j;`) to the end of the block containing the declaration. Recall from Section 3.1 that a block is a group of statements delimited by braces. A formal parameter is essentially a special kind of local variable. Hence the scope of a formal parameter is the entire definition of the method.

If it weren't for scope's ability to limit the accessibility of local variables, we might have been tempted to write class `Min2` as follows.

```
// Min2Bad.java - doesn't work because of scope

class Min2Bad {
  public static void main(String[] args) {
    int    j = 78, k = 3 * 30, m;
    System.out.println("Minimum of two integers Test:");
    m = min();
    System.out.println("The minimum of : "
        + j + " , " + k + " is  " + m);
  }
  static int min() {
    if (j < k)
      return j;
    else
      return k;
  }
}
```

This code won't compile because the variables `j` and `k` can't be referenced outside method `main()`, as we attempted to do in method `min()`. In order for `min()` to compare the values for two local variables in `main()`, those values must be passed as parameters to `min()`, as we did in the correct version earlier.

The scope of a variable declaration in the initialization portion of a `for` loop is the loop body plus the update and loop termination expressions. Declaring the index variable for a `for` loop in the `for` loop is quite common. In that case the loop index variable won't be accessible after the loop, as shown in this example.

```
double squareRoot;
for (int x = 1; x <= 10; x++) {
  squareRoot = Math.sqrt(x);
  System.out.println("the square root of " + x +
        " is " + squareRoot);
}
System.out.println("x = " + x);     //Syntax error
```

Note that the use of declarations inside blocks could result in two variables with the same name having overlapping scopes. Java, however, disallows a local declaration that conflicts with another local declaration. In the following example, the second declaration of `squareRoot` is illegal because there is already a local declaration for `squareRoot` that extends into the block that is the body of the `for` statement. Likewise, the definition of `i` in the `for` statement is illegal. Also, the final print of `square` is illegal because the scope of `square` ends at the brace that ends the `for` statement.

```
// SquareRoots2.java - contains scope errors
public class SquareRoots2 {
  public static void main(String[] args) {
    int i = 99;
    double squareRoot = Math.sqrt(i);

    System.out.println("the square root of " + i +
                        " is " + squareRoot);

    for (int i = 1; i <= 10; i++) {
      double squareRoot = Math.sqrt(i);
      double square = squareRoot * squareRoot;
      System.out.println("the square root of " + i +
                          " is " + squareRoot);
      System.out.println("squaring that yields " + square);
    }
    System.out.println("The final value of square"
                        + " is " + square);
  }
}
```

DISSECTION OF THE SquareRoots2 PROGRAM

■ ```
   public class SquareRoots2 {
     public static void main(String[] args) {
       int i = 99;
       double squareRoot = Math.sqrt(i);
   ```

The scope of these declarations extends to the end of the method `main()`.

■  ```
   for (int i = 1; i <= 10; i++) {
     double squareRoot = Math.sqrt(i);
   ```

The declaration of `i` in the `for` statement initialization part is illegal because `i` was already declared in this method. Likewise the declaration of `squareRoot` is illegal. These declarations are illegal because we can't have two local variables with overlapping scopes that have the same name. Some programming languages allow overlapping, giving precedence to the innermost definition, but Java doesn't. This restriction simplifies the language and adds to program clarity. In this program, the error can easily be eliminated by removing the type declarations so that the two lines become

```
for (i = 1; i <= 10; i++) {
  squareRoot = Math.sqrt(i);
```

■ ```
   double square = squareRoot * squareRoot;
   ```

The scope of this definition of `square` extends only to the end of the `for` statement.
   ```

```
■    System.out.println("the square root of " + i +
                         " is " + squareRoot);
     System.out.println("squaring that yields " + square);
   }

   System.out.println("The final value of square"
                      + " is " + square);
```

The first `println()` involving `square` is within the scope of `square` so it is fine. The second is beyond the scope of `square` and will result in a syntax error at compile time. A solution would be to declare `square` before the `for` statement.

4.5 TOP-DOWN DESIGN

Imagine that you have to analyze some company data represented by a series of integers. As you read each integer, you want to print out the count of integers read, the integer, the sum of all the integers read up to this point, the minimum integer read up to this point, and the maximum integer read up to this point. In addition, suppose that a banner must be printed at the top of the page and that all the information must be neatly printed in columns under appropriate headings. To help you construct this program, we decompose the problem into the following subproblems.

DECOMPOSING THE RUNNING SUM PROGRAM

1. Print a banner.
2. Print the headings over the columns.
3. Read the data and print them neatly in columns.

You can code each subproblem directly as a method. Then you can use these methods in `main()` to solve the overall problem. Note that by designing the code this way, you can add further methods to analyze the data without affecting the program structure.

```
//RunSums.java: top level, main(), calls methods to
//     handle subproblems
import tio.*;
class RunSums {
  public static void main(String[] args) {
    printBanner();
    printHeadings();
    readAndPrintData();
  }
  // printBanner, printHeadings and readAndPrintData
  // definitions will go here
...
}
```

This program fragment illustrates in a very simple way the idea of top-down design. Think of the tasks to be performed and code each task as a method. If a particular task is complicated, you can subdivide it into smaller tasks, each coded as a method. A further benefit is that the program as a whole is more readable and self-documenting. There may be many ways to decompose a problem into methods. Much of the art of program design lies in finding a good decomposition.

Coding the individual methods is straightforward. The first method contains a single `println()` statement.

```
static void printBanner() {
  System.out.println("\n" +
    "*********************************************\n" +
    "*    RUNNING SUMS, MINIMUMS, AND MAXIMUMS   *\n" +
    "*********************************************\n");
}
```

The next method writes headings over columns. Similar to `\n` being used to indicate a newline, `\t` is the escape sequence for a tab character. Words appear separated by a tab.

```
static void printHeadings() {
  System.out.println(
        "Count\tItem\tSum\tMinimum\tMaximum");
}
```

Most of the work is done in `readAndPrintData()`.

```
static void readAndPrintData() {
  int cnt = 0, sum = 0, item, smallest, biggest;

  item = Console.in.readInt();
  smallest = biggest = item;
  while (item != -99999) {
    cnt++;
    sum = sum + item;
    smallest = min(item, smallest);
    biggest = max(item, biggest);
    System.out.println( cnt + "\t" +  item + "\t"
      + sum + "\t" + smallest + "\t" + biggest);
    item = Console.in.readInt();
  }
}
```

If we execute the program and enter data directly from the keyboard, we get the echoing of input characters and the output of the program intermixed on the screen. To prevent this problem, on systems with redirection such as Unix, we create a file called *data* containing the integers

```
19   23   -7   29   -11   17 -99999
```

Most Java IDEs allow you to specify a file to be used for input in place of the keyboard. If you're running Java from a Unix or Windows command line you can use the command

```
java RunSums < data
```

This procedure is called file redirection because you're redirecting the program to read from a file instead of from the keyboard. In Chapter 10 we discuss how to do file I/O more generally. Here's what is printed on the screen.

```
*****************************************
*   RUNNING SUMS, MINIMUMS, AND MAXIMUMS   *
*****************************************

Count    Item    Sum    Minimum Maximum
1        19      19     19      19
2        23      42     19      23
3        -7      35     -7      23
4        29      64     -7      29
5        -11     53     -11     29
6        17      70     -11     29
```

DISSECTION OF THE `readAndPrintData()` METHOD

▪
```
static void readAndPrintData() {
    int cnt = 0, sum = 0, item, smallest, biggest;
```

The header of the method definition is the single line before the brace. The method doesn't return a value, so its return type is `void`. The method takes no arguments. In the method definition, the variables `cnt`, `sum`, `item`, `smallest`, and `biggest` are declared to be of type `int`. The variables `cnt` and `sum` are initialized to zero. The initial value of the variable `item` is taken from the console. The initial values of the variables `smallest` and `biggest` are computed.

▪
```
item = Console.in.readInt();
sum = smallest = biggest = item;
```

The first `item` is read in. The variables `sum`, `smallest`, and `biggest` are assigned the value of `item`. Recall that `biggest = item` is an expression using the assignment operator. The value of such an expression is the same as the expression on the right-hand side of the assignment operator. Thus we can use the expression `biggest = item` as the right-hand side expression assigned to `smallest` and similarly to `sum`.

▪
```
while (item != -99999) {
    cnt++;
    sum = sum + item;
    smallest = min(item, smallest);
    biggest = max(item, biggest);
    System.out.println( cnt + "\t" +  item + "\t"
        + sum + "\t" + smallest + "\t" + biggest);
    item = Console.in.readInt();
}
```

The integer value –99999 is a *sentinel* value intended to terminate the loop. After the first integer has been obtained from the console, we use this `while` loop to find others. Each time the body of this `while` loop is executed, the variable `cnt` is incremented by 1, sum is incremented by the current value of item, smallest is assigned the minimum of the current values of item and smallest, biggest is assigned the maximum of the current values of item and biggest, and all these values are printed in the appropriate columns. Recall that \t prints a tab. Eventually, readInt() is supposed to read -99999 from the console, causing the while loop to end. We investigate in the exercises other ways to end this loop.

4.6   PROBLEM SOLVING: RANDOM NUMBERS

Random numbers have many uses in computers. One use is to serve as data to test code; another use is to simulate a real-world event that involves a probability. The method of simulation is an important problem-solving technique. Programs that use random number methods to generate probabilities are called *Monte Carlo* simulations. The Monte Carlo technique can be applied to many problems that otherwise would have no possibility of solution.

A random number generator is a method that returns numbers that appear to be randomly distributed within some interval. The method Math.random() in the standard package java.lang is provided to do this for the interval 0 to 1. The following program fragment displays some random numbers generated by Math.random().

```
//RandomPrint.java: Print Random numbers  in the
//    range (0.0 - 1.0).
class RandomPrint {
  public static void main(String[] args) {
    int n = 10;

    System.out.println("We will print " + n +
      " random numbers");
    printRandomNumbers(n);
  }
  static void printRandomNumbers(int k) {
    for (int i = 0; i < k; i++)
      System.out.println(Math.random());
  }
}
```

We can add to this class methods for max() and min(), which we've already discussed. We can modify printRandomNumbers() to print out the largest and smallest random number found.

```
static void printRandomNumbers(int k) {
  double r, biggest, smallest;

  r = biggest = smallest = Math.random();
  System.out.print(" " + r);
  for (int i = 1; i < k; i++) {
    if (i % 2 == 0)
      System.out.println();
```

```
      r = Math.random();
      biggest = max(r, biggest);
      smallest = min(r, smallest);
      System.out.print(" " + r);
   }
   System.out.println("\nCount: " + k
      + "  Maximum: " + biggest + "  Minimum: "
      + smallest);
}
```

Before we dissect this method definition, let's see what the output of the program looks like. If we run this program, the following appears on the screen.

```
We will print 10 random numbers
0.016657093696542113 0.9872859969278116
0.033313710157700079 0.5954234589013508
0.667160647102587 0.6878910499886401
0.2268455586583925 0.022606516838095003
0.4565489420647485 0.49292751841170546
Count: 10
Maximum: 0.9872859969278116
Minimum: 0.016657093696542113
```

DISSECTION OF THE printRandomNumbers() METHOD

■
```
static void printRandomNumbers(int k) {
   double r, biggest, smallest;
```

The variable k is a parameter declared to be an int. The variables r, biggest, and smallest are all declared to be of type double.

■
```
r = biggest = smallest = Math.random();
```

The method Math.random() from the class java.lang.Math is used to generate a random number. That number is assigned to the variables r, biggest, and smallest. The random number is between 0.0 and 1.0.

■
```
for (int i = 1; i < k; i++) {
   if (i % 2 == 0)
      System.out.println();
   r = Math.random();
   biggest = max(r, biggest);
   smallest = min(r, smallest);
   System.out.print(" " + r);
}
```

This for loop is used to print the remaining k - 1 random numbers. Because one random number has already been printed, the variable i at the top of the loop is initialized to 1 rather than 0. Whenever i is divisible by 2, the expression

```
i % 2 == 0
```

controlling the `if` statement is true, causing a newline character to be printed. The effect of this is to print two random numbers on each line, except possibly the last which will have only one if an odd number of random numbers are printed. This idiom is commonly used for printing several values on one line.

4.7 A SIMULATION: PROBABILITY CALCULATIONS

A common use of computers is to simulate some activity that goes on in the real world. Computer simulations can often be used in place of a dangerous or costly experiment. Another advantage of computer simulations is that they can compress time. Instead of taking years to watch some natural process, a simulation of that process can be done in minutes or hours. Of course, the simulation generally has to be based on some simplifying assumptions, but the results still can be useful.

Let's use a computer to simulate the repeated tossing of a coin. We want to find the probability that we can toss some number, n, heads in a row. This experiment is neither expensive nor dangerous, but we can compress time with it. In less than a second (not counting the time to write the program) we can simulate tossing a coin millions of times.

This program uses a sequence of random numbers between 0 and 1 to simulate the coin tosses. If the next random number in the sequence is less than 0.5, it will be considered a head; if the number is greater than or equal to 0.5, it will be considered a tail. We will conduct many trials, each trial attempting to "toss" n heads in a row. If the trial succeeds by tossing n heads in a row, we will count the trial as a success. If the trial fails, by tossing a tail before n heads have been tossed, we will count the trial as a failure. The probability that we can toss n heads in a row is approximately the ratio of successful trials to total trials. By increasing the number of trials, we can increase the accuracy of our result.

The following is a pseudocode solution to the problem.

PSEUDOCODE FOR COIN TOSS SIMULATION

```
Input the number of heads in a row for a trial.
Input the number of trials to run.
Perform the specified number of trials.
Print the result.
```

We can refine how to perform the specified number of trials as follows.

PSEUDOCODE FOR PERFORMING THE SPECIFIED NUMBER OF TRIALS

```
initialize the number of successes to 0
while there are more trials to run
  run one trial
  if the trial was a success
    increment the number of successes
end while loop
return the number of successful trials
```

Remember: Pseudocode is an informal notation intended for human beings, not computers. We use indentation to indicate nested statements. We can refine this pseudocode further by detailing how to perform one trial.

PSEUDOCODE FOR PERFORMING ONE TRIAL

```
let numTosses be the number of tosses for a successful trial
initialize the number of heads tossed to zero
while number of heads tossed is less than numTosses
  toss the coin
  if the coin comes up tails
    return failure
  increment the number of heads tossed
end while loop
return success
```

At this point we are almost ready to begin writing the code. As discussed in the preceding section, we can use the method `Math.random()` in the standard package `java.lang` to generate random numbers for the interval 0 to 1. This method will return a value of type `double` that is greater than or equal to 0 and less than 1. If the `double` returned by `Math.random()` is less than 0.5, it will be considered heads; if it is greater than or equal to 0.5, it will be considered tails. The following is the complete program. We coded each section of the pseudocode as a separate method.

```java
//CoinToss.java - Compute the approximate probability
//    of n heads in a row by simulating coin tosses.

class CoinToss {
  public static void main(String[] args) {
    //Input the number of tosses in a row to try for.
    int numTosses = 4;        //Just use 4 for testing

    //Input the number of trials to run.
    int numTrials = 10000;   //Use 10000 for testing

    //Perform the specified number of trials
    int numSuccesses = performTrials(numTosses,numTrials);

    //Print the results
    double probability = numSuccesses / (double)numTrials;
    System.out.println("Probability found in "
          + numTrials + " is  " + probability);
  }
  // return true if numTosses heads are tossed
  // before a tail
  static boolean isAllHeads(int numTosses) {
    double outcome;

    for (int numHeads = 0; numHeads < numTosses; numHeads++) {
      outcome = Math.random();   // toss the coin
```

```
      if ( outcome < 0.5)
         return false;                    // tossed a tail
    }
    return true;                          // tossed all heads
  }
  // perform numTrials simulated coin tosses
  // and return the number of successes
  static int performTrials(int numTosses, int numTrials) {
    System.out.println("Monte Carlo " + numTosses +
                       " in a row heads");
    int numSuccesses = 0;
    for (int trials= 0 ; trials < numTrials; trials++)
      // perform one trial
      if ( isAllHeads(numTosses))
        numSuccesses++;                   // trial was a success
    return numSuccesses;
  }
}
```

DISSECTION OF THE CoinToss PROGRAM

- ```
  class CoinToss {
    public static void main(String[] args) {
      //Input the number of tosses in a row to try for.
      int numTosses = 4;        //Just use 4 for testing

      //Input the number of trials to run.
      int numTrials = 10000;   //Use 1000 for testing
  ```

The code for `main()` follows directly from the pseudocode presented earlier. The comments correspond directly to the pseudocode. When you're actually writing the code, a good first step is to put in the pseudocode as comments. Then either replace the comment/pseudocode with real code, or when appropriate, leave the pseudocode as a comment and add the real code below the comment. In this example we decided to *hardcode* some input, that is, to insert some test values directly into the program. The comments indicate that we should be reading in the parameters for the program, but instead we simply assign some fixed value.We can easily replace these hard-coded assignments with calls to `Console.in.readInt()` or some other input method.

- ```
  //Perform the specified number of trials
  int numSuccesses = performTrials(numTosses,numTrials);
  ```

Here we decided to create a separate method to perform the series of trials. That method will need the number of trials to perform and the number of tosses used to determine whether a trial is a success or a failure. The comment from the pseudocode is almost superfluous because the name of the method and variable names should make clear what is happening. We decided to leave the comment because it emphasizes how we derived this code from the pseudocode.

■
```
//Print the results
double probability = numSuccesses / (double)numTrials;
System.out.println("Probability found in "
                + numTrials + " is  " + probability);
```

We can now compute the estimated probability of tossing numTosses heads in a row by dividing the number of successful trials by the total number of trials. Because numSuccesses and numTrials are both integers, we must first cast one of them into a double. Otherwise, the result of the integer division would always be zero in this example.

■
```
static boolean isAllHeads(int numTosses) {
    double outcome;

    for (int numHeads = 0; numHeads < numTosses; numHeads++)
{
      outcome = Math.random();     // toss the coin
      if ( outcome < 0.5)
        return false;              // tossed a tail
    }
    return true;                   // tossed all heads
  }
```

This method is the key to simulating tossing a coin. If the next numTosses are all heads, then the method returns true. If a tail is tossed before numTosses heads are tossed, then the method immediately returns false. In the exercises, we modify this routine to make other calculations, such as the probability of tossing k - 1 heads in k tosses.

■
```
static int performTrials(int numTosses, int numTrials) {
    System.out.println("Monte Carlo " + numTosses +
                       " in a row heads");
    int numSuccesses = 0;
    for (int trials = 0; trials < numTrials; trials++)
      // perform one trial
      if ( isAllHeads(numTosses))
        numSuccesses++;            // trial was a success
    return numSuccesses;
  }
```

This method directly follows the pseudocode presented for Performing the Specified Number of Trials. Each iteration of the loop performs one trial by calling isAllHeads(), testing the result, and if it was a success, incrementing the count of successful trials stored in numSuccesses.

4.8 INVOCATION AND CALL-BY-VALUE

To call one method from another method in the same class, we write the name of the called method and an appropriate list of arguments within parentheses. We have done so many times, as for example in `isAllHeads(n)` or `min(x,y)`. These arguments must *match in number and type* the parameters in the parameter list in the method definition. The arguments are passed *call-by-value*. That is, each argument is evaluated, and its *value* is used within the called method to initialize the corresponding formal parameter. Thus if a variable is passed to a method, the stored value of that variable in the calling environment won't be changed.

In the following example we attempt to swap the values of two local variables using a method.

```
//FailedSwap.java - Call-By-Value test
class FailedSwap {
  public static void main(String[] args) {
    int numOne = 1, numTwo = 2;

    swap(numOne, numTwo);
    System.out.println("numOne = " + numOne);
    System.out.println("numTwo = " + numTwo);
  }
  static void swap(int x, int y) {
    int temp;

    System.out.println("x = " + x);
    System.out.println("y = " + y);
    temp = x;
    x = y;
    y = temp;
    System.out.println("x = " + x);
    System.out.println("y = " + y);
  }
}
```

The output of this program is

```
x = 1
y = 2
x = 2
y = 1
numOne = 1
numTwo = 2
```

Note that, although we successfully swapped the values of the formal parameters, x and y, doing so had no effect on the actual arguments, numOne and numTwo. The formal parameters are effectively local variables in the method swap() that have their values initialized with the values of the corresponding actual arguments. Five memory locations are identified in this program for storing integers: `numOne`, `numTwo`, `x`, `y`, and `temp`.

In Java we can't write a method `swap()` similar to the one presented that actually swaps the values of two primitive type variables passed as parameters. If `swap()` had actually caused the values in `main()` to change, then we would have said that it achieved its result by causing a *side effect*, instead of returning a value. The side effect would have been the changes in the two actual arguments. Any method with a return type of `void`, must cause some side effect or else be a completely useless method. The method `println()` is an example of a method that does its job via a side effect. In the case of `println()` the side effect is the production of output on the console. In Section 5.2, we will explain how we can cause side effects to data when passing nonprimitive types, such as class types or array types, as parameters.

4.9 PROBLEM SOLVING: A COMPUTER GAME

Most programs begin as imprecise ideas in someone's mind. For very small programs, the person who thinks up the idea may be able just to sit down and enter the code for the program. This approach is not good for anything but the smallest programs. Instead, a program usually goes through a development process. Of the many different software development processes, most roughly follow the software life cycle described shortly. However, the steps don't always follow one after the other. For example, the implementation and testing steps are often performed iteratively, with some testing being performed as implementation proceeds.

THE SOFTWARE LIFE CYCLE

1. Requirements analysis and definition: The requirements for the program are written in a form understandable by those who want the software created. They typically aren't programmers.
2. Design: A detailed design of the software is created. For large programs that involves breaking the program into smaller pieces with precise specification of how the various pieces will interact.
3. Implementation: The code is actually written at this point.
4. Testing: The software must be thoroughly tested. For commercial software, fixing an error before the software has been released for use by the eventual customers is much cheaper than fixing it later.
5. Maintenance: This phase is often the longest and most costly part of the program's life cycle. Rarely is a large program never changed after it is put into use. The changes that occur during the maintenance phase are to fix errors discovered

after a program has gone into use and, because program requirements evolve over time, modify existing features or add new features.

A popular use of computers is for game playing. In this section we demonstrate the first four steps in the software life cycle of a small computer game. The game is called Twenty-One Pickup.

4.9.1 TWENTY-ONE PICKUP: REQUIREMENTS ANALYSIS AND DEFINITION

We begin our requirements analysis with a simple statement of the rules of the game.

> Twenty-One Pickup is a two-player game that starts with a pile of 21 stones. Each player takes turns removing 1, 2, or 3 stones from the pile. The player that removes the last stone wins.

Several requirements need to be specified for this program. To do so, we need to answer the following questions.

1. What is the role of the computer? Will it be one of the players or will it simply enforce the rules and display the progress of a game between two human players?

2. What will be the interface between the human being and the computer? For example, will the program have a graphical user interface or will the interface be a simple text display?

3. Does the program play a sequence of games, keeping track of the number of games won by the various players, or does the program play one game and then exit?

We answer these questions in the following way.

1. The computer will be one of the players with a human being as the other player. The human player will always be allowed to go first.

2. For this version of the program a simple textual interface will be used. The computer will print instructions, prompts, and results at the console and will read user input from the console.

3. The program will play only a single game. There will be no tabulation of winners from one game to the next.

4.9.2 TWENTY-ONE PICKUP: DESIGN

We are now ready to begin designing the actual program. We specify precisely how the user and the computer will interact, and we use top-down design to develop the program structure. We begin the design with pseudocode for the top level of the program.

TOP-LEVEL PSEUDOCODE FOR TWENTY-ONE PICKUP

```
print instructions
create the initial pile with 21 stones
while the game is not over
  have the user move
  if the game is not over
    have the computer move
end while loop
print the outcome
```

This pseudocode reflects the design decision that the user will always get to move first. It also reflects the decision that the program will play only a single game. We continue our design by expanding the "have the user move" and "have the computer move" subproblems.

PSEUDOCODE FOR "HAVE THE USER MOVE"

```
get the user move from the console
remove the stones from the pile
print the user's move on the console
```

This pseudocode reflects the design decision that we will be prompting the user to input his or her move at the console. The pseudocode for the "have the computer move" step is similar.

PSEUDOCODE FOR "HAVE THE COMPUTER MOVE"

```
compute number of stones for the computer to remove
remove the stones from the pile
print the computer's move on the console
```

To make our program robust, we designed a user input routine that checks to make sure the user has entered a valid move. If not, we prompt the user again until a valid move is entered.

PSEUDOCODE FOR "GET THE USER MOVE FROM THE CONSOLE"

```
prompt the user for the user's next move
from the console, read the number of stones to remove
while the number read is not a legal move
  prompt the user again
  read the number of stones to remove
end while loop
return the number of stones to remove
```

We complete the design phase of program development by identifying the inputs and outputs for each of the major methods. In doing so we create a method for each piece of pseudocode presented. The following is the opening comment and method header for each of the major methods except `main()`. These comments are formatted as *javadoc* comments. We briefly discuss *javadoc* in Section 4.13.

```
/**
 * playerMove completes one move by the player.
 * @param numberOfStones
 *     The number of stones reamining in the pile.
 * @return
 *     The number of stones remaining after the
 *     user's move.
 */
static int playerMove(int numberOfStones)

/**
 * computerMove completes one move by the computer.
 * @param numberOfStones
 *     The number of stones reamining in the pile.
 * @return
 *     The number of stones remaining after the
 *     computer's move.
 */
static int computerMove(int numberOfStones)

/**
 * getUserMove reads in the user's move, only
 *     accepting legal inputs.
 * @param numberOfStones
 *     The number of stones reamining in the pile.
 * @return
 *     The number of stones selected for removal by
 *     the user.
 */
static int getUserMove(int numberOfStones)
```

In this design we decided that the `userMove()` and `computerMove()` methods will take the current number of stones as input and return, as a result, the number of stones remaining after the move. We also pass the number of stones remaining to the method `getUserMove()`. That allows `getUserMove()` to make sure that the user doesn't attempt to remove more than the remaining number of stones in the pile.

We are now ready to move to the implementation phase wherein we complete the bodies of the methods.

4.9.3 TWENTY-ONE PICKUP: IMPLEMENTATION

Once we've completed the design we can begin writing the actual code. If we've done the design well, the coding phase will be relatively easy because each of the methods identified in the design will be small. The following is the entire program.

```
// TwentyOnePickup.java

import tio.*;
```

```java
public class TwentyOnePickup {
  /**
   * Play the game of Twenty-One Pickup.
   * The user and the computer take turns removing
   * from 1 to 3 stones from a pile. There are 21
   * stones in the pile to start with.
   * The last one to remove a stone wins.
   */
  public static void main(String[] args) {
    printInstructions();
    // create the initial pile with 21 stones
    int numberOfStones = 21;
    // keep track of who moved last
    boolean playerMovedLast = false;

    while (numberOfStones > 0) {
      numberOfStones = playerMove(numberOfStones);
      playerMovedLast = true;
      if (numberOfStones > 0){
        numberOfStones = computerMove(numberOfStones);
        playerMovedLast = false;
      }
    }
    // print the outcome
    if (playerMovedLast)
      System.out.println("Congratulations, you won.");
    else
      System.out.println("Better luck next time.");
  }
  /**
   * printInstructions prints the initial instructions
   */
  static void printInstructions() {
    System.out.println(
      "The object of this game is to remove the last"
      + " stone.\n"
      + "There are 21 stones in the pile to start with.\n"
      + "You may remove from 1 to 3 stones on each move.\n"
      + "Good Luck!");
  }
  /**
   * playerMove completes one move by the player.
   * @param numberOfStones
   *      The number of stones reamining in the pile.
   * @return
   *     The number of stones remaining after the user's move.
   */
  static int playerMove(int numberOfStones) {
    int move = getUserMove(numberOfStones);

    numberOfStones = numberOfStones - move;
    System.out.println("There are " + numberOfStones
                       + " stones remaining.");
    return numberOfStones;
  }
```

```java
/**
 * computerMove completes one move by the computer.
 * @param numberOfStones
 *     The number of stones reamining in the pile.
 * @return
 *     The numberOfStones remaining after the
 *     computer's move.
 */
static int computerMove(int numberOfStones) {
  int move;

  if (numberOfStones <= 3) {
    move = numberOfStones; /* remove the rest */
  }
  else {
    move = numberOfStones % 4;
    if (move == 0) move = 1;
  }
  numberOfStones = numberOfStones - move;
  System.out.println("The computer removes " + move
      + " stones leaving " + numberOfStones + ".");
  return numberOfStones;
}

/**
 * getUserMove reads in the user's move, only
 *     accepting legal inputs.
 * @param numberOfStones
 *     The number of stones reamining in the pile.
 * @return
 *     The number of stones selected for removal by
 *     the user.
 */
static int getUserMove(int numberOfStones) {
  System.out.println("Your move - how many stones"
                     + " do you wish to remove?");
  int move = Console.in.readInt();

  while (move > numberOfStones || move < 1 || move > 3) {
    if (numberOfStones >= 3)
      System.out.println("Sorry," +
          " you can only remove 1 to 3 stones.");
    else
      System.out.println("Sorry, you can only "
          + "remove 1 to " + numberOfStones + " stones.");
    System.out.println("How many stones"
                       + " do you wish to remove?");
    move = Console.in.readInt();
  }
  return move;
}
}
```

DISSECTION OF THE `TwentyOnePickup` PROGRAM

- ```java
  public static void main(String[] args) {
      printInstructions();
      // create the initial pile with 21 stones
      int numberOfStones = 21;
      // keep track of who moved last
      boolean playerMovedLast = false;
  ```

The method `main()` follows the top-level pseudocode presented in the design section. To keep `main()` short, we placed the statements to print the instructions in a separate method. The pile of stones is represented by the integer `numberOfStones`, initially 21. During the implementation phase we discovered that we needed an additional variable, `playerMovedLast`, to keep track of who moved last—the user or the computer. Without this variable, we didn't know what message to print at the end of the program.

- ```java
  while (numberOfStones > 0) {
      numberOfStones = playerMove(numberOfStones);
      playerMovedLast = true;
      if (numberOfStones > 0) {
          numberOfStones = computerMove(numberOfStones);
          playerMovedLast = false;
      }
  }
  ```

This loop comes directly from the loop in the top-level pseudocode "while the game is not over." The game is over when no more stones remain in the pile. Each time around the loop corresponds to one move by the user and one move by the computer, except possibly the last iteration when the computer doesn't move. When the loop exits, we want to know whether the user or the computer moved last, hence the variable, `playerMovedLast`.

- ```java
  // print the outcome
  if (playerMovedLast)
      System.out.println("Congratulations, you won.");
  else
      System.out.println("Better luck next time.");
  ```

We could have created another method, `printOutcome()`, that contained these statements. Doing so would have made `main()` slightly shorter. We decided that this code was simple enough to leave it directly in `main()`.

- ```java
  static void printInstructions() {
      System.out.println(
          "The object of this game is to remove the last"
          + " stone.\n"
          + "There are 21 stones in the pile to start with.\n"
          + "You may remove from 1 to 3 stones on each move.\n"
          + "Good Luck!");
  }
  ```

We could have placed the call to `System.out.println()` that comprises the entire body of this method directly in `main()`. To keep `main()` short and free from unnecessary details, we decided to create this separate method.

```
static int playerMove(int numberOfStones) {
   int move = getUserMove(numberOfStones);

   numberOfStones = numberOfStones - move;
   System.out.println("There are " + numberOfStones
                      + " stones remaining.");
   return numberOfStones;
}
```

The primary objective of the `playerMove()` method is to remove some number of stones from the pile. Because Java uses call-by-value parameter passing, we can't directly modify the variable `numberOfStones` created in the method `main()`. Instead we return the new value for `numberOfStones` and leave it to `main()` to store the returned value in the variable `numberOfStones` in `main()`. Note that the assignment to `numberOfStones` in the method `playerMove()` doesn't change the value of `numberOfStones` in `main()`, which is a separate variable with the same name. We could replace every occurrence of the identifier `numberOfStones` in `playerMove()` with some other identifier, such as `numStones`, and the program would work exactly the same. We used the same identifier in both `main()` and `playerMove()` because to us it seemed like the most descriptive name. Also, it provided a perfect example of how scope allows the freedom to choose local variables without concern for name conflicts with local variables in other methods.

```
static int computerMove(int numberOfStones) {
   int move;

   if (numberOfStones <=3) {
     move = numberOfStones; /* remove the rest */
   }
   else {
     move = numberOfStones%4;
     if (move == 0) move = 1;
   }
   numberOfStones = numberOfStones - move;
   System.out.println("The computer removes " + move
       + " stones leaving " + numberOfStones + ".");
   return numberOfStones;
}
```

This method exposes the winning logic for the game. If three or fewer stones remain, of course the computer picks them all up, making it the winner. If more than three stones remain, the optimal move is to try to leave the pile with a number of stones that is a multiple of four. If that isn't possible, the computer removes just one stone. As with `userMove()`, `computerMove()` returns the new number of stones in the pile as the result.

```
static int getUserMove(int numberOfStones) {
  System.out.println("Your move - how many stones"
                      + " do you wish to remove?");
  int move = Console.in.readInt();

  while (move > numberOfStones || move < 1 || move > 3){
    if (numberOfStones >= 3)
      System.out.println("Sorry," +
          " you can only remove 1 to 3 stones.");
    else
      System.out.println("Sorry, you can only "
              + "remove 1 to " + numberOfStones + " stones.");
    System.out.println("How many stones"
                        + " do you wish to remove?");
    move = Console.in.readInt();
  }
  return move;
}
```

A simpler version of this method could just call `Console.in.readInt()` and return whatever value it gets. This would work as long as the user always followed instructions and entered legal moves. As indicated during the design phase, we decided to try to make the program work even when the user makes a typing error. A good user interface allows the user to correct errors easily. The loop in this program will continue to loop until the user enters a move that is less than or equal to the number of stones remaining in the pile and that also is between 1 and 3. We need two messages because if less than 3 stones remain, 2 or 3 may not be a legal move, so we can't always say "you can only remove 1 to 3 stones." Even the version presented here is a bit clumsy if only one stone remains. In that case it will print the message, `Sorry, you can only remove 1 to 1 stones`. This problem can easily be remedied with a little more code.

Here is the program output. The values typed by the user are shown in boldface.

```
The object of this game is to remove the last stone.
There are 21 stones in the pile to start with.
You may remove from 1 to 3 stones on each move.
Good Luck!
Your move - how many stones do you wish to remove?
3
There are 18 stones remaining.
The computer removes 2 stones leaving 16.
Your move - how many stones do you wish to remove?
2
There are 14 stones remaining.
The computer removes 2 stones leaving 12.
Your move - how many stones do you wish to remove?
1
```

```
There are 11 stones remaining.
The computer removes 3 stones leaving 8.
Your move - how many stones do you wish to remove?
2
There are 6 stones remaining.
The computer removes 2 stones leaving 4.
Your move - how many stones do you wish to remove?
3
There are 1 stones remaining.
The computer removes 1 stones leaving 0.
Better luck next time.
```

Note that, once we let the computer get the edge, it will always adjust the pile to have a multiple of four stones, making winning hopeless for the user.

4.9.4   TWENTY-ONE PICKUP: TESTING

An in-depth discussion of testing is well beyond the scope of this book. Thorough testing is both difficult and important. In general, you can't possibly test every conceivable input. Even if you restricted your testing to consider that, for all but the last move, the user could enter a value that is too big, a value that is too small, or one of three legal values, you would have approximately 3000 test sequences to verify. Obviously, a more systematic approach to testing is necessary.

One approach is called *statement coverage*. In this approach, you attempt to build a set of test cases such that when all test cases have been executed, each statement in the program has been executed at least once. If the set of tests causes every statement to be executed, the tests verify complete statement coverage. Unfortunately, complete statement coverage doesn't guarantee that the program is correct. For example, if we made the following minor typing error in the while condition in method getUserMove(),

```
while (move > numberOfStones || move < 0 || move > 3)
```

verification of complete statement coverage might not uncover the error. To detect this error we would need to enter a move of 0 and then observe that this erroneous move was allowed.

Another approach is called *branch coverage*. In this approach, you attempt to build a set of test cases such that, when all test cases have been executed, each possible branch has been taken at least once. Branch coverage isn't quite the same as statement coverage. For example, statement coverage doesn't require that a loop be forced to execute zero times, but branch coverage requires that the initial loop test be executed so that it branches both into the loop and around the loop.

For the program TwentyOnePickup, we can begin by building a test set that provides complete statement coverage. We then need to add additional tests to verify that each of the relational expressions is correct. Here is an outline of our test strategy.

- All statements in `main()` will be executed if we include at least one case wherein the user wins (moves last) and one wherein the computer wins.
- For `computerMove()`, all statements will be executed if we have a test case wherein the computer wins (the true branch of the outer `if-else` statement) and a test case wherein the computer removes one stone because `numberOfStones % 4` is 0. In addition, we need a test case where `numberOfStones % 4` isn't 0.
- The method `playerMove()` contains no branching statements, so any execution will cover all statements in the method.
- For `getUserMove()`, all statements will be executed if we provide at least one erroneous input value when more than three stones remain and one erroneous value when less than three stones remain. In addition, we need test cases that include a value that is too big and a value that is too small. We also need to test the end condition when less than three stones remain but the user enters 3.

Thus thorough testing of even this simple program requires a significant number of test cases.

4.10 RECURSION

A method is said to be recursive if it calls itself, either directly or indirectly. In its simplest form the idea of recursion is straightforward. Try the following program.

```
// Recur.java - recursive goodbye
public class Recur {
  public static void main(String[] args) {
    sayGoodBye(5);
  }
  static void sayGoodBye(int n) {
    if (n < 1) //base case
      System.out.println("########");
    else {
      System.out.println("Say goodbye Gracie.");
      sayGoodBye(n - 1); //recursion
    }
  }
}
```

This program prints

```
Say goodbye Gracie.
Say goodbye Gracie.
Say goodbye Gracie.
Say goodbye Gracie.
Say goodbye Gracie.
########
```

The general form of a recursive method body is

```
if (stopping condition)        //base case
   //do whatever at the end;
else {                         //recursive case
   //execute recursive step
   RecursiveMethod(arguments);
}
```

A simple standard recursive method is factorial.

```
static long factorial(int n) {
  if (n <= 1)
    return 1;
  else
    return (n * factorial(n - 1));
}
```

Suppose that we executed x = factorial(4); inside method main(). The sequence of method calls would be

```
main() calls factorial(4).
  factorial(4) calls factorial(3).
    factorial(3) calls factorial(2).
      factorial(2) calls factorial(1).
        factorial(1) returns 1.
      factorial(2) returns 2.
    factorial(3) returns 6.
  factorial(4) returns 24.
  main() continues assigning 24 to x.
```

When the innermost call, factorial(1), is executing, it is like having four different copies of the factorial method that have each been started but none have yet returned. Each has its own copy of the formal parameter n, and each value of n is different. Recall that a formal parameter is like a local variable in that the scope is the body of the method. For this reason, the different versions of n don't interfere with each other.

The following table shows another view of factorial(4). First the base case is considered. Then working out from the base case, the other cases are considered.

Method Call	Value Returned		
factorial(1)	1		= 1
factorial(2)	2 * factorial(1)	or	2 * 1 = 2
factorial(3)	3 * factorial(2)	or	3 * 2 * 1 = 6
factorial(4)	4 * factorial(3)	or	4 * 3 * 2 * 1 = 24

Simple recursive methods follow a standard pattern. Typically, a base case is tested for upon entry to the method. Then there is a general recursive case in which one of the variables, often an integer, is passed as an argument in such a way as to ultimately lead to the base case. In `factorial()`, the variable n was reduced by 1 each time until the base case with n equals 1 was reached.

Most simple recursive methods can be easily rewritten as iterative methods, as in

```
static long factorial(int n) {   // iteratively
  int product = 1;
  for ( ; n > 1; --n)
    product = product * n;
  return product;
}
```

For a given input value, both factorial methods return the same value, but the iterative version requires only one method call regardless of the value passed in. Method call is an expensive operation, so, in general, iterative versions of methods are more efficient than their recursive versions.

4.11 PROBLEM SOLVING: MATHEMATICAL FUNCTIONS

In science, we frequently have an equation that describes some behavior, such as Newton's law; $F = MA,$ for force equals mass times acceleration. For complicated equations, we need to use computation to study their behavior. For example, we might want to visualize an equation. To do so we might graphically plot it or print a table of values for it (see Exercise 17, on page 137).

One interesting property of a function is to find a zero of a function in a given region. We might try to find it by computing a function at many points in the interval and find the point $f(x_{root}) = 0$. Consider finding a root for the quadratic equation $f(x) = x^2 - 2$. This computation might be partly described as follows:

```
// SimpleFindRoot.java - find the root of x*x - 2
//Version 1.0 Won't work- Why?
class SimpleFindRoot {
  public static void main(String[] args) {
    double a = 0.0, b = 10.0, x, step = 0.001;

    x = a; /* start at one end */
    while ( f(x) != 0.0 && x < b) {
      x = x + step;
    }
    if (x < b)
      System.out.println(" root is " + x);
    else
      System.out.println(" root not found");
  }
  static double f(double x){ return (x * x - 2.0);}
}
```

What's wrong with this approach? Although we are examining the interval in fairly small steps, we might not hit a zero exactly. (Try the preceding code.) We might be more likely to identify a zero if we make locating a zero less precise. We leave modifying this code to choose the x so that $f(x)$ is nearest to zero for you to do in Exercise 15, on page 137. This new scheme is guaranteed to find a solution, but it has two weaknesses. One, it is a *brute-force* approach and is computationally expensive. Second, it can fail because a smallest $f(x)$ might not be near a true zero.

A better method searches for a smallest interval that contains a zero, which is much safer numerically. This idea is based on the *mean value theorem* of calculus. Informally, when we plot a function on the x and y axes, keeping our pen on the paper, and on one side of the interval the function is above the x axis and on the other side of the interval the function is below the x axis, the pen must cross the x axis in that interval. In other words, for a continuous function, a zero exists in an interval where $f(x)f(y) < 0$.

In our next method we make use of this observation. Further, we use the method of bisection to search the interval efficiently for a zero. This bisection problem-solving technique recurs in many areas of computer science. The idea is to check on the sign of the function evaluated in the center of the current interval and then to replace the existing search interval by one-half the size. We do so by replacing the relevant endpoint of the interval with the point just evaluated. For the code in this example, we assume that $f(a)$ is negative and $f(b)$ is positive for the initial interval endpoints, a and b. As shown in the figure, if the value of the function at the midpoint, $f((a + b)/2)$, is negative, then the left endpoint, denoted by a, will be replaced with $(a + b)/2$.

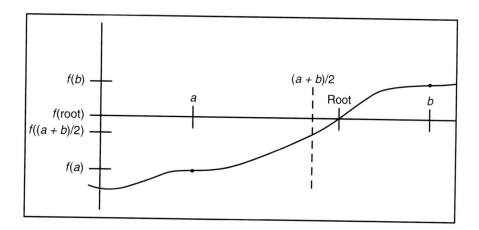

```
//FindRoot.java - use bisection to find a zero
class FindRoot {
  public static void main(String[] args) {
    double a = 0.0, b = 10.0, eps = 0.00001;
    double root = 0.0 , residual;
```

```
        while ( b - a > eps ) {
          root = (a + b) / 2.0;
          residual = f(root);
          if (residual > 0)
            b = root;        // replace right endpoint
          else
            a = root;        // replace left endpoint
        }
        System.out.println(" root is " + root);
      }

      static double f(double x){ return (x * x - 2.0); }
    }
```

Note that improvement in the accuracy of the interval is guaranteed for each evaluation. This improvement works out to a binary digit of accuracy.

4.12 METHOD OVERLOADING

In Section 4.3 we presented `min()` and `max()` methods that work with integer values. If we want these methods to work with values of type `double`, we must rewrite the methods. Here we rewrite `min()` and leave the rewriting of `max()` as an exercise. Instead of a and b, we use the parameters x and y, which is common practice when dealing with `float`s and `double`s:

```
static double min(double x, double y) {
  if (x < y)
    return x;
  else
    return y;
}
```

Because Java supports method overloading, this definition of `min()` and the one from Section 4.3, on page 100, that includes integer parameters can exist in the same class or program. These two definitions are distinguished by their signatures. A *method signature* is the name of the method along with the return type, the number of parameters, and the types of the parameters, in that order. For example, the two `min()` methods have differing signatures,

```
int min(int, int)
```

and

```
double min(double, double)
```

When the Java compiler encounters a call to `min()`, such as `min(expr1, expr2)`, the compiler can determine which of the two `min()` methods to call, based on the types of the expressions, `expr1` and `expr2`. For example, if both expressions result in values of type int, then int min(int,int) would be called; if both are type double, then double min(double,double) would be called. This procedure, known as *signature matching*, is based on the types of the parameters for the method but not on the return type. This ability to define multiple methods with the same name is called *method overloading*.

Overloading is an extremely useful feature. In languages without method overloading, programmers are frequently forced to choose contrived names for methods because another method with the preferred name already exists. Overloading is what makes it possible to call System.out.println() with a String or any of the primitive types. Actually, different println() methods exist for each of the different types. Without overloading, printString(), printInt(), printDouble(), and so on, would be needed.

Returning to our example min(), what would happen if there was a call to min() with one int value and one double value? The Java compiler would convert the int to a double and call the version of min() that takes double parameters. In general, the compiler first tries to find an exact match. If if can't find an exact match, then it performs widening primitive conversions to try to find a match. A *widening primitive conversion* is a conversion from one numeric type to another that is guaranteed to maintain the sign and most significant digits of the value being converted. For example, conversions from int to long or from int to float are widening primitive conversions. The former loses no information, and the latter may lose some significant digits; however, the most significant digits and the sign are preserved. For a detailed description of widening primitive conversion, see Section 2.10.2.

Sometimes the conversions can result in more than one possible match. Multiple matches usually result in a compile-time error, and the call is said to be *ambiguous*, as in

```
//AmbiguousOverload.java: won't compile
class AmbiguousOverload {
  public static void main(String[] args) {
    int i = 1, j = 2;

    System.out.println(ambig(i,j));
  }
  static boolean ambig(float x, int y){
    return x < y;
  }
  static boolean ambig(int x, float y){
    return x < y;
  }
}
```

An int can be converted to a float by a widening primitive conversion. The ambiguity arises because we can either convert i and match the first definition of ambig() or convert j and match the second definition. The definitions aren't inherently ambiguous; it is the call that is ambiguous. If j was instead declared to be a float, then the ambiguity would be eliminated and only the second definition would match the call. Explicit conversions, discussed in Section 2.10.2, can be used to resolve ambiguities such as this one. For example, changing the call to

```
System.out.println(ambig((float)i, j));
```

would result in a call to the first version of `ambig()`.

Sometimes, widening conversions can lead to two matches but not be considered ambiguous. For example, suppose that signature Scall is the signature of the call and there are methods with signatures S1 and S2. If Scall can be converted to S1 using widening conversions and S1 can also be converted to S2 using widening conversions, then S1 is said to be more specific than S2. Visually the conversions looks like this.

Scall ──Widening conversion──▶ S1 ──Widening conversion──▶ S2

In this case the method with signature S1, the more specific signature, will be called. Note that in the preceding example, `AmbiguousOverload`, neither of the two method signatures could be converted to the other by using widening conversions. In the following example, two matches can be found, but one is more specific than the other.

```
//UnambiguousOverload.java: no ambiguity here
class UnambiguousOverload {
  public static void main(String[] args) {
    int i = 1, j = 2;

    System.out.println(unAmbig(i,j));
  }
  static boolean unAmbig(float x, float y){
    return x < y;
  }
  static boolean unAmbig(double x, double y){
    return x < y;
  }
}
```

Although the call could be converted, using widening primitive conversions to match either of the methods, the method that takes two `float` values is more specific and hence is the one called.

4.13 PROGRAMMING STYLE

Breaking a problem into small subproblems that are then coded as methods is crucial to good programming style. To be easily readable, a method should be at most a page of code. Except for a few cases where the purpose of a method is trivially obvious from the choice of identifier names, methods should begin with an opening comment. In this book, however, we generally omit such comments because they would be redundant with the surrounding expository text. The opening comment should include a description of the input parameters and the return value. The parameter names should be chosen to identify clearly the purpose of the parameter. In some cases, well-chosen parameter names can eliminate the need for any further explanation.

To encourage well-documented code, the standard Java tool set includes a program, *javadoc*, that can be used to create automatically HTML formatted documentation from stylized comments. Recall that HTML is the text formatting language for the World Wide Web. Here are sample *javadoc* comments for two of the methods for `CoinToss` presented earlier in this chapter. Note the comments begin with `/**`. The strings beginning with @ are keywords in *javadoc*. There are more keywords for *javadoc* than the two used in this example. Consult the documentation with your system for additional details.

```
public class CoinToss {
  /**
   * Calculate the probability of throwing 4 heads in
   * a row. 10000 trials are run and the probability
   * is estimated as the fraction of trials that
   * successfully tossed 4 heads in a row.
   */
  public static void main(String[] args) {
  ...

/**
   * Simulate an attempt to roll n heads in a row.
   * @param numTosses The number of times to toss the
   *                  coin.
   * @return true if the next numTosses are all heads
   *         false otherwise
   */
  static boolean isAllHeads(int numTosses)
  ...
```

Running *javadoc* on the source file *CoinToss.java* will generate a file *CoinToss.html*. This file can be viewed with any browser. By default, *javadoc* generates documentation only for public classes and public methods. We discuss access modifiers and the keyword `public` in Section 6.4. To get *javadoc* to generate documentation for classes and methods that don't have an access modifier such as `public`, use the command

```
javadoc -package CoinToss.java
```

The flag `-package` is used because a method or class with no access modifier is said to have package access. The following screen shot shows a portion of *CoinToss.html* viewed with Netscape.

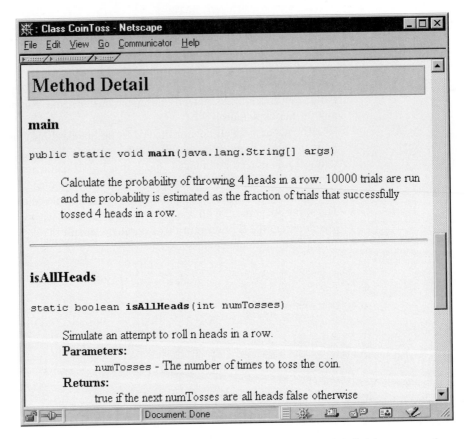

Another stylistic choice is the order in which method definitions occur in a class. It is usually a matter of taste whether a programmer writes `main()` followed by the other method definitions, or vice versa. If a programmer is doing top-down development, however, it is natural to start with `main()`.

It is considered good programming style to have only a few `return` statements in a given method. In fact, the best choice is usually a single return as the last statement in the method. If there are many `return` statements, the logic of the code may be difficult to follow.

Summary

- A simple program is made up of one or more static methods contained in a class, one of them being `main()`. In these simple cases, program execution begins with `main()`. When program control encounters a method name followed by parentheses, the method is called, or invoked. This means that program control passes to the method.

- Structured programming is a problem-solving strategy and a programming method-ology that strives for simple flow of control and involves the use of top-down design. Also referred to as stepwise refinement, top-down design consists of repeat-edly decomposing a problem into smaller problems.

- The software life cycle generally includes requirements analysis and definition, design, implementation, testing, and maintenance.

- A long program should be written as a collection of methods, each one being, in general, no longer than a page. Each method should cover some small task as part of the overall problem.

- A variable declared in the body of a method is called a local variable. The scope of a variable begins at the point it is declared and continues to the end of the block con-taining the declaration. The scope of formal parameters is the entire method body. The scope of a variable declared in the initialization expression of a `for` statement is the entire `for` statement.

- A programmer creates a method by writing a method definition, which consists of a header and a block, also known as the method body. The header consists of the type returned by the method, the method name, and a comma-separated list of declara-tions of parameters enclosed by parentheses. The body consists of a block of state-ments.

- When a method is called, program control is passed to the method. When a `return` statement is executed or the end of the method is reached, control is passed back to the point of the call. If a `return` statement contains an expression, the value of the expression is also passed back to the point of the call.

- In Java, all arguments of primitive types are passed call-by-value. That is, when a variable of primitive type is passed as an argument to a method, although the formal argument in the method can be changed, the value of the actual argument remains unchanged in the calling environment.

- Java provides the method `Math.random()`, for random doubles in the range 0.0 to 1.0.

- A method that calls itself directly or indirectly is said to be recursive. Many pro-gramming problems can be solved with recursion, although an iterative solution is often more efficient.

- Java methods can be overloaded. In other words, several methods can have the same name but with different signatures. The signature includes the name of the method and the parameter types.

Review Questions

1. Within a class, is the order of method definitions important? Why or why not?
2. True or false? When passing parameters, the name of the actual parameter must match the name of the formal parameter.
3. What is the significance of `void` in the following statement?

```
public static void printMessage()
```

4. Give an example of method overloading.
5. What is the output of the following program?

```
class PracticeProblem {
  public static void main (String[] args) {
    int x = 10, y = 5;

    printProduct(x, y);
    x = 2;
    printProduct(x + y, x);
  }
  static void printProduct(int x, int y) {
    System.out.print("The Product of " + x);
    System.out.print(" and " + y + " is ");
    System.out.println(x * y);

  }
}
```

6. A method definition must always specify what important aspect of each formal parameter?
7. Where do you specify the type of expression that must follow the keyword `return`?
8. Does writing a method that has several hundred lines of code in its definition violate top-down programming? Explain.
9. The expression `(int)(n * Math.random()) % 10` generates integers in what range?
10. What is printed by the following program?

```
class Fcn {
  static int foo(int a, int b) { return (a + b); }
  static int goo(int x) { return (x * x); }
  public static void main(String[] args) {
    int i = 2;
    System.out.println("foo = " + foo(i, 3));
    System.out.println("foo = " + foo(i, 4));
    System.out.println("goo = " + goo(i));
    System.out.println("goo = " + foo(goo(i), i++));

  }
}
```

11. What are two static methods you have used from the Java libraries?
12. The *javadoc* program is used for what? When using it, why should you use the comment style `/** Remember Me? */`?
13. What syntax errors are in the following program?

```
class Scope {
  public static void main(String[] args) {
    int x = 1;

    {
      int x = 2;
      int y = 3;

      System.out.println("x = " + x);
      System.out.println("y = " + y);
    }
```

```
        System.out.println("x = " + x);
        System.out.println("y = " + y);
    }
}
```

14. Which step of the software life cycle is often the longest and most costly?
15. Name two different approaches to software testing.
16. What is printed by the following program?

```
class RecursionExercise {
  public static void main(String[] args) {
    for (int i = 0; i < 10; i++)
      System.out.println(recurse(i));
  }
  static long recurse(long n) {
    if (n <= 0)
      return 1;
    else
      return 2 * recurse(n - 1);
  }
}
```

Exercises

1. Rewrite the following class Message so that it prints out a personalized happy birthday greeting.

    Message for FILLIN: Happy Birthday to you!
                         You are XX years old!
                         Have a nice year!

    Be sure that it handles the special case of a one-year-old, printing You are 1 year old!

2. Rewrite the class Message2 to read from the keyboard the value n that will be passed to the method printMessage().

3. Write a static method square() that will take an integer and return its square and a static method cube() that will take an integer and return its cube. Use your square() and cube() methods to write the methods quartic() and quintic() that return the fourth and fifth power of an integer, respectively. Use your methods to write a program that prints a table of powers of integers from 1 to 25. The output of your program should look like

```
A TABLE OF POWERS
-----------------


Integer Square  Cube    Quartic Quintic
------- ------  ----    ------- -------
1       1       1       1       1
2       4       8       16      32
.....
```

4. Write the method static double max(double x, double y). This method can be defined in the same class as static int max(int x, int y) because the argument types of the two methods are different.

5. In class `RunSums`, the method `readAndPrintData()` used a sentinel value −99999 to terminate input. Rewrite the program to ask the user for the number of items and use this positive integer to terminate the input loop.

6. The class `ReadInput` in the package `tio` supplied with this text contains a method `hasMoreElements()` that returns true if there is more input to read. This method can be used to detect the end of input. On Unix machines you indicate the end of input from the keyboard by entering Ctrl+D. On Windows machines you enter Ctrl+Z instead. If you use the method `hasMoreElements()`, the `readAndPrintData()` method in class `RunSums` can read in an arbitrary number of values without the need for a special sentinel value. Rewrite `readAndPrintData()` to use `hasMoreElements()`. The syntax of the loop will be

```
while (Console.in.hasMoreElements()) ...
```

7. Modify `isAllHeads()` to compute the probability using an unfair coin that comes up heads with probability 0.8. How do fair and unfair coins compare for producing five heads in a row? If you know the probability theory for this case, work it out theoretically. Does the theoretical result agree with your computational experiments?

8. Modify `isAllHeads()` to compute `almostAllHeads(int n, int k)`, which is true if at least `k` out of `n` heads are tossed. Test it by computing the probability that you would toss at least 6 of 10 heads.

9. Modify the coin toss simulation to compute the probability that you get 5 of 10 heads exactly.

10. Modify Exercise 15, on page 90, in Chapter 3, to have a method `drawBox()` that takes the width and height of the box in asterisks as formal parameters. Modify the program further to include three methods: `drawLine()`, `drawSides()`, and `drawBox()`. The method `drawLine()` will take two parameters: the length of the line and a `String` that will print length times to draw the line. The method `drawSides()` will take three parameters: the height of the sides, the width of the box that will be formed (both lines must be drawn at the same time), and a `String` used to represent a side. The method `drawBox()` will take three parameters: the width and height of the box and a string used to represent the sides. For example, if called as `drawBox(5,4,"Java")`, the output would be

```
JavaJavaJavaJavaJava
Java                Java
Java                Java
JavaJavaJavaJavaJava
```

11. Write a weather prediction program using the random number generator. Three outcomes should be possible: rain, sun, or cloudy. Assume that each outcome occurs one-third of the time.

12. Write a fortune-telling program, using the random number generator to pick 1 of at least 10 fortunes. Use the `switch` statement in the following way.

```
switch((int)(10 * Math.random()) {
   case 0:  ... break;
   case 1:  ... break;
   //more cases with fortunes
   case 9:  ... break;
}
```

13. Write a program to print the values of $F(x) = x^2 - 2$ for the range $0 < x < 10$. Print the values in this range at a step size of 0.01. Also find the largest and smallest value of $F(x)$ in this interval.

14. Modify `SimpleFindRoot` to find x, such that $F(x)$ is nearest to zero. You can use the `static` method `Math.abs()` to solve this problem.

15. Modify `FindRoot` to solve for a root of $F(x) = e^{x^2} - 10$. Use as your starting interval $(0, 5)$. How do we know this interval will work? (The answer can be found in Section 4.11.) The class `java.lang.Math` has a method `Math.pow(double n1, double n2)` that computes n1 raised to the n2 power. The class also defines the constant `Math.E`.

16. A further method for finding roots employs a Monte Carlo search. A random point in the search interval is chosen. The function is evaluated at this point. If the result is closer to zero than the value of the function for any previous point, then this point is kept as the current candidate solution. The more points evaluated, the greater becomes the confidence in the final solution. This approach is similar to `Simple-FindRoot` and is a brute force, computationally expensive method. It avoids some subtle problems because it chooses its candidate points at random. Write such a method and use 100 points in the interval 0 through 5 to solve for a root of $F(x) = e^{x^2} - 10$. Now try the method with successively 100 and 10,000 points. Observe how slowly the accuracy of the root improves compared to that of the bisection method.

17. Write a program that allows the user to play the game of Craps, which is played with two dice. A simple version of the game between one player and "the house" can be described as follows.

   a. The player bets some amount of money.

   b. The player throws the dice.

   c. If the dice total 2 or 12 the player loses the bet and play starts again at step 1.

   d. If the dice total 7 or 11 the player wins the amount of the bet from the house and play starts again at step 1.

   e. If the dice total any other value, this value is called the point.

   f. The player continues to roll the dice until they total either 7 or the point.

   g. If the dice total is 7 the player loses the bet; otherwise, the player has made the point and wins the amount of the bet from the house. In either case, play starts again at step 1.

   Play continues until the player indicates that he or she wants to quit or until the player runs out of money. Before you begin to write the code for this program, you should develop a design. Convert the description of play to pseudocode and identify the primary methods that you'll need. You may even need to refine the specification some more first. For example, how much money does the player start with? To simulate the roll of the dice, the expression

```
(int)(Math.random() * 6) + 1
```

will evaluate to a random integer of 1 through 6. You must simulate rolling each die separately. Generating a random number in the range 2 through 12 isn't sufficient.

18. Write and test a method that will recursively print all the characters from `'a'` through `'z'`. Remember that each character is one more than the previous.

19. Write and test a method that recursively prints the characters from `first` through `last`:

```
static void printRange(char first, char last)
//example if first = 'c' and last = 'g' then
//prints c d e f g
```

(*Hint:* recur on the variable `first`.)

20. *Fibonacci Recursion*: Many algorithms have both iterative and recursive formulations. Typically, recursion is more elegant and requires fewer variables then does iteration to make the same calculation. Recursion takes care of its bookkeeping by stacking arguments and variables for each invocation. This stacking of arguments, although invisible to the user, is still costly in time and space. Let's investigate efficiency with respect to the calculation of the Fibonacci sequence, which is defined recursively by

$$f_0 = 0, \ f_1 = 1,$$
$$f_{i+1} = f_i + f_{i-1} \ \text{for } i = 1, 2, \ldots$$

Except for f_0 and f_1, every element in the sequence is the sum of the previous two elements. The sequence begins 0, 1, 1, 2, 3, 5, ... Here is a function that computes Fibonacci numbers recursively:

```
static long fibonacci(int n) {
  if (n <= 1)
    return n;
  else
    return (fibonacci(n - 1) + fibonacci(n - 2));
}
```

Write a class that tests this recursive calculation. Choose a large enough n, say, $n = 40$, to see the results of the computation on the screen where the calculation visibly slows. On a 400 megahertz Pentium it is shows up in the range $n > 35$.

Now write an iterative version of this same algorithm and run it up to the same n or larger. It should run instantaneously. Explain why.

Applet Exercise

In the Applet Exercise at the end of Chapter 2, you explored how to do simple drawing using an applet. Methods let you easily create more complicated drawings. For example, the standard java method `drawOval()` from the class `Graphics` can draw an oval of any size, placed anywhere on the visible area of an applet. By creating methods to draw a shape with its size and position controlled by parameters, you can make complicated drawings much more simply. The following applet uses the standard Java method `fillRect()` from the class `Graphics` to draw a simple chair.

```
/* <applet code="DrawChairs.class"
    width=150 height=120></applet> */
import java.awt.*;
import javax.swing.*;
public class DrawChairs extends JApplet {
  public void paint(Graphics g) {
    drawChair(10, 10, 50, 100, g);
    drawChair(70, 10, 25, 50, g);
    drawChair(105, 10, 10, 20, g);
  }
  /**
   * drawChair draws a chair at the specified
   *     position, scaled to the specified size
   * @param left The distance in from the left edge.
   * @param top The distance down from the top.
   * @param width The width of the chair seat.
   * @param height The height of the chair back.
   * @param Graphics The object to draw on.
   */
  void drawChair(int left, int top,
                 int width, int height, Graphics g){
    // thickness of the legs, back and seat
    int thickness = width / 10 + 1;

    // draw the seat
    g.fillRect(left, top + height / 2,
               width, thickness);
    // draw the back and back leg
    g.fillRect(left + width - thickness, top,
               thickness, height);
    // draw the front leg
    g.fillRect(left, top + height /2 ,
               thickness, height / 2);
  }
}
```

DISSECTION OF THE DrawChairs APPLET

-
```
/* <applet code="DrawChairs.class"
    width=150 height=120></applet> */
import java.awt.*;
import java.applet.*;

public class DrawChairs extends JApplet {
```

As with the applet exercises in previous chapters, this code is just part of the template. We explain the details later in Chapters 8 and 9. For your own applets, you need only change the name of the applet DrawChairs to something appropriate. Be sure and change both occurrences of DrawChairs in the template. Also, you may decide to change the width and height of your applet. Unlike the applet in Chapter 3 on page 138, this applet doesn't respond to user input, so you don't need import java.event.* and implements ActionListener as you did in that earlier exercise.

■
```
public void paint(Graphics g) {
    drawChair(10, 10, 50, 100, g);
    drawChair(70, 10, 25, 50, g);
    drawChair(105, 10, 10, 20, g);
}
```

This method is called when it is time for the applet to be displayed. For this particular applet, this is the top-level method, which is somewhat like `main()` in other programs. Here we call our new method `drawChair()` three times, drawing three different-sized chairs in three different locations. Here is what it looks like when executed.

■
```
void drawChair(int left, int top,
               int width, int height, Graphics g)
```

Our method `drawChair()` takes the same four parameters as `drawOval()`: the coordinates of the upper left corner and the width and the height of an imaginary box drawn around the chair. In addition, our `drawChair()` method must be passed the `Graphics` object upon which the drawing is to be made.

■
```
int thickness = width / 10 + 1;
```

To make our chair scale properly, we set the thickness of the chair seat, legs, and back to be about 10 percent of the overall width of the chair. The +1 ensures that the thickness is always at least 1. Recall that, if width is less than 10, then the expression `width / 10` will be 0.

■
```
// draw the seat
g.fillRect(left, top + height/2,
           width, thickness);
// draw the back and back leg
g.fillRect(left + width - thickness, top,
           thickness, height);
// draw the front leg
g.fillRect(left, top + height / 2,
           thickness, height / 2);
```

The method `fillRect()` draws a filled-in rectangle. The parameters for `fill-Rect()` are the same as the parameters for `drawOval()`, namely, the coordinates of the upper left corner of the rectangle, the width, and the height. You can also draw an outline of a rectangle with the method `drawRect()` and a filled-in oval with `fillOval()`. The following drawing shows the relationships of the various values used to draw the chair.

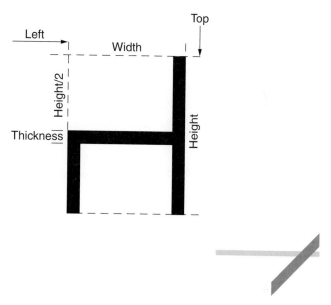

Modify the applet `DrawChairs` to include methods similar to `drawChair()` that draw a table and a vase. Your methods have to allow the shapes to be drawn anywhere and at any size. Each shape should be placed inside an imaginary box. Then use your methods to draw a picture that includes at least two tables, two chairs, and two vases, each a different size. You should first work out your drawing on paper with a figure like the one above for the chair.

5

Arrays

So far we've been dealing with distinct variables for referring to any particular stored value. However, there are countless collections of similar values in everyday situations—for example, students' test scores, the daily temperature at each city in the country, or the social security numbers of all the students at a university. An array in Java is a data structure that stores and processes such related values. An array is a simple form of *container* that holds a related group of values of the same type. For example, you can use an array of integers to represent student test scores or an array of floating point values to represent city temperatures or an array of strings to represent the names of students in a class.

5.1   ONE-DIMENSIONAL ARRAYS

Java, like most programming languages, provides a special syntax for dealing with arrays. In Java, the elements in an array are always numbered 0 through $n - 1$ where n is the number of individual items or elements in the array. The elements in an array are ordered, and the position of an element in the array is called the element's *index*. This position can result in some awkward or ambiguous statements about arrays. For example, when a person talks about the "first" element in an array he or she usually means the element at *index* 0, not the element at *index* 1. The main reason for starting at 0 instead of 1 is to make Java syntax for arrays the same as that of C and C++, which use this convention. The reason that those languages start at 0 has to do with how arrays are arranged in the computer's memory and how an individual element is located. Arrays of values are arranged in contiguous memory locations. The name of the array is viewed as referring to the first element in the array. To find the address in memory of a specific element, the computer can add the element's index to the address of the location of the first element. The following figure shows an array of seven integers having the values 100 through 106. The array is being referred to by the variable data.

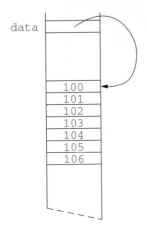

The variable data tells the computer where the first element in the array is located (indicated by the arrow). To find the value at index 3 in the array the computer locates the first element and then moves down three locations. In this case the element at index 3 is 103.

You declare array variables just like any other variable, by specifying a type followed by the name of the variable. For any type T in Java, T[] is the notation for the type: array of Ts. Some examples of array variable declarations are

```
int[]    data;       //reference to array of ints
String[] sentence;  //reference to array of Strings
```

These are reference declarations. As the preceding figure suggests, the memory location most closely associated with an array variable doesn't contain the array data itself. Rather, it contains a reference or pointer to the actual array data. All variables in Java are either primitive type variables or reference variables. *Reference variables* are declared with a class type or are declared with an array type. No actual arrays are created by the declarations shown. Arrays are created by using the operator new, similar to the way that objects or instances of classes are created (see Section 2.4, on page 22). The general syntax for creating an actual array and assigning an array variable to refer to the newly created array is

> *someArrayVariable* = new *type* [*length*] ;

Execution of this statement will evaluate *length*, an integer expression, and then create an array with *length* elements of type *type*. The array variable *someArrayVariable* is assigned to reference this newly created array object. For example, let's assume that we use v = new int[n] to allocate an array v. After this statement has been executed, the int variables v[0], v[1], v[2],..., v[n - 1] come into existence and can be used by the program. Once an array has been created, its size may not be changed. However, an array variable may be changed to refer to a *different* array that is a different size (see Section 5.3 on page 150).

Here are some more examples.

```
data = new int[7];          // 7 int's
sentence = new String[2 * n]; // 2n Strings
```

In the same way that other variables can be declared and assigned initial values in one statement, array variables can be declared and assigned initial values in one statement, as in

```
int[]    data = new int[100];
String[] names = new String[1000];
```

5.1.1 INDEXING AN ARRAY ELEMENT

To manipulate each individual element we use *subscripting* or *indexing*. Let's assume that declarations of the form

```
int[] someArray = new int [length];
int  i;        //used to index or subscript array
```

have been made. Then we can write `someArray[i]` to access an element of the array. More generally, to access an element of the array we may write `someArray[expr]`, where *expr* is an integral expression. We call *expr* a *subscript*, or *index*, of `someArray`. The value of a Java subscript should lie in the range 0 through *length* − 1, where *length* is the number of elements in the array.

5.1.2 ARRAY INITIALIZATION

Arrays have their individual elements automatically initialized when allocated. Primitive numeric types are initialized to 0, and the type `boolean` is initialized to `false`. All other types are reference types and are initialized to the special value `null`, which signifies that the element doesn't currently refer to anything. Once an array has been created, we can assign specific element values using assignment, as in

```
int[] a = new int[2]; //create a[0] = a[1] = 0

a[0] = 10;            //a[0] now has integer value 10
a[1] = 20;            //a[1] now has integer value 20
```

For convenience, Java provides a way to declare, create, and initialize an array in one statement. Arrays can be initialized by a comma-separated list of expressions enclosed in braces. The compiler uses the number of expressions as the size for the array. Hence we can more succinctly declare and initialize the preceding assignments as

```
int[] a = {10, 20}; //allocates and initializes
```

The following simple program initializes an array, prints its values, and computes its sum and average value.

```
// ArraySum.java - sum the elements in an array and
//     compute their average
```

```
class ArraySum {
  public static void main(String[] args) {
    int[] data = {11, 12, 13, 14, 15, 16, 17};
    int sum = 0;
    double average;

    for (int i = 0; i < 7; i++) {
      sum = sum + data[i];
      System.out.print(data[i] + ", ");
    }
    average = sum / 7.0;
    System.out.println("\n\n sum = " + sum
        + " average = " + average);
  }
}
```

DISSECTION OF THE ArraySum PROGRAM

- `int[] data = {11, 12, 13, 14, 15, 16, 17};`

The variable `data` is declared to refer to an array of integers. It is allocated seven integer elements, which are initialized to the values 11 through 17.

- `for (int i = 0; i < 7; i++) {`

The `for` statement declares the local variable `i` to be used as an index or subscript variable. This `for` statement is the most common array code idiom. The initial subscript for array objects in Java is 0, so the subscript variable is usually initialized to 0. The array length is 7, so the terminating condition is usually i < 7 so that the loop will stop after executing the loop body with the array index set to 7 - 1. The last part of the `for` statement header is the increment of the index variable, ensuring that each array element gets processed in turn.

- `sum = sum + data[i];`
  `System.out.print(data[i] + ", ");`

The element `data[i]` is selected by computation of the index value. A common error that results is for the index value to be out of range. These subscripted or indexed elements can be used as simple variables of type `int`. In this code, each element's integer value is added to the variable `sum`. Then, in turn, each element's value is printed.

The output of this program is

```
11, 12, 13, 14, 15, 16, 17,

sum = 98 average = 14.0
```

5.1.3   ARRAY MEMBER LENGTH

Once created, an array stores more than just the elements of the array. The most important extra information now is the length of the array. The expression *arrayVariable*.`length` can be used to determine the number of elements allocated to an array. It will be an integer value greater than or equal to 0. A common use of the length member for an array is in a `for` statement header. Using *arrayVariable*.`length` is preferable to coding a particular integer constant or other expression. In the class `ArraySum`, the `for` statement should be rewritten as

```
for (int i = 0; i < data.length; i++) {
  sum = sum + data[i];
  System.out.print(data[i] + ", ");
}
```

which is our preferred style. It is less error prone than writing an explicit integer or specific integer expression. If we insert additional elements in the array initialization, no other changes are needed.

COMMON PROGRAMMING ERROR

An array subscript value outside the range 0 through *length* − 1 will cause the program to abort with an error message about an `IndexOutOfBoundsException`. When that happens, the condition is called "overrunning the bounds of the array" or "subscript out of bounds." In Chapter 11 we discuss how programs can catch these errors at run time and attempt to recover. Java, unlike some other popular programming languages, is much easier to debug because this common error is caught by the system, which displays an informative message.

A common error that is more difficult to detect is to begin or end the array computation with the wrong element. It is sometimes called the "off-by-one error." The following code shows this error.

```
for (int i = 1; i < data.length; i++)
  sum = sum + data[i];      //forgot to start with i = 0
```

5.2   PASSING ARRAYS TO METHODS

In the previous section, we had code that summed the integer array `data` in `main()`. This standard action is better packaged as a method so that it can be generally reused. The following program contains a method `sum()` to compute the sum of the elements in an array of integers.

```
// ArraySum2.java - sum the elements in an array
//     using a method
class ArraySum2 {
  public static void main(String[] args) {
    int[] data1 = {1, 2, 3, 4, 5, 6, 7};
    int[] data2 = {16, 18, 77};

    System.out.println("data1:" + sum(data1));
    System.out.println("data2:" + sum(data2));
  }

  // sum the elements in an array
  static int sum (int[] a) {
    int sum = 0;

    for (int i = 0; i < a.length; i++)
      sum = sum + a[i];
    return sum;
  }
}
```

The output of this program is

```
data1:28
data2:111
```

The length field of each array allows the sum() code to index properly each array. In the first invocation, sum(data1), the seven array elements of data1 are summed. In the second invocation, sum(data2), the method sums the three elements of data2.

As discussed in Section 4.8, Java passes parameters by value. Recall that arrays are reference types. Thus, although you may casually think of the value of an array such as data1 in the preceding example, as the entire array of values, in fact the "value" of the variable data1 is simply a reference to the array of values. So think of the array variable as storing the address of the actual array data. This address, not the array data, is passed by value when an array is passed to a method.

One of the reasons for this style of parameter passing with arrays is that arrays are often very large. Passing references to the array instead of the entire array of values enables programs to execute much faster. Each time an array is passed as a parameter, all the data values in the array need not be copied into the method—only the address of the array is copied.

An important consequence of the fact that array references, not the entire array of values, are passed is that we can pass an array variable to a method and have the method modify the contents of the array. This result is called a *side effect* because a side effect of calling the method is that the array's contents are changed. The following program contains a method for copying the values of one array into another array.

```
// TestCopy.java - demonstrate that array
//      parameters can be modified
class TestCopy {
  public static void main(String[] args) {
    int[] data1 = {1, 2, 3, 4, 5, 6, 7};
    int[] data2 = {8, 9, 10, 11, 12, 13, 14};

    copy(data1, data2);
    System.out.println("data1:");
    for (int i = 0; i < data1.length; i++)
      System.out.println(data1[i]);
    System.out.println("data2:");
    for (int i = 0; i < data2.length; i++)
      System.out.println(data2[i]);
  }

  static void copy(int[] from, int[] to) {
    for (int i = 0; i < from.length; i++)
      to[i] = from[i];
  }
}
```

The call to copy() changes the integer values stored in the elements of the array data2. The elements of the array to inside copy() are *mutable* or changeable. Recall that a primitive type variable, when passed as a parameter, can't be changed by the called method, although the copy in the called method can be changed. In contrast, use of an array reference parameter can lead to changes in array element values in the calling environment. When a parameter, such as the second parameter to copy(), is used to pass information back to the calling environment, the parameter is called an *output parameter*. It is so called because the parameter is used to send information from the method. This action is shown graphically in the following illustration. The arrows indicate that the array variables are referring to array objects. Although not shown, each array object contains the length of the array, followed by the elements of the array. When the method copy() is called, the *values* in the boxes labeled data1 and data2 are copied into the boxes labeled from and to. Recall also that the value is the reference to the array, not the array of values. The crossed out values show how the old element values in data2 or to (both refer to the same array of values) are replaced during the execution of the body of method copy().

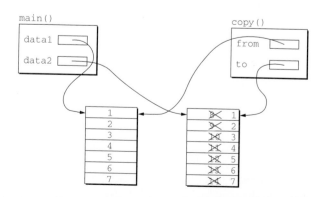

COMMON PROGRAMMING ERROR

As with other variables, direct modification of an array parameter has no effect at the point of the call. To demonstrate this lack of effect, let's suppose that the following method was substituted for the copy() in the class TestCopy.

```
static void copy(int[] from, int[] to) {
  to = from;     // failed attempt to copy an array
}
```

Using this method, as the comment suggests, wouldn't perform the desired copy operation. In fact, calling the latter copy() method would have no effect outside the method. Nor would the arrays data1 and data2 in main() be affected. The result of calling the defective copy() method is shown in the following diagram. It represents the state of the computer's memory after the assignment statement to = from in copy().

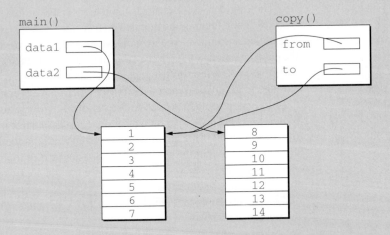

As shown, the variable to is made to refer to the array referred to by the variable from and data1, but no change is made to the contents of either array or to data2.

5.3   ARRAY ASSIGNMENT

Although we can't change the size of an array once it has been allocated, we can assign one array to another. The failed copy() method in the previous section assigned one array variable to another in to = from. If the array referred to by from wasn't the same size as the one originally referred to by to, then we could say the size of to had been changed. Consider the following code excerpt.

```
int[] a1 = {10, 20, 30};        //3 element array
int[] a2 = {1, 2, 3, 4, 5};     //5 element array
a1 = a2;        //now both refer to the same 5 elements
```

Note that this code fragment makes the arrays `a1` and `a2` physically the same array; `a1[0]` is in the same location in the computer's memory as `a2[0]`, and changing one will change the other. If instead you want to create a new array from an old array, you need to allocate a new array and assign each element from one array to the other. The following method could be used to duplicate a one-dimensional array of integers.

```
static int[] duplicate(int[] a) {
  int[] theCopy = new int[a.length];
  for (int i = 0; i < a.length; i++)
    theCopy[i] = a[i];
  return theCopy;
}
```

The following statement could be used to make a duplicate of the array `a2`. Let's assume that `a1` and `a2` were declared as previously shown.

```
a1 = duplicate(a2); //now two arrays containing 1 to 5
```

For one-dimensional arrays, a built-in mechanism produces an identical copy of an array. A method `clone()` is defined for all arrays so that

```
a1 = (int[])a2.clone(); // built in array "copy"
```

has the same effect as the use of `duplicate()`. The method `clone()` always returns a generic reference of type `Object`. The class `Object` is a standard Java class. This generic reference must be cast into the correct type for `a1`. We discuss generic references and this type of casting in Chapter 7.

5.4 FINDING THE MINIMUM AND MAXIMUM OF AN ARRAY

We can use the following program to illustrate some of these ideas. The program reads in an array of values, prints out the values, and finds the minimum and maximum elements.

```
// ArrayTest.java - minimum and maximum of an array
import tio.*;

class ArrayTest {
  public static void main(String[] args) {
    int[] data;
    int n;

    System.out.println("Enter size of data[]:");
    n = Console.in.readInt();
    data = new int[n];
    System.out.println("Enter " + n + " integers:");
    readArray(data);
```

```
    printArray(data, "My Data");
    System.out.println("minimum is " + minimum(data)
        + "   maximum is " + maximum(data));
}

// fill an array by reading values from the console
static void readArray(int[] a) {
  for ( int i = 0; i < a.length; i++) {
    a[i] = Console.in.readInt();
  }
}

// find the maximum value in an array
static int maximum(int[] a) {
  int  max = a[0]; //initial max value
  for (int i = 1; i < a.length; i++)
    if (a[i] > max)
      max = a[i];
  return max;
}

// find the minimum value in an array
static int minimum(int[] a) {
  int  min = a[0]; //initial max value

  for (int i = 1; i < a.length; i++)
    if (a[i] < min)
      min = a[i];
  return min;
}

// print the elements of an array to the console
static void printArray(int[] a, String arrayName) {
  System.out.println(arrayName );
  for (int i = 0; i < a.length; i++)
    System.out.print(a[i] + "   ");
  System.out.println();
}
}
```

Note that this program contains a series of useful methods, all of which are applicable to the basic container class, integer array. The code also shows the power of the `for` statement as an iterator mechanism for traversing the array container, processing each element in turn.

DISSECTION OF THE ArrayTest PROGRAM

■
```
int[] data;
int n;

System.out.println("Enter size of data[]:");
n = Console.in.readInt();
data = new int[n];
```

The array reference variable `data` is initially `null`. We dynamically create the array based on user input, namely, the input assigned to n.

```
■   readArray(data);
    printArray(data, "My Data");
    System.out.println("minimum is " + minimum(data)
        + "   maximum is " + maximum(data));
```

Once again, we utilize the power of structured programming. We solve the original problem by using a series of method calls. Each method is easily coded as a short block.

```
■   static int maximum(int[] a) {
      int  max = a[0]; //initial max value

      for (int i = 1; i < a.length; i++)
        if (a[i] > max)
          max = a[i];
      return max;
    }
```

The maximum value is found by a linear search of the array. One element at a time is tested to determine whether it improves on the maximum value. The term *linear* refers to the fact that computing time is proportional to the size or length of the array. The other methods have similar code, namely, a single `for` statement that processes the entire array.

5.5   A SIMPLE SORTING METHOD

Methods that order information are crucial to searching large databases. Think of a dictionary; it is relatively easy and convenient to use because the information has been sorted and is presented in alphabetic, or lexicographic, order. Sorting is a very useful problem-solving technique. The question of how to sort information efficiently is an important area of computer science theory and practice.

Efficient sorting algorithms typically require approximately $n \log(n)$ comparisons to sort an array with n elements. The selection sort, presented below, is inefficient because it requires n^2 comparisons; nonetheless, for small arrays its performance is usually okay. After presenting the code for `SelectionSort`, we illustrate in detail how the program works on a particular array of integers.

```
// SelectionSort.java - sort an array of integers
import tio.*;

class SelectionSort {
  public static void main(String[] args) {
    int[] a = {7, 3, 66, 3, -5, 22, -77, 2};

    sort(a);
    for (int i = 0; i < a.length; i++){
      System.out.println(a[i]);
    }
  }
```

```
// sort using the selection sort algorithm
static void sort(int[] data) {
  int    next, indexOfNext;

  for (next = 0; next < data.length - 1; next++) {
    indexOfNext = min(data,next,data.length - 1);
    swap(data, indexOfNext, next);
  }
}

// find the index of the smallest element in
// a specified range of indices in an array
static int min(int[] data, int start, int end) {
  int indexOfMin = start; // initial guess

  for (int i = start+1; i <= end; i++)
    if (data[i] < data[indexOfMin])
      indexOfMin = i; // found a smaller value
  return indexOfMin;
}

// swap to entries in an array
static void swap(int[] data, int first, int second){
  int temp;

  temp = data[first];
  data[first] = data[second];
  data[second] = temp;
  }
}
```

DISSECTION OF THE SelectionSort PROGRAM

▪
```
public static void main(String[] args) {
  int[] a = {7, 3, 66, 3, -5, 22, -77, 2};

  sort(a);
  for (int i = 0; i < a.length; i++) {
    System.out.println(a[i]);
  }
}
```

This program creates a sample array, passes the array to the method sort(), and then prints the array. Before the call to sort(), the values in the array are clearly not in increasing numerical order. After the call to sort() the values in the array will be in increasing numerical order.

▪
```
static void sort(int[] data) {
  int    next, indexOfNext;

  for (next = 0; next < data.length - 1; next++) {
    indexOfNext = min(data,next,data.length - 1);
    swap(data, indexOfNext, next);
  }
}
```

This method does the actual sort. It is called a *selection sort* because the algorithm first finds the smallest value in the array, selects it, and puts it in its proper position. The algorithm then selects the smallest value of those remaining and so on until all values have been selected. Each iteration of the `for` loop selects the smallest value of the *remaining* values—those with indices between `next` and `data.length - 1`. The first iteration selects the smallest value from the entire array because `next` will be 0. We have written a method, `min()`, to do the work of finding the index of the smallest element over a range of indices. The method `swap()` moves the selected element, the one with index `indexOfNext`, into its proper position, `next`, by swapping it with whichever element is currently `next`. The operation of `sort()` is illustrated for the data in this program, following this dissection of `SelectionSort`.

■
```
static int min(int[] data, int start, int end) {
  int indexOfMin = start; // initial guess

  for (int i = start + 1; i <= end; i++)
    if (data[i] < data[indexOfMin])
      indexOfMin = i; // found a smaller value
  return indexOfMin;
}
```

This method finds the index of the smallest value in array `data`, considering only the values with indices between `start` and `end`, inclusive. This method is similar to the `min()` method discussed earlier; however, the one here doesn't look at the entire array. For the program `SelectionSort`, we didn't need to be able to specify the upper limit for the indices because the method `sort()` always uses the index of the last element as the upper limit. Writing the method as shown here makes reusing the method easier in other programs where a varying upper limit on the index might be needed.

■
```
static void swap(int[] data, int first, int second){
  int temp;

  temp = data[first];
  data[first] = data[second];
  data[second] = temp;
}
```

To keep the code for `sort()` as short and clear as possible, we provide this method to swap the values stored at two different locations in an array.

The following table shows the elements of the array `a[]` before the first pass of the loop in `sort()` and after each pass of the loop. Recall that `a[0]` is the first element of the array.

Elements of Array `a[]` After Each Pass

Pass	a[0]	a[1]	a[2]	a[3]	a[4]	a[5]	a[6]	a[7]
Unordered data	7	3	66	3	−5	22	−77	2
First	−77	3	66	3	−5	22	7	2
Second	−77	−5	66	3	3	22	7	2
Third	−77	−5	2	3	3	22	7	66
Fourth	−77	−5	2	3	3	22	7	66
Fifth	−77	−5	2	3	3	22	7	66
Sixth	−77	−5	2	3	3	7	22	66
Seventh	−77	−5	2	3	3	7	22	66

The first pass finds that the index of the smallest element is 6. The value at index 6 is swapped with the value at index 0 as shown in the row labeled First. In the second pass, only values with indices 1 through 7 are examined. The next smallest element is at index 4. The value at index 4 is then swapped with the value at index 1. The variable next in method `swap()` keeps track of where the newly selected element is supposed to be placed. This process continues until the entire array has been sorted. Note that, although the elements are actually in order at the end of the sixth pass, the program continues. In fact, during the last pass the element at index 6 is selected as the smallest and swapped with the element at 6, which of course doesn't actually do anything.

5.6   SEARCHING AN ORDERED ARRAY

Let's assume that an array has been ordered with element $a[0] \leq a[1] \leq \ldots \leq a[length - 1]$. Now finding the minimum or maximum element can be done in a fixed number of operations, regardless of the size of the array. The minimum is the value `a[0]`, and the maximum is the value `a[length - 1]`. Finding the minimum and the maximum require linear time for an unordered array. That is, the number of operations is directly proportional to the length of the array.

What if we want to find the position of a given value in a sorted array? This problem is common in searching a large database. For example, most people have an identification code, usually their social security number. Their records, such as a credit or employment history, can be searched by using this identification code. In general, such an identification code is called a *key* when it is used for searching in a database.

Let's write a routine to look for a particular value in an ordered array and, if the value is found, return its position in the array. If the value isn't found, the routine will return –1.

```
static int linearSearch(int[] keys, int v) {
  for (int i = 0; i < keys.length; i++)
    if ( keys[i] == v)
      return i;
  return -1;
}
```

Note how the loop terminates if the element's position is found. If the element isn't found, the entire array will be searched. We call this procedure linearSearch() because the time required to find the desired element is proportional to the length of the array. We haven't really taken advantage of the fact that the array is ordered. For an ordered array, we can improve on this performance by recognizing that, once we have a value larger than v, we can stop looking.

```
static int betterLinearSearch(int[] keys, int v) {
  for (int i = 0; i < keys.length; i++)
    if ( keys[i] == v)
      return i;              //just right
    else if (keys[i] > v)
      return -1;             //too large
  return -1;                 // not found
}
```

For failed searches, this version should terminate on average in roughly half the time of the method linearSearch(). However, we still haven't taken full advantage of the ordering information.

Consider a number guessing game whereby you try to guess a number within a certain interval, using as few guesses as possible. If asked to guess a number between 1 and 100, inclusive, your optimal strategy is to guess 50. If the other person says that your guess is too big, you should next guess 25; if your guess was too small, your next guess should be 75. After each wrong guess reduce the range of possible guesses by half. Using this strategy, you will get the answer in at most seven guesses. The following program uses such an algorithm in the method binarySearch().

```
// BinarySearch.java - use bisection search to find
//    a selected value in an ordered array
class BinarySearch {
  public static void main(String[] args) {
    int[] data = {100, 110, 120, 130, 140, 150};

    int index = binarySearch(data, 120);

    System.out.println(index);
  }
```

```
// find the index of element v in array keys
// return -1 if it is not found
static int binarySearch(int[] keys, int v) {
  int position;
  int begin = 0, end = keys.length - 1;

  while (begin <= end) {
    position = (begin + end) / 2;
    if (keys[position] == v)
      return position;            // just right
    else if (keys[position] < v)
      begin = position + 1;       // too small
    else
      end = position - 1;         // too big
  }
  return -1;
}
}
```

Each time through the `while` loop, the search interval is halved—hence the name `binarySearch()`. Thus the search of an ordered array of keys will make at most $\log(n)$ comparisons for an array with n elements. A search of roughly one thousand elements is accomplished in no more than 10 iterations (recall that 1024 is 2^{10}), and a search of a million elements takes no more than 20 iterations (1,000,000 is approximately 2^{20}).

5.7 BIG-OH: CHOOSING THE BEST ALGORITHM

Our initial method, `find()`, required as many as $n - 1$ comparisons, and our final version, `binarySearch()`, required at most $\log(n)$ comparisons. We say that there are *on the order of n* comparisons in `find()` and *on the order of log(n)* comparisons in `binarySearch()`. Because this concept is so important in computer science, there is a special notation for it. We say that using `find()` to find an element requires $O(n)$ time. Read this expression as "on the order of n" or "order n" or "big-oh of n" time. The notation is called *big-oh notation*.

More precisely, $O(n)$ means that as n increases the quantity being measured is at most $c \times n$ for some constant c. In general, $O(f(n))$ means that the quantity being measured is at most $c \times f(n)$ for some constant c. In our example, the quantity is the number of comparisons.

When we convert an expression that involves several terms into big-oh notation, only the fastest growing term remains. For example, $3n^2 + 20n + 15$ is $O(n^2)$ because $c \times n^2$ is larger than $3n^2 + 20n + 15$ for all values of n greater than 3, if $c = 10$. Similarly, $3n + 20 \log(n)$ is $O(n)$ because n grows faster than $\log(n)$. If an algorithm requires a fixed number of operations, regardless of the size of the problem, it is $O(1)$; it is also known as requiring constant time.

In most cases, an algorithm that requires $O(\log(n))$ time is better than an algorithm that requires $O(n)$ time. However, there may be some small values of n for which the $O(n)$ algorithm is better. Suppose that the actual number of operations for the $O(log(n))$ algorithm was $512\ log(n)$ and the actual number of operations for the $O(n)$ algorithm was $5n$. Then the $O(n)$ algorithm will be faster for all values of n less than 1024.

An algorithm that completes in $O(n)$ time is said to be a linear time algorithm because the running time is bounded by a linear function. Similarly, an $O(log(n))$ algorithm is said to be logarithmic and an $O(2^n)$ algorithm is exponential.

Sometimes, big-oh notation isn't enough to help you choose the best algorithm. It can be proved that $n - 1$ comparisons are needed to find either the minimum or the maximum element in an array. Does that mean that `ArrayTest` finds the minimum and the maximum using the fewest number of comparisons? The answer is *no*. The following method, `minMaxArray()`, shows how to determine the maximum and the minimum of an array, using approximately 25 percent fewer comparisons involving array elements.

```
static int[] minMaxArray(int[] data) {
  int[] minMax = new int[2];     //store min and max
  // the length must be even
  int midPoint = data.length / 2;

  // loop puts the min somewhere in the first half
  // and the max somewhere in the second half
  for (int i = 0; i < midPoint; i++)
    if (data[i] > data[midPoint + i ])
      swap(i, midPoint + i, data);
  // loop finds the min which must be in first half
  minMax[0] = data[0];
  for (int i = 1; i < midPoint; i++)
    if (data[i] < minMax[0])
      minMax[0] = data[i];
  // loop finds the max which must be in second half
  minMax[1] = data[midPoint];
  for (int i = midPoint + 1; i < data.length; i++)
    if (data[i] > minMax[1])
      minMax[1] = data[i];
  return minMax;
}
static void swap(int i, int j, int[] data) {
  int temp = data[i];

  data[i] = data[j];
  data[j] = temp;
}
```

With `minMaxArray()`, we can find the minimum and the maximum value in an array by using $3(n/2 - 1)$ comparisons involving array elements. Each loop executes $n/2 - 1$ comparisons. In the program `ArrayTest`, the two methods used to find the minimum and the maximum use $2(n - 1)$ comparisons involving array elements.

Although the `minMaxArray()` solution requires fewer comparisons involving array operations, it is clearly a more complex solution, and for small values of n it will even take longer to execute. When you use big-oh notation, the algorithms are considered to have the same complexity: Both are $O(n)$.

5.8 TYPE AND ARRAY

So far, most of our examples have involved the `int` type. This approach keeps things simple and in most cases code can also be rewritten to other types. In this section we use one-dimensional arrays of different data types. We also demonstrate techniques and idioms that are common to these different data types.

5.8.1 BOOLEANS: THE SIEVE OF ERATOSTHENES

Let's say that we want to find the prime numbers between 2 and 100. To do so, we write code based on the *sieve of Eratosthenes*. We allocate a boolean array `isPrime` of 100 elements. We set each element to true. Starting with element `isPrime[2]` we use its index value 2 and proceed through the remaining array elements `isPrime[4], isPrime[6],..., isPrime[98]`, setting each value to false. Then we go to `isPrime[3]` and set each element at a spacing of 3 to false. We do this until we reach 10, because 10 is the square root of 100 and is sufficient for checking primality in the range 2 through 100. When we have finished, only those entries that remain true are primes.

```
//Primes.java-Sieve of Eratosthenes for Primes up to 100.
class Primes {
  public static void main(String[] args) {
    boolean[] sieve = new boolean[100];
    int i;

    System.out.println(" Table of primes to 100.");
    for (i = 0; i < 100; i++)
      sieve[i] = true;
    for (int j = 2; j < Math.sqrt(100); j++)
      if (sieve[j])
        crossOut(sieve, j, j + j);
    for (i = 0; i < 100; i++) //print primes
      if (sieve[i])
        System.out.print(" " + i);
  }
  public static void crossOut(boolean[] s,
                int interval, int start)
  {
   for (int i = start; i < s.length; i += interval)
     s[i] = false;
  }
}
```

We can readily generalize this program to an arbitrarily large *n*. The key would be to replace the hardcoded value 100 with a variable *n*. We leave this for you to do as Exercise 2, on page 184.

5.8.2   char: USING A LINE BUFFER

Much of character processing is done by sequentially examining a sequence of characters stored in an array called a *buffer*. For example, in a word processing program we might want the capability to count words. To do so we would store a line of text in a buffer and examine the characters in the buffer. A word might be defined as a sequence of alphabetic characters that are adjacent. We write just this program and dissect the parts of it that are idiomatic of character processing.

```java
//CountWord.java
import tio.*;
public class CountWord {
  public static void main(String[] args) {
    String input;
    char[] buffer;
    System.out.println("type in line");
    input = Console.in.readLine();
    System.out.println(input);
    buffer = input.toCharArray();
    System.out.println("word count is " + wordCount(buffer));
  }

  //words are separated by nonalphabetic characters
  public static int wordCount(char[] buf) {
    int position = 0, wc = 0;
    while (position < buf.length) {
      while (position < buf.length &&
             !isAlpha(buf[position]))
        position++;
      if (position < buf.length)
        wc++;
      while (position < buf.length &&
              isAlpha(buf[position]))
        position++;
    }
    return wc;
  }

  public static boolean isAlpha(char c) {
    return (c >= 'a' && c <= 'z') ||
           (c >= 'A' && c <= 'Z') ;
  }
}
```

DISSECTION OF THE CountWord PROGRAM

■   ```java
    String input;
    char[] buffer;

    System.out.println("type in line");
    input = Console.in.readLine();
    ```
    ```

The `String` variable `input` is used to capture an input line typed at the keyboard. We use the `tio` method `readLine()`, which captures a line after Enter is hit.

▪
```
buffer = input.toCharArray();
System.out.println("word count is " + wordCount(buffer));
```

The `String` method `toCharArray()` converts the `String` to an array of characters. `String`, `StringBuffer`, and `char[]` are all important types that can be used to manipulate sequences of characters. Using a `char[]` is the most fundamental of these schemes and is often the most efficient. We call the method `wordCount()` to count the words in the buffer.

▪
```
public static int wordCount(char[] buf) {
   int position = 0, wc = 0;

   while (position < buf.length) {
      while (position < buf.length &&
            !isAlpha(buf[position]))
         position++;
```

We process this character array `buf[]` from the zeroth character to the `buf.length - 1` character. Our definition of a word is a sequence of alphabetic characters. We advance through the buffer until we find a first alphabetic character. Note that the boolean method `isAlpha()` returns true when the character value passed in as its actual parameter is an English letter. All the characters in the buffer could be nonalphabetic. In that case we need to verify that the word count is zero.

▪
```
if (position < buf.length)
   wc++;
while (position < buf.length && isAlpha(buf[position]))
   position++;
```

If we have reached an alphabetic character before we reach the last position in the buffer, we have a new word and can increment `wc`. We then sequence through adjacent alphabetic characters. We return to the outer loop and check to be sure that we haven't reached the end of the buffer.

▪
```
public static boolean isAlpha(char c) {
   return (c >= 'a' && c <= 'z') ||
          (c >= 'A' && c <= 'Z') ;
}
```

The boolean method `isAlpha()` is by convention named *isSomeProperty*. It relies on the property of the Unicode table wherein the alphabetic characters are in the right order sequentially.

This example should help you understand the `String` and `StringBuffer` classes provided in the Java libraries.

5.8.3   `double`: ACCUMULATE, A GENERALIZATION OF `sum`

One of our first array examples was `sum()`, which worked on an `int` type.

```
//Sum the int elements in an array.
static int sum(int[] a) {
  int sum = 0;

  for (int i = 0; i < a.length; i++)
    sum = sum + a[i];
  return sum;
}
```

This code is also useful for other types. It can be overloaded for the type `double`, as follows.

```
//Sum the double elements in an array.
static double sum(double[] a) {
  double sum = 0.0;

  for (int i = 0; i < a.length; i++)
    sum = sum + a[i];
  return sum;
}
```

To make these changes, we must change the type declaration three places in the code.

We can further generalize this code and make it useful for a wider range of computations. We can sum an array over a range from the first element up to, but not including, the last element. We can also accumulate from a starting value that may be different from the value 0. Such a general algorithm is as follows.

```
//Accumulate the double elements in an array.
static double sum(double[] a, int first, int last,
      double initialValue)
{
  for (int i = first; i < last; i++)
    initialValue += a[i];
  return initialValue;
}
```

This code shows many features of generalizing a basic method by extending its abilities with additional variables.

5.9   TWO-DIMENSIONAL ARRAYS

The arrays in the preceding sections are all one-dimensional arrays; that is, the elements are conceptually in a single row or column. Java allows arrays of any type, including arrays of arrays. Recall that, for any type `T`, `T[]` is the notation for the type array of Ts. The type T can itself be an array. With two bracket pairs, we obtain a two-dimensional array consisting of rows and columns. This idea can be iterated to obtain arrays of higher dimension. With each bracket pair, we add another array dimension, as for example in

```
String[] up;            //one-dimension
double[][] upUp;        //two-dimensions
char[][][] andAway;     //three-dimensions
```

We focus on two dimensions because these arrays constitute the most useful and used of the multidimensional array types. We can conveniently think of a two-dimensional array as a rectangular collection of elements with rows and columns. For example, if we declare

```
int[][] data = new int[3][5];
```

then we can think of the array elements being arranged as follows.

	Col 1	Col 2	Col 3	Col 4	Col 5
Row 1	a[0][0]	a[0][1]	a[0][2]	a[0][3]	a[0][4]
Row 2	a[1][0]	a[1][1]	a[1][2]	a[1][3]	a[1][4]
Row 3	a[2][0]	a[2][1]	a[2][2]	a[2][3]	a[2][4]

To illustrate these ideas, let's write a program that fills a two-dimensional array with some internally generated values.

```
// TwoD.java - simple example of two-dimensional array
class TwoD {
  public static void main(String[] args) {
    int[][] data = new int[3][5];

    for (int i = 0; i < data.length; i++) {
      System.out.print("Row " + i + ":     ");
      for (int j = 0; j < data[i].length; j++) {
        data[i][j] = i * j;
        System.out.print(data[i][j] + ", ");
      }
      System.out.println();
    }
  }
}
```

DISSECTION OF THE TwoD PROGRAM

- `int[][] data = new int[3][5];`

This statement does three things. It declares the variable data to be a reference to a two-dimensional array of integers. It creates an array with three rows and five columns. Finally, it assigns `data` to refer to the newly created array. We don't need to create the array in the same statement that declares the variable. However, we must create an array and assign `data` to refer to that array before we can use `data`. A common mistake is to forget to create the array.

■
```java
for (int i = 0; i < data.length; i++) {
    System.out.print("Row " + i + ":    ");
    ...
    System.out.println();
}
```

This is the outer loop. For multidimensional arrays, we can write an expression to find the size of each dimension. The expression `data.length` evaluates to the length of the first dimension. Each iteration of this loop will print one row of the array.

■
```java
for (int j = 0; j < data[i].length; j++) {
    data[i][j] = i * j;
    System.out.print(data[i][j] + ", ");
}
```

This loop is the inner loop. A pair of nested loops for accessing a two-dimensional array is an important idiom. The expression `data[i][j]` is of type `int`, one of the elements of the array. The expression `data[i]` is of type `int[]`, one of the rows of the array. From it we get the expression `data[i].length` for the row size used inside the inner loop to process each `i`th-row element.

5.9.1 TWO-DIMENSIONAL INITIALIZER LISTS

A two-dimensional array can be explicitly initialized with a set of values. The rows are also contained in a set of braces. Each of the following initializations

```java
int[][]  a = {{1, 2}, {3, 4}, {5, 6}};
int[][]  b = {{1, 2, 3}, {4, 5, 6}};
int[][]  c = {{1, 2, 3, 4, 5, 6}};
int[][]  ragged = {{1,2}, {3, 4, 5}, {6}}
```

creates a two-dimensional array with a total of six elements. But their layout—in other words—their row organization—is completely different. Array `a` has three rows of two elements each. Array `b` has two rows of three elements each. Array `c` has one row of six elements and is a degenerate two-dimensional array. Array `ragged` has three rows, each with a different number of elements.

As this example shows, in Java we can create a two-dimensional array that isn't rectangular. That is, the number of elements in each row can be different. This approach works because a two-dimensional array of integers is really a one-dimensional array of references to one-dimensional arrays of integers. The following diagram shows the layout of array `ragged`.

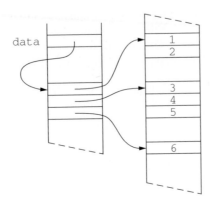

5.10 AN ELEMENTARY SIMULATION: THE "GAME OF LIFE"

The Game of Life is an archetypal checkerboard simulation. It was invented by the English mathematician John H. Conway for exploring certain formal situations involving reproduction and growth (see *Scientific American,* October 1970, p. 120). The game is a successor to the work of John von Neumann on cellular automata.

A checkerboard simulation is a model wherein the world is broken into a rectangular array of cells. Each cell may interact only with its neighboring cells, the interactions occurring once per simulated clock pulse. The rules for a local change are well defined and simple, but predicting global change is impractical without computer simulation. The Game of Life has the following rules.

GAME OF LIFE RULES

1. A cell is either empty, indicated by a blank, or alive, indicated by an X.
2. Each cell is the center of a 3 × 3 square grid of cells, which contains its eight neighbors.

3. A cell that is empty at time t becomes alive at time $t + 1$ if and only if exactly three neighboring cells were alive at time t.
4. A cell that is alive at time t remains alive at time $t + 1$ if and only if either two or three neighboring cells were alive at time t. Otherwise, it dies for lack of company (< 2) or overcrowding (> 3).

5. The simulation is conducted, in principle, on an infinite two-dimensional grid.

A simulation starts with an initial configuration of Xs on the grid. The following example of a simple repeating life form is called a *blinker*, as it repeats every two generations, or time steps.

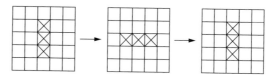

5.10.1   THE GAME OF LIFE: REQUIREMENTS ANALYSIS AND DEFINITION

Following the software development process described in Section 4.9, on page 114, we must first add a few refinements to the specification of the program just described.

- Instead of trying to simulate an infinite two-dimensional grid, simulating a relatively small grid will suffice.
- Because the grid isn't infinite, we must decide how to deal with the borders. To keep the program simple, we will treat the borders as lifeless zones.
- The initial placement of life forms in the grid will be read from the console as a sequence of Xs and dots. The Xs will stand for life forms and the dots will represent empty cells. If the grid was only 5 × 5 as shown in the preceding figure, the initial configuration would be specified at the console by typing

```
. . . . .
. . X . .
. . X . .
. . X . .
. . . . .
```

- The user will specify the size of the grid, which will always be a square grid, and the number of generations to simulate.
- The program should echo the initial generation and then print each new generation simulated.

5.10.2   THE GAME OF LIFE: DESIGN

We are now ready to begin designing the program. The first—and obvious—decision is that we will use a two-dimensional array to represent the grid. We start with pseudocode for the top level.

TOP-LEVEL PSEUDOCODE FOR THE GAME OF LIFE

```
read in the size of the grid
read in the initial generation
read in the number of generations to simulate
print the current generation
for the specified number of generations
  advance one generation
  print the generation
end for loop
```

The most difficult step is "advance one generation" so we need to write some pseudocode for advancing one generation.

PSEUDOCODE FOR ADVANCING ONE GENERATION

```
for each cell
  compute the number of neighbors
  apply the game rules to decide if the cell
    should be alive or dead in the next generation
end for loop
```

Applying the game rules to one cell isn't too hard once we know the number of neighbors. The code will be some `if-else` statement. Either the new cell will be dead or it will be alive. Computing the number of neighbors still looks difficult. However, there are several approaches that we can use to solve this problem. A cell and its neighbors can be viewed as a 3 × 3 subarray. With this in mind, we write the following pseudocode for counting the neighbors.

PSEUDOCODE FOR COMPUTING THE NUMBER OF NEIGHBORS

```
visit each cell in the 3x3 subarray around the cell
keep a count of how many of those are alive
if the center cell is alive
  then return one less than the count found
  else return the count found
```

At this point in the design we need to recognize that we can't simply update the cells in the array as we visit each of them while advancing one generation. A generation is a snapshot of the grid at an instant in time. Changing some of the cells will affect the number of neighbors that another cell observes. This type of unsynchronized updating of the cells might be interesting, but it isn't what Conway intended in his Game of Life. We need to not disturb the current generation while creating the next generation. As is often the case, there are several solutions. The one that we have chosen is to use two arrays: one for the current generation and another for the next generation.

Before moving to the implementation stage, we have to refine two of the sections of our pseudocode.

REFINED TOP-LEVEL PSEUDOCODE FOR THE GAME OF LIFE

```
read in the size of the grid
create two arrays, currentGen and nextGen
read the initial generation into currentGen
read in the number of generations to simulate
print currentGen
for number of generations
  update nextGen using currentGen
  swap currentGen and nextGen
  print currentGen
end for loop
```

Each iteration of the loop fills the cells of nextGen from the values found in currentGen. Then the arrays referred to by nextGen and currentGen are swapped. Note that after the last iteration currentGen will have the data of the most recently computed generation.

REFINED PSEUDOCODE FOR ADVANCING ONE GENERATION

```
input: currentGen and nextGen
output: updated nextGen

for each cell in currentGen
  compute the number of neighbors
  apply the game rules to decide if the cell
    should be alive or dead in the next generation
  store the result, alive or dead, in the
    corresponding cell in nextGen
end for loop
```

5.10.3   THE GAME OF LIFE: IMPLEMENTATION

The parts of the program for which we haven't presented pseudocode are sufficiently simple that we can proceed directly to the complete program at this point. Although some of those parts are nontrivial, the pseudocode for them is almost identical to the final code.

```java
//GameOfLife.java - Conway's Game of Life
import tio.*;

class GameOfLife {
  public static void main(String[] args) {
    // read in the size of the grid and create arrays
    int size = 10; // fix at 10 for testing
    boolean[][]  currentGeneration, nextGeneration;

    currentGeneration = new boolean[size][size];
    nextGeneration = new boolean[size][size];
    readInitialGeneration(currentGeneration);
```

```
      // read in the number of generations to simulate
      int cycles = 4; // fix at 4 for testing
      printState(currentGeneration);
      for (int i = 0; i < cycles; i++) {
        System.out.println("Cycle = " + i + "\n\n");
        advanceOneGen(currentGeneration,
                      nextGeneration);
        printState(nextGeneration);
        // swap current and next generations
        boolean[][] temp = nextGeneration;
        nextGeneration = currentGeneration;
        currentGeneration = temp;
      }
  }

  // read the initial generation from the input
  // a dot means empty and a * means alive
  // any other characters are ignored
  // the border cells are all set to empty
  // the method assumes the array is square
  static void readInitialGeneration(boolean[][] w) {
    for (int i = 0; i < w.length; i++)
      for (int j = 0; j < w[i].length; j++) {
        char c = (char)Console.in.readChar();
        //skip illegal characters
        while (c != '.' && c != '*')
          c = (char)Console.in.readChar();
        if (c == '.')
          w[i][j] = EMPTY;
        else
          w[i][j] = ALIVE;
      }
    //set border cells to be empty
    int border = w.length - 1;

    for (int i = 0; i < w.length; i++){
      w[i][0] = w[0][i] = EMPTY;
      w[i][border] = w[border][i] = EMPTY;
    }
  }

  // print a generation to the console
  static void printState(boolean[][] w) {
    for (int i = 0; i < w.length; i++) {
      System.out.println();
      for (int j = 0; j < w[i].length; j++)
        if (w[i][j] == ALIVE)
          System.out.print('X');
        else
          System.out.print('.');
    }
    System.out.println();
  }
```

```
     // compute the number of alive neighbors of a cell
     static int neighbors(int row, int column, boolean[][] w)
     {
        int neighborCount = 0;

        for (int i = -1; i <= 1; i++)
          for (int j = -1; j <= 1; j++)
            if (w[row + i][column + j] == ALIVE)
              neighborCount = neighborCount + 1;
        if (w[row][column] == ALIVE)
          neighborCount--;
        return neighborCount;
     }

     static void advanceOneGen(boolean[][] wOld,
                               boolean[][] wNew)
     {
        int neighborCount;

        for (int i = 1; i < wOld.length - 1; i++)
          for (int j = 1; j < wOld[i].length - 1; j++) {
            neighborCount = neighbors(i, j, wOld);
            if (neighborCount == 3)
              wNew[i][j] = ALIVE;
            else if (wOld[i][j] == ALIVE &&
                    neighborCount == 2)
              wNew[i][j] = ALIVE;
            else
              wNew[i][j] = EMPTY;
          }
     }

     static final boolean ALIVE = true;
     static final boolean EMPTY = false;
}
```

DISSECTION OF THE GameOfLife PROGRAM

■   `import tio.*;`

We use `Console.in.readChar()` to read in the initial generation. Thus we need to import `tio`.

■   ```
     public static void main(String[] args) {
        // read in the size of the grid and create arrays
        int size = 10; // fix at 10 for testing
        boolean[][] currentGeneration, nextGeneration;

        currentGeneration = new boolean[size][size];
        nextGeneration = new boolean[size][size];
     ```

Following the pseudocode developed earlier, we need to read in the size of the grid and create the arrays. For testing purposes we have fixed the size at 10. In the final version of the program we would replace the assignment of 10 to `size` with a prompt to the user for the desired size and an input statement to read the size from
     ```

the console. We create two square arrays to represent the cells in the world. Each generation, the cells in `currentGeneration` are used to update the cells in `nextGeneration`. Because a cell can only be alive or empty, we use the primitive type `boolean` for the cells. The value `true` means that the cell is alive. Java will initialize all array elements to `false`, which means *empty* in our simulation.

■ `readInitialGeneration(currentGeneration);`

The method `readInitialGeneration()` is used to read an initial world from the console. When the method returns, the cells in `currentGeneration` will have been modified to correspond to user input.

■
```
// read in the number of generations to simulate
int cycles = 4;        // fix at 4 for testing

printState(currentGeneration);
```

This comment from the pseudocode reminds us that we haven't finished the implementation. As with the size of the grid, we've fixed the number of generations to simulate. The method `printState()` will print to the console the initial generation, which is stored in `currentGeneration`.

■
```
for (int i = 0; i < cycles; i++) {
  System.out.println("Cycle = " + i + "\n\n");
  advanceOneGen(currentGeneration, nextGeneration);
  printState(nextGeneration);
  // swap current and next generations
  boolean[][] temp = nextGeneration;
  nextGeneration = currentGeneration;
  currentGeneration = temp;
}
```

This loop is the main simulation loop. Each iteration, the next generation is computed and the state is printed. At the end of each iteration, the array variables referring to the two arrays are reversed so that, at the start of the next iteration, `currentGeneration` points to the most recently updated array and `nextGeneration` refers to the array with the older generation, which subsequently is modified to contain the newest generation. Recall that this swapping of the array variables isn't copying the entire array; it is simply changing the variables to refer to different arrays.

■
```
static void readInitialGeneration(boolean[][] w) {
  for (int i = 0; i < w.length; i++)
    for (int j = 0; j < w[i].length; j++) {
      char c = (char)Console.in.readChar();
      //skip illegal characters
      while (c != '.' && c != '*')
        c = (char)Console.in.readChar();
      if (c == '.')
        w[i][j] = EMPTY;
      else
        w[i][j] = ALIVE;
    }
}
```

The first part of this method reads the initial generation in from the console. The call `Console.in.readChar()` reads one character from the input. The return type of `readChar()` is `int`, which allows for a return value of `-1` to signal that there are no more characters to read. Even if a character were read, the cast to `char` wouldn't lose any information. In this example we haven't checked for the return value of `-1`. We leave that for you to do as an exercise. The `while` loop is used to skip over any white space or other unexpected characters. To make the code more self-documenting, we have defined constants to encode the fact that true will be treated as `ALIVE` and that false will be treated as `EMPTY`. The constants are defined at the end.

■
```
    int border = w.length - 1;

    for (int i = 0; i < w.length; i++){
      w[i][0] = w[0][i] = EMPTY;
      w[i][border] = w[border][i] = EMPTY;
    }
  }
```

As discussed in the design section, the border cells require some form of special treatment because they have fewer than eight neighbors. Recall that we decided to treat the border cells as a lifeless zone. To enforce that we set all border cells to `EMPTY`, ignoring border values that were supplied by the user. This code makes the unchecked assumption that the array is actually square.

■
```
  static void printState(boolean[][] w) {
    for (int i = 0; i < w.length; i++) {
      System.out.println();
      for (int j = 0; j < w[i].length; j++)
        if (w[i][j] == ALIVE)
          System.out.print('X');
        else
          System.out.print('.');
    }
    System.out.println();
  }
```

This routine prints the state to the console, with the output format the same as that used for the input. The code doesn't take advantage of the fact that the elements in the array are actually of type `boolean`. At some later time the decision to use a boolean array might be changed. In that case, only the type of the parameter in the method header would need to be changed. In addition, by using the constant `ALIVE`, the code is self-documenting. It should be clear that `X` is printed if the cell is `ALIVE` and that a dot is printed otherwise.

■
```
  static int neighbors(int row, int column, boolean[][] w) {
    int neighborCount = 0;

    for (int i = -1; i <= 1; i++)
      for (int j = -1; j <= 1; j++)
```

```
        if (w[row + i][column +j] == ALIVE)
          neighborCount = neighborCount + 1;
    if (w[row][column] == ALIVE)
      neighborCount--;
    return neighborCount;
  }
```

This routine counts the number of neighboring cells that are alive. It does so by counting the number of alive cells in the 3×3 subarray that has the specified cell at its center. Then the center cell is removed from the count if it is alive because a cell isn't a neighbor to itself. If this routine is called with a cell on the border of the array, an `IndexOutOfBoundsException` error message is printed. In our program, that never happens because `neighbors()` is never called with the coordinates of a border cell.

```
■   static void advanceOneGen(boolean[][] wOld,
                               boolean[][] wNew)
    {
      int neighborCount;

      for (int i = 1; i < wOld.length - 1; i++)
        for (int j = 1; j < wOld[i].length - 1; j++) {
          neighborCount = neighbors(i, j, wOld);
          if (neighborCount == 3)
            wNew[i][j] = ALIVE;
          else if (wOld[i][j] == ALIVE &&
                  neighborCount == 2)
            wNew[i][j] = ALIVE;
          else
            wNew[i][j] = EMPTY;
        }
    }
```

This method implements the rules of the simulation. The array `wOld` is examined to determine the current number of neighbors for each cell, and then the array `wNew` is set according to the rules. These loops avoid the borders of the array, implementing our design decision that the borders will be lifeless zones.

```
■   static final boolean ALIVE = true;
    static final boolean EMPTY = false;
```

To make the code more self-documenting, the program uses these two constants. Without the constants, we would need to add some comment. For example, without a comment in

```
    wNew[i][j] = true;
```

the user must remember that `true` is used to mark alive cells. A comment would help, but self-documenting code is always preferable. Comments can become out of date when a programmer modifies the code but doesn't update the comments accordingly.

The `GameOfLife` program requires enough input that typing the input in each time would be rather tedious. Instead, you can prepare an input file and then use file redirection to cause the program to read from the file instead of from the keyboard. Suppose that the file *glider* contains

```
. . . . . . . . . .
. . . . * . . . . .
. . . . . * . . . .
. * . . . * . . . .
. . * * * * . . . .
. . . . . . . . . .
. . . . . . . . . .
. . . . . . . . . .
. . . . . . . . . .
. . . . . . . . . .
```

Then we can run `GameOfLife` by having it read characters from glider instead of the keyboard. To have it do so we type the following command at either a Unix or DOS command prompt.

```
java GameOfLife < glider
```

Execution of this command would be followed immediately by the program output. A portion of the output would be

```
. . . . . . . . . .
. . . . X . . . . .
. . . . . X . . . .
. X . . . X . . . .
. . X X X X . . . .
. . . . . . . . . .
. . . . . . . . . .
. . . . . . . . . .
. . . . . . . . . .
. . . . . . . . . .
Cycle = 0
(intermediate cycles deleted to save space)
Cycle = 3
. . . . . . . . . .
. . . X . . X . . .
. . . . . . . X . .
. . . X . . . X . .
. . . . X X X X . .
. . . . . . . . . .
. . . . . . . . . .
. . . . . . . . . .
. . . . . . . . . .
. . . . . . . . . .
```

Note that, after four cycles, the initial configuration has reappeared but has moved to the right by one position. This interesting "life form" is one of many that have been discovered. This one is called a *glider* because it sort of glides across the simulated world.

5.11 ARRAYS OF NONPRIMITIVE TYPES

At the beginning of this chapter we said that an array can be created from any type `T` by using the notation `T[]`. The elements in the arrays presented so far have all been primitive values. As discussed earlier, two-dimensional arrays were actually arrays of arrays, but ultimately the elements of the arrays were always primitive values. In this section we take a brief look at some arrays of nonprimitive elements.

5.11.1 ARRAYS OF STRINGS

The nonprimitive type that we have used the most so far is the type `String`. We can create a variable of type "array of strings" with

```
String[] myStringArray;
```

Recall that, as with other arrays, this statement doesn't create an array but a reference to an array. To create an array of 10 string variables we can use

```
myStringArray = new String[10];
```

Initially each of the `String` variables, `myStringArray[i]`, has the value `null`. To get them to refer to some actual strings, we must assign them values, as for example,

```
myStringArray[0] = "zero";
myStringArray[1] = "one";
...
```

A common mistake is to create an array of references to `String` or some other nonprimitive type, and then forget to create the actual object values and assign them to the elements in the array.

Because Java provides special syntax for creating string literals, the same array initializer notation used earlier can be used with strings. The same effect of creating an array of 10 strings containing the strings for 0 through 9 can be achieved with an array initializer. The following example demonstrates this approach.

```
// StringArray.java - uses a string array initializer
class StringArray {
  public static void main(String[] args) {
    String[] myStringArray = { "zero", "one", "two",
        "three", "four", "five", "six", "seven",
        "eight", "nine"};

    for (int i = 0; i < myStringArray.length; i++)
      System.out.println(myStringArray[i]);
  }
}
```

The output of the program is the words `zero, one, two, ... nine`—one per line.

We now see that the familiar

```
public static void main(String[] args)
```

is actually declaring that the method `main()` is expecting an array of strings as a parameter. The only question that remains is, Where does the array come from?

The answer is that this array will be filled with any strings included after the name of the class used to start a Java program. These are called the *command line arguments* used to run the program. Each element in the array contains one, white space delimited, string from the command line. The following program prints out any command line arguments.

```
// CommandLine.java - print command line arguments
class CommandLine {
  public static void main(String[] args) {
    for (int i = 0; i < args.length; i++)
      System.out.println(args[i]);
  }
}
```

The following line shows the program being started from a Unix or DOS command line prompt, followed by the output.

```
os-prommpt>java CommandLine this is a test
this
is
a
test
```

You can insert spaces in a single command line argument by putting the argument in quotes. This approach is shown in the following execution of the same program.

```
os-prompt>java CommandLine this "is another" test
this
is another
test
```

Note that the quotation marks aren't part of the argument and that the second argument includes a space.

5.11.2   ARRAYS OF POINTS

The class `String` is special because of the extra syntactic support for string literals. The following program is another small example of an array of nonprimitive values. We use the standard Java class `Point` to represent a point in the *xy* plane. We use an array of three `Point` objects to represent a triangle.

```
// PointArray.java-example array nonprimitive values
import java.awt.Point;

class PointArray {
  public static void main(String[] args) {
    Point[] triangle;

    triangle = new Point[3];
    triangle[0] = new Point(10,20);
    triangle[1] = new Point(35,90);
    triangle[2] = new Point(20, 85);
    for (int i = 0; i < triangle.length; i++)
      System.out.println(triangle[i]);
    translate(triangle,100,200);
    for (int i = 0; i < triangle.length; i++)
      System.out.println(triangle[i]);
  }

  public static void translate(Point[] points,
      int deltaX, int deltaY)
  {
    for (int i = 0; i < points.length; i++)
      points[i].translate(deltaX, deltaY);
  }
}
```

DISSECTION OF THE PointArray PROGRAM

- `import java.awt.Point;`

Although `Point` is a standard Java class, it is in a separate *package* called `java.awt`. We discuss packages in Section 12.11. To gain access to many of the standard Java classes, you must use an import statement such as the one here to indicate that you want to use the class. A small number of classes, including `String`, are in a special package that is imported by default, which is why you could use `String` without an import statement.

- `Point[] triangle;`
  `triangle = new Point[3];`

The first line declares that triangle is a reference to an array of points but doesn't create an array of points. The second line actually creates an array of three references to points and assigns `triangle` to refer to that array. We have still not created any `Point` values. After execution of these two statements, all three elements in the array will have the value null to indicate that they aren't referring to any `Point` object. As we showed earlier with other array declarations, we can combine these two statements into the single statement, `Point[] triangle = new Point[3];`.

- `triangle[0] = new Point(10, 20);`
  `triangle[1] = new Point(35, 90);`
  `triangle[2] = new Point(20, 85);`

Finally, we create some actual `Point` objects and place them in the array. In Section 2.4, on page 22, we introduced briefly the use of `new` to create nonprimitive values such as values of type `Point`; we discuss its use in detail in Chapter 6.

▪
```
for (int i = 0; i < triangle.length; i++)
   System.out.println(triangle[i]);
translate(triangle, 100, 200);
for (int i = 0; i < triangle.length; i++)
   System.out.println(triangle[i]);
```

If this were a real program, at this point we would write some code to do something with the triangle. In this example, we first print out all the points and then call a method to translate the triangle 100 units in the *x* direction and 200 units in the *y* direction. To see the effect of the translation, we print the points again after the translation.

▪
```
public static void translate(Point[] points,
      int deltaX, int deltaY)
{
   for (int i = 0; i < points.length; i++)
      points[i].translate(deltaX, deltaY);
}
```

The method translates all of the points in the array by calling the method `translate()`, which is an operation already defined for objects of type `Point`.

The following is the output of the program.

```
java.awt.Point[x=10,y=20]
java.awt.Point[x=35,y=90]
java.awt.Point[x=20,y=85]
java.awt.Point[x=110,y=220]
java.awt.Point[x=135,y=290]
java.awt.Point[x=120,y=285]
```

COMMON PROGRAMMING ERROR

When working with arrays, you need to remember to create the actual array. Fortunately, the compiler will detect any failure to create the actual array for a local variable. For example, if you delete the statement `triangle = new Point[3];` from the preceding example, you will get a compiler error message something like

```
PointArray.java:9: Variable triangle may not have been ini-
tialized.
      triangle[0] = new Point(10,20);
      ^
1 error
```

Once created, an array of references—that is, any nonprimitive type—will be filled with `null` by default. As a result, if you forget to put a value in one or more of the array's cells and then try to do anything with the value in the cell, you'll get an error message at run time, called a `NullPointerException`. For example, if you removed the statement `triangle[2] = new Point(20, 85);` from `Point-Array`, an attempt to translate `points[2]` inside the method `translate` in `PointArray` will cause an error. The following is the output of the program without the statement `triangle[2] = Point(20, 85);`.

```
java.awt.Point[x=10,y=20]
java.awt.Point[x=35,y=90]
null
java.lang.NullPointerException
        at PointArray.translate(PointArray.java:22)
        at PointArray.main(PointArray.java:14)
```

Note that the first attempt to print the three points executes successfully. The method `println()` can handle printing a reference that is null. However, when you attempt to execute the statement `points[i].translate(deltaX, deltaY);` with i equal to 2, a `NullPointerException` occurs and the program aborts with a message similar to the one shown. The numbers 22 and 14 in the error message indicate the line numbers of the statements that were being executed when the error occurred. Line 14 is the call to `translate()` in `main()` and line 22 is the statement

```
points[i].translate(deltaX, deltaY);
```

5.12 PROGRAMMING STYLE

Stylistically the most common array idiom in Java is

```
for (int i = 0; i < d.length; i++)
  computation on d[i]
```

This idiom is preferred to an explicit use of an array upper bound, as in

```
for (int i = 0; i < N; i++)
  computation on d[i]
```

The use of such an explicit bound, N, is more error prone and requires more code maintenance than does the preferred idiom. It is a carryover from C programming style, where arrays don't have a length member.

When computing over an array, you should package the computation as a method, as in

```
static T computeArray(T[] a)   {
    . . .
    for (int i = 0; i < a.length; i++)
       compute on a[i];
    . . .
}
```

5.12.1   COUNTING FROM ZERO

Much of the syntax for Java is derived from the programming language C. For a number of reasons, C programmers tend to write loops that begin with the loop index at 0. One reason is that in C arrays are represented in such a way that they are always indexed from 0. This C idiom has survived into Java so that even loops that are not indexing an array often start from 0.

```
static void printRandomNumbers(int k) {
   for (int i = 0; i < k; i++)
     System.out.println(Math.random());
}
```

However, people more naturally count from 1. Rewriting this code to start from 1 gives

```
static void printRandomNumbers(int k) {
   for (int i = 1; i <= k; i++)
     System.out.println(Math.random());
}
```

Either style is reasonable. You need to be able to write and understand code with both counting styles. Many tricky bugs enter code when the end values of loops are *off by one*.

Summary

- An array is a data type used to represent a large number of homogeneous values. It is an elementary form of container.
- Array allocation starts with element 0. The elements of an array are accessed by the use of index expressions. Therefore an array of *size* number of elements is indexed or subscripted from 0 to *size* – 1, inclusive. The array size can be accessed by using the notation `arrayVariable.length`.
- Allocation is often combined with declaration, as in

  ```
  int[] data = new int[100];
  ```

- The expression `a[expr]`, where *expr* is an integral expression, accesses an element of the array. We call *expr* a subscript, or index, of `a`. The value of a subscript should lie in the range 0 to *length* – 1, inclusive. An array subscript value outside this range will cause an `IndexOutOfBoundsException` error message to be printed.

- Only a reference to an array is passed to a method. That is, the array elements are not copied and passed to the method. Hence the individual elements of an array can be modified by a method passed as an array.
- Java allows arrays of any type, including arrays of arrays. With two bracket pairs, we obtain a two-dimensional array. This idea can be iterated to obtain arrays of higher dimension. With each bracket pair, we add another array dimension, as for example in

```
double[][] upUp;       //two-dimensions
char[][][] andAway;    //three-dimensions
```

- Sorting information is a heavily studied subject in computer science. Inefficient sorts such as selection sort take approximately n^2 operations for n elements. Efficient sorts take approximately $n \log(n)$ operations. When information is sorted, it can be retrieved efficiently. Methods such as `binarySearch()` can retrieve keys in $\log(n)$ operations. Unsorted arrays require linear time searches to retrieve keys.

Review Questions

1. Does the statement `int[] x;` create an array of integers? If you answer *no*, how do you create an array of integers and associate it with the variable `x`? If you answer *yes*, how many elements are in the array?
2. Can you change the size of an array? Explain.
3. Can an array variable be changed to refer to arrays of different sizes? What about arrays that contain different types of primitive elements?
4. Write a single statement that declares `x` to be an array of `int` values, creates an array of 10 integers, and assigns `x` to refer to the newly created array.
5. What is the value of `x[0]` after executing the statement that answers the previous question?
6. What is stored in `s[0]` after executing `String[] s = new String[2];`?
7. In a single statement, create an array of three `String` objects that contains the strings `"one"`, `"two"`, and `"three"`.
8. Assume that `x` refers to an array of `float` values. Write a loop to print the values in `x`, one per line. Don't make any assumptions about the length of the array.
9. Java uses pass-by-value for all parameter passing. That is, a copy of the value of the variable or expression is passed to the method. When the actual parameter is a variable, the variable in the calling statement can't be changed by the method. However, when passing an array variable, the contents of the array can be changed. What makes this change possible?
10. What does the following code fragment print?

```
int[] y = { 2 };    // create an array of length one
mystery(y);
System.out.println(y[0]);
```

Assume `mystery()` is defined to be

```
void mystery(int[] x) {
   x[0] = 1;
}
```

11. What does the following program print?

```
class Review11 {
  public static void main(String[] args) {
    int[] data = {1, 3, 5, 7, 9, 11};
    int sum = 0;
      for (int i = 1; i < data.length; i++) {
        sum = sum + (data[i] + data[i - 1]);
        System.out.println("sum  = " + sum);
      }
  }
}
```

12. Convert each of the following expressions for running times of an algorithm to big-oh notation.

$$3n + 2$$

$$3n + 2\log n + 15$$

$$256n^2 + 19n + 1024$$

13. How many `int` values can be stored in the array created with `new int[6][5]`? How many in `new int[6][5][3]`?

14. What does the following code fragment print?

```
int[] a1 = { 1 , 2 };
int[] a2;
a2 = a1;
a2[0] = 3;
System.out.println(a1[0]);
```

15. Is the following code fragment legal? If so, what does it print?

```
int[] a1 = new int[3];
int[] a2 = new int[10];
a1 = a2;
System.out.println(a1.length);
```

16. What does the following program print?

```
class Review16 {
  static int goo(int i){
    return i + 2;
  }
  static void hoo(int[] d, int n)  {
    for (int i = 0; i < d.length; i++)
      d[i] = goo(n);
  }
  public static void main(String[] args) {
    int i = 2;
    int[] a = {1, 2, 3};
    System.out.println("goo =" + goo(i));
    hoo(a, 1);
    hoo(a, i);
    for (i = 0; i < a.length; i++)
      System.out.println(i + " : " + a[i]);
  }
}
```

17. What does the following program print?

```
class Review17 {
  public static void main(String[] args) {
    int n = 20;
    boolean[] sieve = new boolean[n];
    int i;

    for (i = 0; i < sieve.length;  i++)
      sieve[i] = true;
    for (int j = 2; j < 8; j++)
      if (sieve[j])
        crossOut(sieve, j, j + j);
    for (i = 0; i < sieve.length; i++)
      if (sieve[i])
        System.out.println("i is " + i);
  }

  public static void crossOut(boolean[] s,
         int interval, int start)
  {
    for (int i = start; i < s.length; i += interval)
      s[i] = false;
  }
}
```

Exercises

1. Modify the program CommandLine in Section 5.11.1, on page 177, to print the command line arguments from right to left and to number each of them.

2. Generalize the sieve algorithm in Section 5.8.1, on page 160, to go from 2 through *n*. In the general case, you need only strike out multiples that are less than or equal to the square root of *n*. You also need only strike out factors for values that have not been set to false. For example, striking out multiples of 2 strikes out isPrime[4]. Striking out multiples of 4 won't strike out any elements not already out. Try to improve this program with these ideas.

3. Allocate an array of integers of length 100. Initialize the array to a series of random numbers. Print the contents of the array.

4. Repeat the preceding, but also find the minimum, maximum, and average value in the array.

5. Repeat the previous exercise, but do not print the contents of the array. Instead use an array of length 10,000 and write out how long each action on the complete array takes if you use the method System.currentTimeMillis(). This method returns a long integer that is the current time measured in milliseconds since midnight, January 1, 1970. By computing the difference between the time before and after an action you can determine how long the action took. Try this method for increasingly larger arrays by factors of 10 until your program no longer runs. That will happen when you request too large an integer array size from the heap. The *heap* is a place in the computer's memory where all arrays are stored.

6. A palindrome is a sequence of characters that reads the same both forward and backward. Some examples are

```
"otto"       "121"       "i may yam i"
```

Write a method that takes an array of `char` and returns the boolean value true if the string is a palindrome.

7. Modify your palindrome function from the previous exercise so that blanks and capitals are ignored in the matching process. Under these rules, the following are examples of palindromes.

```
"Huh"       "A man a plan a canal Panama"       "at a"
```

8. Write a different version of `wordCount()` that treats a word as a sequence of characters separated by the white-space characters: `'\t'`, `'\n'`, and `'\b'`.

9. Write a program that inputs a character array and then compiles as an array of strings all the individual words found. Use your instructor's definition of *word*.

10. Write a lexicographic comparison of two character arrays.

```
static boolean isLess(char[] word1, char[] word2) {. . .}
//true if word1 < word2
```

Words should be compared as in the dictionary, so *be*, *bet*, *between*, *bird*, . . . , are in correct order. You first must compare the character in the zeroth position. If two words are of different length and the shorter word is the same as the initial sequence of the longer word, then the longer word is *greater*.

11. Write a routine that sorts character arrays lexicographically. Then modify Exercise 9 not only to capture the words, but also to print a sorted list of all the words found.

12. Modify the previous exercise to produce a list of unique words independent of case. Turn all the words into lowercase before sorting them. After sorting them print only a single instance of any word. You need a test `isEqual()` to readily accomplish this task.

13. Write a program to produce the inner product of two arrays of `double`. Each array should be the same length. Write an overloaded form of this method that generalized it as follows.

```
static double innerProduct(double[] v1, double[] v2,
    int first, int last, double init);
//v1 and v2 must both have positions first and last
//but can otherwise be of different lengths
//init will normally be zero.
```

14. A real polynomial $p(x)$ of degree n or less is given by

$$p(x) = a_0 + a_1 x + a_2 x^2 + \cdots + a_n x^n$$

with the coefficients $a_0, a_1, \ldots, a_n$ representing real numbers. If $a_n ! = 0$, the degree of $p(x)$ is n. Polynomials can be represented in code by an array such as

```
public final int N = 5; /* N is the max degree */
double[]  p = new double[N + 1];
```

Write a method

```
static double evalPoly(double[] p, double x) {
   . . .
```

that returns the value of the polynomial p evaluated at x. Write two versions of the function. The first version should be a straightforward, naive approach. The second version should incorporate Horner's Rule. For fifth-degree polynomials, Horner's Rule is expressed as

$$p(x) = a_0 + x(a_1 + x(a_2 + x(a_3 + x(a_4 + x(a_5)))))$$

How many additions and multiplications are used in each of your two versions of the `eval()` function?

15. Write a method that adds two polynomials.

```
// f = g + h;
static double[] addPoly(double[] f, double[] g ) {
...
```

16. Write an algorithm to multiply two polynomials. Use your function `addPoly()` to sum intermediate results. This approach isn't very efficient, so write a better routine, if you can, to do the same thing.

17. Write a program that reads 10 characters into an array. Then have it print out the letters of the array sorted in alphabetic order.

18. Write a program that reads n letters into an array where n is read in. Then have the program remove adjacent letters that are duplicates.

19. Write a program that reads n strings into an array where n is read in. Then have it print out the strings of the array sorted in alphabetic order. Perform the sort with a method

```
static void sort(String[] names){...}
```

20. A simple encryption scheme is to interchange letters of the alphabet on a one-to-one basis. This scheme can be accomplished with a translation table for the 52 lower-case and uppercase letters. Write a program that uses such a scheme to encode text. Write another program to decode text that has been encoded. This isn't a serious encryption scheme. Do you know why? If you're interested, learn about a more secure encryption system and then program it. (See Section 10.5.)

21. Recall that simulations involving the repeated use of a random number generator to reproduce a probabilistic event are called *Monte Carlo simulations* (after one of the world's most famous gaming casinos). In this exercise, you are to find the probability that at least two people in a room with n people have birthdays that fall on the same day of the year. Assume that there are 365 days in a year and assume further that the chance of a person being born on each day of the year is the same. A single trial experiment consists of filling an array of size n with integers that are randomly distributed from 1 through 365. If any two elements in the array have the same value, then we say that the trial is true. Thus a true trial corresponds to the case when at least two people in the room were born on the same day of the year. Simulate the probability by running, say, 10,000 trials with n people in the room. Do this for $n = 2, 3, \ldots, 100$. You can use the expression

```
(int)(Math.random() * 365 + 1)
```

to compute the day of birth for each person. The number of true trials divided by 10,000 is the computed simulated probability. What value of n yields the probability of at least 0.5 that there are shared birthdays in the room?

22. Consider again the probability question in the previous exercise, but look for three people in a room of *n* people sharing the same birthday. By the way, if there are 3 * 365 people in the room, you are guaranteed (forgetting leap day) to have a probability of 1 for this question.

23. Two matrices can be multiplied, provided that the number of columns of the matrix on the left of the multiplication sign equals the number of rows in the matrix on the right of the multiplication sign. If the left matrix, call it *L,* has *m* rows and *n* columns and the right matrix, call it *R,* has *n* rows and *p* columns, then the result, call it *X,* will be a matrix that has *m* rows and *p* columns, with each element defined by

$$X_{i,j} = \sum_{k=1}^{n} (R_{i,k} \cdot L_{k,j})$$

Write a method `mult()` that takes two two-dimensional arrays of double values representing two matrices and returns the two-dimensional array that results from multiplying the two matrices. The method should return `null` if the matrices can't be multiplied because the number of columns of the first doesn't equal the number of rows in the second.

24. Write a program to play a number guessing game. The player thinks of a number between 1 and 100 and the computer tries to guess. The program prints out how many guesses the computer used. The player must respond to each guess by typing *correct, too big,* or *too small.* Using top–down design, one possible solution has the following top-level pseudocode.

PSEUDOCODE FOR GUESSING GAME

```
set range to be the initial range of 1-100
make an intial guess in the range
while the guess is not correct
   adjust the range based on the feedback
   make a guess in the revised range
print the number of guesses
```

Be sure to break the problem into smaller problems, each of which can be implemented by using a method. To make reasonable guesses, the computer will need to keep track of the current range of possible values. The pseudocode given suggests the creation of a method `adjustRange()` having the following header for the method.

```
static void adjustRange(String response,
                        int[] range,
                        int currentGuess)
```

This method takes as input the user's response (*too big* or *too small*), the current range of possible values, and the current guess. It updates `range` to reflect the new information from the user. The parameter `range` is an input–output parameter and should be an array of length 2. The method modifies the contents of the array to reflect the new information from the user about the current guess. For this program you will need to use the method `equals()` from the class `String` to check the response. If the response is a `String`, then `response.equals("correct")` will be true if response is the string *correct*. Although `response == "correct"` is syntactically correct, it doesn't give the expected result.

Applet Exercise

Using `AppletSum.java`, from the Applet Exercise at the end of Chapter 3, as your template, write an applet version of the word counting program in Section 5.8.2, on page 161. In this version allow the user to type text into a text field and have the word count appear as output.

6

Objects: Data Abstraction

In object-oriented programming languages such as Java, objects are used to represent data values. They are called *objects* because they are often used to model objects in the real world. For example, a computer model of the solar system might have one planet object to describe all the data for each of the planets.

Using Java, we can create a description of an arbitrary planet by writing a class that can be used for declaring planets. With a class `Planet`, we can declare variables of type `Planet` just as we declared variables of type `int` or `String`. In fact, `String` is a class. So a class is also a type, although all types are not classes. Types include the primitive types, such as `int`, which are not classes.

An object from a particular class can be thought of as a value of the type described by that class. For example, if *Earth* is an object from the class `Planet`, we might say that *Earth* is a value of type `Planet`. At other times we might want to emphasize the fact that the Earth is an object and that it belongs to a particular class. In that case we refer to it as an object or an *instance* of the class `Planet`.

A class not only describes the particular data values that make up objects from the class, but it also defines how those objects can be manipulated. In object-oriented terms, objects are defined to accept and respond to certain messages. For example, a planet might respond to the message, *getDiameter* by providing its diameter. It might also respond to a message such as *move to (x, y, z)* by adjusting its internal data values to model being moved to the new position in space.

In this chapter we first describe how to manipulate some objects that belong to classes that are a standard part of Java. We've already used one such class, `String`. We then show how to create new classes of objects.

6.1   STRING: USING A STANDARD CLASS

Different types of objects have different operations that make sense for those objects. If an object is a number, multiplication and addition make sense; if it is a planet, *moveTo(x, y, z)* might make sense. For strings, meaningful operations include combining two strings with concatenation, comparing two strings, or finding where one string is located inside a larger string.

As first introduced in Section 2.4, on page 31, in Java, operations on objects are usually performed by using methods instead of some type of operator symbol, as is done for the primitive types. The one exception is that Java supports the use of the operator symbol + for concatenation of two `String` objects. For all other operations on `String` objects—and all operations on objects for other classes—methods are used. In this section we look at some more of the operations that are available for objects from the class `String`.

6.1.1   AN EXAMPLE: PALINDROME

We begin our discussion of the class `String` with an example that uses two operations defined for `String`: `length()` and `charAt()`. Recall that a string can be viewed as a sequence of characters. The method `length()` is used to find the number of characters in the string. The method `charAt()` is used to select individual characters from a string. The first character in the string is at position zero and the last is at position *length* − 1, where *length* is the number of characters in the string.

We use the `String` class to determine whether a string is a palindrome. A palindrome is a string that reads the same backward or forward. A simple example is the word *eye*. The following is the pseudocode for our solution to the problem.

PSEUDOCODE FOR A PALINDROME

```
compare the first character with the last character
if they are not equal then return false
compare the second character with the next to last
if they are not equal then return false
continue until middle two characters are compared
```

This pseudocode gives the general idea but is a bit far from real code. It isn't quite a trivial task to map this pseudocode into actual code. The following refined version of the pseudocode is closer to real code.

REFINED PSEUDOCODE FOR A PALINDROME

```
set left to index the leftmost or first character
set right to index the rightmost or last character
while left is less than right
  compare the left character with the right character
```

```
      if they are not equal return false
      increment left
      decrement right
   end of the while loop
   return true
```

We can now easily convert this pseudocode to actual Java code.

```java
// Palindrome.java - check if a string is a palindrome
public class Palindrome {
  public static void main(String[] args) {
    String  str1 = "eye", str2 = "bye";

    System.out.println("Palindrome detection");
    System.out.println(str1 + " "
                            + isPalindrome(str1));
    System.out.println(str2 + " "
                            + isPalindrome(str2));
  }

  static boolean isPalindrome(String s) {
    int left = 0;
    int right = s.length() - 1;

    while (left < right) {
      if (s.charAt(left) != s.charAt(right))
        return false;
      left++;
      right--;
    }
    return true;
  }
}
```

This program prints

```
Palindrome detection
eye true
bye false
```

DISSECTION OF THE Palindrome PROGRAM

■
```java
public static void main(String[] args) {
  String  str1 = "eye", str2 = "bye";

  System.out.println("Palindrome detection");
  System.out.println(str1 + " " + isPalindrome(str1));
  System.out.println(str2 + " " + isPalindrome(str2));
}
```

We use the method `main()` to test our `isPalindrome()` method. We declare two variables of type `String` and assign them initial values, as we've done many times before. Except for the objects of type `String`, for which there are string literals, we create all other objects by using the keyword `new`.

■   `static boolean isPalindrome(String s)`

For methods that perform a test and return a boolean, the method's name commonly begins with the prefix *is*.

■   ```
int left = 0;
int right = s.length() - 1;
```

Here the operation `length()` is applied to the `String` variable s. Probably for the same reason that arrays are indexed starting at 0 (see Section 5.1), the position of the first character in a `String` is position, or index 0; therefore, the position of the last character is *length* - 1.

■    ```
while (left < right) {
   if (s.charAt(left) != s.charAt(right))
     return false;
   left++;
   right--;
}
return true;
```

This code follows directly from the pseudocode. The method `charAt()` implements the operation of extracting a single, selected character from a string, based on the position of the character in the string. Each pair of corresponding characters is tested for inequality. The first pair of characters that disagree causes the method to terminate with a value of false. If the iteration reaches the middle of the string without disagreement, the loop terminates. The method then returns with a value of true.

6.1.2   STRING METHODS

The methods `length()` and `charAt()` are called *instance methods* because they operate on a specified instance of the class `String`. Note that in the palindrome example, we preceded the method calls `length()` and `charAt()` with a `String` variable separated by a dot. That's how we specify the object upon which the method is to operate. Note that this method is different from the way we've been passing values to methods in earlier chapters.

In addition to providing instance methods to support operations for the objects from a particular class, classes can also have `static` or *class methods*. These methods are part of the class definition but don't operate on a specified instance of the class. Class methods usually provide some type of operation related to the objects defined by the class. The methods presented in previous chapters have been class methods, indicated by the keyword `static`. We've also used some standard class methods, such as `Math.random()`. In the case of `Math.random()`, the name of the method is preceded by the class name.

The following table lists some of the methods defined in the class `String`. Remember, instance methods for the class `String` are implicitly operating on the `String` object used to invoke the method. This implicit `String` doesn't appear in the parameter list for the methods.

Method Declaration	Type	Action
`boolean equals(Object anObject)`	Instance	Compares this string with another object
`int length()`	Instance	Number of characters in this string
`char charAt(int index)`	Instance	Returns the character at the position `index` within this string
`int compareTo(String str)`	Instance	Returns an integer value, based on lexicographic order
`int indexOf(int ch)`	Instance	Index of where the `ch` occurs in this string or `-1` if not present
`int indexOf(String str)`	Instance	Index of the first character of a matching substring `str`
`String concat(String str)`	Instance	Concatenates this string instance with `str` and returns the result
`String toLowerCase()`	Instance	Returns a copy of this string but in all lowercase
`String toUpperCase()`	Instance	Returns a copy of this string but in all uppercase
`static String valueOf(type prim)`	Class	Returns the `String` representation of primitive value `prim`, where *type* can be any primitive type

In the following test program we use each of the methods listed in the table.

```
// StringTest.java - demo some String methods
public class StringTest {
  public static void main(String[] args) {
    String str1 = "aBcD", str2 = "abcd", str3;

    System.out.println(str1.equals(str2));
    System.out.println(str1.length());
    System.out.println(str1.charAt(1));
    System.out.println(str1.compareTo("aBcE"));
    System.out.println(str1.compareTo("aBcC"));
    System.out.println(str1.compareTo("aBcD"));
    System.out.println(str1.indexOf('D'));
    System.out.println(str1.indexOf("Bc"));
    System.out.println(str1.indexOf("zz"));
```

```
System.out.println(str1.concat("efg"));
str3 = str1.toLowerCase();
System.out.println(str3);
str3 = str1.toUpperCase();
System.out.println(str3);
System.out.println(str1);
str3 = String.valueOf(123);
System.out.println(str3.equals("123"));
    }
}
```

This test program prints

```
false
4
B
-1
1
0
3
1
-1
aBcDefg
abcd
ABCD
aBcD
true
```

DISSECTION OF THE StringTest PROGRAM

- ```
  String str1 = "aBcD", str2 = "abcd", str3;

  System.out.println(str1.equals(str2));
  System.out.println(str1.length());
  System.out.println(str1.charAt(1));
  ```

The method `equals()` is used to compare two strings. Although syntactically correct, the expression `str1 == str2` doesn't in general give the expected result. The `==` operator checks to see whether `str1` and `str2` are referring to exactly the same object, not just two string objects that contain the same characters. We discussed the methods `length()` and `charAt()` in Section 6.1.1.

- ```
  System.out.println(str1.compareTo("aBcE"));
  System.out.println(str1.compareTo("aBcC"));
  System.out.println(str1.compareTo("aBcD"));
  ```

These calls to method `compareTo()` will return –1 if `str1` is lexicographically before the parameter. Essentially, that means alphabetical order, but it also specifies an ordering for nonalphabetic characters. The calls will return 1 if `str1` is lexicographically after the parameter, and they will return 0 if the strings are equal. The output of these three calls is

```
-1
1
0
```

▪
```
System.out.println(str1.indexOf('D'));
System.out.println(str1.indexOf("Bc"));
System.out.println(str1.indexOf("zz"));
```

The method `indexOf()` is overloaded to accept either a `String` or a `char` as a parameter. When the parameter is a `char`, the method returns the index of the first position in the string where the character appears. When the parameter is a `String`, the method returns the index of the position in the `String` operated upon (`str1` in our example) where the parameter `String` appears. If the parameter `String` isn't a substring of the `String` operated upon, the method returns `-1`. The resulting output is

```
3
1
-1
```

▪
```
System.out.println(str1.concat("efg"));
```

This method has exactly the same meaning as `str1 + "efg"`. It is best to think of `str1 + "efg"` as shorthand for `str1.concat("efg")`. This example emphasizes the fact that instance methods actually are operations on object values, for which no special symbols have been assigned.

▪
```
str3 = str1.toLowerCase();
System.out.println(str3);
str3 = str1.toUpperCase();
System.out.println(str3);
System.out.println(str1);
```

All instance methods in the class `String` are *accessor methods*. In other words, they are simply accessing the `String` object as opposed to modifying the object. Methods that modify objects are called *mutator methods*. We present examples of mutator methods shortly. Note that the `String` `str1` is unaffected by the calls to `toLowerCase()` and `toUpperCase()`. These calls return new `String` objects that contain the appropriate characters. The output of these statements is

```
abcd
ABCD
aBcD
```

▪
```
str3 = String.valueOf(123);
System.out.println(str3.equals("123"));
```

The method `valueOf()` is an example of a class method; it isn't an instance method nor does it operate on a `String` object. It is related to the `String` class because it can be used to create `String` objects and thus is defined in the `String` class. The method `valueOf()` is overloaded to accept parameters of any primitive type. In each case, the method returns the `String` representation of the primitive value. The result of the comparison shown is true.

6.2 STRINGBUFFER: USING MUTATOR METHODS

Instances of the class `String` are not modifiable. Some of the security aspects of Java required that the standard `String` objects be immutable. Don't confuse immutable objects with unmodifiable variables. As we showed in the preceding example, we can modify a `String` variable to refer to different objects, but we can't change an actual `String` object to let it contain different characters.

However, the standard Java class `StringBuffer` does provide string objects that are modifiable. Like a `String` object, a `StringBuffer` object represents a sequence of characters. In addition, the class `StringBuffer` provides *mutator methods* that can be used to change the sequence of characters represented by the `StringBuffer`. For example, the method `reverse()` can reverse the character sequence contained in `StringBuffer`. Compare the following code fragment with the example in Section 6.1.2, on page 193, that used `toLowerCase()` from class `String`.

```
StringBuffer str = new StringBuffer("ABCD");
str.reverse();
System.out.println(str);   //prints   DCBA
```

Note that `str.reverse()` doesn't return a new `StringBuffer` that is the reverse of `str`. Instead it actually modifies the `StringBuffer` referred to by `str`.

Like all classes except `String`, `StringBuffer` has no special syntax for creating `StringBuffer` values. New objects are created by using the keyword `new`, as in the preceding example. The keyword `new` is followed by the name of the class for the type of object being created. That in turn is followed by a list of parameters used to construct the initial value of the object. In the `StringBuffer` example, a `StringBuffer` object is being created with a `String` value given as a parameter. Obviously, the `StringBuffer` object will represent the same sequence of characters as the `String` parameter.

A *constructor* is a special type of method used to initialize or "construct" a new object value. A constructor always has the same name as the class. Like other methods, a constructor can be overloaded to take different types of parameters.

It should come as no surprise to readers familiar with arrays that the `StringBuffer` class internally stores the characters of the represented string in an array. (It is not necessary to be familiar with arrays in order to follow the discussion of `StringBuffer`.) Consequently, a `StringBuffer` object has two sizes: One is called the *length* and the other is called the *capacity*. The object's length is just like the length of a `String` object. It is the number of characters in the represented string. The object's capacity is the number of characters that can be stored in the

StringBuffer, before the StringBuffer must do a relatively expensive operation of adding additional storage. This information is helpful to an understanding of some of the methods that are part of the StringBuffer class.

The following table lists of some of the StringBuffer methods and constructors.

Method Declaration	Type	Action
StringBuffer()	Constructor	Initially empty, with capacity 16
StringBuffer(String str)	Constructor	Initialize with str, and remaining capacity 16
String(int capacity)	Constructor	Initially empty with specified capacity
int length()	Accessor	Number of characters in the string represented by this string buffer
int capacity()	Accessor	Total capacity before an expensive operation to expand is performed
char charAt(int index)	Accessor	Return the character at the position index within this string buffer
char setCharAt(int index, char ch)	Mutator	Replace the character at the position index with ch
StringBuffer append(String str)	Mutator	str appended
StringBuffer append(char c)	Mutator	c appended
StringBuffer insert(int offset, String str)	Mutator	Inserts str at offset
StringBuffer insert(int offset, char c)	Mutator	Inserts c at offset
StringBuffer reverse()	Mutator	Reverses the character sequence

Note how many of these methods parallel those found in the class String. Note also how the various method are frequently overloaded to perform similar actions on different types. The following test program demonstrates each of the methods listed in the table.

```
// StringBufferTest.java - demo StringBuffer methods
public class StringBufferTest {
  public static void main(String[] args) {
    StringBuffer sbuf1 = new StringBuffer();
    StringBuffer sbuf2 = new StringBuffer("abcd");
    StringBuffer sbuf3 = new StringBuffer(30);

    System.out.println(sbuf1.length());
    System.out.println(sbuf2.length());
    System.out.println(sbuf3.length());
    System.out.println(sbuf1.capacity());
```

```
System.out.println(sbuf2.capacity());
System.out.println(sbuf3.capacity());
System.out.println(sbuf2.charAt(1));
sbuf2.setCharAt(2,'Z');
System.out.println(sbuf2);
sbuf2.append("xyz");
System.out.println(sbuf2);
sbuf2.append('?');
sbuf2.insert(4, "---");
sbuf2.insert(2, '+');
System.out.println(sbuf2);
sbuf2.reverse();
System.out.println(sbuf2);
System.out.println("sbuf2 capacity " + sbuf2.capacity());
System.out.println("sbuf2 length " + sbuf2.length());
    }
}
```

The output of this test program is

```
0
4
0
16
20
30
b
abZd
abZdxyz
ab+Zd---xyz?
?zyx---dZ+ba
sbuf2 capacity 20
sbuf2 length 12
```

DISSECTION OF THE StringBufferTest PROGRAM

■
```
StringBuffer sbuf1 = new StringBuffer();
StringBuffer sbuf2 = new StringBuffer("abcd");
StringBuffer sbuf3 = new StringBuffer(30);
```

The first statement constructs an empty StringBuffer with a capacity of 16. The second constructs a StringBuffer containing the four characters with a total capacity of 20. The capacity is 20 because this constructor always leaves room for 16 more characters. The third statement constructs an empty StringBuffer with a capacity of 30 characters before needing to create more internal space for any characters that may be added.

```
■  System.out.println(sbuf1.length());
   System.out.println(sbuf2.length());
   System.out.println(sbuf3.length());
   System.out.println(sbuf1.capacity());
   System.out.println(sbuf2.capacity());
   System.out.println(sbuf3.capacity());
```

These statements confirm what we indicated before: The length is the number of actual characters represented, and the capacity is the total space currently available. Except for performance reasons, the capacity can be ignored. `StringBuffer` will automatically increase the capacity if necessary. In most cases, the additional cost of expanding a `StringBuffer` will be negligible. The output of these six statements is

```
0
4
0
16
20
30
```

```
■  System.out.println(sbuf2.charAt(1));
```

This method is identical to the method with the same name in class `String`.

```
■  sbuf2.setCharAt(2, 'Z');
   System.out.println(sbuf2);
```

The method `setCharAt()` is an example of a mutator method. It actually modifies the internal data for the `StringBuffer` object referred to by `sbuf2`. The output is

```
abZd
```

```
sbuf2.append("xyz");
System.out.println(sbuf2);
sbuf2.append('?');
sbuf2.insert(4, "---");
sbuf2.insert(2, '+');
System.out.println(sbuf2);
```

These are more examples of mutator methods. The method `append()` adds the characters to the end of the `StringBuffer`. The method is overloaded to append either a `String` or a single character. The method `insert()` inserts either a string or a character, starting at a specified index position in the `StringBuffer`. The output of these statements is

```
abZdxyz
ab+Zd---xyz?
```

```
■  sbuf2.reverse();
   System.out.println(sbuf2);
```

As discussed earlier, `reverse()` is also a mutator method. The output of these statements is

```
?zyx---dZ+ba
```

```
▪  System.out.println("sbuf2 capacity " + sbuf2.capacity());
   System.out.println("sbuf2 length " + sbuf2.length());
```

These statements again reinforce the difference between capacity and length. The length of `sbuf2` increased as we appended and inserted characters. Because we haven't yet exceeded the initial capacity of 20, the capacity is unchanged. If we continue to add characters, the capacity will eventually be increased automatically. The output of these two statements is

```
sbuf2 capacity 20
sbuf2 length 12
```

6.3 THE ELEMENTS OF A SIMPLE CLASS

As discussed at the beginning of this chapter, a class describes the data values that make up an object from the described class and any operations that can be applied to that object. The data values are stored in *instance variables*, which are also called *data members* or *fields*. The operations are described by *instance methods,* which are also called *procedure members.*

Typically, a class implements a user-defined data type needed to solve a programming problem. For example, suppose that we needed a class `Counter` that would count sequentially from 0 through 99. Each time the counter is "clicked" it should increase by 1. When the counter reaches 99 and is clicked it returns to 0. Such counters are common in everyday life: The sweep second hand on a watch is a counter that counts from 0 through 59, and the trip odometer on a car is a counter. Our counter has values 0 through 99 and needs an operation *click*. We might also need to be able to *reset* the counter to 0 and to have a *get* operation that gets the current value of the counter. The following example uses our proposed `Counter` object. We then present the actual definition of the `Counter` class.

```
// CounterTest.java - demonstration of class Counter
class CounterTest {
  public static void main(String[] args) {
    Counter c1 = new Counter(); //create a Counter
    Counter c2 = new Counter(); //create another

    c1.click();  // increment Counter c1
    c2.click();  // increment Counter c2
    c2.click();  // increment Counter c2 again
    System.out.println("Counter1 value is " + c1.get());
    System.out.println("Counter2 value is " + c2.get());
```

```
        c1.reset();
        System.out.println("Counter1 value is " + c1.get());
    }
}
```

The output of this program is

```
Counter1 value is 1
Counter2 value is 2
Counter1 value is 0
```

The methods `click()` and `reset()` are mutator methods: They modify the values of the `Counter` objects upon which they operate. The definition of the class `Counter` is as follows.

```
//Counter.java - a wrap around counter
class Counter {
    int value;                          //0 to 99

    void reset() { value = 0; }
    int get()    { return value; }   //current value
    void click() { value = (value + 1) % 100; }
}
```

DISSECTION OF THE CLASS Counter

- `class Counter {`

The first thing to note about the class `Counter` is that there is no method `main()`. `Counter` by itself isn't a program. It is instead a class or new type that can be used in other Java programs. As we showed in `CounterTest`, we can declare variables of type `Counter`.

- `int value;`   `//0 to 99`

Here we are declaring an *instance variable*. Each object or instance of the class `Counter` contains an integer used to represent the value of the `Counter`. Note that this variable declaration isn't in the body of any method. This variable is visible to all the instance methods of the class.

- `void reset() { value = 0; }`

This method is an instance method. Note that the keyword `static` is absent from this method definition. The methods that we've been writing until now have been static or class methods. Class methods don't implement operations on objects. This method appears to have no parameters and no return value. In fact it has one implicit parameter: the object upon which this operation is being performed. That implicit parameter is the object named in the method invocation—for example, `c1` in `c1.reset()`. This method demonstrates that the instance variable `value` can be accessed from inside an instance method.

- `int get()    { return value; }    //current value`

This method is an accessor method. It simply returns the integer value that represents the value of the `Counter` object. Again, the instance variable is referenced from inside an instance method.

- `void click() { value = (value + 1) % 100; }`

This method is another mutator method. It uses the modulus operator, `%`, to keep the value of the `Counter` within the range 0 through 99. In general, including numbers such as the 100 in the statement isn't a good idea. The use of symbolic constants is preferable. We discuss symbolic constants in Section 6.12.

Note that there is one instance of the integer variable `value` for each instance of the class `Counter`. In the program `CounterTest`, there are two copies of `value`: one for the `Counter` object referred to by `c1` and one for the `Counter` object referred to by `c2`. As discussed in the preceding dissection, in the method call `c1.click()`, the object referred to by `c1` is passed as an *implicit first parameter* to the method. In this way, the method knows which `value` to increment.

The following diagram shows a portion of the computer's memory just before the first two calls to `println()`. By following the arrows, you can get from a variable such as `c1` to a particular object. From there you can find the methods for the class.

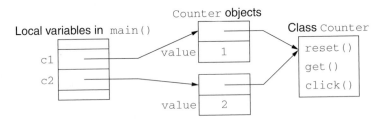

An *abstract data type* (ADT) is a user-defined type with a set of methods to manipulate objects of that type. In the case of `Counter`, we've methods such as `get()` and `click()`. There is also an implementation of the values needed to describe the object's state—in this case, the instance variable `value`. Decoupling implementation from manipulation via accessor and mutator methods has important advantages. For example, we can have a program use a `Counter` without knowing whether the internal value is represented as an `int`, `long`, `byte`, or possibly some other class. This capability allows the implementer to develop an optimal implementation. At the same time it allows a client, or user of the implementation, the opportunity to develop an application using `Counter` without being concerned about the internal details of `Counter`.

Note that in the preceding discussion we said the "object referred to by `c1`," not "the object `c1`." Recall that variables declared to be a nonprimitive type are referred to as reference variables. They don't directly store the object but in fact store a *pointer* or *reference* to the object, as shown in the preceding diagram. However, when the fact that the variable is actually a reference is unimportant to the discussion, we say, "the object `c1`." In Section 6.10, we explain the circumstances under which it is important that the variable is actually a reference.

6.4 ACCESS `public` AND `private`: DATA HIDING

As a general rule, each class should be defined in a separate file. The name of the file should be the same as the name of the class with the suffix *.java*—for example, *Counter.java*. Many files with the *.java* suffix can reside in a common directory. By default, all classes in the same directory are part of the same unnamed package. (We describe packages in Section 12.11.) With appropriate syntax, methods for one class can refer to class variables, instance variables, class methods, and instance methods for any other class in the same package, provided that the variable or method declaration being referenced isn't preceded by the keyword `private`. For the example to work correctly, the files *Counter.java* and *CounterTest.java* would need to be in the same directory and hence in the same unnamed package.

Because the declaration of the instance variable `value` in class `Counter` isn't preceded by the keyword `private`, any method in another class in the same directory can perform a manipulation, such as

```
Counter c = new Counter();
c.value = 100;
```

Such a manipulation isn't consistent with our original description of `Counter`. In this case, the value isn't between 0 and 99, inclusive. To prevent this from happening, we can declare `value` as `private`. The `private` access modifier restricts the use of the variable to methods that are defined in the same class. Methods in other classes can't use a privately declared variable. In data hiding terms, instance variables should be private to prevent misuse. Methods can be written to give access to the object's values in a controlled and safe manner.

Although we want to protect or hide the internal state of the `Counter` class, we want to be able to reuse the `Counter` class as widely as possible. That is, we want classes outside the current directory or package to be able to create `Counter` objects and manipulate them using the methods `reset()`, `click()`, and `get()`. We can use the access keyword `public` to do so. This approach becomes more important as you begin to build your own packages. Until then, you won't be able to observe any difference in behavior between public access and the default access when no access keyword appears. This is called *package access*. The class `Counter` is modified to include the preferred access modifiers as follows.

```
// Counter.java - a simple wrap around counter
public class Counter {
    //instance variables -fields -- hidden
    private int value;

    //methods -- exposed
    public void reset() { value = 0; }
    public int get()    { return value;}
    public void click() {value = (value + 1) % 100;}
}
```

This implementation makes certain access to the field `value`, such as the assignment `c.value = 100`, a compiler error if attempted from outside the methods in class `Counter`. The use of private fields for implementation is a common technique in building ADTs and is referred to as the *principle of data hiding*. It enforces on the client or user of the ADT the discipline of using only the public fields and methods, also called the *interface* of the ADT.

6.5 CONSTRUCTOR METHODS AND OBJECT CREATION

When we want a `Counter` object we must allocate it with `new`, as in

```
Counter c1 = new Counter();
```

This allocation creates a `Counter` object and calls a constructor, which initializes `c1.value` to 0 implicitly. The constructor in this example has an empty argument list; that is, there is nothing between the parentheses in `new Counter()`. This constructor is called the default, no-arg constructor. It is provided automatically by the compiler when it isn't explicitly written by the programmer. In the following program fragment, we provide `Counter` with two explicit constructors: one that initializes the counter with an integer value, and the second which is the no-arg constructor.

```
public class Counter {
    //constructors
    public Counter() { }
    public Counter(int v) { value = v % 100; }
    .....
}
```

A *constructor* is like a method with two special characteristics: It has no return type, and in place of an arbitrary method name, has the class name. We don't need to do anything in the no-arg constructor because the field `value` is automatically initialized to 0. All numeric fields are automatically initialized to 0, which is different from local variables that are not automatically initialized.

The constructor with the integer argument uses the argument to initialize the counter value. To ensure that the counter value is valid, based on our definition of a counter, we use the modulus operator. Its use guarantees that the value will be between 0 and 99, inclusive.

The code in a constructor should stick to the purpose of initialization. In general, it should use its arguments as the means for initializing the instance variables of the object being created. Constructors are frequently overloaded because there are many useful ways to initialize objects. Overloading for constructors is the same as for methods. Recall that overloading allows us to write several methods with the same name, distinguished by the number and types of their parameters. Our style is to group constructors at the head of the class definition. For initialization to work correctly, acceptable values must be used in the fields of the object. Good practice involves testing whether a value in the correct range is being used to initialize an object's fields. For example, if our counter can only hold nonnegative values, we should verify that they are initialized with values greater than or equal to 0. When we discuss exceptions in Section 11.6, we also use the constructor to check that the initial state is valid.

COMMON PROGRAMMING ERROR

Keep in mind that the default no-arg constructor is provided by the compiler *only if* no constructor is explicitly coded in the class. If we had added the constructor `public Counter(int v)`, but not the no-arg constructor, to our class `Counter`, then the declaration

```
Counter c1 = new Counter();
```

would be a syntax error, generating a message similar to

```
No constructor matching Counter() found in class Counter.
```

6.6 STATIC FIELDS AND METHODS

As we discussed earlier in the sections on `String` and `StringBuffer`, static or class methods are part of a class definition but don't operate on specific instances of the class. The keyword `static`, as part of a method header, means that the method doesn't have an implicit first parameter as we had when calling the methods of class `Counter`. We've made extensive use of static methods as a way to organize simple programs. We've also used various static methods from other classes, such as `Math.random()` and `String.valueOf()`. Note that, from outside the class in which it is defined, you call a static method by preceding the method name with the name of the class separated by a dot.

Java also has static fields called class variables. A *class variable* is independent of the objects for the class. There is only one instance of a class variable no matter how many objects from the class you have created. The value `Math.PI` is a `static` or class variable in the class `Math`. Class variables are referenced just like class methods, by preceding the variable name with the class name. Some static fields are defined so that they can't be changed, thereby turning them into constants. This is the case for `Math.PI`.

For example, we can add a static variable to our `Counter` class to track how many counter instances have been created.

```
public class Counter {
  //instance variables -fields -- hidden
  private int value;
  private static int howMany = 0;

  //methods -- exposed
  public Counter(){ howMany++; }
  public void reset() { value = 0; }
  public int get()    { return value; }
  public void click() { value = (value + 1) % 100; }
  public static int howMany() { return howMany; }
}
```

Each time a `Counter` object is created, the `static` variable howMany is incremented. Unlike the field value, which can have a different value for each instance of `Counter`, the static field howMany is universal to the class. Here you can see some justification for the choice of the word `static`. A static field is created once, or *statically*, when the Java virtual machine first encounters the class. A new instance variable is created *dynamically* each time a new instance of the class is created with the operator `new`. The following test program demonstrates the difference between class variables and instance variables.

```
// CounterTest2.java - demonstration of static field
class CounterTest2 {
  public static void main(String[] args) {
    System.out.println(Counter.howMany());
    Counter c1 = new Counter();
    Counter c2 = new Counter();
    c1.click();
    c2.click();
    c2.click();
    System.out.println("Counter1 value is " +
          c1.get()); //prints Counter1 value is 1
    System.out.println("Counter2 value is " +
          c2.get()); //prints Counter2 value is 2
    System.out.println(Counter.howMany());// prints 2
  }
}
```

We modified `CounterTest` to print `Counter.howMany()` at the beginning and end of `main()`. The first statement prints out `0` because no `Counter` objects have been created and therefore the `Counter` constructor hasn't been called to increment the variable `howMany`. The last statement prints `2` because the constructor for `Counter` was called twice, each time incrementing the static variable `howMany` in the class `Counter`. The following diagram is based on the one in Section 6.3, on page 202, which illustrates this action. Here it has been modified to reflect the presence of the class variable `howMany` when execution has reached the end of `main()` in `CounterTest2`.

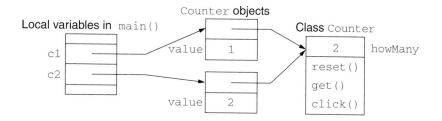

You can't access instance variables directly or call instance methods from static methods. You can't access instance variables from a static method because there is no object from which to get the variable. You can't call instance methods using the *methodName(argument-list)* syntax because there is no object to pass as the implicit first parameter required by instance methods. But you can, of course, call instance methods by using variables that reference objects, as we did in `CounterTest` when calling `c1.click()`. The object referenced by `c1` will be the implicit first parameter to `click()`.

For example, you would create a syntax error if you tried to reference the instance variable `value` from within the static method `howMany()`. The method `howMany()` when called with `Counter.howMany()` wouldn't know which instance of `value` to use. The reason is that the method isn't operating on any object.

From within instance methods you can reference both static and nonstatic members (fields or methods) within the same class as the method. From within the class in which a static member is defined, you normally access the member by specifying only its name, as for instance variables.

We've now discussed all the concepts needed to explain fully the expression `System.out.println()`. `System` is a standard Java class from the package `java.lang`. The class `System` contains a static field named `out`, so `System.out` refers to the value stored in that static field. The value `System.out` is an object, or an instance, of the class `PrintStream` from the standard Java package `java.io`. All you need to know for the current discussion is that the class `PrintStream` has an instance method `println()`. So `System.out.println()` calls the `println()`

method associated with the `PrintStream` object referred to by the static field `out` in the class `System`, as illustrated in the following diagram.

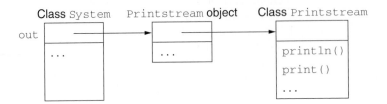

COMMON PROGRAMMING ERROR

A common mistake is to forget to use `static` for a variable that is referenced from within a method declared to be `static`. This error generates a message from the compiler similar to

```
Attempt to reference a nonstatic variable from a static
method.
```

You'll get a similar message if you attempt to call an instance method from a class method within the same class if you use only the name of the method.

6.7 CALLING METHODS—A RECAP

There are three ways to call methods. How you call a method depends on two things: whether the method is an instance method or a class method, and whether the method is in the same class as the method containing the call.

6.7.1 CALLING A METHOD IN THE SAME CLASS

The simplest form of method call has the form we used primarily in earlier chapters: *methodName* (*argument-list*). You simply give the name of the method followed by the actual argument list, as we did for all the methods we wrote in previous chapters. You can use this form to call one class method from another, to call one instance method from another, or to call a class method from an instance method. You can't call an instance method from a class method in this way, even if the methods are in the same class.

Recall that instance methods have an implicit first parameter that specifies the object to which the operation applies. For example, the method `click()` in class `Counter` needs to know "click what?" When calling one instance method from another, the same implicit first parameter is used. For example, we could have implemented the `click()` method in `Counter` by calling `get()`, as in

```
void click() { value = (get() + 1) % 100; }
```

The call to `get()` will have the same implicit first parameter as the method `click()`. In this case both operate on the same copy of the instance variable `value`.

There is no implicit first parameter for class methods. Therefore any attempt to call an instance method from a class method, even in the same class, must provide the object that will be the implicit first parameter. The notation for calling an instance method from a class method is the same as calling an instance method of a different class.

6.7.2 CALLING INSTANCE METHODS

To call a nonstatic or instance method in a different class we used, for example, `str1.charAt()` to call the instance method `charAt()`. The method `charAt()` is defined, without the keyword `static`, in the class `String`, a different class from `StringTest` where the call is located. The method name in this case is preceded by an expression that evaluates to a value from the class that contains the method definition. In the example given, `str1` must evaluate to a value from the class `String`. A simple variable name is the most common expression used in this form, but any expression that evaluates to an appropriate value can be used. For example, we could write `str1.toUpperCase().charAt(1)`. In this case, the expression `str1.toUpperCase()` evaluates to a value of type `String`. The method `charAt()` will be implicitly passed the `String` that appears before the name of the method in the call.

6.7.3 CALLING CLASS METHODS

In Chapter 5, all the methods we wrote were static or class methods. As explained in Section 6.7.1, when the call is from one method to another in the same class, we can simply use the name of the method. If the method is in a different class, we precede the name of the method with the name of the class. Superficially, doing so appears similar to calling an instance method. However, instead of preceding the name of the method with an expression that evaluates to a value from the class, we precede it with the name of the class. For example, we used `Math.sqrt(x)` to call the class method `sqrt()` from class `Math`.

6.8 PROBLEM SOLVING: MAKING CHANGE

Earlier we developed a simple program for making change. We can encapsulate the logic of that program in a class. The new class can then be used in a larger program for making change.

We can look at change as an object returned when we have a purchase. We have to decide which data members are needed for making change. Generally, objects mimic the real world. In this case we need members that track the number of coins of each denomination. We also need actions that are useful with these types. For example, what would be the value of a set of coins containing three quarters and two dimes?

```java
//Change.java
class Change {
  private int dollars, quarters, dimes, pennies;
  private double total;
  Change(int dlrs, int qtr, int dm, int pen) {
    dollars = dlrs;
    quarters = qtr;
    dimes = dm;
    pennies = pen;
    total = dlrs + 0.25 * qtr + 0.1 * dm + 0.01 * pen;
  }

  static Change makeChange(double paid, double owed) {
    double diff = paid - owed;
    int dollars, quarters, dimes, pennies;

    dollars = (int)diff;
    pennies = (int)((diff - dollars) * 100);
    quarters = pennies / 25;
    pennies -= 25 * quarters;
    dimes = pennies / 10;
    pennies -= 10 * dimes;
    return new Change(dollars, quarters, dimes, pennies);
  }

  public String toString() {
    return ("$" + total + "\n"
            + dollars + " dollars\n"
            + quarters + " quarters\n"
            + dimes + " dimes\n"
            + pennies + " pennies\n");
  }
}
```

DISSECTION OF THE Change PROGRAM

- ```
  private int dollars, quarters, dimes, pennies;
  private double total;
  ```

Here we declare the various data members bundled inside a Change object. We gave them private access to protect them from arbitrary manipulations by nonmember methods.

- ```
  Change(int dlrs, int qtr, int dm, int pen) {
      dollars = dlrs;
      quarters = qtr;
      dimes = dm;
      pennies = pen;
      total = dlrs + 0.25 * qtr + 0.1 * dm + 0.01 * pen;
  }
  ```

As currently defined, the only way to construct a Change object is by specifying the number of each type of coin. We chose not to use nickels or half-dollars, just to keep the code shorter. Because there's no no-arg constructor in this class, we can't create a Change object by using the expression new Change(). As discussed earlier, doing so would result in a syntax error. We intentionally left the no-arg constructor out because, as currently implemented, there is no use for it.

- ```
  static Change makeChange(double paid, double owed) {
      double diff = paid - owed;
      int dollars, quarters, dimes, pennies;

      dollars = (int)diff;
      pennies = (int)((diff - dollars) * 100);
      quarters = pennies / 25;
      pennies -= 25 * quarters;
      dimes = pennies / 10;
      pennies -= 10 * dimes;
      return new Change(dollars, quarters, dimes, pennies);
  }
  ```

This method is a static method because it isn't operating on a Change object. Instead, it is a helper function, used to compute change for an amount paid and an amount owed. Once we've computed the numbers of each of the coin types, we then create a new Change object, using the values. This new Change object is then returned as the result of the method. Note that we are using an object to encapsulate many related values—the amounts of the various coins. The return type, rather than being a single primitive value, is an object. This type allows a complex calculation to bundle and return many related values as an object.

- ```
  public String toString() {
      return ("$" + total + "\n"
              + dollars + " dollars\n"
              + quarters + " quarters\n"
              + dimes + " dimes\n"
              + pennies + " pennies\n");
  }
  ```

As we demonstrate later, all classes include a method `toString()`, which returns a string representation of the class. If we don't provide the method, the Java system provides one by default—but it isn't useful for most purposes. It simply returns the name of the class of which the object is an instance and the address of the object in the computer's memory. One version of the method `println()` takes as an argument any reference. The method then prints whatever the `toString()` method for the referenced object returns. Here we use string concatenation to build the result string. This `toString()` method gives slightly nonstandard output for values when no pennies are involved. For example, the total for $1.50 will print out as $1.5, with no trailing 0. We discuss a way to correct this formatting problem in Section 10.4.

The following simple program uses the class `Change`.

```
public class ChangeTest {
  public static void main(String[] args) {
    double owed = 12.37;
    double paid = 15.0;

    System.out.println("You owe " + owed);
    System.out.println("You gave me " + paid);
    System.out.println("Your change is " +
            Change.makeChange(15.0, 12.37));
  }
}
```

The output of this program is

```
You owe 12.37
You gave me 15.0
Your change is $2.63
2 dollars
2 quarters
1 dimes
3 pennies
```

6.9   ACCESSING ANOTHER OBJECT'S PRIVATE FIELDS

Using the abstraction capability provided by classes, you can easily make manipulating complex objects as easy as manipulating simple values. For example, you can easily modify the `Change` class from Section 6.8, on page 210, to support addition and subtraction of two `Change` objects. You do so by adding methods to support each of the operations. The following example shows how this new capability is used.

```
public class ChangeTest2 {
  public static void main(String[] args) {
    Change c1 = new Change(10, 3, 4, 3);
    Change c2 = new Change(7, 2, 2, 1);
    Change sum = c1.add(c2);

    System.out.println(sum);
  }
}
```

After creating two sets of change, c1 and c2, we add them, using c1.add(c2). The following method must be added to the class Change to implement this new operation.

```
public Change add(Change addend) {
  Change result = new Change(dollars + addend.dollars,
                   quarters + addend.quarters,
                   dimes + addend.dimes,
                   pennies + addend.pennies);

  return result;
}
```

The method simply creates a new object, initializing its data members to the sum of the corresponding members from the object upon which the method was invoked, c1 in this example, and the parameter, c2 in this example. This new Change object is then returned as the result of the method. Note that this method, when invoked on one object, can access the private fields of another object from the same class. The implementation details are hidden from other classes, but not from other objects in the same class. We leave adding a method for subtraction of Change values as Exercise 10, on page 229, for you to do.

We could have created a static method with two explicit parameters, as in

```
public static Change add(Change augend,Change addend) {
  Change result =
    new Change(augend.dollars + addend.dollars,
               augend.quarters + addend.quarters,
               augend.dimes + addend.dimes,
               augend.pennies + addend.pennies);

  return result;
}
```

Such a method, when called from another class, would have required including the name of the class in the call, as in

```
Change sum = Change.add(c1,c2);
```

Static methods don't support the object-oriented model of "sending messages to objects." Specifically, static methods don't allow for *dynamic method dispatch*, which we discuss in Section 7.2, on page 320. As we show later, we can "send a message" to an object—that is, invoke a method—when we don't know its exact type or class. The appropriate method is determined dynamically, which can be a powerful technique.

6.10 PASSING OBJECTS: REFERENCE TYPES

In Section 6.9, on page 213, the method add() in class Change had a parameter that was type Change and also returned a value that was type Change. The syntax was identical to the syntax used for passing and returning primitive type values. Despite the apparent similarity, there is one important difference.

As discussed in Section 4.8, primitive values are passed using call-by-value. In other words, the *value* of the actual parameter (the expression at the point of the method call) is passed. In particular, we showed that, when the actual parameter is simply a variable, the value stored in the variable can't be changed by the called method.

Recall that variables declared with a class type are referred to as references. A reference variable doesn't store an object directly but instead stores a reference to an object. This technique was shown graphically in the diagram in Section 6.3, on page 202. Consequently, when a reference type variable is passed using call-by-value, the "value" passed is the reference, not the actual object.

The result is that, when a reference type variable is passed to a method, the method receives a reference to the *same* object. This result in turn means that, if the referenced object is modified, the change will be observed back at the point of the call. The following program uses the class StringBuffer to demonstrate this behavior.

```
// PassingReferences.java - object parameters can be modified

class PassingReferences {
  public static void main(String[] args) {
    StringBuffer sbuf = new StringBuffer("testing");

    System.out.println("sbuf is now " + sbuf);
    modify(sbuf);
    System.out.println("sbuf is now " + sbuf);
  }

  static void modify(StringBuffer sb) { sb.append(", 1 2 3");
  }
}
```

The output of this program is

```
sbuf is now testing
sbuf is now testing, 1 2 3
```

This behavior is illustrated in the following diagram. The arrows indicate that the variables are referring to a StringBuffer object. When modify() is called, the value in the box labeled sbuf is copied to the box labeled sb. The values in the

labeled boxes are the references to the actual object. When the `append()` method
for the `StringBuffer` is called, the `StringBuffer` object is changed.

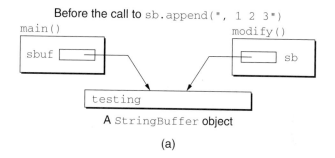

Before the call to `sb.append(", 1 2 3")`

A `StringBuffer` object

(a)

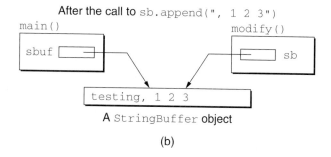

After the call to `sb.append(", 1 2 3")`

A `StringBuffer` object

(b)

If you think of the object as the parameter, this way of passing a parameter can be
called *call-by-reference*. The reason is that a reference to the object is passed, not a
copy of the object itself, as in call-by-value. However, if you think of the variable as
the parameter, this way of passing a parameter *is* properly referred to as call-by-
value. The important thing to remember is that you can't change the value stored in a
variable for a primitive type as a result of being passed as a parameter to a method.
However, you can change the object referred to by a variable for a reference type by
passing that variable to a method. Also, you can't modify the actual reference variable
by passing it as a parameter. The following program emphasizes this distinction.

```
// ModifyParameters.java - you can't modify the actual
//      arg even when it is a reference

class ModifyParameters {
  public static void main(String[] args) {
    StringBuffer sbuf = new StringBuffer("testing");

    System.out.println("sbuf is now " + sbuf);
    modify(sbuf);
```

```
    System.out.println("sbuf is now " + sbuf);
  }

  static void modify(StringBuffer sb) {
    sb = new StringBuffer("doesn't work");
  }
}
```

The output of this program is

```
sbuf is now testing
sbuf is now testing
```

The attempt to modify `sbuf` by making an assignment to `sb` in method `mod-ify()` has no effect outside the method. To understand why, refer to the figure in Section 6.10, on page 215. Can you redraw the figure to show what it would look like immediately after the assignment of the new `StringBuffer` to `sb`? Try it.

6.11 SCOPE

In Section 4.4 we discussed the scope of local variables. Recall that the scope of a local variable starts at the point of declaration and continues to the end of the block containing the declaration. Class variables and instance variables also have a defined scope—that is, the range of statements over which the declaration is visible.

The scope of both class variables and instance variables is the entire class, regardless of where the declaration appears. A local variable must be declared before its first use. In contrast, instance variables and class variables can be declared at the end of a class and still be referenced by methods defined earlier. For example, in the class `Counter`, we could place the declaration of the instance variable value at the end, as in

```
class Counter {
  void reset() { value = 0; }
  int get()    { return value; }              //current value
  void click() { value = (value + 1) % 100; }
  int   value;                                 //0 to 99
}
```

Note that we referenced `value` before defining it. We can do so because, as just stated, the scope of an instance variable is the *entire* class.

When a local variable and a class variable or an instance variable have the same name, the local variable takes precedence and the class variable is hidden. A hidden class variable can still be accessed by using the qualified name of the class variable, which is the name of the class followed by a dot followed by the class variable name. A hidden instance variable can be accessed by using the keyword `this`, discussed shortly. There is no way to refer to local variables from outside the method in which the local variable was declared. Consider the following program.

```
//Scope2.java: class versus local scope
class Scope2  {
  public static void main(String[] args) {
    int x = 2;

    System.out.println("local x = " + x);
    System.out.println("class variable x = " + Scope2.x);
  }

  static int x = 1;
}
```

In this program the declaration, where `x = 1`, declares a class variable, `x`. The scope of this variable is the entire class, even though it appears at the end of the class definition. This class variable could be referenced from any method defined in this class, not just `main()`. The declaration of `x` inside `main()` is a local variable. This declaration of `x` hides the class variable so that the first `println()` prints `local x = 2`. The second `println()` shows how the class name can be used to access the class variable when there is a local variable with the same name. If the local declaration of `x` were eliminated, the program would still be legal and both `println()` statements would print the value of `x` as `1`.

The keyword `this` provides a reference to the implicit first parameter for instance methods—that is, the object upon which the instance method is operating. For example, in a call such as `c1.add(c2)`, the implicit first parameter to `add()` is `c1`, which can be referenced with the keyword `this` inside the method. Let's return to `Change` and recode some methods using the `this` reference.

```
Change(int dollars, int quarters, int dimes, int pennies) {
  this.dollars = dollars;
  this.quarters = quarters;
  this.dimes = dimes;
  this.pennies = pennies;
  total = dollars + 0.25 * quarters + 0.1 * dimes + pennies;
}
```

In our earlier definition of the constructor for `Change`, we had to make up alternative names for the formal parameters to avoid having them conflict with the names of instance variables. The result of this approach is often that either the instance variable or the formal parameter have an unnatural choice of identifiers for a name. However, by using the `this` reference, we can use the most descriptive name for both.

We can always add the `this` reference to an instance variable reference from within an instance method, but we normally do so only when necessary to resolve an ambiguity. Without the `this` reference, we would have to find alternative names or be unable to access the instance variables.

Later we show that there are other situations in which we need the `this` reference. In those situations, there is no alternative, such as renaming local or instance variables. That occurs when, from within an instance method, we need to pass a reference to `this` object to some other method. Without the `this` reference we couldn't pass the current object to another method.

6.12 KEYWORD `final` AND CLASS CONSTANTS

As suggested earlier, making the instance variables in a class public is generally not a good idea. A better approach is to provide accessor methods and keep the actual instance variables hidden. Doing so allows us to be sure that the instance variables aren't set in such a way as to compromise the correctness of the class. For example, we made `value` private in our `Counter` class so that we could be sure it was always between 0 and 99, inclusive. There is one situation when instance variables are commonly made public: when the instance variable represents some constant value for the class.

An example from a standard Java class is the value `Math.PI`, which is a class constant. In the class `Math`, this constant is declared, as in

```
public static final double PI = 3.14159265358979323846;
```

The keyword `final` indicates that this variable can't be changed once it has been initialized, effectively making it a constant. Any further attempt to make an assignment to `Math.PI` will result in an error message from the compiler.

As a matter of style, such final values, or constants, are generally given identifiers that are all uppercase letters. Embedded words are separated with the underscore. For example, `Integer.MAX_INT` is a constant in the class `Integer`, which defines the largest possible integer value.

In addition to providing helpful values such as `Math.PI` and `Integer.MAX_INT`, constants can also be used to make a program easier to modify and understand. In general, numeric literals shouldn't be scattered throughout a program. Such numeric literals are often referred to derogatorily as "magic numbers." Someone reading the code might see such a number and wonder, Where did that number come from? By turning the numbers into named constants, the program becomes self-documenting and all uses of the particular value can be changed by just changing the definition of the constant. To illustrate, we replace the magic number 100 in our earlier example of the `Counter` class.

```
class Counter {
  int value;                          //0 to MDOULUS-1

  void reset() { value = 0; }
  int get()    { return value; }    //current value
  void click() { value = (value + 1) % MODULUS; }

  private static final int MODULUS = 100;
}
```

In this very short example, using 100 directly might seem fine. However, when the class becomes more complicated, we may find other methods using the modulus value of 100. For example, we might add a method to set the value or a constructor to give it an initial value. In either of those situations, we would still want to be sure that the value was properly in range. Using a constant makes the code easier to read and lets us easily change the modulus to something else.

6.13 ARRAYS OF OBJECTS

Let's assume that we want to write a program to play poker. One object we would want is a playing card. Once we had a playing card we could create a deck by having an array of 52 cards properly initialized. In this chapter we've avoided using arrays because we wanted to make the study of arrays and classes independent. If you haven't yet read Chapter 5 on arrays you may want to skip this section until you do.

Each card has a value from 1 through 13, where 1 stands for ace, 11 stands for jack, 12 stands for queen, and 13 stands for king. A card also has a suit value of clubs, diamonds, hearts, or spades. We use a number of classes to develop this application. First we present a class encapsulating suit information.

```
//Suit.java - a playing card attribute
class Suit {
  static final int CLUBS = 1;
  static final int DIAMONDS = 2;
  static final int HEARTS = 3;
  static final int SPADES = 4;
  int suitValue;

  Suit(int i) { suitValue = i; }

  public String toString() {
    switch (suitValue) {
      case CLUBS: return "clubs";
      case DIAMONDS: return "diamonds";
      case HEARTS: return "hearts";
      case SPADES: return "spades";
      default: return "error";
    }
  }
}
```

Note how for this class we use named constants to represent the four card suits. We also used this approach with the standard classes—for example, with the constant `Math.PI`. This class also has the usual `toString()` method, which we use to obtain a `String` representation of the `Suit` object.

We use the next class to represent card values. These are the card values 2 through 10 and the special cards, jack, queen, king, and ace. The spots on playing cards are called pips, so we name the class `Pips`.

```java
//Pips.java - a playing card attribute
class Pips {
  int p;

  Pips(int i) { p = i; }
  public String toString() {
    if (p > 1 && p < 11)
      return new Integer(p).toString();
    else if (p == 1)
      return "Ace";
    else if (p == 11)
      return "Jack";
    else if (p == 12)
      return "Queen";
    else if (p == 13)
      return "King";
    else return "error";
  }
}
```

A playing card combines a suit value with a pip or card value. Note how, by properly mimicking the problem domain, we quickly develop a set of objects that allows us to represent card play easily.

```java
//Card.java - a playing card
class Card {
  Suit suit;
  Pips pip;

  Card(Suit s, Pips p) { suit = s; pip = p; }
  Card(Card c) { suit = c.suit; pip = c.pip; }

  public  String toString() {
    return pip.toString() + ":" +  suit.toString()+ " ";
  }
}
```

A deck of cards is 52 individual cards of the right suits and pips or card values. Here's where arrays of objects prove useful.

```java
//Deck.java - a deck of playing cards
class Deck {
  Card[] deck;

  Deck() {
    deck = new Card[52];
    for (int i = 0; i < deck.length; i++)
      deck[i] = new Card(new Suit(i / 13 + 1),
                         new Pips(i % 13 + 1));
  }

  void shuffle() {
    for (int i = 0; i < deck.length; i++) {
      int k = (int)(Math.random() * 52);
      Card t = new Card(deck[i]);
      deck[i] = deck[k];
      deck[k] = t;
    }
  }

  public  String toString()  {
    String t = "";

    for (int i = 0; i < 52; i++)
      if ( (i + 1) % 5 == 0)
        t = t + "\n" + deck[i];
      else
        t = t + deck[i];
      return t;
  }
}
```

Two important methods in this class are the constructor, which must correctly initialize all the playing cards, and the shuffling method, which must reorder the cards in the deck. We focus on these routines in the dissection of the class Deck.

DISSECTION OF THE CLASS Deck

■   `Card[] deck;`

The internal representation of a deck is an array of cards, which is a natural representation. An understanding of how the various classes build on each other is important. We use Suit and Pips to define Card.

■
```java
Deck() {
  deck = new Card[52];
  for (int i = 0; i < deck.length; i++)
    deck[i] = new Card(new Suit(i / 13 + 1),
                       new Pips(i % 13 + 1));
}
```

The deck is constructed of 4 suits of 13 cards each. We use the integer arithmetic operators to ensure that all the distinct 52 cards are created. After a call to this constructor, the first card in the deck is an ace of clubs. The clubs are created in sequence, then diamonds, hearts, and finally spades with the card `deck[51]` being the king of spades.

```
■   void shuffle() {
      for (int i = 0; i < deck.length; i++) {
        int k = (int)(Math.random() * 52);
        Card t = new Card(deck[i]);
        deck[i] = deck[k];
        deck[k] = t;
      }
    }
```

We used the random number generator to rearrange a card deck. The following pseudocode describes this shuffle.

PSEUDOCODE FOR `shuffle()`

```
randomly select one card from the deck
    and swap it with the first card
randomly select another card from the deck
    and swap it with the second card
continue until this has been done 52 times
```

```
■   public  String toString()  {
      String t = "";
      for (int i = 0; i < 52; i++)
        if ( (i + 1) % 5 == 0)
          t = t + "\n" + deck[i];
        else
          t = t + deck[i];
      return t;

    }
```

Recall that every class has a `toString()` method. If one isn't defined explicitly, a simple `toString()` method is provided automatically via inheritance. (We describe inheritance in Chapter 7.) It converts the user-provided class type to a string. Among other uses, `toString()` is used by `println()` to generate an output representation. The `if` statement is used to generate a newline for each five card values. In the expression `t + deck[i]`, the string representation of the card `deck[i]` is implicitly generated, using `toString()` from class `Card`, before concatenation to `t` happens.

We test these classes as follows.

```
//CardTest.java testing the shuffling method.
public class CardTest {
  public static void main(String argv[]) {
    Deck deck = new Deck();

    System.out.println("\nNew Shuffle\n" + deck);
    deck.shuffle();
    System.out.println("\nNew Shuffle\n" + deck);
    deck.shuffle();
    System.out.println("\nNew Shuffle\n" + deck);
  }
}
```

Observing how well the shuffling method works by checking the results of successively shuffling the deck is important. This method should approximate the common real-world experience of shuffling and dealing a deck of cards.

6.14 OBJECT-ORIENTED DESIGN

Object-oriented programming (OOP) is a balanced approach to writing software, with data and behavior packaged together. This encapsulation creates user-defined types, which extend and interact with the native types of the language. *Type-extensibility* is the ability to add user-defined types to the language so that they are as easy to use as native types.

An abstract data type such as a string is a description of the ideal public behavior of the type. From the documentation of the class String, the user knows that operations, such as determining whether two strings are equal or converting a string to uppercase, are public behaviors supported by the class. These operations are implemented by the methods equals() and toUpperCase() from class String. *Encapsulation* is the ability to hide internal detail while providing a public interface to a user-defined type. Java uses class declarations in conjunction with the access keywords private and public to provide encapsulation.

Object-oriented programing terminology is strongly influenced by the Smalltalk programming language. The Smalltalk designers wanted programmers to break with their past habits and embrace a new programming methodology. They invented terms such as *message* and *method* to replace the traditional terms *function invocation* and *member function*.

Public members are available to any function within the scope of the class declaration and provide the type's interface. Private members are available for use only by other member functions of the class. Privacy allows the implementation of a class type to be hidden, which prevents unanticipated modifications to the data. Restricted access, or *data hiding*, is a feature of OOP.

The design of object-oriented programs can be aided by a diagramming process. Several object-oriented design (OOD) notations exist, and a number have been incorporated in computer-aided software engineering tools (CASE). The most comprehensive diagramming process is based on the Universal Modeling Language (UML) pioneered by Rational Software. We also describe a related low-tech scheme that we've found useful. It is based on class-responsibility-collaborator (CRC) cards.

A *responsibility* is an obligation that the class must keep. For example, the designer of the class `Rectangle`, from the standard package `java.awt`, decided that this class had the responsibility to provide a method that could be used to determine whether a rectangle "contains point *p*." Likewise, our class `Counter` has the responsibility to provide a method to "click the counter."

A *collaborator* is another class that cooperates with the class represented by the CRC card. For example, the class `Rectangle` must collaborate with the class `Point` to provide the "contains point *p*" method. However, the collaborator relationship isn't necessarily symmetric. For example, the CRC card for `Point` might not list `Rectangle` as a collaborator. The collaboration between `Point` and `Rectangle` is important only to the `Rectangle` class.

An index card or piece of paper is used to represent each class being developed. If the information can't be made to fit easily on a single card or page, the class is too complicated and the design needs to be modified. The name of the class, the responsibilities of the class, and the collaborators for that class are arranged on the front of the card. The back of the card can be used to describe implementation details. The front of the card corresponds to public behavior.

As the design process proceeds, the cards are rewritten and refined. They gradually become more detailed and closer to a set of methods. The attractiveness of this scheme is its flexibility and simplicity.

The design process begins by identifying the most obvious classes needed for the program and creating a CRC card for each. Next, various scenarios are proposed. Each scenario is designed to answer one or more "what-if" questions. As the scenarios are followed, existing CRC cards are modified and new cards are created.

As an example, let's consider the design of a simple e-mail program. We begin by displaying a menu of options. The options include reading an existing e-mail message or sending a new message, as shown in the `MainWindow` CRC card.

MainWindow	Collaborators
Display main menu Read mail Send new message	EmailSender EmailReader

The `EmailReader` class is responsible for retrieving e-mail messages from the e-mail server and then displaying either the headers of all messages or the text of a single message. Each message is represented by an instance of the class `Message`. The class `EmailServer` handles actual communication with the e-mail server.

EmailReader	Collaborators
Display headers	
Display a selected message	Message
Get e-mail messages from server	EmailServer

The `EmailSender` class is responsible for creating and sending a new message. It must allow for the editing of all the fields of a message. The actual transmission of the message to the e-mail server is handled by the `EmailServer` class.

EmailSender	Collaborators
Send the completed message	
Edit message text	Message
Edit message subject	EmailServer
Edit message "to" field	
Edit message "cc" list	

Each e-mail message is represented by an instance of class `Message`.

Message	Collaborators
Get/set subject	None
Get/set to	
Get/set cc	
Get/set text	

At this point we examine usage scenarios to determine whether new classes are needed or whether existing classes need modification. For example, what if the user is reading a message and wants to send a response? The subject and to fields should be filled in automatically. In addition, quite often the user will want to include part of the original message in the response. One solution would be to add the responsibility of "create an initial response message" to the EmailSender class and add the responsibility of "respond to selected message" to the EmailReader class.

6.15 PROGRAMMING STYLE

We prefer to write our Java classes with public members first and private members last. Applying this so-called need to know rule inserts first what everyone uses and needs to know and inserts last what only the implementers need.

```java
public class Counter {

  //public members - the interface to the class first
  //constants first then constructors then methods
  //overloaded methods are together

  public static final int MODULUS = 100;

  public Counter() { howMany++; }

  public Counter(int v) {
    value = v % MODULUS;
    howMany++;
  }

//methods are alphabetical
  public void click() {value = (value + 1) % MODULUS;}

  public int get()     { return value;}

  public static int howMany() { return howMany; }

  public void reset() { value = 0; }

//private members - implementation
  private int value;
  private static int howMany = 0;
}
```

Summary

- An object is an instance of a class. In Java, it is normally created by the use of new. A class can have both instance variables, called fields, and methods. Instance variables are used to describe the value or state of an object, and the method members are the operations that can be applied to the object.

- Methods that access only the state of an object are called accessor methods. Methods that modify the state of an object are called mutator methods.
- A class can have both static and nonstatic methods. Nonstatic methods are invoked as

reference.method(parameters)

except when calling the method from another nonstatic method in the same class. In that case the object reference value *reference* can be dropped. In this latter situation, the `this` reference for the called method is the same as the `this` reference for the method making the call.
- An abstract data type (ADT) is a user-defined type with a set of methods to manipulate objects of that type. In the case of `Counter`, these methods include `get()` and `click()`. Public behavior is the interface of the ADT. There is also an implementation, usually private, of the values needed to describe the object's state. In the `Counter` example, we made the field `value` private. In ADTs, we decouple implementation from manipulation.
- A constructor is used to create a class instance. Constructors have two special characteristics: They have no return type, and they have, in place of a method name, the class name. One further rule to keep in mind is that the default no-arg constructor is provided by the compiler only if no constructor is explicitly coded in the class.
- The keyword `this` provides a self-reference within a method to the object that the method acts on. Unless needed in referring to members to avoid confusion with other names or to pass this object as a parameter to some other method, the keyword `this` is usually omitted.
- The keyword `static` as part of a method header means that the method doesn't act on an implicit object. In other words, the method can't use the `this` reference. In previous chapters, we made extensive use of static methods in organizing simple programs.
- Java also has static fields or class variables. A static field isn't duplicated in each instance of a class. There is just one instance of a static field, which is shared by all parts of the program that can access it.

Review Questions

1. Does the statement `String s;` create a `String` object?
2. If you answered *no* to Question 1, how can an object be associated with the variable `s`?
3. What is meant by the default constructor?
4. Write a default constructor for class `Counter` that sets `value` to the largest possible `int` that is consistent with the specification of `Counter`. Why is the text's default constructor preferable?
5. What is meant by an accessor method? What is meant by a mutator method?
6. Give an example from this chapter of data hiding.
7. What is meant by the interface to a class?
8. Another term for a static field is a(n) _____ variable. Another term for a nonstatic field is a(n) _____ variable.
9. How is a static field different from an nonstatic field? Can a nonstatic field be referenced without direct or indirect reference to an object?

10. How can the `this` reference be used? Give an example where, in a class member, it is necessary to use the `this` reference. Briefly explain the conditions that require the use of `this`.

Exercises

1. Change and test `isPalindrome()` in Section 6.1.1, on page 191, to return true even when letters are of different case. Therefore "eyE" would still be a palindrome.

2. Change the `isPalindrome` program in Section 6.1.1, on page 191, to ignore space characters. Therefore "e   Ye" would still be a palindrome, or "A man a plan a canal Panama" would also be a palindrome.

3. Write a recursive form of the `isPalindrome()` method in Section 6.1.1, on page 191.

4. Add the method `increment(int i)` to the class `Counter` in Section 6.15, on page 226. The method adds `i` to the internal counter value. It must use the % modulus operation to guarantee a legal value in the field `value`. Write a program to test your modified `Counter` class.

5. Add a method `toString()` to the class `Counter` in Section 6.15, on page 226. The method should convert a counter value to a string for output. You will need to declare the method `public`. Write a program to test your modified `Counter` class.

6. Add a constructor to the class `Counter` in Section 6.15, on page 226, that takes two parameters. The first parameter is an `int` that specifies the intial value for the counter. The second parameter is an `int` that specifies the modulus for the counter.

7. Create a class to represent a pair of integer values. The no-arg constructor should leave both integers at the default value of 0. Include a constructor that can take one value *n*, setting one of the values of the pair to *n* and the other to 0. Include a constructor taking two values, setting both values of the pair. Note how useful it is to design a set of overloaded constructors that conveniently initialize the object pair. Have accessor methods that return `first` and `second`, the two values of the pair. Also have mutator methods that allow you to change the two values of a pair separately. Write a program to test your new class.

8. Write a method `minMax()` that takes as input an array of integers and returns the minimum and the maximum value in the array. The method should return the two integers by using the integer pair class from the previous exercise. Write a program to test your method.

9. Create a class `Rectangle` that represents a rectangular region of the plane. A rectangle should be described using four integers: two to represent the coordinates of the upper left corner of the rectangle, giving its location; one for the width; and one for the height. Your rectangle class should include

   ■ appropriate constructors,
   ■ a `toString()` method,
   ■ a method `translate()` that takes two integer parameters, `deltaX` and `deltaY`, used to translate the location of the rectangle,
   ■ a method `contains()` that takes two integer parameters, `xCoord` and `yCoord`, and returns true if the point (`xCoord`, `yCoord`) lies within the rectangle, and

- a method `intersection()` that takes a `Rectangle` as a parameter and returns a new `Rectangle` that forms the intersection of the `Rectangle` upon which the method is operating, and the `Rectangle` parameter.

Write a program to test the class `Rectangle`.

10. Add a method `sub()` to the `Change` class in Section 6.8, on page 210. The method should be an instance method with one `Change` object as a parameter, returning a new `Change` object as the result. This method is similar to the `add()` method discussed in Section 6.8, on page 213. Write a program to test the new method.

11. Rewrite the class `Change` in Section 6.8, on page 210, to include half-dollars and nickels. Include a `toString()` method appropriate to this class.

12. Write a `MyString` class that mimics the behavior of the standard class `String`. To do so you should have already studied arrays. Use a private array of characters to implement this class.

13. Code the class `Clock`. It is to have a set of methods that let you keep time. You want to be able to initialize a `Clock` to a given time in hours, minutes, and seconds. Include a method `tick()` that advances the `Clock` one second. Also include the ability to add two `Clock` values. When you add two `Clock` values, the first value will represent a time of day and the second will represent a time interval. Thus 2:15 plus 1:30 is 3:45 or one hour thirty minutes later than 2:15. Use 24-hour time so that midnight is hour 0 and noon is hour 12. Include a method `toString()` for output.

14. Recode `Clock` from the previous exercise to have a clock display time in terms of AM/PM. How much of the previous implementation did you retain? Keep all these examples in mind when you read about inheritance (Chapter 7) as a way to reuse and factor code.

15. Create a class to represent complex numbers. Complex numbers have two parts: a real part and an imaginary part. So a complex number value could be $(1, 1.5i)$, where 1 is the real part and $1.5i$ is the imaginary part. You should be able to add, subtract, and multiply two complex numbers. The rules for these operations are

$$(a, bi) + (c, di) = (a + c, (b + d)i);$$
$$(a, bi) - (c, di) = (a - c, (b - d)i);$$
$$(a, bi) \times (c, di) = (ac - bd, (ad + bc)i)$$

Hint: The `add()` method in your class `Complex` should be like the one with one explicit parameter in Section 6.9, on page 213, not like the static method in Section 6.9, on page 213, with two explicit parameters.

16. Develop a class `Person`. It should have fields for first and last name, address, social security number, and telephone number. Be careful in your choice of types for each field. The address field should itself be an ADT defined as class `Address`.

17. Create a class `Hand` that represents a hand of cards. Add a method `dealHand()` to the `Deck` class in Section 6.13, on page 221, that deals a hand of 7 cards from a card deck. If you've read the array chapter, use an array of `Card` objects to implement the class `Hand`. Otherwise, you can include seven instance variables, one for each of the seven cards.

18. Add a method `isflush()` to the class `Hand` from the previous exercise. The method should return a `boolean` value. The result should be true if the hand has five cards of the same suit. Use this method to compute the probability of getting a flush by dealing out 1000 hands and computing how often a hand is a flush.

19. Use the same ideas to produce the probability of getting a straight. A straight is a sequence of five cards with successive pip values. Remember that an ace can be either before a 2 or after a king.

20. Write a program to play the number guessing game described in Exercise 24, on page 187 in Chapter 5. Instead of using an array of length 2 to represent the range, use the class that you created in Exercise 7, on page 228, and call the class `Range`. In this way you can have methods such as `adjustRange()` that return a new `Range` object.

21. Create a class `Polynomial`. A polynomial has the form

$$a_i \cdot x^i + a_{i-1} \cdot x^{i-1} + \cdots + a_1 \cdot x + a_0$$

You should represent a polynomial as an array of coefficients. Your class should include a constructor that takes an array of coefficients as a parameter, a method to evaluate the polynomial at a particular point, and a `toString()` method.

22. Add an `add()` method to the `Polynomial` class that you created in the previous exercise. This method will take one `Polynomial` as a parameter and return a new `Polynomial` that is the result of adding the `Polynomial` upon which the `add()` method was invoked and the parameter.

23. Add a method `findRoot()` to the `Polynomial` class that you created in the previous exercise. The `findRoot()` method should be passed two parameters that correspond to the left and right ends of the interval in which to search for a root. The method can assume that the values of the polynomial at the two endpoints differ in sign. That is, if the value of the polynomial at one end is positive, the value of the polynomial at the other end must be negative. From the Mean Value Theorem we know that the polynomial must cross the x axis somewhere in the interval. That point is a root of the polynomial. The following is a simple root-finding algorithm.

PSEUDOCODE FOR FINDING THE ROOT OF A POLYNOMIAL

```
assume a and b are the endpoints of the interval
assume p is the polynomial to be evaluated
while the absolute value of (a - b) < epsilon
  root = (a + b) / 2     // guess the midpoint
  error = p(root)        // how close to 0 are we
  if (error > 0)
    set the positive endpoint (a or b) to be root
  else
    set the negative endpoint (a or b) to be root
end while
return root
```

The root found by this algorithm may not be exact, but it will be within epsilon of the root. By making epsilon arbitrarily small, you can get arbitrarily close to the exact root. Note that each iteration of the loop will cut the size of the interval containing the root in half, maintaining the requirement that the polynomial at the endpoints results in values having different signs.

Applet Exercise

Write an applet version of the number guessing game described in Exercise 24, on page 187 in Chapter 5. The applet should contain at least three buttons and a text field. The text field should be used to display the computer's current guess. The buttons should be labeled, "too small," "too big," and "correct." Each time the user clicks one of the buttons, the text field should be updated to display either the new guess or a message when the correct answer is guessed.

A button is implemented with the class JButton. A JButton is like a JLabel, except that you can respond to button clicks using an actionPerformed() method, just as we did for the JTextFields in the class AppletSum in the Applet Exercise at the end of Chapter 3. The following applet creates two buttons and a text field. When you click one of the buttons, the label on the button is displayed in the text field.

```java
/* <applet code="ButtonApplet.class"
    width=420 height=100></applet> */
//ButtonApplet.java - using buttons
import java.awt.*;
import java.awt.event.*;
import javax.swing.*;
public class ButtonApplet extends JApplet
    implements ActionListener
{
  JButton buttonOne = new JButton("Button One");
  JButton buttonTwo = new JButton("Button Two");
  JTextField output = new JTextField(20);
  public void init() {
    Container pane = getContentPane();

    pane.setLayout(new FlowLayout());
    pane.add(buttonOne);
    pane.add(buttonTwo);
    pane.add(output);
    buttonOne.addActionListener(this);
    buttonTwo.addActionListener(this);
  }

  public void actionPerformed(ActionEvent e) {
    String cmd = e.getActionCommand();
    output.setText(cmd);
  }
}
```

DISSECTION OF THE CLASS ButtonApplet

▪
```
/* <applet code="ButtonApplet.class"
    width=420 height=100></applet> */
//ButtonApplet.java - using buttons
import java.awt.*;
import java.awt.event.*;
import javax.swing.*;
public class ButtonApplet extends JApplet
    implements ActionListener
{
  JButton buttonOne = new JButton("Button One");
  JButton buttonTwo = new JButton("Button Two");
  JTextField output = new JTextField(20);
```

This example follows the same template used in earlier applet excercises. This time we create two buttons and a text field. We give the buttons labels when we create them.

▪
```
public void init() {
  Container pane = getContentPane();

  pane.setLayout(new FlowLayout());
  pane.add(buttonOne);
  pane.add(buttonTwo);
  pane.add(output);
  buttonOne.addActionListener(this);
  buttonTwo.addActionListener(this);
}
```

Here we add the two buttons and the text field to the applet. The last two statements state that the `actionPerformed()` method in this applet should be called whenever either of the buttons is clicked.

▪
```
public void actionPerformed(ActionEvent e) {
  String cmd = e.getActionCommand();
  output.setText(cmd);
}
```

This method will be called when either button is clicked. To determine which button was clicked, we call the method `getActionCommand()` for the `ActionEvent` parameter. This call will return the string used to label the button. We then display this string in the text field.

See Exercise 20, on page 230, for an additional suggestion about implementing this game.

7

Inheritance

A key element in object-oriented programming (OOP) is the ability to derive new classes from existing classes by adding new methods or redefining existing methods. The new class can inherit much of its implementation from the existing class. This process of deriving new classes from existing classes is called *inheritance*. This mechanism of one class inheriting some functionality from another class results in an *inheritance hierarchy*, just like the hierarchy that results if you look at the offspring of a person or other organism. The following diagram shows a hierarchy for two generations from a parent.

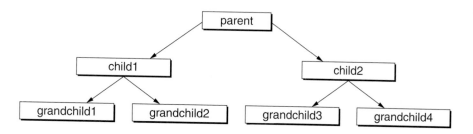

The usefulness of inheritance is apparent when we examine how taxonomic classification compactly summarizes large bodies of knowledge. For example, knowing the concept "mammal" and knowing that an elephant and mouse are both mammals allows our descriptions of them to be considerably more succinct than they would be otherwise. The root concept contains the information that mammals are warm-blooded, higher vertebrates and that they nourish their young using mammary glands. This information is inherited by the concept of both "mouse" and "elephant," but it is expressed only once: in the root concept. In Java terms, both elephant and mouse are derived from the superclass mammal.

Many useful types are variants of one another, and producing the same code for each is frequently tedious and error prone. A derived class, called a *subclass*, inherits all methods and fields from the parent, or *superclass*. The subclass can then be used to add fields or methods. Existing methods can also be redefined, which is called *overriding*.

7.1 A STUDENT "IS A" PERSON

Suppose that you needed to develop a system for tracking people at a university or college. You might want to maintain information about students, faculty, and staff. The records for these subgroups would have many things in common, but they would also each have specialized fields that apply only to each subgroup. Let's begin with a base class that contains the common information.

```java
//Person.java - characteristics common to all people
class Person {
  Person(String name)        { this.name = name; }

  void setAge(int age)        { this.age = age; }
  void setGender(char gender){ this.gender = gender; }
  void setName(String name)   { this.name = name; }
  int getAge()                { return age; }
  char getGender()            { return gender; }
  String getName()            { return name; }

  public String toString() {
    return ("Name: " + name +
      ", Age: " + age + ", Gender: " + gender);
  }

  private String name;
  private int age;
  private char gender; //male == 'M' , female == 'F'
}
```

The class `Person` has constructors, methods, and data members. The implementation details are hidden by declaring the fields to be private. All access is done through methods such as `setAge()`. This approach is in accordance with OOP methodology, which stresses the separation of implementation from abstraction or concept. We can now create new classes for students, faculty, and staff by extending `Person`. Here we work with only the derived class `Student`. We choose not to include a default constructor, thus forcing a name field to be specified for all `Person` objects. Including a constructor that allows all fields to be initialized is desirable; we leave that for you to do in Exercise 1, on page 267.

A class can be derived from an existing class by using the form

```
class class-name extends subclass-name {
...
}
```

The new class is a subclass of the class from which it is derived, its superclass. The keyword `extends` defines this relationship. The subclass being defined automatically inherits all the data members and methods of its superclass. The keyword `super` is used to refer to the superclass object that is implicitly part of the subclass object.

```
//Student.java - an example subclass
class Student extends Person  {
  Student(String name) {  super(name); }

  void setCollege(String college) { this.college = college; }
  void setGpa(double gpa)    { this.gpa = gpa; }
  void setYear(byte year)    { this.year = year; }
  String getCollege()        { return college; }
  double getGpa()            { return gpa; }
  byte getYear()             { return year; }
  public String toString() {
    return(super.toString() + "\n  " +
      "College: " + college +
      ", GPA: " + gpa +
      ", Year: " + year);
  }

  static final byte FROSH = 1;
  static final byte SOPH = 2;
  static final byte JUNIOR = 3;
  static final byte SENIOR = 4;
  private String college = "Unknown";
  private byte year;  // FROSH, SOPH, ...
  private double gpa; //0.0 to 4.0
}
```

The subclass `Student` has three new fields: `college`, `year`, and `gpa`. New methods are used to set and access those fields, for example `getYear()` and `setYear()`. The subclass `Student` also overrides the definition of the method `toString()`.

DISSECTION OF THE Student CLASS

- `class Student extends Person`

We use the keyword `extends` to declare that a new class will extend an existing class.

- `Student(String name) {  super(name); }`

All normal methods are inherited, but constructors are never inherited. A constructor can invoke the constructor of the superclass, by making what appears to be a method call but with the keyword `super` as the name of the method. The call to `super()` must be the first statement in the constructor. If there is no call to `super()`, then the default constructor for the superclass is called automatically before executing the body of the constructor of the derived class. Although not shown in this example, the call to `super()` can be followed by any other legal Java statements, as with any other constructor.

■
```
    void setCollege(String college)
        { this.college = college; }
    void setGpa(double gpa)    { this.gpa = gpa; }
    void setYear(byte year)    { this.year = year; }
    String getCollege()        { return college; }
    double getGpa()            { return gpa; }
    byte getYear()             { return year; }
```

We provide accessor and mutator methods for each of the fields added by class `Student`. In general, providing methods for accessing fields is preferable to exposing the fields for direct manipulation. Although we haven't done so here, by using methods for all access we can later easily add code to verify that only legal values are used for setting the fields. If an illegal value is passed to one of the mutator methods, we could generate an exception, as described in Chapter 11.

■
```
    public String toString() {
      return(super.toString() + "\n   " +
        "College: " + college +
        ", GPA: " + gpa +
        ", Year: " + year);
    }
```

When a subclass such as `Student` redefines a method found in the superclass, it is called *overriding*. That is what we do with the method `toString()`. We can still access the overridden version in the superclass by using the keyword `super`, as shown in this example. Here we use the superclass version of `toString()` to get the string representation of the fields inherited from the class `Person`, and then we append the string representation of the new fields.

■
```
    static final byte FROSH = 1;
    static final byte SOPH = 2;
    static final byte JUNIOR = 3;
    static final byte SENIOR = 4;
```

We provide constants so that code that sets the field `Year` will be self-documenting, as shown in the next example. Recall that the primitive type `byte` can represent small integers from -128 to 127 and requires only 1 byte of memory for storage. We use it to save storage because a type `int` would require 4 bytes of storage.

Keep in mind that every `Student` object is also a `Person` object. This "is a" relation will always hold between a derived class and its superclass. All method calls that could be made for a `Person` object can be made with a `Student` object, as shown in the following program.

```
//StudentTest.java
class StudentTest {
  public static void main(String[] args) {
    Student student = new Student("Jane Programmer");

    student.setAge(21);
    student.setGender('F');
    student.setCollege("UCSC");
    student.setYear(Student.FROSH);
    student.setGpa(3.75f);
    System.out.println(student.toString());
  }
}
```

The output of this program is

```
Name: Jane Programmer, Age: 21, Gender: F
   College: UCSC, GPA: 3.75, Year: 1
```

Note that, although the class `Student` doesn't explicitly declare the methods `set-Age()` or `setGender()`, those methods can be called. They are automatically inherited from the class `Person`.

BENEFITS OF USING A SUBCLASS

- Code is reused. The `Student` type uses existing, tested code from `Person`.
- The hierarchy reflects a relationship found in the problem domain. When we speak of a "person," the special grouping "student" reflects the real world and its treatment of this group.
- Various mechanisms will allow other code to treat `Student` as a subtype of `Person`, simplifying the code while granting it the benefits of maintaining these distinctions among subtypes.

COMMON PROGRAMMING ERROR

Forgetting to use `super` when overriding methods can lead to incorrect code. For example, if we mistakenly code the `Student.toString()` method as

```
public String toString() {
  return(toString() + "\n  " +
    "College: " + college + ", GPA: " + gpa);
}
```

the internal call of `toString()` would be a recursive call, leading to a nonterminating method execution. Why wouldn't the compiler know that we want to reference the super method `Person.toString()`? The reason is that, when a name isn't qualified by an object reference, a class name, `super`, or `this`, the compiler always looks for a definition in the current class before looking for an inherited method. When using inheritance, you have to be careful to select the right name if you've defined an identifier in both the superclass and subclass.

7.2 OVERRIDING INSTANCE METHODS

As shown in the preceding example with the method `toString()`, Java supports *overriding methods*, which are declared in one class and redefined in a subclass. The class hierarchy that results from the use of inheritance creates a related set of user types. Instances of any subclass of a given superclass may be referenced by a superclass variable. For example, an object of type `Student` may be referenced by a variable of type `Person`. The reverse isn't true. Because such referencing is valid in Java, the following *subtype principle* holds for all subclasses.

A subclass object can always be used where an object of its superclass is expected.

This principle holds because all the methods needed for the superclass are available for the subclass object. Look at the example of `Person` and `Student`. The methods you might call if you thought you had a `Person` object include `setName()`, `setAge()`, `setGender()`, and `toString()`. These methods are all defined by virtue of inheritance for any `Student` object, in addition to those added to `Student`.

When calling a method that has been overridden, the Java run-time system selects the method definition that corresponds to the actual type of an object, regardless of the type of variable used to reference the object. The object being referred to carries around type information so that this distinction can be made dynamically, a feature typical of OOP languages. Each object "knows" how it is to be acted on. This capability is variously called *dynamic typing, dynamic method dispatch,* or *pure polymorphism.* Both the noun *polymorphism* and the adjective *polymorphic* come from *poly-,* meaning "many," and *-morphic,* meaning "having such a form"; in this case a polymorphic variable or object can take many forms.

Suppose that we added the following two lines to the end of the example declaring a `Student` object for "Jane Programmer" at the end of Section 7.1, on page 237.

```
Person anyPerson = student;
System.out.println(anyPerson.toString());
```

Here we've assigned the variable `anyPerson`, which is declared to be a reference to a `Person` object, to point to the same object referred to by the variable `student`. The object is in fact a `Student` object. But as just described, this duplication is fine.

Any student is also a person, both in real life and as modeled by Java in this example. We can't call the methods in class `Student` by using the reference `anyPerson` in the following manner.

```
anyPerson.setYear(Student.FROSH); // illegal
```

A compiler can't, in general, figure out that this particular `Person` object is in fact also a `Student`. However, at run time the Java virtual machine can figure it out, so when you make a call to an overridden method such as `toString()` that is defined in both classes, the one for the actual type of the object is called. Therefore the call to `anyPerson.toString()` above will return the result of calling `toString()` as defined in class `Student`, not the one in class `Person`. The output of the statement will be the same as for the earlier print.

```
Name: Jane Programmer, Age: 21, Gender: F
  College: UCSC, GPA: 3.75, Year: 1
```

Distinguishing overriding from overloading is important. Recall our discussion of overloading in Section 4.12. We showed that in overloading several methods can differ only in their signatures, that is, in the number and type of formal parameters. We also demonstrated that the compiler can resolve overloading and select the appropriate method at compile time.

In contrast, overriding involves two methods with the same signatures except for differences in the *implicit* first parameter, that is, the one before the dot in expressions such as `x.methodName(...)`. In overriding, or pure polymorphism, determination of the actual method to call must be postponed until execution time. Then the actual type of the implicit parameter can be determined from the type information associated with all objects.

7.2.1   CALLING `print()` AND `println()` WITH ANY OBJECT

The dynamic determination of methods resulting from overriding is what makes possible the calling of methods `print()` and `println()` with any legal Java value. These methods are overloaded to accept one parameter that matches any of the primitive types or a parameter of type `Object`. All Java classes are implicitly derived from the class `Object`, except `Object` itself, which has no superclass. The class `Object` includes a method `toString()`. When `print()` is called with a primitive type, overloading allows the compiler to insert machine code to call the proper method. When `print()` is called with *any* reference type, the implementation of `print()` first calls the `toString()` method for the object. Just as our call to `toString()` called the method in `Student` instead of the method in `Person`, the call inside `print()` calls the `toString()` method for the actual class of which the object is an instance. Thus our statements involving `println()` for `anyPerson` could just as well—and in fact more properly—be written like

```
System.out.println(anyPerson);
```

There is nothing special about toString(), other than the fact that it is defined in the class Object. This dynamic type resolution works for any method that is overridden in a subclass. The following contrived example shows this same dynamic selection of methods.

```
//SuperClass.java - a sample super class
class SuperClass {
  public void print() {
    System.out.println(" inside SuperClass");
  }
}

//SubClass.java - a subclass of SuperClass
class SubClass extends SuperClass {
  public void print() {
    System.out.println(" inside SubClass");
  }
}

//TestInherit.java - overridden method selection.
class TestInherit {
  public static void main(String[] args) {
    SuperClass s =  new SuperClass();
    s.print();
    s = new SubClass();
    s.print();
  }
}
```

The output of this program is

```
inside SuperClass
inside SubClass
```

In the first s.print() call, s is referring to a SuperClass object; therefore the print() in SuperClass is called. In the second s.print() call, s is referring to a SubClass object; therefore the print() in SubClass is called.

7.3　THE ACCESS MODIFIERS private AND public REVISITED

Java has four different protection modes for fields and methods. The one that we have used the most is the default protection mode, called *package access*, that is in effect when no protection modifier is specified. Package access allows a field or method to be accessed by code in any method in any class within the same package. We discuss packages in Section 12.11.

The access mode private, signified by the keyword private, means that the method or the field can be referenced only from methods in the same class as the definition of the private field or method. This protection mode is preferred for most fields. When necessary, access should be provided to private fields through methods. In this way the implementation details of the class can be modified without affecting code that uses the class. Recall that this approach is known as data hiding.

The designation `public` is used to export fields and methods so that they can be accessed outside the package in which they are defined. As we haven't been building packages, we've generally not used the keyword `public`. In two specific cases we were forced to use the keyword `public`. In the first case, we had to make the method `main()` public so that the part of the Java virtual machine that starts a program could access the method. That is, we needed to export the method `main()` outside the default unnamed package in which it is defined.

In the second case, we needed to use `public` for the method `toString()`. As previously discussed, the method `toString()` is defined for the class `Object`, which is a superclass of all classes. In Java, we aren't allowed to use overriding to decrease the accessibility of an inherited method. Because `toString()` is inherited by every class and has the most accessible designation—namely, `public`—no overriding definition can specify anything other than public access. Without this restriction, the important principle that a subclass object can always be used where a superclass object is expected would be violated. For example, if our class `Student` overrode the method `toString()` to be `private`, then the statement

```
System.out.println(anyPerson.toString());
```

with `anyPerson` pointing at the `Student` object for Jane Programmer, would compile but fail at run time. The dynamic typing system would determine that `anyPerson` was referring to an object of type `Student` and attempt to call `toString()`, but `toString()` is private, making access illegal.

Classes can have only two designations: `public` or package access, which is signaled by no modifier.

COMMON PROGRAMMING ERROR

Narrowing access isn't legal when you're declaring an overridden method. An example is as follows.

```
class Point {
  int x, y;

  public String toString() {
      return String.valueOf(x) + " , " +
          String.valueOf(y);
  }
}
```

```
class ColorPoint extends Point {
  int color; // 0 = white, 1 = red, 2 = blue
  String toString() {
    return super.toString() + "  color is " + color;
  }
}
```

The compiler reports that you attempted to narrow the access of the overridden `ColorPoint.toString()`. This method needs to be labeled `public`, as it was in the class `Point`.

7.4 THE ACCESS MODIFIER PROTECTED

When you're not extending existing classes from other packages, the three access levels, package, private, and public, are all that apply. You can use a fourth access level when designing a class for export from a package. A *package* is a collection of classes, and classes are placed in a package by adding a declaration to the beginning of the class. All classes with no package declaration are part of a single, unnamed package. If you expect classes in other packages to extend a class that is part of a named package, the use of the access modifier `protected` may be helpful; it can be applied to both methods and fields.

Access to a protected member from within the same package is the same as package access. That is, adding `protected` to a field or method has no affect on the accessibility of the field or method from classes in the same package.

Access to a protected member from classes defined outside the package containing the class with the protected member is permitted only if the accessing class is a subclass of the class with the protected member. That is, from outside the package, a protected member is like a private member unless the method doing the accessing is part of a class derived from the class with the protected member. This description is a slight simplification; for elaboration see the Common Programming Error at the end of this section on page 244.

Let's consider our example class `Person` further. Suppose that we were designing a package that would include `Person` and possibly some classes derived from `Person`, such as `Student`. If we believed that others might want to derive their own subclasses of `Person`, we might decide to give protected access to the fields, declaring them as

```
public class Person {
  ...
  protected String name;
  protected int age;
  protected char gender; //male == 'M' , female == 'F'
}
```

Note that we also added the keyword `public` to the class definition. This addition is necessary if we want to export the class from the package containing it. We also add `public` to the method definitions. Changing the fields from `private` to `protected` has two effects. First, it makes them accessible anywhere in the package, which weakens data hiding. We can no longer freely change the names of these fields or their implementations. We must now consider the impact of such a change on the rest of the package. Second, the switch to protected access makes these fields accessible outside the package, but only in classes that extend `Person`. Suppose that the class `Person` was part of a package called `people`; then we could have

```
import people.*;

class Driver extends Person {
  ...
  public boolean needsDriverEd() {
    if (age < 25)
      return true;
    else
      return false;
  }
  ...
}
```

The class `Driver` is assumed to be defined outside the package `people`. Because the field `age` has protected access, it can be directly accessed in the subclass `Person`.

As a general rule, you should avoid protected access because it seriously erodes data hiding. Once you have exported a protected field, you can't change the field without considering any class that imports the package containing the class with the protected member.

Let's review the access levels.

1. Private—Use this level whenever possible. You can make changes to private members by examining only the class containing the member. This restriction provides maximum information hiding.

2. Package—Use this level when one class needs to be aware of some implementation details of another class in the same package. You may use package access for fields that are used heavily by other classes in the same package. You may use this option instead of access methods such as $setX()$ and $getX()$, which should almost always be used to provide access to fields from outside a package.

3. Protected—Use this level when designing a class to be reused via inheritance from outside the package in which it is defined. You should carefully consider any decision to export a protected member. Such exporting seriously weakens information hiding and makes program maintenance significantly more difficult and error prone.

4. Public—Reserve use of this level for the required interface elements to a class or package. You should never expose unnecessary implementation details with public access. Exporting a field with public access is very unusual, unless the field is also declared to be `final`.

COMMON PROGRAMMING ERROR

Our description of protected access was slightly oversimplified. Let's consider the following program fragment.

```
//SomeSuper.java
// assume this is part of the package PKG1
public class SomeSuper {
  protected int prot;
  ...
}

//SomeSub.java - not in package PKG1
import PKG1.*;

class SomeSub {
  void ok(...) {
    prot = 0; // this would be ok
  }

  void alsoOk(SomeSub subReference) {
    subReference.prot = 0; // this is also ok
  }

  void notOk(SomeSuper superReference) {
    superReference.prot = 0;
  }
}
```

The assignment to prot in method ok() is fine. This assignment is to the prot field inherited by the object on which the method ok() is operating. The assignment to prot in method alsoOk() also is okay. In this case the assignment is made to a protected field by a reference of type SomeSub. The assignment to prot in method notOk() shows how our earlier description of protected was oversimplified. In this last case we are attempting to make an assignment to a protected field by using a reference of type SomeSuper. In fact, a subclass may access a protected member of a superclass only when that access is made with a reference to a subclass object. In method ok() we are implicitly using the SomeSub reference this. In method alsoOk() we are explicitly using the SomeSub reference subReference. In method notOk() we are trying to reference the protected field by using a SomeSuper reference, not a SomeSub reference.

7.5 TYPE Object AND INHERITANCE

As we discussed earlier, in Java everything inherits from class Object. Thus Object is generic, in that any operation applicable to an instance of the class Object is applicable to an instance of any class. This characteristic enables us—

through inheritance—to write generic methods. A *generic method* is a method that has at least one parameter that can be an instance of several different types. We presented an example of this capability in how the `println()` method uses `toString()` to attempt to print any object's string representation. Java style is to have a `toString()` method as an overridden method in a class for output and debugging purposes.

Another `Object` method is `equals()`. This method is supposed to return `true` if elements have the same value. The default method defined in class `Object` takes the strictest interpretation of equals. It returns `true` if and only if the two references refer to the same object. This definition of *equals* is also the only one that could be implemented in the class `Object`. Other classes that are designed to be used in comparisons using equals can override the method `equals()` to be less strict. For example, two `Counter` objects could be considered equal if they contained the same value field, which isn't the same as having two references to the same `Counter` object.

We can use the method `equals()` to create a method to count the number of items in an array that have a particular value. The following method is called a generic method because it works for any array of nonprimitive values.

```
//Count the number of times obj is found in array.
static int howManyCopiesOf(Object obj, Object[] array) {
  int count = 0;

  for (int i = 0; i < array.length; i++)
    if (obj.equals(array[i]))
        count++;
  return count;
}
```

Because of the subtype principle, this method can be passed an array of *any* type of nonprimitive objects. There will always be some method `equals()`, but, as previously discussed, the one defined in class `Object` may not always give the desired result. The following contrived program shows `howManyCopiesOf()` being called with two different types of arrays.

```
//EqualsTest.java -
class EqualsTest {
  public static void main(String[] args) {
    // Create and fill an array of Strings
    String[] stringArray = new String[10];

    for (int i = 0; i < stringArray.length; i++)
      stringArray[i] = "String " + i;

    // Create and fill an array of Counters
    Counter[] counterArray = new Counter[5];

    for (int i = 0; i < counterArray.length; i++)
      counterArray[i] = new Counter();
```

```
        // Make two entries refer to the same Counter
        counterArray[2] = counterArray[0];

        System.out.println(
          howManyCopiesOf(counterArray[0], counterArray));
        System.out.println(
          howManyCopiesOf("String 1", stringArray));
    }
    //Count the number of times obj is found in array.
    static int howManyCopiesOf(Object obj, Object[] array) {
      int  count = 0;

      for (int i = 0; i < array.length; i++)
        if (obj.equals(array[i]))
            count++;
      return count;
    }
}
```

When we use the class `Counter` from Chapter 6, the preceding code will print 2 and then 1. Although the `Counter` objects are all set to 0, we haven't defined an `equals()` method for the class, so the default `equals()` method in `Object` is used. That method simply checks to see whether the references are to the exact same physical object. For the class `String` there is an `equals()` method; therefore one entry in the `stringArray` array contains a `String` equal to `"String 1"` as determined by the method `equals()`. How will the output change if we add an `equals()` method to the class `Counter`? See Exercise 16, on page 268.

7.6 WRAPPER CLASSES

Java includes wrapper classes for all the primitive types. A *wrapper class* wraps a single primitive value inside an object. This action makes it possible to treat primitive values like objects by first wrapping the primitive value in an object.

For example, the class `Integer` is a *wrapper class* for `int` because it wraps a primitive `int` value inside an object. Thus, we could create an array of `Integer` objects that might get processed by the `howManyCopiesOf()` method in the previous section. Without these wrapper classes, numeric types could not be processed with generic methods.

The class `Number` is the superclass for the wrapper classes for the primitive numeric types. The class `Number` provides methods for conversion to `byte`, `double`, `float`, `int`, `long`, and `short` through the use of the corresponding *type*-`Value()` method, such as `intValue()` or `doubleValue()`. Therefore, with types that are convertible, `Number` can be used to provide generic routines for standard calculations, such as finding the minimum element of an array.

```
static Number elementMin(Number[] array) {
  Number  min = array[0];

  for (int i = 1; i < array.length; i++)
    if (array[i].doubleValue() < min.doubleValue())
      min = array[i];
  return min;
}
```

This method will work so long as the loss of precision in converting to `double` doesn't affect the selected minimum.

The use of superclasses such as `Object` and `Number` provides a powerful generic mechanism for writing code. Such a method can also be called polymorphic, in that it can operate on different types of objects.

7.7 ABSTRACT CLASSES

A root of a class hierarchy often contains methods that all subclasses must override. There may be no meaningful way to implement such a method in the root class. In that case the root class is declared to be abstract, and any methods that must be over-ridden in the subclasses are also declared to be abstract.

An *abstract method* is used to defer the implementation decision of the computation to a subclass. In OOP terminology it is called a *deferred method*. A class that contains abstract methods is an abstract class, which has the form

```
abstract class class-name {
  abstract type method-id(argument-list);
  .....//other concrete and abstract methods
}
```

It is often useful for the root class in a type hierarchy to be an abstract class. By *root* here we mean a local root because in Java there is only one type hierarchy and it has `Object` as the root. When implemented as an abstract class, a local root defines the basic common properties of its derived classes but can't itself be used to create objects. Reference variables can be declared with an abstract type. Such a reference will always point to an actual object that is a subtype of the abstract type.

For example, we could create a collection of different types of counter classes, all with some common features. Here is an abstract counter class.

```
abstract public class AbstractCounter {

  abstract public void click();
  public int get() { return value; }
  public void set(int x) { value = x; }
  public String toString() { return String.valueOf(value); }
  protected int value;
}
```

Using this abstract class as a superclass, we can derive our earlier `Counter` class as follows.

```
public class Counter extends AbstractCounter {
  public void click() { value = (value + 1) % 100; }
}
```

We could also create a counter that counts by 2, using

```
public class CountByTwo extends AbstractCounter {
  public void click() { value = (value + 2) % 100; }
}
```

We might then have a program that needed a counter. Under user control, the program might sometimes operate with a count-by-2 counter and sometimes with a count-by-1 counter. In that case we could write the program to just assume some type of counter. The following code fragment shows a method that expects a parameter that is any subclass of AbstractCounter.

```
void sampleMethod(AbstractCounter counter) {
  ...
  counter.click();
  ...
}
```

Although we can't create an AbstractCounter object by using new, we can declare parameters and variables of type AbstractCounter. Recall that the subtype principle says that a subtype can be used anywhere the supertype is expected. Here we expect an AbstractCounter, so any subtype of AbstractCounter is allowed to be used. Thus, we can call sampleMethod(), passing it a reference to either a Counter object or a CountByTwo object.

These two subclassses of AbstractCounter added the minimum amount of implementation possible. We can also override the methods provided by the abstract base class. The following class extends AbstractCounter, overriding the method set(), in addition to providing an implementation for click().

```
class Timer extends AbstractCounter {
  public Timer(int v) { set(v); }

  public void click() {
    value++;
    seconds = value % 60;
    minutes = value / 60;
  }

  public void set(int v) {
    value = v;
    seconds = v % 60;
    minutes = v / 60;
  }

  public String toString() {
    return minutes + " minutes, " + seconds + " seconds";
  }

  private int seconds, minutes;
}
```

This class treats each click as a second of time. It maintains the total number of seconds in `value`, as well as the amount in the usual format of minutes and seconds. The class overrides `set()` and `toString()` and defines the required method `click()`.

Note that the preceding implementation of the class `Timer` may not be the best if `Timer` is clicked much more frequently than it is displayed. Each click requires a division and a modulus operation. The following is an alternative implementation that has the same visible behavior, although the internal implementation details are different.

```
class Timer extends AbstractCounter {
  public Timer(int v) { set(v); }
  public void click() { value++; }

  public String toString() {
    return (value / 60) + " minutes, " +
           (value % 60) + " seconds";
  }
}
```

The choice of which is the proper implementation depends on how you're going to use the class. The nice thing about the data abstraction provided by Java and other OOP languages is that at any time you can substitute an alternative implementation without making any changes to the rest of the program.

7.8 AN EXAMPLE: PREDATOR–PREY SIMULATION

Object-oriented programming was originally developed as a simulation methodology, using the programming language Simula 67. Hence many of the ideas underlying OOP are best understood in terms of modeling a particular reality. In this section we use a set of classes and inheritance to simulate an artificial ecology.

The world in our example has different forms of life that interact. We derive classes for modeling the life forms from a single abstract class, `Living`. Our simulation includes foxes as an archetypal predator, with rabbits as prey; the rabbits eat grass. The resulting class hierarchy is

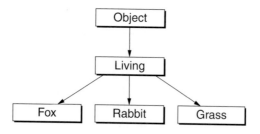

Our simulated world consists of a two-dimensional array of life forms. In this simple version, we use a single character to display each life form: 'F' for fox, 'R' for rabbit, 'G' for grass, and '.' for an empty cell in the two-dimensional world.

During each cycle of the simulation, certain rules are applied to determine which life form will occupy a cell in the next cycle. The rules are based on the populations in the neighborhood of a given cell. This approach is similar to Conway's Game of Life simulation.

In addition to the classes representing the life forms, we use the class World to represent the world in general. As already indicated, the world consists primarily of a two-dimensional array of life forms. In addition, the World class provides operations for initially filling a world with life forms and for advancing from one step to the next in the simulation. The simulation actually consists of two World objects: One represents the current state of the world, and the other is used to store the state of the world in the next cycle. The following pseudocode is for the top level of the simulation.

PSEUDOCODE FOR PREDATOR–PREY SIMULATION

```
create two worlds, current and next
initialize one with some life forms
print the initial world
for each step of the simulation
  update next based on current
  print the next world
  switch the roles of current and next
end of for loop
```

A key element of the rules used to compute which life form will occupy a cell in the next cycle is the number of various life forms in adjacent or neighbor cells. To handle this, each class that implements a life form must contain a static count to store the count of that particular life form. Using these counts in the various life form classes, we can use the following pseudocode to describe how we compute the count of neighbors for a single cell.

PSEUDOCODE FOR COUNTING NEIGHBORS

```
set the count for all life form types to 0
for each of the current cells 8 immediate neighbors
  if the neighbor is type LifeType
  then increment the count for LifeType
```

Because the counting neighbors code is the same for all life forms, we implement this operation as computeNeighbors() in the abstract class Living. In this way, all life form classes will inherit this operation.

We are now ready to look at the actual implementation of the classes. We begin at the top, with the class PredatorPrey, which is simply a place to put the method main() for the program.

```java
//PredatorPrey.java - top level class
class PredatorPrey {
  public static void main(String[] args) {
    World odd = new World(10), even = new World(10);
    int i, cycles = 10;

    even.eden();                    //generate initial World
    System.out.println(even); //print initial state
    for (i = 0; i < cycles; i++) {
      System.out.println("Cycle = " + i + "\n\n");
      if (i % 2 == 1) {
        even.update(odd);
        System.out.println(even);
      }
      else {
        odd.update(even);
        System.out.println(odd);
      }
    }
  }
}
```

Any of several approaches may be used to cycle between the two World objects. In the preceding implementation we elected to name one of the worlds even and the other odd. Thus when the cycle number is even, even is the current world and odd is the next world. In the next cycle—when the cycle number is odd—the roles are reversed. The code indicates that the class World must contain the methods eden(), update(), and toString(). We also decided to have the world always be a square array. Therefore the constructor for World accepts only a single parameter, which is the number of cells in a row or column.

```java
//World.java - square grid of life form cells
class World {

  World(int n) {
    size = n; cells = new Living[n][n];
    for (int i = 0; i < size; i++)
      for (int j = 0; j < size; j++)
        cells[i][j] = new Empty(i,j);
  }

  public void clearNeighborCounts() {
    Fox.neighborCount.set(0);
    Rabbit.neighborCount.set(0);
    Grass.neighborCount.set(0);
    Empty.neighborCount.set(0);
  }

  void eden() { // left as an excercise }
  public String toString() { // left as an exercise }
```

```
public void update(World oldWorld) {
  //borders are taboo
  for (int i = 1; i < size - 1; i++)
    for (int j = 1; j < size - 1; j++)
      cells[i][j] =
          oldWorld.cells[i][j].next(oldWorld);
}

Living[][] cells;
private int size;  //set in constructor
}
```

The pseudocode for "counting neighbors" includes the line "set the count for all life form types to 0." Only the class World knows about all the possible life forms in a particular simulation. Therefore the class World provides the operation clear-NeighborCounts(). This method sets the static field, neighborCount, found in each life form class, to 0.

The method update() visits each cell in the previous world passed as a parameter to update(), invoking the next() operation on the cell. The result of next() is stored as the state of the cell in the new world, which is the one upon which update() was invoked. Note that update() doesn't visit any of the cells on the outer border. This omission avoids an index out of bounds error when the neighbors are counted. Note that border cells are missing some neighbors. As a result, the state of a border cell never changes. This oversight can be corrected with a bit more logic in the computeNeighbors() method of Living. We leave that for you to do as Exercise 14, on page 268.

As discussed earlier, all life form classes are derived from an abstract class Living.

```
//Living.java - the superclass for all life forms
abstract class Living {

  abstract Count getCount();
  abstract Living next(World world);
  abstract char toChar(); // character for this form

  void computeNeighbors(World world) {
    world.clearNeighborCounts();
    world.cells[row][column].getCount().set(-1);
    for (int i = -1; i <= 1; i++)
      for (int j = -1; j <= 1; j++)
        world.cells[row+i][column+j].getCount().inc();
  }

  int row, column; //location
}
```

In this simulation, a life form "knows" its location, as represented by the two integer instance variables row and column. For each new life form, implementations for getCount(), next(), and toChar() must be provided. We discuss these methods in the dissection of the class Fox.

The method `computeNeighbors()` is used by each of the classes derived from `Living`. The code for `computeNeighbors()` follows directly from the pseudocode presented earlier. This code uses the method `getCount()` to get a reference to the `Count` object used in counting neighbors. The class `Count` is a simple wrapper for an integer, with methods to get, set, and increment the count. There is one `Count` object in each class derived from `Living`. The double `for` loop increments the count for the current cell, as well as the counts for each of the neighbors. We don't want to count the current cell as a neighbor, so we set the count for the current cells type to `-1` initially. We leave implementation of the class `Count` for you to do in Exercise 11, on page 267.

We are now ready to present the implementation of the actual life form classes. In addition to the three life forms fox, rabbit, and grass, we need to provide a class that extends `Living` to represent an empty cell, which becomes the class `Empty`. The rules of the simulation are contained in the `next()` methods of these classes. Each implementation of `next()` begins by computing the counts of neighbors, using the method `computeNeighbors()` inherited from `Living`. Then each life form class can query the various other life form classes to determine how many neighbors of a particular type exist. Most life forms care only about some of the other life forms. For example, in our rules, the `Fox` class only cares about how many foxes and how many rabbits are nearby. The `Fox` class doesn't care about how much grass is nearby.

```java
//Fox.java - prey class
class Fox extends Living {
  Fox(int r, int c, int a ) {
    row = r;
    column = c;
    age = a;
  }

  Living next(World world) {
    computeNeighbors(world);
    if (Fox.neighborCount.get() > 5 ) //too many Foxes
      return new Empty(row, column);
    else if (age > LIFE_EXPECTANCY)    //Fox is too old
      return new Empty(row, column);
    else if (Rabbit.neighborCount.get() == 0)
      return new Empty(row, column);  // starved
    else
      return new Fox(row, column, age + 1);
  }

  public String toString(){ return "Fox age " + age; }
  char toChar() { return 'F'; }
  Count getCount() {  return neighborCount; }
  static Count neighborCount = new Count();

  private int age;
  private final int LIFE_EXPECTANCY = 5;
}
```

DISSECTION OF THE Fox CLASS

- ```
  class Fox extends Living {
      Fox(int r, int c, int a ) {
          row = r;
          column = c;
          age = a;
      }
  ```

Each life form "knows" where it is located. We create a Fox by specifying the coordinates of the cell in which it will be placed and giving it an initial age.

- ```
  Living next(World world) {
      computeNeighbors(world);
      if (Fox.neighborCount.get() > 5 )   //too many Foxes
          return new Empty(row, column);
      else if (age > LIFE_EXPECTANCY)      //Fox is too old
          return new Empty(row, column);
      else if (Rabbit.neighborCount.get() == 0)
          return new Empty(row, column);    // starved
      else
          return new Fox(row, column, age + 1);
  }
  ```

The method next() contains the rules for what happens in the next cycle to a cell that currently contains a fox. In our simple rules the fox will die if there are too many foxes nearby, if the fox is too old, or if there are no rabbits for the fox to eat.

- ```
  public String toString(){ return "Fox age " + age;}
  ```

Although not used in our simulation, we include the standard toString() method, which might be used in debugging. Unlike the simple one-character representation used in our display, the String representation includes the age of the fox.

- ```
  char toChar() { return 'F';}
  ```

We use the method toChar() in the method toString() of World to create a simple representation of the world.

- ```
  Count getCount() { return neighborCount;}
  static Count neighborCount = new Count();
  ```

For each class that extends Living, a method getCount() must be implemented. Although the count is stored in a static variable, we use an instance method to access the count. This approach allows us to take advantage of dynamic method dispatch so that the code in the method computeNeighbors() in Living can get the counter for a particular class, using an instance of the class.

- ```
  private int age;
  private final int LIFE_EXPECTANCY = 5;
  ```

These two fields, along with the row and column fields inherited from Living, constitute the state of a particular Fox object. In our simulation all foxes die after five cycles, if not sooner. We could easily change this parameter to some random value over a range of values.

The classes `Rabbit`, `Grass`, and `Empty` are essentially the same as `Fox`, except that the rules in `next()` are different.

```java
//Rabbit.java - prey class
class Rabbit extends Living {
  Rabbit(int r, int c, int a ) { row = r; column = c; age = a;}

  Living next(World world) {
    computeNeighbors(world);
    if (Fox.neighborCount.get() >=
        Rabbit.neighborCount.get() )
      return (new Empty(row, column));   // eat Rabbits
    else if (age > LIFE_EXPECTANCY)
      return (new Empty(row, column));   // too old
    else if (Grass.neighborCount.get() == 0)
      return (new Empty(row, column));   // starved
    else
      return (new Rabbit(row, column, age + 1));
  }

  public String toString() {return "Rabbit age " + age;}
  char toChar() { return 'R'; }
  Count getCount() { return neighborCount; }

  static Count neighborCount = new Count();
  private int age;
  private final int LIFE_EXPECTANCY = 3;
}

//Grass.java - something for the rabbits to eat
class Grass extends Living {
  public Grass(int r, int c) { row = r; column = c; }

  public Living next(World world) {
    computeNeighbors(world);
    if (Grass.neighborCount.get() >
        2 * Rabbit.neighborCount.get())
      // rabbits move in to eat the grass
      return (new Rabbit(row, column, 0));
    else if (Grass.neighborCount.get() >
             Rabbit.neighborCount.get())
      // grass remains
      return (new Grass(row, column));
    else
      // rabbits eat all the grass
      return (new Empty(row, column));
  }

  public String toString() { return "Grass"; }
  char toChar() { return 'G'; }
  Count getCount() { return neighborCount; }

  static Count neighborCount = new Count();
}
```

```
//Empty.java - representation of an empty cell
class Empty extends Living {
  Empty(int r, int c) { row = r; column = c; }

  Living next(World world) {
    computeNeighbors(world);

    if (Rabbit.neighborCount.get() > 2)
      return (new Fox(row, column, 0));
    else if (Grass.neighborCount.get() > 4)
      return (new Rabbit(row, column, 0));
    else if (Grass.neighborCount.get() > 0)
      return (new Grass(row, column));
    else
      return (new Empty(row, column));
  }

  public String toString() { return "."; }
  char toChar() { return '.'; }
  Count getCount() {  return neighborCount; }

  static Count neighborCount = new Count();
}
```

Note that, except for methods `eden()` and `clearNeighborCounts()` in `World`, the classes `PredatorPrey`, `World`, and `Living` are completely independent of the specific life-form classes. Hence we can easily add new life forms without changing the existing life-form classes. Here the only change required is to add a line for each new life form to the method `clearNeighborCounts()`. We also need to provide some way to get the new life forms into the world. We could do so either via `eden()` or via the rules in one or more of the existing life-form classes. For example, we might add a new class `Clover` and modify the rules in class `Empty` to create `Clover` if there is nothing nearby.

You may wonder why we didn't place the code

```
Count getCount() { return neighborCount; }
static Count neighborCount = new Count();
```

in class `Living`. These two lines appear, without change, in each of the classes derived from `Living`, so why not just put them in the superclass and let them be inherited? The problem is that we want one `Count` object for each class derived from `Living`. If we place the two lines of code in `Living`, there will be only one `Count`, not one for each derived class. Although we can't create instances of an abstract class such as `Living`, the behavior of a static field in an abstract class is the same as a static field in other classes. Specifically, there will be only one instance of a static field, no matter how many instances of the class we create. The same restriction applies to both abstract and nonabstract classes.

We leave for you to do Exercise 12, on page 267, the writing of `toString()` and `eden()` in the class `World`.

7.9 INTERFACES

Java has a classlike form called an *interface* that can be used to encapsulate only abstract methods and constants. Think of an interface as a blueprint or a design specification. A class that uses this blueprint is a class that *implements* the interface. Another way of thinking of an interface is as a pure abstract class, wherein all implementation details are deferred. An interface is allowed to have only abstract methods and constants. Interface methods can't be `static`.

Let's consider a simulation like the one in the previous section. Suppose that not all life forms have the same notion of what it means to be a neighbor. For example, the neighborhood for a fox is probably different than that for a rabbit. If that's the case, our superclass `Living` wouldn't be able to implement `computeNeighbors()` for all derived classes. In this case we could use an interface instead of an abstract class. The interface for `Living` might be

```
interface Living {
  Living next(World world);
  char toChar();
  void computeNeighbors(World world);
  Count getCount();
}
```

An interface is allowed to have only public methods, and by convention the keyword `public` is omitted. Because all methods in an interface are abstract, the keyword `abstract` is also omitted. Implementing an interface is like extending an abstract class. A new class implementing the interface uses the keyword `implements`. The class that implements the interface must provide an implementation for all methods in the interface. When we use this interface instead of the earlier abstract class, our class `Fox` might become

```
//Fox.java - prey class
class Fox implements Living {
  // everything will be the same as before with the
  // addition of the following and changing
  // all methods from Living to be public

  // now each life form must provide this method
  // each can do it differently
  public void computeNeighbors(World world) {
    world.clearNeighborCounts();
    world.cells[row][column].getCount().set(-1);
    for (int i = -2; i <= 2; i++)
      for (int j = -2; j <= 2; j++)
        if (row + i > 0 &&
            row + i < world.cells.length &&
            column + j > 0 &&
            column + j < world.cells[0].length)
        {
          world.cells[row + i][column + j].getCount().inc();
        }
  }
}
```

```
// an interface doesn't contain data fields
// so row and column must be declared here
// we can now make these members private
private int row, column;
}
```

Note that we changed the neighborhood of a fox to be a 5 × 5 neighborhood from the 3 × 3 neighborhood used earlier. Other life forms might have the earlier 3 × 3 neighborhood or something different. Because we're using a larger neighborhood, we also added code to be sure that we don't go beyond the bounds of the array.

Of course, we could have overridden the definition of `computeNeighbors()` in the class `Fox`, even when it was derived from the earlier abstract class `Living`. In this example, there is no particular advantage to using an interface rather than an abstract class. However, the difference between an interface and an abstract class becomes very important when you want to create a class that implements more than one interface. You can't extend more than one class, but you can use a class to implement many interfaces, in addition to extending one class.

We use interfaces extensively when we discuss graphical user interfaces in Chapter 8. In the next section we present a brief example in which abstract classes can't be used but interfaces can.

7.10 MULTIPLE INHERITANCE

Let's revisit the tracking system for a university presented earlier in this chapter. The system contains records for students, faculty, and staff. Some parts of the system operate only on student records, others only on faculty records, and so on; some parts operate on the records for any type of person. As described so far, the system might be modeled with a type hierarchy like the one shown in the following diagram.

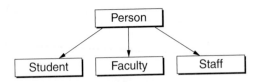

What happens when a student is also a staff member? We could create two records for the person—a student record and a staff record—but that could cause problems. Parts of the system dealing with person records might treat the staff record and the student record as two different people.

We need the ability to create a single record that sometimes can be treated as a student, sometimes as a person, and sometimes as a staff member. We can use interfaces to create such a record. Our university record system then might include the following interfaces.

```
//Person.java
interface Person {
  void setAge(int age);
  void setGender(char gender);
  void setName(String name);
  int getAge();
  char getGender();
  String getName();
}

//Student.java
interface Student extends Person {
  void setCollege(String college);
  void setGpa(double gpa);
  void setYear(byte year);
  String getCollege();
  double getGpa();
  byte getYear();
  static final byte FROSH = 1;
  static final byte SOPH = 2;
  static final byte JUNIOR = 3;
  static final byte SENIOR = 4;
}

//Staff.java
import java.util.Date;
interface Staff extends Person {
  void setSalary(double salary);
  void setStartDate(Date start);
  void setEndDate(Date end);
  void setSSN(String ssn);
  double getSalary();
  Date getStartDate();
  Date getEndDate();
  String getSSN();
}
```

An interface can extend another interface, and an interface can include static final data members. However, an interface can't include other types of data members. For this reason, the keywords `static` and `final` on the data member declarations in interface `Student` could be omitted, just as we omitted `public` and `abstract` from the methods in an interface. When we use interfaces, we don't inherit method implementations, only their specification. We can now create classes that implement these various interfaces. The following class can be used to store student employee records, something we couldn't do before.

```
import java.util.Date;
class StudentEmployee implements Student, Staff {
  // methods required by Person
  public void setAge(int age){...}
  public void setGender(char gender){...}
  public void setName(String name){...}
  public int getAge(){...}
  public char getGender(){...}
  public String getName(){...}
```

```
// methods required by Student
public void setCollege(String college){...}
public void setGpa(double gpa){...}
public void setYear(byte year){...}
public String getCollege(){...}
public double getGpa(){...}
public byte getYear(){...}

// methods required by Staff
public void setSalary(double salary){...}
public void setStartDate(Date start){...}
public void setEndDate(Date end){...}
public void setSSN(String ssn){...}
public double getSalary(){...}
public Date getStartDate(){...}
public Date getEndDate(){...}
public String getSSN(){...}
}
```

Of course, the method bodies must be filled in, but the preceding example clearly shows that multiple interfaces can be implemented. This approach is different from extending a class because only a single class can be extended. Some OOP languages permit multiple inheritance of classes, but various subtle complexities arise when code is inherited directly from several different classes. The developers of Java decided to avoid those complexities by not permitting multiple inheritance of classes. However, many of the programming problems that might otherwise be solved with multiple inheritance of classes can be solved by using Java's multiple inheritance of interfaces. Note that we are talking about multiple inheritance from more than one immediate superclass. But multiple inheritance means more than simply having multiple superclasses. For example, if Student extends Person and Person extends Object, that isn't multiple inheritance. Only when a class *directly* extends two or more classes is it called multiple inheritance, and only then do the problems that we've alluded to arise.

Instances of the class StudentEmployee can be passed to methods that expect as parameters any of StudentEmployee, Student, Staff, or Person. Although we've gained the ability to create classes that implement many different interfaces, we've given up some degree of code reuse. Hence, we need to provide implementations of methods such as setAge() in every class that implements the interface Person, directly or indirectly. The class StudentEmployee implements the Person interface indirectly because StudentEmployee implements Student and Student extends Person.

COMMON PROGRAMMING ERROR

You can use interfaces just like classes when declaring variables or formal parameters. The key difference is that you can't actually create an instance of an interface. For example, for the interface declarations in the preceding code, the following statement would generate a syntax error.

```
Staff staff = new Staff(); // illegal
```

But this statement is legal:

```
Staff staff = new StudentWorker();
```

Of course, you should make such an assignment only if you expect later to have staff refer to some object that isn't a StudentWorker. Otherwise, you should declare staff to be type StudentWorker.

7.11 INHERITANCE AND DESIGN

At one level, inheritance is a code-sharing technique. At another level it reflects an understanding of the problem; that is, it reflects relationships between parts of the problem space. Much of inheritance is the expression of an "is a" relationship between the superclass and derived classes. A student *is a* person. This relationship is the conceptual underpinning for making Person a superclass and allowing the behavior described by its public member functions to be interpretable on objects within its type hierarchy; in other words, subclasses derived from it share its interface.

There is no way to specify a completely optimal design. Design involves trade-offs between the various objectives that a programmer wants to achieve. For example, generality is frequently at odds with efficiency. Using a class hierarchy that expresses "is a" relationships increases our understanding of how to compartmentalize coding relationships and potentially introduces coding inefficiencies by having various layers of access to the (hidden) state description of an object. However, a reasonable "is a" decomposition can simplify the overall coding process. For example, a shape-drawing package need not anticipate the need for future additional shapes. Through inheritance, the class developer implements the superclass "shape" interface and provides code that implements operations such as "draw." What is primitive or held in common remains unchanged. Also unchanged is the client's use of the package.

An undue amount of decomposition imposes its own complexity and ends up being self-defeating. There is a granularity decision, where highly specialized classes don't provide enough benefit and are better folded into a larger concept.

Single inheritance (SI) conforms to a hierarchical decomposition of the key objects in the domain of discourse. Multiple inheritance (MI) is more troubling as a modeling or problem-solving concept. In MI we are saying that the new object is composed of several preexisting objects and is usefully thought of as a form of each. The term *mixin* is used to mean a class composed via MI, whereby each inherited class is orthogonal. Much of the time there is an alternate *"has a"* formulation. For example, is a vampire bat a mammal that happens to fly, a flying animal that happens to be a mammal, or both a flying animal and a mammal? Depending on the code available, developing a proper class for vampire bat might involve an MI derivation or an SI implementation with appropriate "has a" members. Interfaces in Java generally take the form of mixins providing "has a" relationships. In our example of the student employee, the interface `Staff` is essentially stating that a `Student-Employee` object *has a* social security number, salary, and start–end dates. `Staff` doesn't actually implement any of these fields. Nor are we inheriting any code from `Staff`. Instead, we are stating that some methods exist in any class that implements the interface.

7.12 THE OPERATOR `instanceof` AND CASTING NONPRIMITIVE TYPES

The operator `instanceof` can be applied to an object to determine its type. The operator returns a boolean value. An example is

```
if (x instanceof Shape)
  // x is a Shape, act accordingly
else
  // x is not a Shape, act accordingly
```

The `instanceof` operator is used when ordinary polymorphism with overridden methods is inappropriate. An example is

```
if (x instanceof Point)
  System.out.println("Point has no area" + x);
else
  System.out.println("Area is " + x.area());
```

Here we've two behaviors: a polymorphic behavior for shapes, which involves computing their area, and the special case of `point` not having an area calculation.

In Section 2.10.2, we showed how to use casting to convert one primitive type to another. We can use the same syntax for casting one reference type to another; the type can be any Java type. Recall that a cast is a type enclosed by parentheses. The following example shows how to cast a `Person` object to a `Student` object, provided that the object is in fact a `Student`. In this example `Student` is our original class `Student`, not the interface `Student`.

```
Person person = new Student();
...
if (person instanceof Student) {
  Student student = (Student)person;
  // code to operate on student object here
}
```

Not all casts are legal, and some illegal casts can be detected by the Java compiler. Other illegal casts are detected at run time, in which case a `ClassCastException` error will be reported. The following example is an illegal cast that will be detected at run time. In it we use the classes `Student` and `Person` from Section 7.1, not the interfaces `Student` and `Person`.

```
Person person = new Person();
Student student = (Student)person; // illegal
```

Because of this dynamic type checking, you can safely cast from a superclass to a subclass without violating the type safety of Java. That is, you can never treat an object as something it really isn't. Recall that an object of `TypeA` is also an object of `TypeB` when `TypeB` is any superclass of `TypeA`. In the preceding example, a `Student` object is also a `Person` object and an `Object` object.

By combining the operator `instanceof` and casting, we can operate on *generic containers* in a completely safe way. A generic container is a container, such as an array, that may contain different types of objects. You can use the operator `instanceof` to determine the type of the object stored in the container and then cast the object into the appropriate type. This choice is the proper one if you expect the object to be one of several different types and you can't use ordinary polymorphism with overridden methods. Alternatively, you can try to cast the object and then catch the exception, if there is one. (We discuss catching exceptions in Chapter 11.) This choice would be the appropriate one if most of the time you expected the object to be of one type, but on rare occasions other types are expected. We use the exception handling mechanism of Java to handle the exceptional case. As shown in the following example, you can create an array that contains both strings and numbers by using the classes `String` and `Integer`.

```java
// GenericArray.java - demonstrate generic array container
class GenericArray {
  public static void main(String[] args) {
    Object[] array = new Object[4];

    array[0] = "String 1";
    array[1] = new Integer(1);
    array[2] = "String 2";
    array[3] = new Integer(2);
    for (int i = 0; i < array.length; i++) {
      if (array[i] instanceof String) {
        String temp = (String)array[i];
        System.out.println("Processing string " + temp);
        // do something appropriate for strings
      }
      else if (array[i] instanceof Integer) {
        Integer temp = (Integer)array[i];
        System.out.println("Processing Integer " + temp);
        // do something appropriate for an Integer
      }
      else {
        System.out.println("Unexpected type " + array[i]);
        // do something to handle unexpected cases
      }
    } // end of for loop
  }
}
```

7.13 PROGRAMMING STYLE

Inheritance should be designed into software to maximize reuse and allow a natural modeling of a problem. With inheritance, the key elements of the OOP design methodology are as follows.

OOP DESIGN METHODOLOGY

1. Decide on an appropriate set of types.
2. Design in their relatedness and use inheritance to share code.
3. Use overridden methods to process related objects polymorphically.

When overriding methods in a subclass, you should have the subclass method call the associated superclass method, if appropriate. The same is true for subclass constructors. The rationale is that this procedure maintains a conceptual link between related pieces of code. Then, if the superclass method or constructor is changed, the subclass constructor or method is similarly updated.

```
//in Person
public String toString() {
  return ("Name: " + name +
    ", Age: " + age + ", Gender: " + gender);
}

//in Student
public String toString() {
  return(super.toString() + "\n   " +
    "College: " + college +
    ", GPA: " + gpa +
    ", Year: " + year);
}
```

Now, if a change is made to how `Person` is converted to a `String`, that change is propagated automatically to `Student`.

Summary

- Inheritance is the mechanism used to derive a new class from existing classes. That is, the existing classes can be added to or altered to create the subclass. Through inheritance, a hierarchy of related, code-sharing abstract data types (ADTs) can be created.
- A class can be derived from an existing class by using the keyword `extends`. The derived class is called a subclass. The class that it is derived from is called its superclass.
- The keywords `public`, `private`, and `protected` are available as accessibility modifiers for class members. A `public` member is accessible anywhere. A `private`

member is accessible from other methods within its own class. A `protected` member is accessible from methods within its package and within any class immediately derived from it. If no access keyword is used this is called package access. A member with package access is accessible from any class in the same package. By default, classes in the same directory are in the same, "unnamed" package.

- Constructors are never inherited. The default superclass constructor is called implicitly as the first statement in a constructor, unless an explicit superclass constructor is called. To call a superclass constructor other than the default, no-args constructor, use the keyword `super`. A subclass is a subtype of its superclass. An object of the subclass can in many ways be treated as if it were the superclass type. A variable of the superclass type can reference objects of the subclass type.

- Overriding is a mechanism to dynamically select at run time the appropriate method from among superclass and subclass methods. This ability to select dynamically a method appropriate to an object's type is a form of polymorphism.

- Inheritance provides for code reuse. A subclass inherits superclass code, and the subclass typically modifies and extends the superclass. Inheritance also creates a type hierarchy. It allows for run-time selection of overridden methods. Facilities that allow the implementation of ADTs, inheritance, and the ability to process objects dynamically are the essentials of object-oriented programming (OOP).

- An abstract method is one whose body is undefined. Such a method must be overridden in a subclass and given a concrete definition. In OOP terminology it is called a deferred method. A class that has abstract methods is an abstract class and must be declared as such. It is useful for the root class in a type hierarchy to be an abstract class. It defines the interface for its derived classes, but can't itself be used to create objects.

- Java provides the `interface` construct, which is similar to abstract classes. An interface can contain only abstract methods and static final fields. A class may implement multiple interfaces, in addition to extending one class.

Review Questions

1. Inheritance allows the programmer to _____code.
2. A reason to have private fields is _____.
3. An abstract method has a declaration but doesn't have _____.
4. Redefining the same method name in a given class is called over____. Redefining the same method name with the same signature in a subclass is called over_____.
5. An interface can have abstract methods but can't have _____.
6. A class can extend ____ class(es) and implement ____ interface(s).
7. The keyword `super` can be used in two different ways. Give an example of each. Why is it needed?
8. What is the principle of data hiding?
9. Discuss public, package, protected, and private access. Write a simple example that shows their differences.

10. `Object` provides an `equals()` method. In the following code what gets printed?

```
public class Review10 {
  public static void main(String[] args) {
    Integer m = new Integer(3), n = new Integer(3);
    System.out.println(m);
    System.out.println(m.equals(n)+ " : " + (m == n));
  }
}
```

11. For the following class definitions, what is printed when the method `main()` in class `Review11` is executed?

```
class ClassOne {
  public void print() {
    System.out.println( "ClassOne");
  }
}

class ClassTwo extends ClassOne {
  public void print() {
    System.out.println( "ClassTwo");
  }
}

class Review11 {
  public static void main(String[] args) {
    ClassOne one = new ClassOne();
    ClassTwo two;

    one.print();
    one = new ClassTwo();
    one.print();
    two = (ClassTwo)one;
    two.print();
  }
}
```

12. For the class definitions in the previous question, will the following code compile? If not, what error message results? If so, what does it print when executed?

```
class Review12 {
  public static void main(String[] args) {
    ClassOne one = new ClassOne();

    one.print();
    ClassTwo two = (ClassTwo)one;
    two.print();
  }
}
```

13. For the class definitions in Review Question 11, will the following two classes compile? If not, what error message results? If so, what does it print when executed?

```
class ClassThree extends ClassOne {
  public void print() {
    System.out.println( "ClassThree");
  }
}

class Review13 {
  public static void main(String[] args) {
    ClassThree three = new ClassThree();

    three.print();
    ClassTwo two = (ClassTwo)three;
    two.print();
  }
}
```

Exercises

1. Add a constructor to class `Person` in Section 7.1, on page 234, that allows all fields to be given initial values. Do the same for `Student`.

2. Derive a class from `Person` in Section 7.1, on page 234, that has fields appropriate to a staff member in a company. Call the class `Employee`.

3. Derive a class from `Student` in Section 7.1, on page 235, called `GradStudent`. Add members for the graduate student's department and thesis topic. Then write appropriate constructors. Include a `toString()` method.

4. Write a program with a method `reducedFare()` that takes one parameter of type `Person`. The method should return true if the age of the person is less than 12 or greater than 64. Test the method by calling it first with a `Person` object and then with a `Student` object, using the classes `Student` and `Person` in Section 7.1, on page 234. This exercise shows you the importance of inheritance and polymorphism in using related types.

5. If you've already studied arrays write a program that lexicographically sorts an array of students by their last name. You can recode `Student` to have a first name member and a last name member.

6. Modify the program in the previous exercise to break ties by using the first name when there is more than one person with the same last name.

7. Add a method `hours()` to class `Timer` in Section 7.7, on page 248, that returns the number of hours for a given value of a `Timer` object.

8. Create a class `Clock` that is derived from `Timer` and has a member `hours`. Override the methods of `Timer` to manipulate, access, and print out hours, minutes, and seconds.

9. Create a class `CountBy3` that extends `AbstractCounter` and counts by 3s.

10. Create a class `CountByN` that extends `AbstractCounter` to count by a designated value *n*. Let the user specify this value as part of the constructor.

11. Implement the class `Count` needed by the Predator–Prey simulation in this chapter.

12. Complete the definition of the class `World` in Section 7.8, on page 251, by writing the methods `toString()` and `eden()`. One way to compute the garden-of-eden position is to use a random number to pick the type of life form that goes in each cell.

13. Add a new life form to the Predator–Prey simulation.

14. Modify the method `computeNeighbors()` of the class `Living` to allow for updates of the border cells.

15. Complete the implementation of `PredatorPrey` by using the interface for `Living`, as described in Section 7.9, on page 257, instead of the abstract class `Living` in Section 7.8, on page 252. Use at least two different notions of neighborhood when implementing `countNeighbors()` in the various classes that implement `Living`.

16. Add a method `equals()` to the class `Counter` in Section 6.3, on page 200. This method should return true if the counters are set to the same value. Test your method and dynamic typing by using your new `Counter` class in the program `EqualsTest` in Section 7.5, on page 245.

17. Create a class `Point` with two coordinates. Include a method `lineLength()` that takes another `Point` as a parameter and returns the length of the line segment connecting the two points (the parameter and the implicit point upon which the method was called). Extend `Point` to create a class `ThreeDPoint` that also has a z coordinate. Overload the `lineLength()` method in `ThreeDPoint` to work with a `ThreeDPoint` parameter. Discuss the advantages and disadvantages of having `ThreeDPoint` extend `Point` versus having two independent classes.

CHAPTER

8

Graphical User Interfaces: Part I

The main program examples presented so far have obtained their input by reading keystrokes typed at the keyboard, and their output has been in the form of text, printed to the computer console. Most computer programs today, however, have a *graphical user interface* (GUI), which includes both a graphical output capability and a pointing device to allow the user to select items on the computer screen. Java contains a completely portable and reasonably easy to use graphical library. In early versions of Java, the collection of classes used for building graphical user interfaces was called the *abstract window toolkit* (AWT). It is still part of standard Java, but it has been expanded with a new collection of classes called *Swing*. This addition makes inclusion of a GUI in any Java program relatively easy.

The standard Java packages, `java.awt` and `javax.swing`, together contain a collection of classes that implement a wide assortment of GUI elements. Although we can build GUIs by using only components from `java.awt`, because of the added power and flexibility that comes with the components in `javax.swing`, we describe building GUIs with both AWT and Swing. Some examples of simple GUI elements are buttons, menus, and scrolling text windows. For some GUI elements, we can obtain the appearance and behavior we want by creating instances of standard Java classes. In other cases we need to create new components. Using inheritance (see Chapter 7) allows us to add our desired behavior to existing components.

The objects that make up a GUI built with Swing are called *components*. Some components are containers that can be used to group and arrange several components. Some examples of predefined components are `JButton`, `JLabel`, and

JCheckbox. The following screen shot shows the GUI for a sample Java program that uses two JLabel components, three JCheckBox components, and a JButton. All six of the components in this GUI are contained in a single JFrame, which forms the outline of the GUI.

Recall that one of the attractions of Java is that special Java programs called applets can be distributed across the Internet and run inside an Internet browser such as Netscape or Internet Explorer. Applets essentially always have a graphical user interface.

In this chapter we present the fundamental concepts used in building Java programs that include a GUI. At the end of the chapter we introduce Java applets. You may have already worked some with applets and Swing components in the optional exercises in earlier chapters. If you did any of those exercises, some of the material presented in this chapter will be a review for you.

8.1 "HELLO, WORLD!" BUTTON

Our first GUI example is the graphical equivalent of the traditional "Hello, world!" program (see Section 2.1, on page 15).

```
//HelloButton.java
import java.awt.*;
import javax.swing.*;

class HelloButton {
  public static void main(String[] args) {
    JFrame frame = new JFrame("HelloButton");
    Container pane = frame.getContentPane();
    JButton hello = new JButton("Hello, world!");
    pane.add(hello);
    frame.pack();
    frame.show();
  }
}
```

When run, this program creates a new window on your computer desktop titled HelloButton. Inside the window will be a button labeled "Hello, world!" If you click the button, its appearance changes to show the button being pushed in and then released. Nothing else will happen. It looks like this.

The window created for the GUI is too small to show the full title, `HelloButton`, which appears just as `He....` We didn't tell the program to do anything when you push the button. The only result that you see at the moment is the default behavior of an object of type `JButton`. Shortly, we show you how to get the button actually to do something. If you enlarge the window, you can see the full text of the title.

DISSECTION OF THE CLASS `HelloButton`

- ```
  import java.awt.*;
  import javax.swing.*;
  ```

The standard Java classes used so far have been from the package `java.lang`. This package is automatically imported into every Java program. Thus you can refer to the classes in the package without having to tell the Java compiler that you're doing so. For all other packages, whether standard Java packages or those you write yourself, you must use an import statement like the ones shown here to tell the Java compiler to look in the specified package for classes. You can either list the specific classes that you're using from the package or you can do as is done here and use an asterisk to indicate to the compiler that it can use any of the classes from the specified packages.

- ```
  JFrame frame = new JFrame("HelloButton");
  ```

Here we create a `JFrame` that corresponds to the window on the computer's desktop. The string `"HelloButton"` is used to title the window. The class `JFrame` is from the package `javax.swing`. The fully qualified name of the class is `javax.swing.JFrame`. Because we import `javax.swing.*`, we can just use the name `JFrame`. In future discussions, we will use the fully qualified name of a class when we first introduce it, so you will know which package it is from. In subsequent usage of the class, we will use only the simple class name.

- ```
  Container pane = frame.getContentPane();
  ```

A container is a component to which we can add other components. A `JFrame` is actually a container, but you shouldn't attempt to add components directly to a `JFrame`. Instead, you should add all components to a special container in the
  ```

JFrame. Use the method getContentPane() to get a reference to the JFrame's special container.

■ JButton hello = new JButton("Hello, world!");

Here we create a javax.swing.JButton object and give it a string that will be used as a label. The constructor for JButton takes a single parameter, which specifies the label for the JButton. Because of the import statement at the beginning of the program, we can just use the simple name JButton.

■ pane.add(hello);

The method add() in the class Container is used to add a component to the JFrame's content pane. This method is part of every container component. In this example we don't tell the container how to arrange the components in the container or where in the container this particular component should be displayed. We show how to do so later.

■ frame.pack();
  frame.show();

These two calls tell the JFrame to pack all the objects in the JFrame appropriately and then cause the window to show up on the screen. In this example there is only one visible component, the JButton, so the JFrame will adjust itself to be just large enough to hold the JButton.

The initially displayed window was too small. However, we can change its size by applying the method setSize() to the JFrame as follows.

```
//remove frame.pack() -- use
frame.setSize(300, 200);
```

This methods sets the horizontal length of the window to 300 pixels and the vertical length of the window to 200 pixels. Pixels are a standard unit for windowing and drawing components (see Section 8.5). The method pack() needs to be removed; otherwise, it will compress the window to the smallest size necessary to display the frame contents.

8.2 LISTENING TO EVENTS

If you run the program HelloButton, the program won't terminate, although main() has finished. You will need to use your computer's facility for aborting programs to end the program. What was going on?

Any program that uses Swing to create a window implicitly creates a separate thread of execution that enters into an infinite loop, looking for events such as mouse movement, button clicks, or key presses. It's like having two workers on the job, one following the instructions in `main()` and the methods it calls and the other watching for events and calling various methods to respond to those events. This type of program is called *event driven*. Hence, once `main()` has finished, all program behavior is in response to events.

All Swing components are *event sources* that can be observed or "listened to." In order to do something when an event is generated at some source, you need to tell the source which object to notify when the event occurs. To do so, use the method add*Something*`Listener()`, where *Something* is some event type. This event model is called a *delegation model*, wherein specific objects are delegated the responsibility of handling specific events.

By default, the `JButton` object in the preceding example responds to mouse clicks by changing its appearance. `JButton` objects are also the source of `java.awt.event.ActionEvent` objects. An `ActionEvent` is generated by a button whenever you click the button with the mouse.

PRESS, PRESS, PRESS . . .

In order to do something when an event is generated, you need to tell the source of the event—for example, the `JButton` in `HelloButton`—where to send the event. Objects that can receive events are called *listeners*. Different types of events have different types of listeners. Objects that generate `ActionEvents` contain the method `addActionListener()` that indicates which object or objects should receive the events. The `ActionEvent` listener must *implement* the `java.awt.event.ActionEventListener` *interface*. To implement an interface, a class must define all the methods specified in the interface. Thus a class that implements the `ActionEventListener` interface must contain an `actionPerformed()` method. (Recall our discussion of interfaces in Section 7.9. Although helpful, you don't have to read that section before proceeding with the remainder of this chapter.)

Whenever you generate an `ActionEvent` by clicking a button, the `action-Performed()` method for each `ActionEventListener` that was added to the button is called with the `ActionEvent` object as a parameter, as shown in the following diagram.

In the following program we show how to add a listener to our "Hello, world!" button.

```
//HelloGoodBye.java -
import java.awt.*;
import javax.swing.*;

class HelloGoodBye {
  public static void main(String[] args) {
    JFrame frame = new JFrame("HelloGoodBye");
    Container pane = frame.getContentPane();
    Button hello = new Button("Hello, world!");
    GoodBye listener = new GoodBye();

    hello.addActionListener(listener);
    pane.add(hello);
    frame.pack();
    frame.show();
  }
}
```

The class `HelloGoodBye` is almost the same as `HelloButton`; the only difference is the addition of two lines. First, we create an instance of the class `GoodBye`, which we use to listen for action events from the button. Then we add the listener as an action listener for the button, using

```
hello.addActionListener(listener);
```

We have called `addActionListener()` for the button, passing it a new `GoodBye` object. The missing piece is the class `GoodBye`, which we implement as

```
//GoodBye.java
import java.awt.event.*;

class GoodBye implements ActionListener  {
  public void actionPerformed(ActionEvent e) {
    System.out.println("Goodbye!");
    System.exit(0);
  }
}
```

DISSECTION OF THE CLASS GoodBye

- `import java.awt.event.*;`

We need to import an additional package, which contains the definition of the various event listener interfaces. Recall that interfaces are used to indicate that a class contains certain methods. In this example we use the interface `ActionListener` to indicate that `GoodBye` contains the method `actionPerformed()`.

- `class GoodBye implements ActionListener`

Here we indicate that the class `GoodBye` contains all methods specified in the interface `ActionListener`. That is, we say that the class `implements` the interface `ActionListener`.

▪
```
public void actionPerformed(ActionEvent e) {
  System.out.println("Goodbye!");
  System.exit(0);
}
```

This method is called when the button is clicked. It prints a message and then forces the program to exit. In this example, the method doesn't use the `ActionEvent` parameter passed to the method. We use this parameter in later examples.

To summarize, the following steps are needed to "listen" or respond to button presses.

1. Create a button with `new JButton("some label")`.
2. Get the `Container` for the `JFrame` using `getContentPane()`.
3. Add the button to the content pane of the `JFrame` with `add()`.
4. Create an `ActionEventListener` class by
   (a) adding `implements ActionEventListener` to the class declaration and
   (b) defining an `actionPerformed()` method.
5. Add the listener object to the list of listeners for the button by calling `button.addActionListener(listener)`, where `button` is a reference to the button created in step 1 and `listener` is a reference to an instance of the class created in step 4.

As we stated at the beginning of this section, programs that use Swing implicitly create a separate thread of execution, which enters an infinite loop. When that infinite loop detects a mouse click with the cursor over a `JButton`, a specific method in the `JButton` object is called. This method in turn generates the `ActionEvent` and calls the method `actionPerformed()` of any listeners that have been added to the `JButton`. The following pseudocode is for the hidden internal loop. This loop is activated as part of starting up any program that uses Swing components.

PSEUDOCODE FOR SWING EVENT LOOP

```
while(true)
  wait for next event;
  determine event type, call it T;
  determine GUI object where event occurred, call it O;
  call appropriate method in each T listener added to O;
end while loop
```

8.3 TEXT AND NUMERICAL INPUT

We demonstrated the response to a mouse click on a button, but what about reading in numbers or strings? `TextInput` is essentially the same as `HelloGoodBye`, except that it reads from a text field. Instead of a `JButton` object, we create a `javax.swing.JTextField` object. When you type into the text field and then hit Return while the cursor is in the text field, an action event will be generated. The resulting `ActionEvent` object is passed to the method `actionPerformed()` and can be used to determine what text is in the field. Here is the class `TextInput`.

```
//TextInput.java
import java.awt.*;
import javax.swing.*;

class TextInput {
  public static void main(String[] args) {
    JFrame frame = new JFrame("TextInput");
    Container pane = frame.getContentPane();
    JTextField input = new
        JTextField("Edit this text then hit <return>");
    Echo listener = new Echo();

    input.addActionListener(listener);
    pane.add(input);
    frame.pack();
    frame.show();
  }
}
```

You can create an empty text field by specifying the width of the field in characters, or you can specify some initial text, as in the preceding example. Here is what the initial display looks like.

You can use the mouse to select the text in the window and type your own message. For example, you could change the window to the following.

If you hit Return after editing the text, the message you typed would appear on the console as

```
os-prompt>java TextInput
Java programming is fun.
```

The action listener we use is called `Echo`.

```
//Echo.java
import javax.swing.*;
import java.awt.event.*;

class Echo implements ActionListener {
  public void actionPerformed(ActionEvent e) {
    JTextField source = (JTextField)e.getSource();
    String text = source.getText();
    System.out.println(text);
  }
}
```

The class `Echo` is similar to the listener class `GoodBye`. However, instead of exiting, we echo whatever is in the text field by using `println()`. The class `ActionEvent` has a method that can be used to find the source of the event. The method `getSource()` returns a generic reference that must be cast into a `JTextField`. (We discussed generic references and this type of casting in Section 7.12.) This operation is safe in that Java generates an exception if the reference isn't in fact referencing a `JTextField` object. In this case, it is always a `JTextField` because that's the only object to which we are listening. In more complicated programs we could use the operator `instanceof` (see Section 7.12) to determine the type of the object returned by `getSource()`.

Once we have a reference to the `JTextField` object, we can use its `getText()` method to retrieve the text. At this point, if we were expecting a number, we could use methods from the various numeric classes to parse the string into a number. For example, if we were expecting an integer, we could turn the variable `text` into an `int` with

```
int value = Integer.parseInt(text.trim());
```

As we discuss later in Section 10.3.2, we use the method `trim()` from class `String` to trim away any leading or trailing white space. We need to do so because `parseInt()` generates an exception if it gets any characters that aren't part of the integer, including white space.

Note that we have again created a program that never ends. You can combine the techniques from `Echo`, `GoodBye`, `HelloGoodBye`, and `TextInput` to create a program that accepts text or numeric input and then quits when a button is clicked. We leave that for you to do as an exercise.

COMMON PROGRAMMING ERROR

If you omit the cast in the method `actionPerformed()`,

```
JTextField source = e.getSource();
```

you get the syntax error message `Explicit cast is needed to convert a java.lang.Object to javax.swing.JTextField`. The method call `e.getSource()` returns an `Object`, which holds the value for the event source. It must be properly cast to the type `JTextField`.

8.4 USING SEVERAL COMPONENTS

Most GUIs have more than a single button to click or a single text field. As a result, we face two new questions: How do we arrange the GUI components when there is more than one? How do we respond to events from several different components?

To control the arrangement of GUI components, Java uses layout managers. A *layout manager* is an object that determines the location of components. One type of layout manager is implemented by the class java.awt.GridLayout. As the name implies, GridLayout arranges the components in a two-dimensional grid. We specify the number of rows and columns in the grid and then add the components, one at a time. Each new component is added into the next available cell in the grid.

In the following program we use a GridLayout to arrange the components of a minicalculator, which is capable of adding and subtracting two numbers. The program includes two buttons: one for adding and one for subtracting. The Action-Listener determines which button is clicked.

```
//MiniCalc.java - demo GridLayout
import java.awt.*;
import javax.swing.*;

class MiniCalc {
  public static void main(String[] args) {
    JFrame frame = new JFrame("MiniCalc");
    Container pane = frame.getContentPane();
    // create the major components
    JTextField firstNumber = new JTextField(20);
    JTextField secondNumber = new JTextField(20);
    JTextField result = new JTextField(20);
    JButton addButton = new JButton("Add");
    JButton subButton = new JButton("Subtract");
    // there will be 4 rows of 2 components each
    pane.setLayout(new GridLayout(4, 2));
    // add all of the components to the content pane
    pane.add(new JLabel("Enter a number"));
    pane.add(firstNumber);
    pane.add(new JLabel("Enter a number"));
    pane.add(secondNumber);
    pane.add(new JLabel("Result"));
    pane.add(result);
    pane.add(addButton);
    pane.add(subButton);
    // setup the listener, listening to the buttons
    DoMath listener =
        new DoMath(firstNumber, secondNumber, result);
    subButton.addActionListener(listener);
    addButton.addActionListener(listener);
    frame.pack();
    frame.show();
  }
}
```

The initial display looks like this.

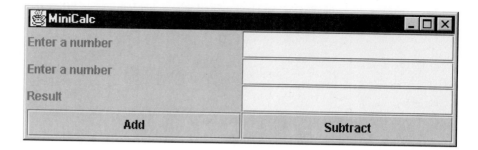

DISSECTION OF THE CLASS MiniCalc

- ```
  import java.awt.*;
  import javax.swing.*;

  class MiniCalc {
    public static void main(String[] args) {
      JFrame frame = new JFrame("MiniCalc");
      Container pane = frame.getContentPane();
  ```

This program begins like our other GUI examples so far. The imports are needed because we use `JFrame`, `JButton`, `JTextField`, and `JLabel` from the package `javax.swing` and `Container` from `java.awt`. We create a `JFrame`, which is the top-level window, and get the content pane to which we add the other GUI components.

- ```
  JTextField firstNumber = new JTextField(20);
  JTextField secondNumber = new JTextField(20);
  JTextField result = new JTextField(20);
  JButton addButton = new JButton("Add");
  JButton subButton = new JButton("Subtract");
  ```

Here we create the `JButton` and `JTextField` components that are to be part of the GUI. The `JTextField` components are wide enough to display 20 characters.

- ```
  pane.setLayout(new GridLayout(4, 2));
  ```

To have the content pane use a `GridLayout` manager, we must set the layout manager as shown. We discuss two other layout managers, `BorderLayout` and `Flow-Layout`, later.

- ```
  pane.add(new JLabel("Enter a number"));
  pane.add(firstNumber);
  pane.add(new JLabel("Enter a number"));
  pane.add(secondNumber);
  pane.add(new JLabel("Result"));
  pane.add(result);
  pane.add(addButton);
  pane.add(subButton);
  ```

We can now add the components to the grid. Instead of specifying a row and column number for each component, we simply add them one at a time. The components are added to the grid beginning in the upper left corner, filling the rows from left to right, and moving to the next row when a row is full. Each of the `JTextField` components is placed in a row with a `JLabel` component, which is text that serves as a label. We haven't bothered to save a reference to the `JLabel` components in local variables because we don't need to refer to the labels after we've added them to the GUI.

■
```
DoMath listener =
    new DoMath(firstNumber, secondNumber, result);
subButton.addActionListener(listener);
addButton.addActionListener(listener);
```

Here we create an instance of the class `DoMath`. The constructor for `DoMath` is passed the three text fields, which it needs in order to perform its task. The `DoMath` listener object is added as an `ActionListener` for both buttons.

■
```
frame.pack();
frame.show();
```

Now that we've added all the components to our GUI, we call `pack()`, which tells the `JFrame` to arrange the components according to the layout manager that we specified—in this case, a grid of four rows and two columns. Finally the `JFrame` is ready to be shown.

We have now shown one way to control the arrangement of multiple components—with a `GridLayout`. We use the class `DoMath` to show how an object can listen to multiple buttons and determine which button was clicked.

```java
//DoMath.java - respond to two different buttons
import javax.swing.*;
import java.awt.event.*;

class DoMath implements ActionListener {

  DoMath(JTextField first, JTextField second,
         JTextField result)
  {
    inputOne = first;
    inputTwo = second;
    output = result;
  }

  public void actionPerformed(ActionEvent e) {
    double first, second;
    first = Double.parseDouble(inputOne.getText().trim());
    second = Double.parseDouble(inputTwo.getText().trim());
    if (e.getActionCommand().equals("Add"))
      output.setText(String.valueOf(first + second));
    else
      output.setText(String.valueOf(first - second));
  }
```

```
        private JTextField inputOne, inputTwo, output;
}
```

DISSECTION OF THE CLASS DoMath

■
```
import javax.swing.*;
import java.awt.event.*;

class DoMath implements ActionListener
```

This class uses `JTextField` from `javax.swing` and `ActionListener` and `ActionEvent` from `java.awt.event`. As with the other listener classes that we've created, the class `DoMath` must implement the interface `ActionListener`.

■
```
DoMath(JTextField first, JTextField second,
        JTextField result)
{
  inputOne = first;
  inputTwo = second;
  output = result;
}
```

Previously, the listener classes have had no explicit constructors, relying on the default constructor. An instance of `DoMath` needs references to the three text fields in the GUI—two for input and one for output. Each is saved in a private instance variable.

■
```
public void actionPerformed(ActionEvent e) {
  double first, second;
  first = Double.parseDouble(inputOne.getText().trim());
  second = Double.parseDouble(inputTwo.getText().trim());
```

Regardless of which button is clicked, we need to get the text strings from each of the input text fields and convert those strings to numbers. Here we chose to convert them to primitive `double` values. The call `inputOne.getText()` returns the `String` object corresponding to the text typed into the `JTextField` component. We use the method `trim()` from the class `String` to eliminate any extraneous spaces a user may type before or after the number. This call isn't required, provided the user doesn't accidentally type any spaces in the text field. However, including it makes our program more robust, that is, less likely to generate an error when we could have given a normal response. The call `Double.parseDouble(...)` converts a `String` to a primitive `double` value.

■
```
if (e.getActionCommand().equals("Add"))
  output.setText(String.valueOf(first + second));
else // must be the "Subtract" button
  output.setText(String.valueOf(first - second));
```

The class `ActionEvent` defines the method `getActionCommand()`. When the event is generated by a button, this call returns the *action command string* associated with the button. By default, the action command string is the same as the label on the button. The action command string can be different from the label, if the method `setCommandString()`, which is defined for the class `JButton`, is called. By testing the command string, we can determine which button was clicked. Once we know which button was clicked, we perform the appropriate operation and call `output.setText()` to set the text string displayed in the output text field. The call `String.valueOf()` is used to convert the `double` value to a `String`, as required by `setText()`.

■ `private JTextField inputOne, inputTwo, output;`

Here we declare the private data members of the class that are initialized in the constructor.

8.5 DRAWING WITH SWING

We have shown how to create an application that uses a GUI containing label, button, and text field components. We have also shown how to respond to button press events and events generated when Return is hit in a text field. In addition to displaying and receiving text, GUI components are also available for displaying arbitrary images. Drawing in Java is always done on an instance of the class `Graphics`. We demonstrate shortly how to obtain an object on which to draw.

Java uses a coordinate system that places the origin, (0, 0), in the upper left corner of the window, with positive displacements being down and to the right. You draw rectangles by specifying the coordinates of the upper left corner of the rectangle and the rectangle's width and height. All values are in units of pixels. A *pixel*, short for picture element, is one dot on your computer's screen. For a black and white image, each pixel requires only one bit of storage: 0 for white and 1 for black. When you use more bits, each pixel can represent shades of gray or different colors. Eight or 16 bits per pixel, allowing for 256 or 65,536 (64K) colors, are common today.

In the following figure, the outer rectangle represents the border of the drawing window. Given a `java.awt.Graphics` object g, you would draw the inner rectangle with the call `g.drawRect(50, 20, 100, 40)`. It is 50 pixels in from the left edge, 20 pixels down from the top, 100 pixels wide, and 40 pixels high. The left (50) plus the width (100) gives the first coordinate of the lower right corner (150). Similarly the top (20) plus the height (40) gives the second coordinate of the lower right corner (60).

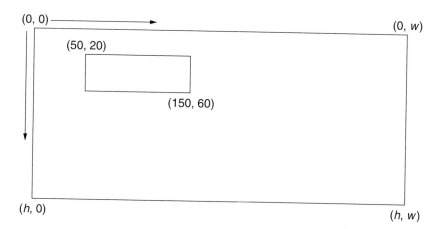

The class `Graphics` includes methods for drawing arcs, lines, ovals, and polygons. All but lines can be drawn in outline or filled in. You can also change the color, draw text strings, change the font used for text strings, and perform several other drawing-related operations.

Drawing is normally done by *extending* the class `JComponent`. As discussed in Chapter 7, you extend an existing class by adding additional methods to the original class or by overriding some of the methods that exist in the original class. Once you've created a class that extends `JComponent`, you simply add an instance of that class to a GUI. The class `Star` draws a starburst. The following simple program displays the starburst in a `JFrame`.

```
//StarTest.java - display a starburst
import java.awt.*;
import javax.swing.*;
class StarTest {
  public static void main(String[] args) {
    JFrame frame = new JFrame("StarTest");
    Container pane = frame.getContentPane();
    Star star = new Star();

    pane.add(star);
    frame.pack();
    frame.show();
  }
}
```

The preceding program is similar to others that we've already presented. The only difference is that we add an instance of the class `Star` to the content pane instead of a `JButton` or other standard Java component. The class `Star` is as follows.

```
//Star.java - draws a starburst
import java.awt.*;
import javax.swing.*;

class Star extends JComponent {
  public void paint(Graphics g) {
    double x1, x2, y1, y2;
    for (double angle = 0; angle < Math.PI;
        angle = angle + Math.PI / 16) {
      // compute coordinates of endpoints of a line
      // cosine and sine range from -1 to 1
      // multiplying by RADIUS gives changes the
      // range to be from -RADIUS to RADIUS
      // adding RADIUS gives the final range of
      // 0 to 2 * RADIUS
      x1 = Math.cos(angle) * RADIUS + RADIUS;
      y1 = Math.sin(angle) * RADIUS + RADIUS;
      x2 = Math.cos(angle + Math.PI) * RADIUS +RADIUS;
      y2 = Math.sin(angle + Math.PI) * RADIUS +RADIUS;
      g.drawLine((int)x1, (int)y1, (int)x2, (int)y2);
    }
  }

  // make the JComponent big enough to show the image
  public Dimension getMinimumSize() {
    return new Dimension(2 * RADIUS, 2 * RADIUS);
  }

  public Dimension getPreferredSize() {
    return new Dimension(2 * RADIUS, 2 * RADIUS);
  }

  private static final int RADIUS = 100;
}
```

The output of this program is

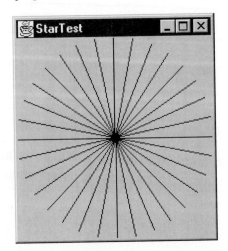

DISSECTION OF THE CLASS Star

- ```
  import java.awt.*;
  ```

  ```
  class Star extends JComponent
  ```

The class `JComponent` is a standard Java component. By extending it, we create a class that already includes all the methods defined for `JComponent`. This includes the methods required of every GUI component.

- ```
  public void paint(Graphics g)
  ```

The main thing we need to do in our extension of `JComponent` is redefine the method `paint()`, which is where we issue any desired drawing commands. This method is called indirectly in response to the call to `show()` for the `JFrame` that will eventually contain this `Star` object. Note that `paint()` is passed a reference to a `Graphics` object. As mentioned earlier, the class `Graphics` actually implements the various drawing methods. In this example we use only one method from `Graphics`, the method `drawLine()`. The `Graphics` object passed to `paint()` is part of the `JComponent` that we are extending. In fact all components have a `Graphics` object stored internally as a private field. The `Graphics` object itself isn't a component, and therefore it can't be added to a GUI or displayed. The `Graphics` object is part of the `JComponent`, like the `String` object representing a name might be part of a `Student` object or like the `String` that is part of a `JButton` object. In the case of a `String`, the value is a collection of characters. In the case of a `Graphics`, the value is a collection of pixel values and various other parameters that we discuss later. The methods defined for `Graphics` allow us to modify those pixel values.

- ```
  for (double angle = 0; angle < Math.PI;
          angle = angle + Math.PI / 16) {
      // compute coordinates of endpoints of a line
      // cosine and sine range from -1 to 1
      // multiplying by RADIUS gives -RADIUS to RADIUS
      // adding RADIUS gives the final range of
      // 0 to 2 * RADIUS
      x1 = Math.cos(angle) * RADIUS + RADIUS;
      y1 = Math.sin(angle) * RADIUS + RADIUS;
      x2 = Math.cos(angle + Math.PI) * RADIUS + RADIUS;
      y2 = Math.sin(angle + Math.PI) * RADIUS + RADIUS;
      g.drawLine((int)x1, (int)y1, (int)x2, (int)y2);
  }
  ```

You don't need to understand the mathematics in this example. The main thing to note is that there is a loop and that each iteration of the loop draws one line. The `angle` of the line drawn is changed with each iteration, resulting in the starburst of lines shown in the output. The calls to `Math.cos()` and `Math.sin()` compute values that correspond to two points on opposite sides of a circle with radius one and centered at the origin, (0, 0). The multiplication by `RADIUS` expands the lines to be
  ```

2 * RADIUS long instead of length 2. The addition of RADIUS is used to translate the lines so that the center of the imaginary circle is moved to the point (RADIUS, RADIUS). The angle is in radians and is the angle of the diagonal of the circle produced by connecting the two points. The method drawLine() takes four parameters: the *x* and *y* coordinates of the first point and the *x* and *y* coordinates of the second point, in that order. The parameters to drawLine() must be integers, so we use an explicit cast to convert the double values to int.

```
public Dimension getMinimumSize() {
    return new Dimension(2 * RADIUS, 2 * RADIUS);
}
public Dimension getPreferredSize() {
    return new Dimension(2 * RADIUS, 2 * RADIUS);
}
```

When the method pack() for a JFrame is called, for each component the layout manager of the content pane will call one of the methods getMinimumSize() or getPreferredSize(). The choice of which to call depends on the layout manager and other factors. The value returned by this method call is used to adjust the size and placement of the component. The class JComponent includes definitions of these methods, but by default they simply return a Dimension value that is height equals 0 and width equals 0. Here we redefine those methods so that the layout manager will provide enough area for our entire starburst image to show. The class Dimension is a standard Java class that simply encapsulates two integers, treated as the width and height.

COMMON PROGRAMMING ERROR

In drawing applications you can easily get the dimensions wrong. If the size of the frame displayed on your screen is too small, important drawing details may be lost. In the preceding application, see what happens when the methods get-MinimumSize() and getPreferredSize() are omitted. The resulting window won't be large enough to display the star. You can use the mouse to enlarge the window so that the star will be displayed in full.

8.6 THE LAYOUT MANAGER FlowLayout

The layout manager GridLayout used by the class MiniCalc earlier is fine if all the components are to be the same size. If the components need to be different sizes, a different layout manager must be used. Several different layout managers are standard classes in Java. The default layout manager for the content pane of a `JFrame` is called `BorderLayout`. We discuss the class `BorderLayout` in Section 9.1.1.

One of the simplest layout managers is `java.awt.FlowLayout`. It lays out the components in rows like lines of text, putting as many components as will fit in a single row. The rows of components can be aligned left, right, or center, just like lines of text. If the window is resized, the rows are adjusted accordingly.

The following example uses a `FlowLayout` manager. The code shows the alignment being set to center when the `FlowLayout` is constructed.

```
//FlowLayoutTest.java
import java.awt.*;
import javax.swing.*;

class FlowLayoutTest {
  public static void main(String[] args) {
    JFrame frame = new JFrame("FlowLayout.CENTER");
    Container pane = frame.getContentPane();

    pane.setLayout(new FlowLayout(FlowLayout.CENTER));
    pane.add(new JButton("Button 1"));
    pane.add(new JLabel("Label 2"));
    pane.add(new JButton("Button 3"));
    pane.add(new JLabel("Label Four (4)"));
    pane.add(new JButton("Button 5"));
    frame.pack();
    frame.show();
  }
}
```

The following screen shot shows the output of the program. When initially drawn, the window was just big enough to contain all the buttons and labels on one row, as in

To show the flow of buttons, we made the window narrower. We used our normal desktop windowing facility to adjust the size of the window to get

If we change `FlowLayout.CENTER` to `FlowLayout.LEFT` and again make the window narrower after the program starts, we get

If instead we change `FlowLayout.CENTER` to `FlowLayout.RIGHT` and again make the window narrower after the program starts, we get

Note that, unlike the arrangement with `GridLayout`, the components aren't all the same width, and they don't form nice columns.

Using a `FlowLayout`, we can add a Quit button to our starburst drawing program as in

```
//StarTestQuit.java - added a quit button to StarTest
import java.awt.*;
import javax.swing.*;
class StarTestQuit {
  public static void main(String[] args) {
    JFrame frame = new JFrame("StarTest");
    Container pane = frame.getContentPane();
    Star star = new Star();
    //Changes from StarTest are below here
    JButton quit = new JButton("Quit");
    pane.setLayout(new FlowLayout());
    quit.addActionListener(new GoodBye());
    pane.add(quit);
    //Changes from StarTest are above here
    pane.add(star);
    frame.pack();
    frame.show();
  }
}
```

This program uses the class `GoodBye` discussed earlier. The changes from the earlier class `StarTest` are the lines that create the button, change the layout, add the listener to the button, and add the button to the content pane. The following screen shot shows the output of the program. Clicking the Quit button causes the program to exit normally.

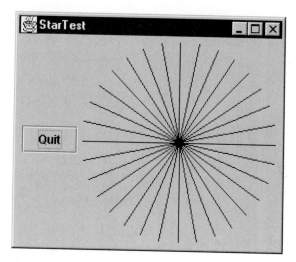

8.7 A SIMPLE DRAWING PROGRAM

One of the earliest applications of a graphical user interface with a mouse involved using the mouse to draw on the screen. The following program allows us to draw on the screen by holding down the mouse button and "painting with the mouse." The program consists of three classes: The class `SimplePaint` contains `main()`, creates the `JFrame`, and adds the drawing component to the frame; the class `Drawing-Canvas` extends `JComponent`; and the class `PaintListener` responds to mouse motion and draws on the canvas.

First, let's consider the code for the class `SimplePaint`.

```java
//SimplePaint.java - a program to draw with the mouse
import java.awt.*;
import javax.swing.*;

class SimplePaint {
  public static void main(String[] args) {
    JFrame frame = new JFrame("SimplePaint");
    Container pane = frame.getContentPane();
    DrawingCanvas canvas = new DrawingCanvas();
    PaintListener listener = new PaintListener();
    canvas.addMouseMotionListener(listener);
    pane.add(canvas);
    frame.pack();
    frame.show();
  }
}
```

The class `SimplePaint` doesn't need much explanation. It's nearly identical to previous examples that created a `JFrame`. The main difference is that the listener this time is a `java.awt.event.MouseMotionListener`, so we use the method `addMouseMotionListener()` instead of `addActionListener()`. We discuss shortly the interface `MouseMotionListener` in the dissection of `PaintListener`.

Next, let's consider the code for the class `DrawingCanvas`.

```java
// DrawingCanvas.java - a blank Canvas
import java.awt.*;
import javax.swing.*;

class DrawingCanvas extends JComponent {
  public Dimension getMinimumSize() {
    return new Dimension(SIZE, SIZE);
  }
  public Dimension getPreferredSize() {
    return new Dimension(SIZE, SIZE);
  }
  private static final int SIZE = 500;
}
```

The only thing we need to do in `DrawingCanvas` is to define the methods used to determine the size of the `DrawingCanvas`. There isn't even a `paint()` method, so all the work of this program is done in `PaintListener`.

Finally, let's consider the code for the class `PaintListener`.

```java
//PaintListener.java - do the actual drawing
import java.awt.*;
import java.awt.event.*;

public class PaintListener implements MouseMotionListener {
  public void mouseDragged(MouseEvent e) {
    DrawingCanvas canvas = (DrawingCanvas)e.getSource();
    Graphics g = canvas.getGraphics();
    g.fillOval(e.getX() - radius, e.getY() - radius,
               diameter, diameter);
  }
  public void mouseMoved(MouseEvent e){}
  private int radius = 3;
  private int diameter = radius * 2;
}
```

The following screen shot shows the output of one run of the program `Simple-Paint`. We used our computer's desktop facilities to reduce the size of the window to save space. When initially displayed, the window was as tall as it is wide.

DISSECTION OF THE CLASS PaintListener

- ```
  import java.awt.*;
  import java.awt.event.*;

  public class PaintListener implements MouseMotionListener
  ```

This class is similar to the other listener classes that we've created. However, it implements a different type of listener—a `MouseMotionListener`. The `Action-Listeners` that we created were required to define the method `actionPer-formed()`. That method was called when the button was clicked or Return was hit in the text field. A `MouseMotionListener` must define two methods: `mouse-Moved()` and `mouseDragged()`. The method `mouseMoved()` is called when the mouse is moved without a button being pressed. The method `mouseDragged()` is called when the mouse is moved while a button is being held down.

- ```
  public void mouseDragged(MouseEvent e) {
      DrawingCanvas canvas = (DrawingCanvas)e.getSource();
  ```

Each time the mouse is moved—while positioned over the component that this listener is listening to—`mouseDragged()` is called. Each change in position detected by the system generates another call to `mouseDragged()`. In other words, a single stroke of dragging the mouse across the screen can result in many calls to `mouse-Dragged()`. Each call is passed a `MouseEvent` object that contains, among other things, a reference to the component that generated the event and the coordinates of the mouse at the time the event was generated. The call `e.getSource()` returns a generic reference to the component that generated the event. In general, the event could have come from any component, not just a `DrawingCanvas`. Here we explicitly cast the reference to a reference to a `DrawingCanvas` object.

■   `Graphics g = canvas.getGraphics();`

We can use the reference `canvas` to the `DrawingCanvas` object to obtain a reference to the `Graphics` object contained in the canvas. This `Graphics` object is analogous to the `Graphics` object that was passed to the method `paint()` in the class `Star`, which we discussed earlier. Although not explicitly defined in our class `DrawingCanvas`—because it extends `JComponent`—`DrawingCanvas` automatically includes the method `getGraphics()`, inherited from `JComponent`.

■   `g.fillOval(e.getX() - radius, e.getY() - radius,`
                        `diameter, diameter);`

The `MouseEvent` parameter `e` contains the x and y coordinates of where the mouse was when the event was generated. We use `getX()` and `getY()` to obtain those coordinates and then draw a small circle, of diameter 6, centered on those coordinates. To draw a circle we use the method `fillOval()`, which needs four `int` parameters. The first two specify the coordinates of the upper left corner of a rectangle. The last two specify the width and height of the rectangle. The oval is inscribed in the rectangle. By specifying the width and height to be equal, we get a circle. If the center of the circle is at (x, y), then the upper left corner of the bounding box will be at $(x\ radius, y\ radius)$.

■   `public void mouseMoved(MouseEvent e){}`

Although we're not interested in doing anything when the mouse is moved with the button up, a `MouseMotionListener` is still required to provide a definition of the method `mouseMoved()`. As shown here, the method does nothing.

■   `private int radius = 3;`
    `private int diameter = radius * 2;`

To make the code more self-documenting and to make changing the size of the circle drawn easier, we capture the size of the circle in these two variables.

A problem with the paint program just described occurs when a portion of the drawing surface is obscured by another window and then is brought back to the front. Any drawing done in the obscured area is lost; that portion of the window will be blank.

If we want to be able to restore the obscured portion of the canvas, we need somehow to remember all the previous drawing operations. One approach would be to save all the coordinates of the points used for drawing the small circles. For example, we could save them in an array. Then we could add a `paint()` method to `DrawingCanvas` that would redraw all the circles, using the saved coordinates from the array. An alternative is to create an offscreen image of what was drawn. Then we could add a method `paint()` to `DrawingCanvas` that transfers this offscreen image to the screen. Java provides direct support for the latter approach, and we demonstrate it in the following program. This program is almost the same as the `SimplePaint` program. It consists of three classes: `SimplePaint2`, `DrawingCanvas2`, and `PaintListener2`. The class `SimplePaint2` is nearly identical to `SimplePaint`. The only difference is that the identifiers `Drawing-Canvas` and `PaintListener` have been changed to `DrawingCanvas2` and `PaintListener2`, so we don't include it here.

The class `DrawingCanvas2` is as follows.

```java
//DrawingCanvas2.java - remember drawing operations
// using an offscreen image
import java.awt.*;
import javax.swing.*;

class DrawingCanvas2 extends JComponent {
  // transfer the offscreen image to the screen
  public void paint(Graphics g) {
    if (offscreenImage != null)
      g.drawImage(offscreenImage, 0, 0, SIZE, SIZE, null);
  }

  // return the offscreen image, if one doesn't exist
  // create one
  public Image getOffscreenImage() {
    if (offscreenImage == null)
      offscreenImage = createImage(SIZE, SIZE);
    return offscreenImage;
  }

  public Dimension getMinimumSize() {
    return new Dimension(SIZE, SIZE);
  }

  public Dimension getPreferredSize() {
    return new Dimension(SIZE, SIZE);
  }

  private static final int SIZE = 500;
  private Image offscreenImage;
}
```

DISSECTION OF THE CLASS `DrawingCanvas2`

■
```java
import java.awt.*;

class DrawingCanvas2 extends JComponent {
  // transfer the offscreen image to the screen
  public void paint(Graphics g) {
    if (offscreenImage != null)
      g.drawImage(offscreenImage, 0, 0, SIZE, SIZE, null);
  }
```

If anything has been drawn, an `offscreenImage` has been created. The method `paint()` calls `g.drawImage()` to transfer the offscreen memory image to the computer's screen. The first parameter for `drawImage()` is a reference to the offscreen image. The next two are the coordinates where the upper left corner of the image should be placed on the canvas. We are filling the entire canvas, so we place the upper left corner of the image at the upper left corner of the canvas, or (0, 0). The next two parameters are the width and height of the image as it will appear in the canvas—in this case the width and height of the canvas. Another time we might choose to stretch or shrink the image to fit a smaller rectangular area of the screen. We can do so by simply adjusting the width and height parameters in the call to `drawImage()`. The entire image is always drawn but is adjusted to fit the rectangle by either stretching or shrinking either or both the width and height.

- ```
  public Image getOffscreenImage() {
     if (offscreenImage == null)
       offscreenImage = createImage(SIZE, SIZE);
     return offscreenImage;
  }
  ```

This method is used by the listener to get a reference to the offscreen image. The listener needs a reference to the image so that it can draw on the image. The first time that `getOffscreenImage()` is called, the offscreen image is created by calling `createImage()`. The method `createImage()` is implicitly defined for `DrawingCanvas2` because it extends `JComponent` and `createImage()` is already defined in `JComponent`. This method is used to create an offscreen image suitable for transfer to a `JComponent`. We placed `createImage()` here instead of in the `DrawingCanvas2` constructor because, at the time the constructor is called, the `JComponent` may not yet be ready to create an offscreen image. Once the `JComponent` has been displayed on the screen as a result of the call to `show()` in `SimplePaint2`, the `JComponent` is ready to create an image. Calling `createImage()` in the constructor for `DrawingCanvas2` simply returns `null`.

- ```
  public Dimension getMinimumSize()
     . . .
  private Image offscreenImage;
  ```

The remainder of `DrawingCanvas2` is the same as `DrawingCanvas`, with the addition of the private instance variable `offscreenImage`.

The class `PaintListener2` is as follows.

```
// PaintListener2.java - paints on an DrawingCanvas2,
// and its associated offscreen image.
import java.awt.*;
import java.awt.event.*;

public class PaintListener2 implements
    MouseMotionListener
{
```

```
public void mouseDragged(MouseEvent e) {
  DrawingCanvas2 canvas = (DrawingCanvas2)e.getSource();
  Graphics g = canvas.getGraphics();
  g.fillOval(e.getX() - radius, e.getY() - radius,
          diameter, diameter);
  // duplicate the drawing on the offscreen image
  Image image = canvas.getOffscreenImage();
  g = image.getGraphics();
  g.fillOval(e.getX() - radius, e.getY() - radius,
          diameter, diameter);
}

public void mouseMoved(MouseEvent e){}

protected int radius = 3;
protected int diameter = radius * 2;

}
```

DISSECTION OF THE CLASS PaintListener2

- ```
  // PaintListener2.java - paints on an DrawingCanvas2,
  // and it's associated offscreen image.
  ...
      Graphics g = canvas.getGraphics();
      g.fillOval(e.getX() - radius,  e.getY() - radius,
              diameter, diameter);
  ```

The first part of PaintListener2 is the same as the first part of PaintListener, except for the name change. The last two lines of this first part draw directly on the DrawingCanvas2 object, which go directly to the screen.

- ```
  Image image = canvas.getOffscreenImage();
  g = image.getGraphics();
  g.fillOval(e.getX() - radius, e.getY() - radius,
          diameter, diameter);
  ```

After drawing directly on the screen, we duplicate the drawing operation, this time drawing on the offscreen image. An Image object can't be added to a GUI; it is simply a representation of an image in the computer's memory. The Image object contains a Graphics object for the actual drawing, in the same way that the DrawingCanvas object contains a Graphics object for drawing on the screen. Once we have a reference to the proper Graphics object, the drawing call is the same as before.

- ```
  protected int radius = 3;
  protected int diameter = radius * 2;
  ```

In anticipation of extending PaintListener2 to add additional features (see Section 9.6, on page 328), we changed the access modifier on these two instance variables to be protected. Thus any class that extends PaintListener2 will have
  ```

access to these fields. We use this approach to add the ability to change the size of
the circle drawn with each stroke of the virtual pen.

8.8   APPLETS

One of the attractions of Java is that a special type of Java program, called an *applet*,
can be embedded in an HTML document. Recall that HTML is the notation used for
creating documents for display in an Internet browser. Recall also that the name *applet*
is derived from *application*, suggesting a "little application." Although applets can be
relatively small programs, there is no practical limitation on their size.

We place an applet in an HTML document by using an *applet tag*. Then when a
browser displays the page containing that tag, the compiled applet is downloaded
onto the computer where the browser is running and executed there. The output is
displayed in the browser. The following simple HTML file contains an applet tag for
the `MiniCalcApplet` discussed later in this section.

```
<html>
<body>
Below is the beginning of an applet calculator. This calculator
can be used only for addition and subtraction. You enter a
number in each of the first two fields and then click either
"Add" or "Subtract". You can continue to change the values in
the first two fields. Whenever you want the new sum or
difference computed, just click the appropriate button.
<p>
<center>
<applet code="MiniCalcApplet.class" width=200 height=100>
</applet>
<p>
MiniCalcApplet
</center>
</body>
</html>
```

Although the details of HTML are beyond the scope of this book, we provide a
brief dissection of this small HTML file.

DISSECTION OF THE FILE *minicalcapplet.html*

■   ```
<html>
<body>
```

These are two examples of HTML tags, all of which are set off with angle brackets.
Most tags come in pairs with a beginning tag, such as <body>, and an ending tag,
```

such as `</body>`. Although not strictly required, all HTML files should begin with an `<html>` tag, indicating that the file is in fact an HTML file. An HTML file can have several parts, but in this file there is only one major part: the body.

- ```
  Below is ...
  <p>
  ```

We place text in the HTML file by simply entering the text. To indicate a new paragraph we can use the paragraph tag, `<p>`. Unlike most tags, the paragraph tag doesn't need a matching `</p>` tag.

- ```
  <center>
  ...
  </center>
  ```

This pair of tags surrounds a section of the document, indicating that the browser should attempt to center the section horizontally on the page.

- ```
  <applet code="MiniCalcApplet.class" width=200 height=100>
  ```

This part of the file is the only part that you really need to understand for the time being. The beginning applet tag `<applet>` contains three named parameters: `code`, `width`, and `height`. All three of them are required, and each is assigned a value. As their names imply, they specify the name of the file that contains the applet code and the width and height of the screen area needed by the applet. In order to work correctly as specified here, the file *MiniCalcApplet.class* must be in the same directory as the file *MiniCalcApplet.html*. Then, when a browser fetches and displays *MiniCalcApplet.html*, the browser will know to go back to the same place and look for the applet file *MiniCalcApplet.class* and execute the program it contains. Because this tag is between the centering tags, the applet will appear centered in the browser window.

- ```
  <p>
  MiniCalcApplet
  ```

We place a caption under the applet by starting a new paragraph and then entering the text of the caption. This material is still between the centering tags, so this line is also centered horizontally.

- ```
  </center>
  </body>
  </html>
  ```

These tags are like closing parentheses. They mark the end of the centered section, the body of the document, and the entire document, respectively.
  ```

The following screen shot shows the file *MiniCalcApplet.html* being viewed with the HotJava browser.

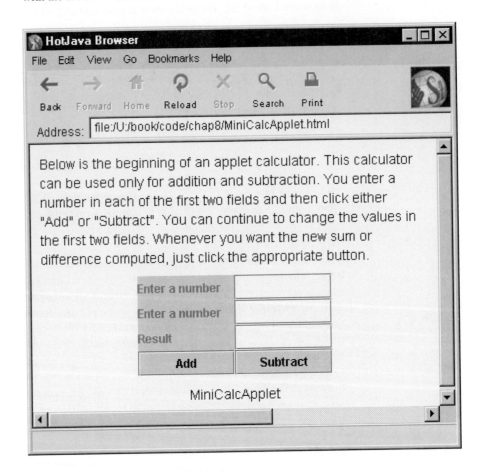

An *applet* is a Java class that extends either the class `java.applet.Applet` or the class `javax.swing.JApplet`. Because we are interested in using Swing components, we extend `JApplet`. Unlike conventional Java applications, applets don't have a `main()` method. Instead, an applet contains several methods that are called at appropriate times by the Internet browser that is viewing the HTML document with the embedded applet and hence executing the applet.

The applet method `init()` is probably the closest thing to `main()` in an application. The `init()` method is called after the applet object has been constructed but before any other applet methods are called. Many operations that we might be tempted to place in a constructor for an applet belong in `init()` instead. We want to invoke operations of an applet in our method `init()` that can't be invoked until the applet has been fully constructed and possibly manipulated by the browser.

An applet is like a `JFrame` in that it has a content pane that can contain Swing components such as buttons and text fields. The following code is our `MiniCalc` application, redone as an applet.

```
// MiniCalcApplet.java
/* <applet code="MiniCalcApplet.class"
     width=200 height=100></applet> */
import javax.swing.*;
import java.awt.*;

public class MiniCalcApplet extends JApplet {
  public void init() {
    Container pane = getContentPane();
    // create the major components
    JTextField firstNumber = new JTextField(20);
    JTextField secondNumber = new JTextField(20);
    JTextField result = new JTextField(20);
    JButton addButton = new JButton("Add");
    JButton subButton = new JButton("Subtract");

    // there will be 4 rows of 2 components each
    pane.setLayout(new GridLayout(4, 2));
    // add all of the components to the content pane
    pane.add(new JLabel("Enter a number"));
    pane.add(firstNumber);
    pane.add(new JLabel("Enter a number"));
    pane.add(secondNumber);
    pane.add(new JLabel("Result"));
    pane.add(result);
    pane.add(addButton);
    pane.add(subButton);
    // setup the listener, listening to the buttons
    DoMath listener =
        new DoMath(firstNumber, secondNumber, result);
    subButton.addActionListener(listener);
    addButton.addActionListener(listener);
  }
}
```

DISSECTION OF THE CLASS `MiniCalcApplet`

- ```
  /* <applet code="MiniCalcApplet.class"
       width=200 height=100></applet> */
  ```

This comment contains an HTML applet tag suitable for displaying a `MiniCalcApplet`. Placing the applet tag in a comment at the beginning of the Java source file for the applet serves two purposes: First, it documents, with the applet source, appropriate values for the applet tag parameters; and second, as an aid in program development, the *appletviewer* program can be used to view applets outside a standard browser. The program *appletviewer* can be passed the name of any text file
  ```

containing an applet tag, and it will attempt to display the applet. Thus, on systems wherein Java programs are run from a command line, such as Unix and Windows, the following command can be used to execute this applet.

```
appletviewer MiniCalcApplet.java
```

Note that the source file `MiniCalcApplet.java`—not the compiled file `MiniCalcApplet.class`—is given to *appletviewer*. We still have to compile the program before attempting to run it. We eventually want to create an HTML file, such as the one just dissected, *MiniCalcApplet.html*, containing the applet tag for viewing with a Web browser. If we had already created the HTML file, we could also use it with *appletviewer* as in

```
appletviewer MiniCalcApplet.html
```

The program *appletviewer* won't display the entire HTML document—only the applet portion.

■
```
import javax.swing.*;
import java.awt.*;
```

As with other Swing-based programs, we must import `javax.swing.*` and `java.awt.*`.

■
```
public class MiniCalcApplet extends JApplet
```

In our earlier Swing examples we often extended the class `JComponent`. Similarly, we can extend the class `JApplet` to create `MiniCalcApplet`. As a result, our new class automatically contains definitions of all the methods defined for `JApplet`. Many methods are required of all applets. Note also that this declaration of the class includes the modifier `public`. We've avoided using `public` when it wasn't required, which it hasn't been for most of the classes created so far. When displayed inside a browser, the class `MiniCalcApplet` is instantiated inside another Java program that is part of the browser. Therefore the applet class must be declared to be `public`.

■
```
public void init() {
    Container pane = getContentPane();
    // create the major components
    JTextField firstNumber = new JTextField(20);

    // code omitted in dissection - see listing above

    DoMath listener =
        new DoMath(firstNumber, secondNumber, result);
    subButton.addActionListener(listener);
    addButton.addActionListener(listener);
}
```

Note that the body of this method is almost identical to the body of `main()` in `MiniCalc` in Section 8.4, on page 278. Here are the changes.

1. We deleted the first line, `JFrame frame = new JFrame("MiniCalc");` from `MiniCalc.main()`. The `JApplet` itself acts like the frame or top level window.

2. We eliminated the last two lines from MiniCalc.main(), pack() and show(). The browser that is running the applet takes care of packing and showing the applet when init() returns.

This applet version of the program uses exactly the same listener class, DoMath.

The preferred way to add graphical output to a JApplet is to add some appropriate component to the content pane for the applet. For example, we could add an instance of the class DrawingCanvas2 in Section 8.7, on page 293, to an applet, to create an applet you can draw on.

In the applet exercises at the ends of Chapter 2 and 4, we overrode the paint() method of JApplet, to draw directly on the applet. This works fine, provided you don't try to add any components to the JApplet. However, overriding paint(), as we did in those early chapters, will prevent any components added to the applet from being properly displayed. The following program is the applet version of SimplePaint2 from Section 8.7.

```java
//SimplePaintApplet.java - applet version of program
//      that draws with the mouse
/* <applet code="SimplePaintApplet.class"
      width=500 height=500> </applet> */
import java.awt.*;
import javax.swing.*;

public class SimplePaintApplet extends JApplet {
  public void init() {
    Container pane = getContentPane();
    DrawingCanvas2 canvas = new DrawingCanvas2();
    PaintListener2 listener = new PaintListener2();

    canvas.addMouseMotionListener(listener);
    pane.add(canvas);
  }
}
```

8.9 PROGRAMMING STYLE

In the examples presented in this chapter we used separate classes for each aspect of the programs they implement. For example, the program SimplePaint is represented by three classes.

1. SimplePaint contains the method main().
2. PaintListener implements the mouse listener needed to do the drawing.
3. DrawingCanvas extends JComponent, creating a new component class.

Each of these classes is placed in a separate file, but all three could be placed in a single file. The only Java requirement is that there be no more than one `public` class per file. In general we recommend that you follow our examples and place each class in its own file. Doing so makes finding the definition of a class easier—just look for the file with the corresponding name. Reusing the class in another program is also easier.

In the following program, we incorporate all the functionality of the three classes from `SimplePaint` into a single class.

```java
//SimplePaintCombined.java - combine all of the
//  features of SimplePaint, PaintListener, and
//  DrawingCanvas into a single class.
//  This style of programming isn't recommended.

import java.awt.*;
import javax.swing.*;
import java.awt.event.*;

class SimplePaintCombined
  extends JComponent implements MouseMotionListener
{
  public static void main(String[] args) {
    JFrame frame = new JFrame("SimplePaint");
    Container pane = frame.getContentPane();
    SimplePaintCombined canvas = new SimplePaintCombined();
    canvas.addMouseMotionListener(canvas);
    pane.add(canvas);
    frame.pack();
    frame.show();
  }

  public void mouseDragged(MouseEvent e) {
    SimplePaintCombined canvas =
      (SimplePaintCombined)e.getSource();
    Graphics g = canvas.getGraphics();
    g.fillOval(e.getX() - 3, e.getY() - 3, 6, 6);
  }

  public void mouseMoved(MouseEvent e) {}

  public Dimension getMinimumSize() {
    return new Dimension(SIZE, SIZE);
  }

  public Dimension getPreferredSize() {
    return new Dimension(SIZE, SIZE);
  }

  private static final int SIZE = 500;
}
```

Although possibly convenient for small programs, this style of combining many distinct capabilities into a single class is generally a bad idea and should be avoided.

Even more than combining multiple classes into a single file, combining many features into a single class can interfere with the ability to reuse parts of your programs. As shown in the minicalculator example, by creating the separate `DoMath` listener, we were able to reuse the `DoMath` listener class, *with no changes*, in our applet version of the minicalculator.

Summary

- Java programs that use Swing use a delegation event model, involving event sources and event listeners. The sources are components such as `JButton` and `JTextField`. The listeners implement one or more interfaces, which include methods that are called when particular events occur in the component. Once a listener has been added to a component, the event delegation model calls the method in the listener when the event occurs. For example, `JButton` objects are the source of `ActionEvent` objects. By adding an `ActionListener` to a `JButton` object, whenever the button is pressed the `actionPerformed()` method of the `ActionListener` is called automatically, passing it an `ActionEvent` object.
- Swing includes many GUI components. In the examples in this chapter, we used the Swing components `JButton`, `JTextField`, `JLabel`, and `JComponent`.
- Although technically a component as well, `JApplets` aren't normally added as components of a GUI. Instead, the `JApplet` is the top-level window, like `JFrame`.
- All drawing is done on an instance of the class `Graphics`. This class includes methods for drawing rectangles, ovals, and lines. Later we discuss methods for drawing arcs, polygons, and strings.
- All drawing routines use a coordinate system that places the origin in the upper left corner of the component. Positive displacements are down and to the right. All distances are in pixels.
- We can draw on a component in one of two ways. The first approach is to extend an existing class, such as `JComponent`, and then redefine the method `paint()` to do the desired drawing. The other approach is to obtain a reference to the `Graphics` object for the component by calling `getGraphics()` and then make the desired drawing calls with this `Graphics` object. However, with this approach, the drawing is lost if the component is obscured by another window.
- The method `getActionCommand()` can be used with the `ActionEvent` passed to an `actionPerformed()` method to determine which button was clicked.
- A class that implements `MouseMotionListener` can be used to perform an action when the mouse is moved without a button being pressed, or is moved when a button is pressed. Moving the mouse with the button held down is called dragging.
- A Swing applet is a Java class that extends the class `JApplet`. Instead of having a `main()` that creates the `JApplet` object, applets are run by incorporating them into an applet viewer or Web browser. An HTML <applet> tag is used to place an applet in a Web page. The browser will create the `JApplet` object and then call `init()` to initialize the applet.

Review Questions

1. In `HelloButton` the following three lines draw the window:

   ```
   pane.add(hello);
   frame.pack();
   frame.show();
   ```

   Write comments for each of these three lines and describe the result to the window.

2. What do each of the GUI elements `JFrame`, `Container`, and `JButton` do?

3. What method must be defined in order to implement the `ActionListener` interface?

4. What steps do you need to perform to create a program that responds to button clicks?

5. What event delivery model does Swing use? Describe it.

6. What kind of event is generated by a `JTextField` when you hit Return?

7. The call `drawRect(0, 0, 10, 10)` will draw a 10×10 pixel square in which corner of the drawing area?

8. How do routines such as `paint()` and `actionPerformed()` get called?

9. What method gets called when the mouse is dragged? What kind of a listener would implement this method?

10. What would happen if the methods `getMinimumSize()` and `getPreferredSize()` were deleted from the class `DrawingCanvas` in Section 8.7, on page 290?

11. What is the purpose of an applet tag?

12. What method in an applet is most similar to `main()` in a stand-alone application?

Exercises

1. Experiment with `setSize()` and determine the largest size of window that can be displayed on your system.

2. Write or obtain a four-line poem, such as "Roses are red, Violets are blue, Coding is a test, Java is best," by Anon. Then display it in a window with an appropriate title. (*Hint*: You may want to use the following code.)

   ```
   // there will be 4 rows of 1 component
   pane.setLayout(new GridLayout(4, 1));
   ```

3. Use an array of `String`s to store the poem in the previous excercise in N lines. Use an array of `JTextField` objects to display the poem.

4. Write a passive window for displaying the results of a computation of two or more arguments. The window should have an appropriate title such as "Roots of a quadratic." It would display the quadratic and then have two result boxes for the potentially distinct roots.

5. Redo the previous exercise to include event listeners. They should allow the user to select arguments and display the results. In the case of a quadratic equation, new coefficients would be input and a mouse click or other event would cause the result to be displayed.

6. Write a program with a window that takes as input a string. Then parse the string into words and display each individual word in its own text box. Assume that the string will have no more than eight words.

7. Modify the program in the previous excercise so that the words are displayed lexicographically.

8. Modify `MiniCalc` in Section 8.4, on page 278, to include additional buttons for multiplication and division.

9. Modify `MiniCalc` in Section 8.4, on page 278, to operate more like a conventional infix calculator. In `MiniCalc`, the only way to add three numbers is to add the first two, copy the answer in the result field into one of the input fields, and put the third number in the other input field. Instead, your calculator program should have a single `JTextField` that is used for both input and output. Your calculator will need an `Equals` button and buttons for each of the arithmetic operators. For example, to add three numbers you would enter the first number and click the `Add` button (nothing would appear to change). You would then enter the second number and click the `Add` button again; this time the sum of the first two numbers should be displayed. Finally you would enter the third number and click `Equals` to display the sum of the three numbers.

10. Instead of having it add and subtract, revise `MiniCalc` to produce the greatest common divisor of two integers.

11. Redesign the `MiniCalc` program to perform an arbitrary function of two arguments. The constructor for the new `MiniCalc` should take a parameter of type `Function` where `Function` is the following interface.

```
interface Function {
  double eval(double x, double y);
}
```

For example, to have the new `MiniCalc` perform addition, you could pass it a reference to an instance of

```
class MyAdder implements Function {
  double eval(double x, double y) {
    return x + y;
  }
  public String toString() {
    return "add";
  }
}
```

The classes the implement `Function` should include a method `toString()` so that the calculator can display the name of the function.

12. Create a regular Java application with a `JFrame` that draws a picture like the one described in the Applet Exercise on page 188 in Chapter 4.

13. Use a `GridLayout` to create a `JFrame` with three buttons along the diagonal. You can use `new Label("")` to create an apparently empty grid position.

14. Run the `FlowLayoutTest` program, using all three alignment parameters. Use your normal desktop mechanism for resizing the window and observe how the components are moved around.

15. Create a Tic-Tac-Toe board with a 3 × 3 grid of buttons. Create an `ActionListener` that changes the button label to an X or an O when it is clicked. The `ActionListener` should remember whether the next click is an X or an O.

Initially, all the buttons should have blank labels. If `e` is the parameter passed to the method `actionPerformed()`, then you can use `e.getSource()` to get a reference to the button that was clicked. You can then use `setLabel()` from the class `JButton` to change the label. You should have only one `ActionListener`, which listens to all the buttons, not one listener per button. Display your Tic-Tac-Toe board in an application or an applet.

16. Using the GUI from the previous exercise, write a program to play Tic-Tac-Toe with the computer as one of the players.

17. Add a `Clear` button to the program `SimplePaint` that paints the entire window white. If `graphics` is an instance of `Graphics`, then

    ```
    graphics.setColor(Color.white);
    ```

    will do all subsequent drawing in white until changed. You will need to use `Color.black` to set the drawing color back to black. The call

    ```
    graphics.fillRect(left, top, width, height);
    ```

    will draw a filled-in rectangle.

18. Modify the program `SimplePaint` to include a button that toggles between painting in black and painting in white. Think of painting in white as erasing. The previous exercise shows how to change the color.

19. Modify the program `SimplePaint` to include buttons for selecting several different pen widths. You change the width of the pen by changing the size of the circle drawn when the mouse motion is detected.

20. Instead of having many different buttons to select different pen widths, as described in the previous exercise, modify `SimplePaint` to use a `JComboBox` object. The class `JComboBox` is described in Appendix D.2. When the user clicks and changes the item selected by the `JComboBox` object, an `ItemEvent` will be generated. The `ItemListener` interface specifies one method: `itemStateChanged()`. This method is passed one parameter: an `ItemEvent`. Calling the method `getItem()` for the `ItemEvent` object returns the string associated with the selected item.

21. Write a program to play a number guessing game as described in Chapter 5, Exercise 24, on page 187. Use a GUI that includes a text field to show the computer's current guess and three buttons labeled `Correct`, `Too Big`, and `Too Small`. As an added feature, allow the user to specify the initial range before generating the first guess. You can do so with two additional text fields. Be sure to use labels on the text fields to make your program easy to use. After the user clicks the `Correct` button, the game should start over.

22. Use the following interface, `HasImage`, to rewrite `SimplePaintApplet` and `SimplePaint2` to use the new listener class `PaintImageListener`. The class `PaintImageListener` will be similar to `PaintListener2`, but the occurrences of `DrawingCanvas2` will be replaced with `HasImage`.

    ```java
    import java.awt.*;
    interface HasImage {
      Graphics getGraphics();
      Image getOffscreenImage();
    }
    ```

Graphical User Interfaces: Part II

In Chapter 8 we introduced the basics of creating graphical user interfaces with standard Java classes from the packages `java.awt` and `javax.swing`. In this chapter we describe some additional capabilities that you can use to build GUI-based applications.

A complete discussion of the features and GUI components that are part of Swing would require an entire book. Instead of describing additional Swing components, in this chapter we focus on additional capabilities that you can use to create quality applications. For example, using only the material from the previous chapter, you'd have very limited control over the arrangement of components in the GUI for your application. Most applications today use a menu bar with cascading menus. The applications often contain several panes or areas in which you can do various things. They often use tool bars, which are collections of buttons, in addition to menus. Many applications can also be resized, with the GUI components adjusting themselves to the window size selected by the user.

9.1 ARRANGING COMPONENTS IN A GUI

In Chapter 8 we introduced the classes `GridLayout` and `FlowLayout`. You can use them to arrange components in a container such as the content pane obtained from either a `JFrame` or a `JApplet`. Another common layout manager is the `Border-Layout`. In fact, it is the default layout manager for both `JFrame` and `JApplet`. To obtain more sophisticated layouts, you can nest containers inside other containers, associating a different layout manager with each container. We will demonstrate this below.

9.1.1 THE CLASS BorderLayout

The class `java.awt.BorderLayout` allows for placement of as many as five components in a container—one in the center, and one on each of the four borders, hence the name `BorderLayout`. The following simple program demonstrates the use of `BorderLayout`.

```
//BorderLayoutTest.java
import java.awt.*;
import javax.swing.*;

class BorderLayoutTest {
  public static void main(String[] args) {
    JFrame frame = new JFrame("BorderLayout");
    Container pane = frame.getContentPane();

    pane.add(
      new JButton("North Button"), BorderLayout.NORTH);
    pane.add(
      new JButton("South Button"), BorderLayout.SOUTH);
    pane.add(
      new JButton("East Button"), BorderLayout.EAST);
    pane.add(
      new JButton("West Button"), BorderLayout.WEST);
    pane.add(
      new JButton("Center Button"), BorderLayout.CENTER);
    frame.pack();
    frame.show();
  }
}
```

The display for this program is

This program doesn't set the layout manager for the content pane because `BorderLayout` is the default. Recall that `FlowLayout` and `GridLayout` required only a single parameter when calling the `add()` method for the associated container. However, when adding a component to a container using `BorderLayout`, you must pass in a second parameter that indicates where to place the component. The constant `BorderLayout.NORTH` is defined in the class `BorderLayout`. Similar constants are defined for the other locations, as shown in the program.

9.1.2 NESTING CONTAINERS IN OTHER CONTAINERS

Suppose that we want a panel of buttons down the left side of the GUI, with a large display area in the center for either text or graphics. Let's use the center to display the star that we drew in Section 8.5, on page 284. We can then nest containers, as follows.

```
//Nesting.java - nest a JPanel container in a JFrame
import java.awt.*;
import javax.swing.*;

class Nesting {
  public static void main(String[] args) {
    JFrame frame = new JFrame("Nesting containers");
    Container pane = frame.getContentPane();
    JPanel panel = new JPanel();

    panel.setLayout(new GridLayout(4, 1));
    panel.add(new JButton("One"));
    panel.add(new JButton("Two"));
    panel.add(new JButton("Three"));
    panel.add(new JButton("Four"));
    pane.add(panel, BorderLayout.WEST);
    pane.add(new Star(), BorderLayout.CENTER);
    frame.pack();
    frame.show();
  }
}
```

The display for this program is

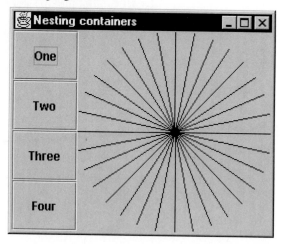

In this example we used a `javax.swing.JPanel`, which is a type of container, to contain the four buttons. We set the layout manager for the `JPanel` to be a `GridLayout` with a single column of four rows. We then added the buttons to the `JPanel` instead of directly to the content pane of the `JFrame`. Finally, we added the `JPanel` as a single component to the west border of the main content pane.

In the preceding two examples, the buttons were resized to just fill their allotted spaces. The `BorderLayout` layout manager always attempts to adjust the sizes of the components to fill the space. Likewise, the `GridLayout` layout manager also attempts to fill each grid cell completely. Not all layout managers do so. For example, the program using a `FlowLayout` in Section 8.6 doesn't expand the buttons to fill the available space.

This process of grouping components in a container and then adding the container to another container can be repeated as much as necessary to achieve the desired arrangement of components.

9.2   GETTING A COMPONENT TO RESIZE

Although some layout managers attempt to resize a component, the components that we have created so far by extending an existing component have had a fixed size. The classes `Star` and `DrawingCanvas` are two such examples. The size of the components derived from `JComponent` is determined by the size returned by the methods `getMinimumSize()` and `getPreferredSize()` defined in the classes. If the window manager attempts to resize a component such as `Star` or `DrawingCanvas`, the resizing will be ignored. For example, if we use the mouse on our computer to adjust the size of the window for the program `Nesting` previously described, we get the following display.

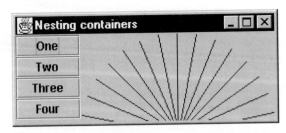

We used the mouse to make the window shorter. The result is that part of the starburst is cut off. Note that the buttons were properly resized to just fill the space. We can modify the class `Star` so that when the user attempts to resize the window, the starburst will be redrawn to fit inside the new window. The program for this new class, `Star2`, is as follows.

```
//Star2.java - draws a resizable starburst
import java.awt.*;
import javax.swing.*;

class Star2 extends JComponent {

  public void paint(Graphics g) {
    // exactly the same as Star except RADIUS was
    // replaced by radius
    // omitted to save space
  }

  public void setBounds(int x, int y, int width, int height)
  {
    radius = Math.min(width, height) / 2;
    super.setBounds(x, y, width, height);
    repaint();
  }

  // make the Canvas just big enough to show the image
  public Dimension getMinimumSize() {
    return new Dimension(2 * radius, 2 * radius);
  }

  public Dimension getPreferredSize() {
    return new Dimension(2 * radius, 2 * radius);
  }

  private int radius = 100;
}
```

The only modifications made in Star to obtain Star2 were to change RADIUS to radius, make radius a variable instead of a constant, and add the method setBounds().

The following display is generated by this program. The original display for Star2 is the same as the one for the original Star in Nesting. But now when we shrink the window, the starburst is made smaller also.

DISSECTION OF THE METHOD setBounds() FOR Star2

- public void setBounds(int x, int y, int width, int height)

The method setBounds() is defined for JComponent (and all components). It is called by the layout manager for the container that holds a component to tell the component where it is being placed and how much of the screen it is being given.

The method is passed the location of the upper left corner, of where the layout manager is moving the component. The method is also passed the width and height of the rectangular area that the layout manager has allocated for the component. By overriding the method we can intercept these changes by the layout manager and adjust our component to fit the new space.

■ `radius = Math.min(width, height) / 2;`

Here we ignore the new location and use only the new `width` and `height`. We can use them to adjust the `radius`. Because our code can draw only a symmetric starburst, we choose the minimum of the `width` and `height` as the new diameter, setting the `radius` to be one-half the diameter.

■ `super.setBounds(x, y, width, height);`

The `JComponent` from which our class is derived must also know about the size and position of the component from the layout manager. Once we have obtained the information we need, we pass the information along to the version of `setBounds()` in the parent class, which is `JComponent` in this example. We do so by using the keyword `super`, which we discussed in Section 7.1.

■ `repaint();`

Once the component has been resized, we need to request that it be repainted as soon as possible. This call to `repaint()` results in an eventual call to the method `paint()`.

9.3 PROBLEM SOLVING: PLOTTING DATA

An important application of computers is the visualization of data. A common visualization of data is a plot or graph of a function. Let's say that we want to create a component that can be used to plot an arbitrary function of one variable. We also want to be able to add the component to a GUI as we would any other component. The following is a complete specification of the problem.

1. The plot component must be able to plot any function of one variable.
2. The plot component will be given a range of values over which to plot the function (e.g. plot the value of the function between 0 and 100).
3. The plot component will have a default size and will adjust the scaling of the plot so that it just fills the allotted screen space.
4. When resized, the plot component will readjust its scaling values so that the plot continues to just fill the allotted screen space.

In Section 9.2, we showed how to get a component to adjust its size when we resize the window. We can apply that same technique here. The main difference is that before we knew exactly what we were going to draw. For this problem, the component needs to use another object to figure out what to draw. The question we have to answer is: How do we represent a function so that different functions can be specified without changing the plot component?

The answer is to use an interface. (We discussed interfaces in Section 7.9. If you skipped it earlier, this would be a good time to go back and read that material.) We can create an interface that describes an arbitrary function in a way that's useful for our plot component. All the plot component needs is the ability to evaluate the function at an arbitrary point. Therefore the following interface will suffice.

```java
//Function.java
interface Function {
  public double valueAt(double x);
}
```

This interface simply specifies that any class implementing it must have a method `valueAt()`, which is to be used to determine the value of the function at the specified point.

The class `Plot` is similar to the class `Star2` discussed earlier. It extends `JComponent` and contains the same methods—`paint()`, `setBounds()`, `getMinimumSize()`, and `getPreferredSize()`—although the bodies of the methods are different. It also has two helper methods that are used to handle the scaling and positioning of the plot.

```java
//Plot.java
import java.awt.*;
import javax.swing.*;

public class Plot extends JComponent {
  public Plot(Function f, double start, double end,
              double deltaX)
  {
    function = f;
    delta = deltaX;
    from = start;
    to = end;
    findRange();        // find max and min of f(x)
    setSize(200, 100); // default width, height
  }
  public void paint(Graphics g)
  {
    double x = from;
    double f_of_x = function.valueAt(x);
    while (x < to - delta) {
      double f_of_x_plus_delta;
      f_of_x_plus_delta = function.valueAt(x + delta);
      drawLine(g, x, f_of_x, x + delta, f_of_x_plus_delta);
      x = x + delta;
      f_of_x = f_of_x_plus_delta;
    }
    drawLine(g, x, f_of_x, to, function.valueAt(to));
  }
```

```java
public void setBounds(int x, int y, int width, int height) {
  xScale = (width - 2) / (to - from);
  yScale = (height - 2) / (fmax - fmin);
  dim = new Dimension(width, height);
  super.setBounds(x, y, width, height);
  repaint();
}

public Dimension getMinimumSize() {
  return dim;
}

public Dimension getPreferredSize() {
  return getMinimumSize();
}

// scale and translate the points from the
// user's coordinate space to Java's
private void drawLine(Graphics g,
                      double x1, double y1,
                      double x2, double y2)
{
  g.drawLine((int)Math.round((x1 - from) * xScale),
             (int)Math.round((fmax - y1) * yScale),
             (int)Math.round((x2 - from) * xScale),
             (int)Math.round((fmax - y2) * yScale));
}

// determine the minimum and maximum values of
// f(x) with x varying between from and to
private void findRange() {
  fmin = fmax = function.valueAt(from);
  for (double x = from + delta;
       x < to - delta;
       x = x + delta)
  {
    double f_of_x = function.valueAt(x);
    if (f_of_x < fmin)
      fmin = f_of_x;
    if (f_of_x > fmax)
      fmax = f_of_x;
  }
}

private Dimension dim;
private double fmin, fmax;
private double xScale, yScale;
private double from, to, delta;
private Function function;
}
```

Before presenting the dissection of the class `Plot`, we present a test program that uses `Plot`. For it we need two more classes. The first, `SinFunction`, implements the interface `Function`. As the name suggests, the values returned will correspond to sin(*x*). The second, `PlotTest`, is where `main()` is located.

```java
//SinFunction.java
class SinFunction implements Function {
  public double valueAt(double x) {
    return Math.sin(x);
  }
}

//PlotTest.java
import java.awt.*;
import javax.swing.*;
class PlotTest {
  public static void main(String[] args) {
    Function f = new SinFunction();
    JFrame frame = new JFrame("PlotTest");
    Container pane = frame.getContentPane();
    Plot plot = new Plot(f, 0, 2 * Math.PI, 0.1);

    pane.add(plot);
    frame.pack();
    frame.show();
  }
}
```

In this code we specified that a `Plot` component be created that plots the function specified by the `SinFunction` object `f`. We further specified that the plot let *x* go from 0 to 2π, in steps of 0.1. The following screen shots show the output. Image (a) shows the initial display. Image (b) shows how the plot is adjusted when the window is resized.

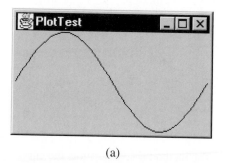

(a)

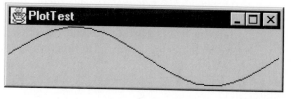

(b)

DISSECTION OF THE CLASS Plot

- ```java
  //Plot.java
  import java.awt.*;
  import javax.swing.*;

  public class Plot extends JComponent {
     public Plot(Function f, double start, double end,
                 double deltaX)
     {
        function = f;
        delta = deltaX;
        from = start;
        to = end;
        findRange(); // find max and min of f(x)
        setSize(200, 100); // default width, height
     }
  ```

The class `Plot` needs a constructor to specify the parameters of the plot. To plot a function $f(x)$, we must know the function, the range of x, and the distance between successive x values. The constructor simply stores all these values in instance variables. We also set a default size. The method `setSize()` is inherited from the class `JComponent`. The call to `setSize()` eventually leads to a call to the method `setBounds()`, which is defined in the class `Plot`. This procedure is different from the one in `Star2`, where we specified the initial size by setting some instance variables. The reason we need to call `setSize()` here but didn't in `Star2` is that in `Plot` we need to have `setBounds()` called even if the window isn't resized. We set the scaling parameters in `setBounds()`.

- ```java
  public void paint(Graphics g)
  {
     double x = from;
     double f_of_x = function.valueAt(x);
     while (x < to - delta) {
        double f_of_x_plus_delta;
        f_of_x_plus_delta = function.valueAt(x+delta);
        drawLine(g, x, f_of_x,
                 x + delta, f_of_x_plus_delta);
        x = x + delta;
        f_of_x = f_of_x_plus_delta;
     }
     drawLine(g, x, f_of_x, to, function.valueAt(to));
  }
  ```

The method `paint()` plots the curve by repeatedly drawing a line from $(x, f(x))$ to $(x + delta, f(x + delta))$. Because *delta* may not evenly divide the range of x values, we make sure that the last point is at $(to, f(to))$. To avoid computing the value of the function twice at the same point, we copy `f_of_x_plus_delta` into `f_of_x` when we increment x. The private function `drawLine()` converts from the coordinate space of the function to the coordinate space of Swing and then calls the standard method `drawLine()` from the class `Graphics`.

```
■  public void setBounds(int x, int y, int width, int height) {
     xScale = (width - 2) / (to - from);
     yScale = (height - 2) / (fmax - fmin);
     dim = new Dimension(width, height);
     super.setBounds(x, y, width, height);
     repaint();
   }
```

As in `Plot2`, this function is called when the layout manager places the `Plot` component in its container or if we resize the window containing our plot, using the desktop facilities of our computer. By computing the scaling and setting the `Dimension` variable `dim` inside `setBounds()`, our `Plot` component automatically resizes itself. After adjusting the scale factors and changing `dim`, we call `repaint()` to have the graph recomputed. In this example, we placed the `Plot` object in a `JFrame` with a content pane that uses a `BorderLayout` manager. The `BorderLayout` manager attempts to adjust the size of the `Plot` object to fill the `JFrame`.

```
■  private void drawLine(Graphics g,
                         double x1, double y1,
                         double x2, double y2)
   {
     g.drawLine((int)Math.round((x1 - from) * xScale),
                (int)Math.round((fmax - y1) * yScale),
                (int)Math.round((x2 - from) * xScale),
                (int)Math.round((fmax - y2) * yScale));
   }
```

In Swing, positive vertical distance is *down*, but normal plotting uses *up* for positive vertical distance. In addition, we need to adjust the origin, and scale all values so that the graph just fills the display. We use `Math.round()` from the standard package `java.lang`, which returns a `long` when passed a `double`. We then cast the `long` to an `int` as required by method `drawLine()`. The method `drawLine()` in the class `Graphics` draws a line between two points. The first two parameters to `drawline()` are the *x* and *y* coordinates of the first point, and the last two parameters are the coordinates of the second point. (See Section 9.4.1 for another way to draw lines.)

```
■  private void findRange() {
     fmin = fmax = function.valueAt(from);
     for (double x = from + delta;
          x < to - delta;
          x = x + delta)
     {
       double f_of_x = function.valueAt(x);
       if (f_of_x < fmin)
         fmin = f_of_x;
       if (f_of_x > fmax)
         fmax = f_of_x;
     }
   }
```

To calculate yScale, we need to know the range of values for $f(x)$ in the interval being plotted. To get it we simply iterate over the range of points at which the function is to be plotted and record the minimum and maximum values computed.

9.4 THE CLASS Graphics

Basic drawing in Java is done on an instance of the class Graphics. You can call the method getGraphics() on any component to get the Graphics object for that component. However, you should normally do your drawing within the method paint(). Any drawing on the Graphics object done outside the method paint() is replaced by the actions of paint() the next time the window manager senses that the window needs updating.

We have used several drawing primitives in the examples so far. We used draw-Line() to draw the lines of the starburst in Star. We used fillOval() to draw the small filled circles for our brush strokes in DrawingCanvas. In addition, the class Graphics includes methods for drawing filled and unfilled rectangles, unfilled ovals, filled and unfilled polygons, and text strings. For the unfilled shapes the outline of the shape is always drawn with a 1 pixel–wide line.

9.4.1 DRAWING LINES

The simplest thing you can draw is a line; you merely specify the coordinates of the two ends of the line. The unit of measure is the pixel, the origin is in the upper left corner, and positive displacements are down and to the right. You can change the color of the line but not its width or style (e.g., dashed). All lines are 1 pixel thick. To draw thicker lines or dashed lines you need to use the enhanced capabilities of the class java.awt.Graphics2D, which we discuss later.

The following example draws a triangle by drawing three lines. You could also use drawPolygon(), which we also discuss later. In this example we demonstrate the use of drawPolyline(), which connects several points in a single call. You could, for example, use drawPolyline() to plot data stored in an array. The program has the same basic structure as the starburst drawing program discussed in detail earlier. We don't discuss the details here, focusing only on the new methods from the class Graphics. As with the starburst there are two classes, one containing main() and the other extending JComponent.

The method drawLine() takes four parameters: the x and y coordinates of the first point and the x and y coordinates of the second point, in that order. The method drawPolyline() takes three parameters: an int array for the x coordinates, an int array for the *y* coordinates, and the number of points to draw. The number of points must be less than or equal to the length of the shorter of the two arrays.

```java
//DrawingLines.java - demo drawLine() and drawPloyline()
import java.awt.*;
import javax.swing.*;

class DrawingLines {
  public static void main(String[] args) {
    JFrame frame = new JFrame("DrawingLines");
    Container pane = frame.getContentPane();

    pane.add(new DrawTriangle());
    frame.pack();
    frame.show();
  }
}
```

```java
//DrawTriangle.java - two ways to draw a triangle
import java.awt.*;
import javax.swing.*;

class DrawTriangle extends JComponent {

  public void paint(Graphics g) {
    g.drawLine(10, 10, 100, 60);
    g.drawLine(100, 60, 50, 80);
    g.drawLine(50, 80, 10, 10);
    int[] x = {120, 140, 160, 180, 200};
    int[] y = {10, 80, 10, 80, 10};
    g.drawPolyline(x, y, 5);
  }

  public Dimension getMinimumSize() { return dim; }

  public Dimension getPreferredSize() { return dim; }

  private Dimension dim = new Dimension(220, 100);
}
```

The output of the program is

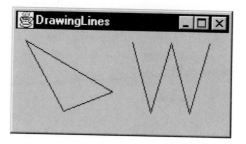

9.4.2 DRAWING RECTANGLES

You can draw rectangles by using either `fillRect()`, for filled rectangles, or `drawRect()`, for outlined rectangles. As discussed in Section 8.5, you specify the four values *left*, *top*, *width*, and *height* to place and size the rectangle.

You can also draw rectangles with rounded corners by using `drawRound-Rect()` and `fillRoundRect()`. In addition to the four values for regular rectangles, you must also specify the width and height of the arcs placed at the corners. In the following example, we included a gray oval with width 40 and height 20 superimposed over one of the corners to show how the arc width of 40 and height of 20 are used to round the corner. We discuss changing the color later in this section.

For this example and the remaining examples in this section covering the class `Graphics`, the programs are almost identical in form to the classes `DrawingLines` and `DrawTriangle`, except for the method `paint()`. We therefore present only the method `paint()`.

```
public void paint(Graphics g) {
  g.drawRect(0, 0, 100, 60);
  g.drawRoundRect(110, 0, 100, 60, 40, 20);
  g.setColor(Color.gray);
  g.drawOval(170, 40, 40, 20);
}
```

The output of the program is

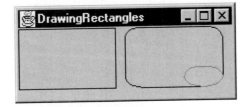

9.4.3 DRAWING OVALS

Ovals are drawn very much like rectangles. You specify a rectangle, and the largest oval that will fit inside the rectangle is drawn. There are just two methods: `drawOval()` and `fillOval()`. The following code excerpt shows how an oval is drawn inside a rectangle.

```
public void paint(Graphics g) {
  g.drawRect(10, 10, 100, 60);
  g.drawOval(10, 10, 100, 60);
}
```

The output of the program is

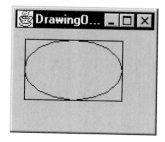

9.4.4   DRAWING ARCS

Arcs are incomplete ovals. As with an oval, you specify a bounding rectangle. In addition, you specify the starting angle and the arc angle, giving both angles in integer degrees. A starting angle of 0° corresponds to 3 o'clock, and positive angles correspond to counterclockwise rotation. Arcs can be filled or drawn in outline.

In this example we draw an unfilled arc starting at 0° (3 o'clock) and then sweeping counterclockwise for 160°. We then draw a filled arc starting at 45° and then sweeping 135° clockwise to finish at 6 o'clock.

```
public void paint(Graphics g) {
  g.drawArc(0, 0, 100, 60, 0, 160);
  g.fillArc(110, 0, 60, 60, 45, -135);
}
```

The output of the program is

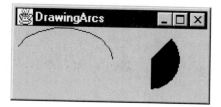

9.4.5   DRAWING POLYGONS

You draw a polygon by first creating a `java.awt.Polygon` object. You then add points to the polygon one at a time with the method `addPoint()`, each of which specifies the coordinates of a vertex. A polygon can be filled or drawn in outline. The class `Polygon` also has a method `translate()` that you can use to translate all the points vertically and horizontally, as shown in the following example. You can also draw a polygon by using two integer arrays: one for the *x* coordinates of the vertices and one for the *y* coordinates of the vertices. This is also shown in the example.

```
public void paint(Graphics g) {
  Polygon p = new Polygon();

  p.addPoint(10, 10);
  p.addPoint(60, 30);
  p.addPoint(40, 50);
  p.addPoint(25, 40);
  g.drawPolygon(p); // draw a Polygon object
  // draw a polygon using 2 arrays
  int[] x = {110, 160, 140, 125};
  int[] y = {10, 30, 50, 40};
  g.fillPolygon(x, y, 4);
  //move 200 pixels right and 20 down
  p.translate(200, 20);
  g.drawPolygon(p); // draw translated polygon
}
```

The output of the program is

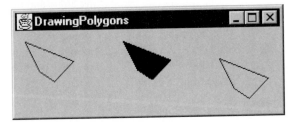

9.4.6   DRAWING TEXT

You can use labels and text areas to place text in a GUI. Sometimes you may want or need to add text to a component that you're drawing on. In that event you can use the method drawString() from the class Graphics. It takes three arguments: the string and the two coordinates of the starting point. You can also change the font. In the following example we added small filled rectangles at the coordinates of the starting points for the drawString() calls. Note how the position of the text relates to the starting point.

The call to setFont() needs a java.awt.Font object, which we obtain by constructing a new font. We specify the name of the font as a string, a parameter used to modify the font (making it bold in this case), and the size of the font in points. Points are a unit of measure originally used by typesetters (72 points/inch). The normal text in this book is 10 points.

```
public void paint(Graphics g) {
  g.drawString("Starts at (10, 20)", 10, 20);
  g.fillRect(10, 20, 4, 4);
  g.setFont(new Font("TimesRoman", Font.BOLD, 20));
  g.drawString("20pt bold starting at (100, 40)", 100, 40);
  g.fillRect(100, 40, 4, 4);
}
```

The output of the program is

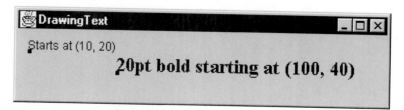

9.4.7 USING COLORS

You can easily change the color of the objects drawn by any of the methods discussed. To do so, call setColor() for the Graphics object before calling the drawing method. You can use the standard class java.awt.Color to create almost any color. You can create your own color by specifying the amounts of red, green, and blue needed to form the color. You do so in the constructor for Color, passing it three integers, each in the range 0 to 255, inclusive. These are the red, green, and blue intensities, respectively, also called the *RGB values*. For any Color object you can also call the methods brighter() or darker() to return a new color that is brighter or darker than the original color.

The class Color also includes some predefined colors that you can use by name—for example, Color.red, Color.green, Color.white, and Color.black. Each of these predefined colors is declared to be a public static final Color value. In the following example we use the standard color Color.gray, a darker shade of gray obtained by calling darker(), and a brighter shade of gray obtained by calling brighter(). The expression Color.gray.darker() returns a Color object that can again have the method darker() invoked on it, as in Color.gray.darker().darker().

```
public void paint(Graphics g) {
  g.setColor(Color.gray.brighter());
  g.fillRect(10, 10, 200, 100);
  g.setColor(Color.gray);
  g.fillRect(20, 20, 180, 80);
  g.setColor(Color.gray.darker());
  g.fillRect(30, 30, 160, 60);
  g.setColor(Color.black);
  g.drawRect(10, 10, 200, 100);
}
```

The output of the program is

9.5 CHANGING THE STROKE USED IN DRAWING

The class `java.awt.Graphics2D`, which extends `Graphics`, adds many sophisticated drawing operations to Java. One example is the ability to control the brush stroke used in drawing lines and shapes. The parameters of a brush stroke that we can control are

- the width of the brush,
- the dash pattern of the brush,

- the shape of the end of a brush stroke,
- what happens when two ends join, and
- for dashed lines, where in the dash pattern does the stroke begin.

The following program is a brief introduction to creating and setting the stroke used in drawing operations.

```java
//StrokeSampler.java - examples of some Java2D strokes
import java.awt.*;
import javax.swing.*;

class StrokeSampler extends JComponent {

  public void paint(Graphics g) {
    Graphics2D g2d = (Graphics2D)g;

    // draw some rectangles with wide lines
    g2d.setStroke(wideStroke);
    g2d.drawRect(10, 10, 100, 60);
    g2d.setStroke(mediumStroke);
    g2d.drawRoundRect(120, 10, 100, 60, 40, 20);

    // draw some lines with round ends/joints
    int[] xcoords = {30, 60, 90};
    int[] ycoords = {90, 140, 90};
    g2d.setStroke(wideRound);
    g2d.drawPolyline(xcoords, ycoords, 3);

    // draw some lines with bevel joints
    for (int i = 0; i < xcoords.length; i++)
      xcoords[i] = xcoords[i] + 110;
    g2d.setStroke(wideBevel);
    g2d.drawPolyline(xcoords, ycoords, 3);

    // use a dot-dash stroke
    g2d.setStroke(dotDashStroke);
    g2d.drawRect(10, 170, 100, 60);
    g2d.drawRoundRect(120, 170, 100, 60, 40, 20);
  }

  static final BasicStroke wideStroke =
    new BasicStroke(8.0f);
  static final BasicStroke mediumStroke =
    new BasicStroke(4.0f);
  static final BasicStroke wideRound =
    new BasicStroke(16.0f,
          BasicStroke.CAP_ROUND /* end style */,
          BasicStroke.JOIN_ROUND /* join style */);

  static final BasicStroke wideBevel =
    new BasicStroke(16.0f,
          BasicStroke.CAP_BUTT /* end style */,
          BasicStroke.JOIN_BEVEL /* join style */);
  static float[] dotDash = {10.0f, 5.0f, 5.0f, 5.0f};
```

```
   static final BasicStroke dotDashStroke =
     new BasicStroke(4.0f /*width*/,
             BasicStroke.CAP_BUTT /*end style*/,
             BasicStroke.JOIN_MITER /*join style*/,
             1.0f /*miter trim limit */,
             dotDash /* pattern array */,
             0.0f /* offset to start of pattern */);

 public Dimension getMinimumSize() {
   return new Dimension(230, 240);
 }

 public Dimension getPreferredSize() {
   return getMinimumSize();
 }
}
```

When added as the only component in a `JFrame`, the class `StrokeSampler` generates the following display.

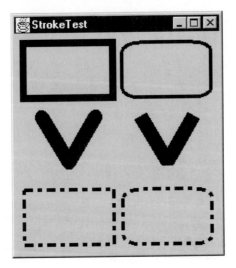

DISSECTION OF THE CLASS StrokeSampler

▪
```
import java.awt.*;
import javax.swing.*;

class StrokeSampler extends JComponent {
  public void paint(Graphics g) {
    Graphics2D g2d = (Graphics2D)g;
```

This sample class extends `JComponent`, as in other examples. Here we cast the `Graphics` object to a `Graphics2D` object. The class `Graphics2D` extends the class `Graphics`, so we can still do anything we could do before with `Graphics`.

The method `paint()` is designed to take a parameter of type `Graphics` instead of type `Graphics2D` for compatibility and historical reasons.

■
```
g2d.setStroke(wideStroke);
g2d.drawRect(10, 10, 100, 60);
g2d.setStroke(mediumStroke);
g2d.drawRoundRect(120, 10, 100, 60, 40, 20);
```

Here we draw rectangles as before, but we first set the stroke that is to be used. Once set, a stroke continues to be used until changed again.

■
```
// draw some lines with round ends/joints
int[] xcoords = {30, 60, 90};
int[] ycoords = {90, 140, 90};
g2d.setStroke(wideRound);
g2d.drawPolyline(xcoords, ycoords, 3);

// draw some lines with bevel joints
for (int i = 0; i < xcoords.length; i++)
  xcoords[i] = xcoords[i] + 110;
g2d.setStroke(wideBevel);
g2d.drawPolyline(xcoords, ycoords, 3);
```

Here we draw two multisegment lines. Each polyline consists of two line segments, forming a V. These statements are used to demonstrate how a stroke can be defined to have different end and join shapes.

■
```
g2d.setStroke(dotDashStroke);
g2d.drawRect(10, 170, 100, 60);
g2d.drawRoundRect(120, 170, 100, 60, 40, 20);
```

The final two drawing calls in this class draw two rectangles, using a dot–dash pattern. We describe shortly the stroke `dotDashStroke`.

■
```
static final BasicStroke wideStroke =
  new BasicStroke(8.0f);
static final BasicStroke mediumStroke =
  new BasicStroke(4.0f);
```

The single parameter for the `BasicStroke` constructor used here is the width of the stroke. The value is a floating point value. Again, the units are in pixels.

■
```
static final BasicStroke wideRound =
  new BasicStroke(16.0f,
        BasicStroke.CAP_ROUND /* end style */,
        BasicStroke.JOIN_ROUND /* join style */);
```

Here we construct a `BasicStroke`, specifying the width and style to be used where the ends of two line segments join. The result—previously shown in the output of the program—is that the ends of the line are rounded and that the corner where the two line segments join is also rounded.

```
▪  static final BasicStroke wideBevel =
      new BasicStroke(16.0f,
             BasicStroke.CAP_BUTT /* end style */,
             BasicStroke.JOIN_BEVEL /* join style */);
```

For contrast, here we construct a `BasicStroke` that uses different end and join styles. The difference, as shown in the output of the program, is obvious.

```
▪  static float[] dotDash = {10.0f, 5.0f, 5.0f, 5.0f};
   static final BasicStroke dotDashStroke =
      new BasicStroke(4.0f /*width*/,
             BasicStroke.CAP_BUTT /*end style*/,
             BasicStroke.JOIN_MITER /*join style*/,
             1.0f /*miter trim limit */,
             dotDash /* pattern array */,
             0.0f /* offset to start of pattern */);
```

Here we construct a `BasicStroke`, specifying a dash pattern by an array of `float` values. The line is drawn by alternating marks and spaces. The length of the first mark is specified by `dotDash[0]`. The length of the first space is specified by `dot-Dash[1]`, the length of the second mark is specified by `dotDash[2]`, and so on. When the end of the array is reached, the pattern goes back to the beginning. The array `dotDash` specifies a pattern that is a 10-pixel line, a 5-pixel space, a 5-pixel line, a 5-pixel space, a 10-pixel line, and so on. The miter trim limit isn't directly related to the dash pattern, but we must specify it when specifying a pattern. The miter limit controls how much a bevel join can extend to make a clean bevel. We left it at the minimum legal value, which is 1. The last parameter can be used to control starting the stroke somewhere other than at the beginning of the pattern. For example, if we had specified the offset to be `15.0f` instead, the stroke would begin with a short, 5-pixel mark because that is 15 pixels into the pattern.

9.6 ADDING MENUS TO A GUI

A standard feature on most GUI-based programs today is a menu. In this section we present a brief introduction to the support in Java for menus. We do so by adding a menu to the `SimplePaint2` program discussed in Section 8.7. We could add many features via a menu, but here we add only two menus. The first is the standard `File` menu found in most programs today. In the `File` menu we add only a single item, `Exit`. The second menu is `Options`. Here we add the ability to change the diameter of the virtual pen tip used to do the drawing. This addition appears in the following screen shot, where we have just selected the large pen size option.

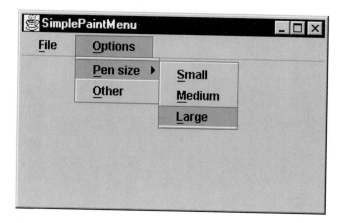

The program consists of five classes and one interface. The method `main()` is in `SimplePaintMenu`. The class `PaintListener3` extends `PaintListener2`, adding a method used to set the pen size. The interface `Painter` is used to isolate the mouse motion listener, `PaintListener3`, which does the painting, from the action event listener, `PenAdjuster`, which responds to the menu selections. The program also uses `DrawingCanvas2` from Section 8.7 with no changes. The following code lacks only `DrawingCanvas2` and `PaintListener2`, which are presented in Section 8.7.

```java
// SimplePaintMenu.java - add a menu to SimplePaint2
import java.awt.*;
import javax.swing.*;
import java.awt.event.*;

class SimplePaintMenu {
  public static void main(String[] args) {
    JFrame frame = new JFrame("SimplePaintMenu");
    Container pane = frame.getContentPane();
    // create the canvas and mouse listener
    // just as in SimplePaint2
    DrawingCanvas2 canvas = new DrawingCanvas2();
    PaintListener3 painter = new PaintListener3();

    canvas.addMouseMotionListener(painter);
    pane.add(canvas);

    // create the menu bar and top level menus
    JMenuBar menuBar = new JMenuBar();
    JMenu fileMenu = new JMenu("File");

    fileMenu.setMnemonic('F');
    JMenu optionsMenu = new JMenu("Options");
    optionsMenu.setMnemonic('O');
    menuBar.add(fileMenu);
    menuBar.add(optionsMenu);
    frame.setJMenuBar(menuBar);
```

```java
            // add items to the fileMenu
            JMenuItem exit = new JMenuItem("Exit",'x');
            fileMenu.add(exit);
            exit.addActionListener(new GoodBye());

            // create and add items to the optionsMenu
            // the first item is a submenu for pen size
            JMenu penAdjusterMenu = new JMenu("Pen size");
            penAdjusterMenu.setMnemonic('P');
            // create and add items to the pen size sub menu
            JMenuItem smallPen = new JMenuItem("Small", 'S');
            JMenuItem mediumPen = new JMenuItem("Medium",'M');
            JMenuItem largePen = new JMenuItem("Large", 'L');
            penAdjusterMenu.add(smallPen);
            penAdjusterMenu.add(mediumPen);
            penAdjusterMenu.add(largePen);
            // add a listener to the pen selection items
            PenAdjuster penAdjuster = new PenAdjuster(painter);
            smallPen.addActionListener(penAdjuster);
            mediumPen.addActionListener(penAdjuster);
            largePen.addActionListener(penAdjuster);
            optionsMenu.add(penAdjusterMenu);
            // for demo purposes add second (unused) item
            optionsMenu.add(new JMenuItem("Other", 'O'));

            frame.pack();
            frame.show();
    }
}

// PaintListener3.java - paints on an DrawingCanvas2,
// and it's associated offscreen image.
// Adds a setPenSize() method to PaintListener2.
import java.awt.*;
import java.awt.event.*;

public class PaintListener3 extends PaintListener2
    implements Painter
{
  // specify one of three pen sizes, Small, Medium, or Large
  // radius and diameter are inherited
  public void setPenSize(String size) {
    if (size.equals("Small")) {
        radius = 0;
        diameter = 1;
    }
    else if (size.equals("Medium")) {
      radius = 3;
      diameter = radius * 2;
    }
    else if (size.equals("Large")) {
      radius = 6;
      diameter = radius * 2;
    }
  }
}
```

```
// PenAdjuster.java - pass pen adjustment requests
//      to the painter
import java.awt.event.*;

class PenAdjuster implements ActionListener {
  private Painter painter;
  PenAdjuster(Painter thePainter) {
    painter = thePainter;
  }
  public void actionPerformed(ActionEvent e) {
    painter.setPenSize(e.getActionCommand());
  }
}

// Painter.java -
//    in practice this interface would contain
//    additional methods such as for changing pen
//    shape, color, pattern etc.
interface Painter {
  public void setPenSize(String size);
}
```

DISSECTION OF THE CLASS `SimplePaintMenu`

- ```
  // SimplePaintMenu.java - add a menu to SimplePaint2
  import java.awt.*;
  ...
      PaintListener3 painter = new PaintListener3();
      canvas.addMouseMotionListener(painter);
      pane.add(canvas);
  ```

  The first part of this class is the same as `SimplePaint2`, with the exception of the name change to `PaintListener3`.

- ```
  JMenuBar menuBar = new JMenuBar();
  JMenu fileMenu = new JMenu("File");
  fileMenu.setMnemonic('F');
  JMenu optionsMenu = new JMenu("Options");
  optionsMenu.setMnemonic('O');
  menuBar.add(fileMenu);
  menuBar.add(optionsMenu);
  frame.setJMenuBar(menuBar);
  ```

  To create a menu, we first create a `javax.swing.JMenuBar`, which is a type of container. We can then add `javax.swing.JMenu` objects to the `JMenuBar`. Finally we add the `JMenuBar` to the `JFrame`, using the special method `setJMenuBar()`. When we create menus, we give them names. In addition, in this example we show how to create easily a keyboard shortcut by using the method `setMnemonic()` for `JMenu`. As the screen shot at the beginning of this section shows, the letter passed to the method `setMnemonic()` is underlined in the menu as a reminder to the user. Using the default key-bindings, the menus can be activated by hitting Alt and the selected key at the same time. For example, Alt+O will cause the `Options` menu to be displayed.

■
```
JMenuItem exit = new JMenuItem("Exit", 'x');
fileMenu.add(exit);
exit.addActionListener(new GoodBye());
```

Here we add a `JMenuItem` to one of the existing menus. The constructor for `JMenuItem` allows us to specify both the name to be displayed as the menu item and the mnemonic key. A `JMenuItem` is a special kind of button. Like `JButton` that we used in the previous chapter, we add an `ActionListener` to the menu item in order actually to do something when we select the menu item. Here we just use the class `GoodBye` from Section 8.2. When invoked, the method `actionPerformed()` in `GoodBye` forces the program to exit by using `System.exit()`.

■
```
JMenu penAdjusterMenu = new JMenu("Pen size");
penAdjusterMenu.setMnemonic('P');
// create and add items to the pen size submenu
JMenuItem smallPen = new JMenuItem("Small",'S');
JMenuItem mediumPen = new JMenuItem("Medium",'M');
JMenuItem largePen = new JMenuItem("Large",'L');
penAdjusterMenu.add(smallPen);
penAdjusterMenu.add(mediumPen);
penAdjusterMenu.add(largePen);
```

A `JMenu` can contain both `JMenuItems` and other `JMenus`, which is how we obtain cascading menus. The `Options` menu eventually contains two items. The first is the `Pen size` submenu created here. The second, discussed later, is just a dummy item, `Other`, that is used to show that the menu could contain additional items. The `penAdjusterMenu` contains three items. We create and add these items to the menu as we did previously for the `Exit` item in the `File` menu.

■
```
PenAdjuster penAdjuster = new PenAdjuster(painter);
smallPen.addActionListener(penAdjuster);
mediumPen.addActionListener(penAdjuster);
largePen.addActionListener(penAdjuster);
```

We dissect the class `PenAdjuster` shortly. It implements `ActionListener`. We use one instance of `PenAdjuster` to listen to all three pen adjustment menu items.

■
```
optionsMenu.add(penAdjusterMenu);
// for demo purposes add second (unused) item
optionsMenu.add(new JMenuItem("Other", 'O'));
```

Here we add the `penAdjusterMenu` to the top-level `optionsMenu`. We then add a second dummy menu item that doesn't do anything. Thus we can mix submenus and regular menu items in a single menu.

■
```
frame.pack();
frame.show();
```

As always, the method `main()` ends by calling these two methods.

DISSECTION OF THE CLASS `PaintListener3`

- ```java
  import java.awt.*;
  import java.awt.event.*;

  public class PaintListener3 extends PaintListener2
      implements Painter
  {
  ```

The only change from `PainterListener2` is the addition of a method that can be used by some other class to change the pen size used by `PaintListener3` when it draws in response to mouse motion events. We could have just copied `PainterListener2` and modified it. Instead, we used the inheritance mechanism in Java to extend `PaintListener2`. In this way, any improvements or corrections we make to the class `PaintListener2` will automatically be incorporated in the class `PaintListener3`. The interface `Painter` specifies that the class `PaintListener3` contains a method `setPenSize()`. We discuss `Painter` further shortly.

- ```java
  public void setPenSize(String size) {
      if (size.equals("Small")) {
          radius = 0;
          diameter = 1;
      }
      else if (size.equals("Medium")) {
          radius = 3;
          diameter = radius * 2;
      }
      else if (size.equals("Large")) {
          radius = 6;
          diameter = radius * 2;
      }
  }
  ```

The method `setPenSize()` expects to be passed one of three strings. If one of the expected strings is passed, the `radius` and `diameter` of the pen are adjusted appropriately. If the parameter doesn't match any of the strings, the pen size is left unchanged. The instance variables `radius` and `diameter` were declared to be `protected` in `PaintListener2`. That allows us to modify and use them from a derived class such as `PaintListener3`. Recall that `radius` and `diameter` are used to specify the shape to be drawn. The following statement from `PaintListener2` does the actual drawing.

```java
g.fillOval(e.getX() - radius, e.getY() - radius,
                  diameter, diameter);
```

DISSECTION OF THE CLASSES PenAdjuster AND Painter

▪
```
import java.awt.event.*;

class PenAdjuster implements ActionListener {
  private Painter painter;
  PenAdjuster(Painter thePainter) {
    painter = thePainter;
  }
}
```

A `PenAdjuster` object acts like an intermediary between a menu item that it is listening to and a `Painter` object that can have its pen size adjusted. The `PenAdjuster` must be passed a reference to the `Painter` when it is created. The menu item knows about the `PenAdjuster` when it is added to the menu item as an action listener.

▪
```
public void actionPerformed(ActionEvent e) {
  painter.setPenSize(e.getActionCommand());
}
```

One instance of `PenAdjuster` is created, and that object is added as an action listener to each of the pen adjustment menu items, `Small`, `Medium`, and `Large`. When the method `actionPerformed()` is called, the `PenAdjuster` passes the string it gets from the menu item to the `Painter` associated with this `PenAdjuster`. As with `JButton` objects, the default action command string for a `JMenuItem` is the same as the string used to label the `JMenuItem`. All that `PenAdjuster` has to do is pass the string to the method `setPenSize()` of the `Painter`. As we showed earlier, the `Painter` object will examine the string and possibly change the pen size.

▪
```
interface Painter {
  public void setPenSize(String size);
}
```

We didn't really need the interface `Painter`. We could have defined `PenAdjuster` to contain a reference to a `PaintListener3` instead of a `Painter`. However, the class `PenAdjuster` doesn't need to know that `PaintListener3` has methods for mouse motion events. Furthermore, we can reuse `Painter` and `PenAdjuster` in other programs, or we can decide to change the name of `PaintListener3`. In either case, we wouldn't need to make any changes to `Painter` or `PenAdjuster`.

9.7 EVENT LISTENERS AND ADAPTERS

In Section 8.2 we introduced the concept of event listeners. Recall that they are used to respond to events generated from a specific event source, such as a `JButton`, and that the various event listener types are specified by interfaces. As we discussed in Section 7.9, an interface specifies the methods that a class must implement and nothing more. For this reason, one class can implement multiple interfaces. To do so, however, the class must include the union of all methods in the interfaces.

In the following program we show how a single class can handle all the events for a program. The event handler class, GameEventHandler, handles action events from a Quit JButton and mouse clicks in a JComponent. The JComponent is intended to represent a generic game board as might be used with the Predator–Prey simulation in Section 7.8. Mouse clicks on the JComponent are used to change the states of the cells. The entire program consists of three classes. GameTest contains main(). Its contents should be rather familiar to you by this time, so we won't discuss it further. GameBoard extends JComponent and has much in common with Plot, which we discussed in Section 9.3. The listeners are implemented in GameEventHandler.

```java
//GameTest.java
import java.awt.*;

class GameTest {
  public static void main(String[] args)
  {
    byte[][] state = new byte[20][20];

    Frame display = new Frame("GameTest");
    GameBoard board = new GameBoard(400, 400, state);
    GameEventHandler actor = new GameEventHandler();
    board.addMouseListener(actor);
    display.add(board, BorderLayout.CENTER);
    Button quit = new Button("Quit");
    quit.addActionListener(new GoodBye());
    display.add(quit, BorderLayout.NORTH);
    display.pack();
    display.show();
  }
}

//GameBoard.java
import java.awt.*;

class GameBoard extends Canvas {
  // the example supports only two valid states
  public static final byte INVALID = -1;
  public static final byte STATE0 = 0;
  public static final byte STATE1 = 1;

  public GameBoard(int width, int height, byte[][] board) {
    this.board = board;
    setSize(new Dimension(width, height));
  }

  // draw the cells of the board
  public void paint(Graphics g) {
    for (int row = 0; row<board.length; row++)
      for (int col=0; col < board[row].length; col++){
        select_color(g, board[row][col]);
        g.fillRect(col * cellWidth,
                   row * cellHeight,
                   cellWidth, cellHeight);
      }
  }
}
```

```
/* The default update() redraws the entire display
 * using the background color, then calls paint().
 * To avoid the flicker of background color,
 * we override update() to just call paint().
 * This is recommended whenever paint() redraws
 * all pixels.
 */
public void update(Graphics g) {
  paint(g);
}

public Dimension getMinimumSize() {
  return dim;
}

public Dimension getPreferredSize() {
  return getMinimumSize();
}

public void setBounds(int x, int y, int width, int height)
{
  dim = new Dimension(width, height);
  //adjust cell size to fill the new board size
  cellWidth = Math.round((float)width / board.length);
  cellHeight = Math.round((float)height / board[0].length);
  super.setBounds(x, y, width, height);
  repaint();
}

public void setCell(int row, int col, byte value) {
  board[row][col] = value;
}

public byte getCell(int row, int col) {
  return board[row][col];
}

public int getCellWidth() { return cellWidth; }
public int getCellHeight() { return cellHeight; }
private void select_color(Graphics g, byte cell) {
  if (cell == STATE0)
    g.setColor(Color.white);
  else
    g.setColor(Color.black);
}

private byte[][] board;
private int cellWidth, cellHeight;
private Dimension dim;
}
```

```java
// GameEventHandler.java
import java.awt.event.*;

class GameEventHandler implements MouseListener {
  public void mouseClicked(MouseEvent e)
  {
    GameBoard board = (GameBoard)e.getSource();
    int row = e.getY() / board.getCellHeight();
    int col = e.getX() / board.getCellWidth();

    if (board.getCell(row, col) == board.STATE0)
      board.setCell( row, col, board.STATE1);
    else
      board.setCell( row, col, board.STATE0);
    board.repaint();
  }

  public void mouseEntered(MouseEvent e) {};
  public void mouseExited(MouseEvent e) {};
  public void mousePressed(MouseEvent e) {};
  public void mouseReleased(MouseEvent e) {};
}
```

Here is what the display looks like after we click five different places on the screen.

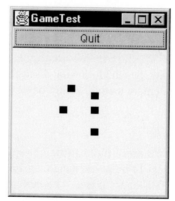

DISSECTION OF THE CLASS GameEventHandler

■   class GameEventHandler implements MouseListener

For this program we're interested in mouse click events, which requires us to implement the interface MouseListener.

```
■   public void mouseClicked(MouseEvent e) {
      GameBoard board = (GameBoard)e.getSource();
      int row = e.getY() / board.getCellHeight();
      int col = e.getX() / board.getCellWidth();
      if (board.getCell(row, col) == board.STATE0)
        board.setCell( row, col, board.STATE1);
      else
        board.setCell(row, col, board.STATE0);
      board.repaint();
    }
```

This method is one of the five specified in the `MouseListener` interface. It is the only one we actually care about. From the event `e` we can obtain the `GameBoard` object and the coordinates of the cursor at the time the mouse button was clicked. We use them to select one cell in our `GameBoard` and then toggle the state in the selected cell. To have the change be reflected immediately on the screen, we call `repaint()`. If this listener was listening to more than one `MouseEvent` source, we could use the `instanceof` operator to determine whether it was indeed a `Game-Board` before doing the cast.

```
■   public void mouseEntered(MouseEvent e) {};
    public void mouseExited(MouseEvent e) {};
    public void mousePressed(MouseEvent e) {};
    public void mouseReleased(MouseEvent e) {};
```

These are the other four methods required of any class that implements the interface `MouseListener`. We aren't interested in any of these events, so the methods do nothing. See the following discussion of adapter classes for a way to avoid including these empty method definitions.

We don't have sufficient space in this book to cover all the AWT listener classes. To help you handle specific events, we included the following table of the AWT listener classes. The table lists the methods specified in each interface and some of the classes of objects that can generate the events for the particular listener.

Class derived from EventListener...	methods ...	can be added to any ...
ActionListener	actionPerformed()	JButton, JList, JTextField, JMenuItem
AdjustmentListener	adjustmentValueChanged()	JScrollBar
ComponentListener	componentHidden(), componentMoved(), componentResized(), componentShown()	JComponent
ContainerListener	componentAdded(), componentRemoved()	Container

Class derived from EventListener...	methods . . .	can be added to any . . .
FocusListener	focusGained(), focusLost()	Component
ItemListener	itemStateChanged()	JList, JCheckBox, JCheckboxMenuItem
KeyListener	keyPressed(), keyReleased(), keyTyped()	JComponent
MouseListener	mouseClicked(), mouseEntered(), mouseExited(), mousePressed(), mouseReleased()	JComponent
MouseMotionListener	mouseDragged(), mouseMoved()	JComponent
TextListener	textValueChanged()	JTextArea, JTextField
WindowListener	windowClosed(), windowClosing(), windowDeactivated(), windowDeiconified(), windowIconified(), windowOpened	JFrame

9.7.1 LISTENER ADAPTER CLASSES

For each AWT listener interface that specifies more than one method, AWT also provides an adapter class. An *adapter class* implements the corresponding interface, defining each method to do nothing—purely for convenience. Because the adapters are classes, you can't combine two adapters into a single class. Recall that Java doesn't allow multiple inheritance (see Section 7.10). However, you can combine one adapter and multiple interfaces.

For example, we could have implemented our GameEventHandler by using the MouseAdapter.

```
// GameEventHandler2.java - demo MouseAdapter
import java.awt.event.*;

class GameEventHandler2 extends MouseAdapter {
  public void mouseClicked(MouseEvent e) {
    GameBoard board = (GameBoard)e.getSource();
    int row = e.getY() / board.getCellHeight();
    int col = e.getX() / board.getCellWidth();
    if (board.getCell(row, col) == board.STATE0)
      board.setCell(row, col, board.STATE1);
    else
      board.setCell(row, col, board.STATE0);
    board.repaint();
  }
}
```

Because the class `MouseAdapter` provides "do nothing" implementations of all of the interface `MouseListener` methods, we need only redefine the one we care about.

9.8 PROGRAMMING STYLE

For large applications, you need to design the graphical user interface carefully. One useful technique involves the use of story boards. *Story boards* are mock-ups of screen shots from a program. These story boards can be used to test the ease of use of a GUI before you write any code.

To test a GUI using story boards, first create a series of mock-up screen shots, showing the screen as it should appear when a user performs a particular task. Then show a test user the first screen and ask the user to perform a particular task. The user says out loud what he or she would do—for example, "click on the button labeled open." When the user does this, display the story board showing the new appearance of the screen to the user. Continue this process until the user successfully completes the task or tries to do something inappropriate or unexpected. Unexpected behavior may signal the need for changes in the design of the GUI.

You can create story boards with pencil and paper, a computer drawing program, or a GUI builder. Many GUI builders for Java allow you to arrange quickly graphical components in a frame or applet. Some even allow automatic creation of connections between event sources and event listeners by using direct manipulation of the components as displayed on the screen. Using these tools, you can quickly put together a GUI. As with a paper story board, you should test these GUIs long before you build the rest of the program by having someone try the GUI. When the user clicks the button, you may need to bring up a different display if the action associated with the button can't be built quickly with the GUI builder.

Summary

- The class `BorderLayout` is the default layout manager for the content pane of a `JFrame`. A `BorderLayout` manager places one component on each border and one in the center.
- With a single container, you are limited to a single layout, such as `BorderLayout` or `GridLayout`. By nesting one container inside another, you can create many different layouts. The standard plain container class is `JPanel`.
- A layout manager may attempt to resize—for example, when the user resizes the window on the desktop. The layout manager calls the method `setBounds()` for the component, indicating the new location and size of the component. By defining `setBounds()` in a class that extends `JComponent`, you can have a custom component make adjustments so that any drawing done by the component still fits within the resized screen area.

- All drawing is done on an instance of the class `Graphics`. This class has methods for drawing lines, rectangles, ovals, arcs, polygons, and strings. It also has methods for setting the color and font.
- The basic drawing pen supported by the class `Graphics` draws lines and shapes with only a 1-pixel-wide line. The class `Graphics2D`, which extends `Graphics`, adds, among other things, the ability to draw wide lines and dashed lines.
- You can add a `JMenuBar` to a `JFrame` with the method `setMenuBar()`. A `JMenuBar` is a special container that can hold several `JMenu` objects. Each `JMenu` can contain sub-`JMenu` objects or `JMenuItems`. You can use these three classes together to create the standard menu bars found at the tops of many applications. When selected, a `JMenuItem` generates an `ActionEvent` just like a button.
- There are different event listener interfaces for the different types of events that can occur. Some event listener interfaces specify several methods. In those cases, there is also an adapter class, which defines each method in the interface to do nothing. The adapters are strictly for convenience and provide no additional functionality.

Review Questions

1. What is the default layout manager for the content pane of a `JFrame` object?
2. How could you create a GUI that has a column of buttons along the left edge and then two large display areas on the right? The outline of the components should look like

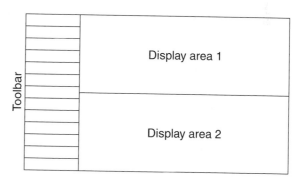

3. What type of event listener should you use to respond to selection of a menu item?
4. How does an event listener, listening to multiple sources, know where the event came from?
5. What is the difference between `MouseListener` and `MouseAdapter`?
6. How do you create cascading menus?
7. What sort of dashed or dotted line would result from creating a stroke with the following pattern array?

```
float[] pattern = { 10.0f, 4.0f, 4.0f, 4.0f, 4.0f, 4.0f };
```

8. What do you need to do if you want to draw thick lines?

9. There are two different ways to draw polygons using drawPolygon(). Describe them. Which should you use if you want to draw the same polygon in several places on the display?

Exercises

1. In a first attempt to create three buttons, we came up with

```java
//HelloButton3.java
import javax.swing.*;
import java.awt.*;
public class HelloButton3 {
   public static void main(String[] args) {
      JFrame frame = new JFrame("HelloButton");
      Container pane = frame.getContentPane();
      JButton hello = new JButton("Hello, world 1!");

      pane.add(hello);
      JButton more = new JButton("Hello, world 2!");
      pane.add(more);
      JButton end = new JButton("Hello, world 3!");
      pane.add(end);
      frame.pack();
      frame.show();
   }
}
```

Can you explain why only one button is displayed? Try to rewrite this code and have the buttons displayed in a nonoverlapping manner.

2. Add axes and labels to the class Plot defined in Section 9.3, on page 313.

3. Use the class Plot defined in Section 9.3, on page 313, to plot $2x^2 + 3x + 4$ in a stand-alone application using JFrame.

4. Redo the previous exercise using a JApplet instead of a JFrame.

5. Create a bar-chart component that extends JComponent. The constructor for the bar chart should take a single parameter that is an array of integer values corresponding to the lengths of the bars. Select a default size for the component and then scale the bars so that the longest bar is as tall as the component is high. Also scale the width of the bars so that they just fill the width of the bar chart. Include a method setBounds() so that, if the user resizes the component, the width and height of the bars are adjusted to continue to just fill the component. Write a simple program to test your component.

6. Create a bar-chart drawing class like the one in the previous exercise, but with the added ability to superimpose bars for two different arrays of data simultaneously by drawing them in different colors. (*Hint*: Always draw the longer bar first and then change the color and draw the shorter bar.) You can use predefined constants Color.red and Color.blue. Test your class in an applet or an application.

7. Use the class GameBoard as a starting point and create a GUI for the Predator–Prey simulation in Section 7.8. Use a 10×10 square to represent each cell in the world.

Fill the square with green for grass, red for fox, and pink for rabbits. The user can change any square by clicking it. Each click should change the square to the next value in the cycle of possible values (empty, grass, fox, or rabbit). For example, if a square is empty, clicking on it twice will change it to a fox. Control the progress of time with a button. Each click of the button should advance time one generation. You can use a `BorderLayout`, with the world in the center, a Quit button on one border, and the Next generation button on another border.

8. Modify the program in the previous exercise to use a menu. The menu bar should include a `File` menu with the option `Exit` and a `LifeForm` menu with the options `Empty`, `Grass`, `Fox`, and `Rabbit`. The currently selected life form is used to set a square when the user clicks on a square.

9. Use the following code to draw a series of smaller enclosed rectangles of different colors.

```
public void paint(Graphics g) {
  g.setColor(Color.white);
  g.fillRect(...); //fill in values
  g.setColor(Color.yellow);
  g.fillRect(...);
  g.setColor(Color.green);
  g.fillRect(...);
  g.drawRect(...);
}
```

Display your result in a window.

10. Create an application or applet that can be used to experiment and create colors. The program display should contain a rectangular area in the selected color, six buttons, and three text fields. Two buttons and a text field are associated with each of the three colors, red, green, and blue. Clicking one of the buttons will increase the associated color component, and clicking the other button will decrease it. The text field should display the current color component value, which should be in the range 0–255. Also, allow the text fields to be edited directly. Each time a component is changed, an area of the display should be filled to display the selected color. Create the color with the expression `new Color(red, green, blue)`, where `red`, `green`, and `blue` are integer values in the range 0–255.

11. Redo the previous exercise using a menu bar with three menus—one for each of the colors red, green, and blue. Each menu should contain items `More`, `Less`, `Max`, and `None`.

12. Draw a hexagon whose sides are all the same length. Such a figure is called a *regular hexagon*. In drawing the hexagon, color the interior red and leave the exterior white.

13. Use a `GridLayout` to draw a series of regular polygons down the screen. Start at the top with a triangle and end with an octagon.

14. Investigate the fonts available on your Java system. Redo the previous exercise, labeling each regular polygon with a text field that uses a different font. Your system should support the fonts Helvetica and Roman in plain, bold, and italic.

15. Develop a simple text window that has a pull-down menu and submenus. Label the chief menu `Format` and the submenus `Font`, `Size`, and `Style`. When these various options are selected, change the text window accordingly. This procedure is similar to most editing and desktop publishing programs that allow you to change fonts.

16. Create an application or applet for plotting arrays of data using drawPolyLine().

17. Given the position and velocity of a ball, you can approximate the new position and velocity of the ball after time *delta* with the equations

$$x_{t+delta} = x_t + vx_t \times delta;$$

$$y_{t+delta} = y_t + vy_t \times delta;$$

$$vx_{t+delta} = vx_t;$$

$$vy_{t+delta} = vy_t - 32.$$

Write an application or an applet to simulate a bouncing ball. To begin you can control the simulation by clicking a button for each tick of the clock. At each tick, compute the new position of the ball and draw it. Assume that the ball is in a box and reverse the sign of the *y* velocity component whenever the ball hits the top or bottom of the box. Likewise, reverse the sign of the *x* velocity component whenever the ball hits either side of the box. To get your simulation to run automatically, you can use the following template. (The method sleep() is discussed in Section 13.7.) The class Ball is similar to the sample drawing classes such as Star and others.

```
//BouncingBall.java - driver for ball simulation
class BouncingBall {
  public static void main(String[] args)
      // the following is needed when calling sleep
      // see Chapter 11 for more about exceptions
      throws InterruptedException
  {
    Ball ball = new Ball();
    // code to create a JFrame, add ball to its
    // container pane and show the JFrame goes here
    Thread self = Thread.currentThread();
    while (true) {
      //call some method in Ball to set new position
      ball.repaint();
      self.sleep(100); //pauses 1/10th second
      // code to update position and velocity here
    }
  }
}
```

18. Create an application or an applet that lets the user select from a list of functions, specify a range of values and a delta, and then plot the function. Provide a menu of functions from which the user can choose.

19. A JButton can be used to select one of several options by changing the label of the JButton. Create a test program that uses a button to cycle among four labels: empty, grass, rabbit, and fox. Each time the button is clicked the label should be changed to the next label in the cycle. Use an ActionListener to echo to the console the currently selected label.

10

Reading and Writing Files

In our programs so far, user input has been from the keyboard or mouse. All output has been printed to the console or displayed in a graphical user interface. In this chapter we show you how to read data from a file and write data to a file.

Excluding graphical input and output, all input and output (I/O) in Java is done with streams. A Java *stream* is a sequence of bytes. An input stream can come from a file, from keystrokes at the console, or from a network. Likewise, an output stream may go to a file, to the console screen, or out over a network. At the top level, the same classes are used for all types of stream input and output. The primary differences among the various classes we present are caused by the need for different byte streams to be reassembled differently to form meaningful values inside a program.

If you have some sequence of 32 bits, the meaning of those 32 bits depends on whether they correspond to an `int`, a `float`, two 16-bit Unicode characters, or something else. In the same way, you can interpret a stream of bytes in different ways. You must be careful to match the method used to write the stream with the method used to read the stream.

10.1 TYPES OF FILES

In Java, as with most operating systems today, files can be broken into two broad categories: text files and binary files.

In a *text file*, each byte is interpreted as a single character. In most cases the character set is the ASCII character set. You can display a text file by using almost any editor on your computer. A text file may use special sequences of characters to encode text formatting or other information. For example, HTML files used on the Internet are text files with tags for formatting. Recall that HTML tags are generally enclosed by angle brackets `<like this>`. The source files for Java programs are text files.

The other broad category of files is *binary files*, which includes everything but text files. Binary files typically use the same bit patterns to represent data as those used to represent the data in the computer's main memory. These files are called binary files because the only thing they have in common is that they store the data as sequences of 0s and 1s. There are a huge number of different binary file formats—Java class files, executable images for your computer, the normal file format for most word processors, the image and audio files used for the Internet, and many more.

For example, suppose that you wanted to store a sequence of `int` values in a file. You know that an integer is 32 bits, or 4 bytes, long, so you could just place the 4 bytes for each integer in the file, one after another, to create a binary file. That would also be a very compact way of storing the integers. However, if you tried to look at this file with a normal editor, you would just get garbage on your screen. The reason is that the editor expects characters and wouldn't recognize that you were encoding integers. The editor would interpret each byte as an ASCII character that in no way resembles the text representation of the corresponding integer. For example, the `int` value 1234 occupies 32 bits, or 4 bytes. The binary representation of 1234 is the sequence of 0s and 1s in the following figure. The 32-bit sequence has been divided into the four 8-bit bytes.

Byte 0	Byte 1	Byte 2	Byte 3
00000000	00000000	00000100	11010010

If each byte is viewed as an integer (see Appendix A.1), you would get the following:

Byte 0	Byte 1	Byte 2	Byte 3
0	0	4	210

Unlike Java, most text editors use ASCII values instead of Unicode. To a text editor, none of these 4 bytes correspond to printable ASCII characters. For comparison, here are the four bytes needed to represent the text string `"1234"`.

Byte 0	Byte 1	Byte 2	Byte 3
49	50	51	52

The ASCII code for the digit 1 is 49, the code for the digit 2 is 50, and so on. If what you cared about was space on the disk for storing the numbers, the binary representation might be the right choice. Although 1234 takes 4 bytes in either format, any integer value greater than 9999 will require more than 4 bytes when stored as text. Recall that 4 bytes are sufficient to store numbers as large as 2 billion, or 10 decimal digits, when stored in binary form.

Instead of writing the 4 bytes of an `int` to a file, you can write the sequence of text characters used to represent the number. Such sequences would include the 10 digits and possibly the minus sign. You would also have to use some special character to separate one number from the next—for example, a space or a comma. This format would be a text file, which would use much more space on your computer's disk. If you wanted to be able to view or modify the file with an editor or use e-mail to send the numbers to someone else, this format might be preferable.

Java's standard package `java.io` contains classes that support the reading and writing of both binary and text files.

10.2 WRITING TEXT FILES

The simplest way to write text to a file requires the use of two different classes—`PrintWriter` and `FileWriter`—both from the standard package `java.io`. The class `PrintWriter` has the familiar methods `print()` and `println()` that we've been using to write to the console. To create a `PrintWriter` object that is associated with a particular file, we must first create a `FileWriter` object for that file. This object is then passed to the constructor for the `PrintWriter` as shown in the following example.

```java
//HelloFile.java - writing to a file
import java.io.*;

class HelloFile {
  public static void main(String[] args)
        throws java.io.IOException
  {
    PrintWriter out =
      new PrintWriter(new FileWriter("hello.txt"));
    out.println("Hello, file system!");
    out.close();
  }
}
```

If you run this program, it will create a file, *hello.txt*, which you can view with any text editor. The contents of the file will be the one line "Hello, file system!".

DISSECTION OF THE CLASS HelloFile

■ `import java.io.*;`

We must import the package `java.io`. That is where the `PrintWriter` and `FileWriter` classes are defined.

■   `public static void main(String[] args)`
           `throws java.io.IOException`

Many of the methods for I/O can generate an I/O exception. As discussed in Chapter 11, an exception is something unexpected that occurs. Often an exception is really an error. In this example, if the output file couldn't be opened for some reason, an `IOException` would be generated. A statement or method that generates an exception is said to throw an exception. The class `IOException` is defined in the package `java.io`. We can either give the full name of the exception, `java.io.IOException`, as in this example, or because we are importing `java.io.*` we can use the shorter name, `IOException`.

■   `PrintWriter out =`
     `new PrintWriter(new FileWriter("hello.txt"));`

The class `FileWriter` needs the name of the file as a string. This name can include directory information, which is platform dependent. When no directory information is specified, the file is created in the operating system's notion of the current directory. The resulting `FileWriter` object is used to construct a `PrintWriter` object.

■   `out.println("Hello file system!");`
    `out.close();`

Anything that we can do with `System.out.print()` or `System.out.println()` we can do with the corresponding method from `PrintWriter`. Closing the file when the program terminates is essential. Failure to close the `PrintWriter` stream may cause some or all of the output not to appear in the file.

Why do we need the two classes `PrintWriter` and `FileWriter`? The reason is that the Java I/O package is designed to support many different types of input–output processing. Think of the classes in the package as building blocks. By assembling the correct set of building blocks, you can meet many different I/O processing needs. You can use the class `FileWriter` to write a stream of text characters into a file, but the methods in `FileWriter` are fairly primitive and support only the writing of text from `String`, `char`, and `char[]` values. The class `PrintWriter` from the same package can generate a stream of text characters from any value. The primary methods in class `PrintWriter` are the familiar `print()` and `println()` used for writing to the console. By passing a `FileWriter` object to the constructor of a `PrintWriter`, you are logically creating a sequence or pipeline of processing steps, as shown in the following figure.

You can use the class `PrintWriter` to create text streams that go somewhere other than to a file. For example, you can also use a `PrintWriter` to write over a network or to write to a character array. The output of the `PrintWriter` is sent to the stream specified in the constructor. In this case, it is a `FileWriter`.

10.3 READING TEXT FILES

Reading a text file is as easy as reading from the keyboard. All along we've been using the class `tio.ReadInput` to read from the console. The expression `Console.in` is just a convenient variable provided in the package `tio`. It refers to a `ReadInput` object that is reading from `System.in` (the standard input stream), which is the keyboard unless we've used some type of file redirection. We can create additional `ReadInput` objects by passing the constructor a `String` that will be interpreted as the name of a file from which to read. Recall that the package `tio` isn't a standard Java package. After showing you how to read from a file with `tio`, we show you how to do so with standard Java. The following program reads in the file that we wrote in `HelloFile`.

```
//HelloFileRead.java - reading a text file
import tio.*;

class HelloFileRead {
  public static void main(String[] args)
  {
    ReadInput in = new ReadInput("hello.txt");
    System.out.println(in.readLine());
  }
}
```

The method `readLine()` is used to read an entire line of input as a `String`, stopping when it encounters a newline character. The newline character isn't included in the resulting string. As we showed when reading from `Console.in`, we can use a `ReadInput` object to read numbers and white-space delimited words. In the next example, we use a `ReadInput` object to read one `int`, one `double`, and one word from the file *sample.txt*.

```
//FileReadInput - reading primitive values from a file
import tio.*;

class FileReadInput {
  public static void main(String[] args)
  {
    ReadInput in = new ReadInput("sample.txt");
    int x = in.readInt();
    double y = in.readDouble();
    String s = in.readWord();
    System.out.println("x = " + x);
    System.out.println("y = " + y);
    System.out.println("s = " + s);
  }
}
```

The first thing in the file *sample.txt* is expected to be a sequence of characters representing an integer, the next a floating point value, and, finally, anything. The method `readWord()` returns the next white-space-delimited sequence of characters in the input. If the file *sample.txt* contains the single line

```
-1234 0.0001234 1234 567
```

the output would be

```
x = -1234
y = 1.234E-4
s = 1234
```

The third input item, `1234`, was actually read as a string. Note that it stopped at the white space between `1234` and `567`.

The next program counts the number of words in a file.

```
//WordCount.java - count the words in a file
import tio.*;

class WordCount {
  public static void main(String[] args)
  {
    ReadInput in = new ReadInput("sample.txt");
    int count = 0;
    while (in.hasMoreElements()) {
      String word = in.readWord();
      count++;
    }
    System.out.println("There were " + count + " words.");
  }
}
```

The class `ReadInput` has the methods

```
int readInt()
long readLong()
float readFloat()
double readDouble()
String readWord()
char readChar()
String readLine()
boolean hasMoreElements()
```

The method `hasMoreElements()` is used to determine whether there are any non-white-space characters left in the input. It is intended to be used with the first five *read* methods. White space is used to delimit consecutive input values, except for `readChar()` and `readLine()`. The method `readChar()` returns the next character, even if it is a white-space character. The method `readLine()` reads all characters up to the next newline. The newline character is read and discarded because it isn't part of the return value. The number-reading routines will generate an error if the next white-space delimited sequence of characters in the input isn't a proper numeric value of the requested type. The error is reported by throwing a `java.lang.Error` exception. Unless caught (see Section 11.1), this exception will print a descriptive error message and abort the program.

10.3.1 READING A TEXT FILE WITH STANDARD JAVA CLASSES

Two difficulties are introduced when we want to read text files by using only standard Java packages. The first is similar to the minor difficulty we encountered with writing text files when we needed the two classes `PrintWriter` and `FileWriter`. The standard class `java.io.FileReader` provides methods only for reading one character at a time or reading in a character array. To convert this input stream of characters into a string, we can use the class `java.io.BufferedReader`, which has a method `readLine()`. This method works just like its namesake in the class `tio.ReadInput`. Unlike `ReadInput`, when using `BufferedReader` we need to declare that our method could throw the exception `java.io.IOException`. In `ReadInput`, all `IOExceptions` are turned into errors that don't require a `throws` clause (see Section 11.7). Here is our original code for reading from a file, redone using these two standard Java classes.

```
//HelloFileRead2.java - using standard classes to read
import java.io.*;

class HelloFileRead2 {
  public static void main(String[] args)
        throws IOException
  {
    BufferedReader in = new BufferedReader(
              new FileReader("hello.txt"));
    System.out.println(in.readLine());
  }
}
```

The following illustration shows how the byte stream from the file is first processed by the `FileReader` and then turned into a string by the `BufferedReader`.

10.3.2 PARSING TEXT STREAMS

The second difficulty associated with using standard Java classes to read text files arises from trying to pull numbers from strings. Several alternatives don't involve the use of `ReadInput`. The easiest of the alternatives works only if the input file or input stream has only one number on each input line. In this case we can use the `BufferedReader` shown earlier to read an entire line as a string with the method `readLine()`. We can then use methods in the classes `Integer`, `Long`, `Float`, and `Double` to convert the string to the appropriate value.

Type represented by String s	Convert with
int	Integer.parseInt(s.trim())
long	Long.parseLong(s.trim())
float	Float.parseFloat(s.trim())
double	Double.parseDouble(s.trim())

The method `trim()` from the class `String` trims any leading or trailing white space. The methods parse*Type*`()` will throw a `NumberFormatException` if they encounter white space in the string being converted.

If limiting files to only one number per line isn't acceptable, some method must be found for pulling out the strings that represent each of the numbers. For some applications, using the class `java.io.StreamTokenizer` may be appropriate. Another option is to do something similar to what we did in class `ReadInput`. A complete version of `ReadInput` is included in Appendix C.1.

10.4   FORMATTING TEXT OUTPUT

Most programming languages provide some form of formatted output. However, the lack of this capability is another serious deficiency in the current Java packages. For example, there is no simple way to print a large set of numbers to a text file with the numbers lined up in columns below column headings. This deficiency is probably the result of Java's focus on graphical user interfaces.

Formatted output takes two general forms. In one form, some type of formatting information is included in the statement that does the printing. For example, the programming language C allows the printing of three integers `i`, `j`, and `k` in columns 10 characters wide with

```
printf("%-10d %-10d %-10d", i, j, k);
```

The first parameter for the procedure `printf()` (recall that a procedure is like a method) is a format string. The percent sign marks the format specification for one value to be printed. The `-10d` indicates that the value is an integer (`d` for decimal) in a field 10 characters wide that is left-justified in the field. The specification `%10d` makes the value right-justified in the field. Similar format specifications are provided for printing strings, floating point values, and other types.

The second general form of formatting is for stream output. In this form, the stream has an internal state that remembers how certain values should be formatted and a mechanism for changing the formatting information in the stream. This approach is used by stream output in the programming language C++. For example, to print the same three integers i, j, and k in columns 10 characters wide, using C++ streams, we would use

```
cout << setw(10) << i << j << k;
```

In C++ `cout` is the name of the standard output stream, which is analogous to `System.out` in Java. The symbol `<<` is an operator that sends its right operand to the stream that is the left operand. The value of the expression `stream << value` is the stream after doing whatever it is supposed to do with `value`. Thus, when evaluated from left to right, the expression first sends out the formatting command `setw(10)`, which sets the width of the subsequent output fields to be 10 characters wide. Then the integers i, j, and k are sent in order.

We believe that this form is the best match for Java's existing stream classes. The package `tio` includes the class `FormattedWriter` that implements basic text formatting. It includes the ability to specify

- the width of a field,
- left or right justification in the field,
- the fill character, and
- the number of digits to print to the right of the decimal point in floating point values.

The complete source for `FormattedWriter` can be found Appendix C.2.

DISSECTION OF THE CLASS `FormattedWriter`

- ```
  package tio;
  import java.io.*;

  public class FormattedWriter extends PrintWriter
  ```

Part of the `tio` package, `FormattedWriter` extends `PrintWriter` by adding methods to do formatted printing. For each method `print()` or `println()` in `PrintWriter`, we add the formatted version `printf()` or `printfln()`. In using `FormattedWriter` in our own work, we discovered that we wanted to retain the unformatted print routines to allow formatted and unformatted printing to be easily mixed.

- ```
  public static final int LEFT = 1;
  public static final int RIGHT = 2;
  ```

We declare class constants that are used to specify left or right justification, using the method `setJustify()`. Using class constants makes programs more readable.

```
■ public FormattedWriter(OutputStream os) {
    super(os, true); // make default auto-flushing
  }
  public FormattedWriter(FileWriter writer) {
    super(writer, true);
  }
  public FormattedWriter(String filename)
    throws java.io.IOException
  {
    this(new FileWriter(filename));
  }
```

No additional initialization is needed beyond that done by the constructors in `PrintWriter`. We simply invoke the appropriate constructor in `PrintWriter` by using `super()`. The third constructor is for convenience only. Using the second constructor, we could construct a `FormattedWriter` for a file using

```
new FormattedWriter(new FileWriter(filename))
```

```
■ public void setWidth(int width) {
    if (width < 0)
      this.width = 0;
    else if (width > MAX_WIDTH)
      this.width = MAX_WIDTH;
    else
      this.width = width;
  }
```

This method is used to tell the stream how wide the current field should be. All formatted output will be padded to fill a field `width` characters wide until changed by a subsequent call to `setWidth()`. We chose to specify a maximum width for padded fields.

```
■ public void setDigits(int places) {
    decimalPlaces = places;
    form.setMaximumFractionDigits(decimalPlaces);
  }
```

This method remembers the number of decimal places and sets the number formatting object `form`, appropriately. These are used when printing `float` or `double` values. We discuss the private instance variable `form` shortly.

```
■ public void setJustify(int leftOrRight) {
    if (leftOrRight != LEFT && leftOrRight != RIGHT)
      throw new IllegalArgumentException(
        "use FormattedWriter.LEFT or" +
        " FormattedWriter.RIGHT");
    justify = leftOrRight;
  }
```

This method first checks to determine that the user has specified a legal value. If so, the value is recorded; if not, an exception is thrown. The `IllegalArgumentException` is a standard Java exception from `java.lang`.

```
▪ public void setPadChar(char pad) {
    if (pad == ' ')
      padding = spaces;
    else if (pad == '0')
      padding = zeros;
    else
      padding = buildPadding(MAX_WIDTH, pad);
  }
```

For efficiency, a string of zeros and a string of spaces are precomputed for use as padding. If any other pad character is selected, a string of MAX_WIDTH pad characters is created. These strings of pad characters are used to fill out the field.

```
▪ public void printf(String s) {
    if (s.length() >= width)
      super.print(s);
    else if (justify == LEFT)
      super.print(s +
        padding.substring(0, width - s.length()));
    else
      super.print(
        padding.substring(0, width - s.length()) + s);
  }
```

This method adds the appropriate number of spaces to the beginning or end of the string s and then prints it by using the method print() inherited from Print-Writer. The padding is done by extracting an appropriately long substring from padding, which is just a long string of padding characters. The method call x.substring(start, end) extracts a substring from x, starting with the character at position start and continuing to, but not including, the character at position end. In our example, if width is 10 and s.length() is 6, the substring of padding starting with position 0 and continuing to but not including position 4 would be used, for a total of 4 spaces. If the string s is wider than the field, the entire string is printed.

```
▪ public void printf(boolean value) {
    printf(String.valueOf(value));
  }
```

There are methods like this one for char, char[], int, long, and Object. Each converts its parameter to a string and passes the result to printf(String) to do the actual padding. In this way the code to do the padding isn't duplicated.

```
▪ public void printf(double value) {
    printf(trimDigits(String.valueOf(value)));
  }
```

The work of trimming and rounding decimal places is handled by trimDigits(). The method printf(float) is similar to printf(double).

```
▪ public void println(String s) {
    printf(s);
    println();
  }
```

There are methods like this one for `char`, `char[]`, `int`, `long`, `float`, `double`, and `Object`. Each uses the corresponding `printf()` method to format the output and then adds a newline by calling `println()`.

■
```
private String trimDigits(String value) {
   int places;

   if (decimalPlaces == -1)
      return value;
   int pos = value.indexOf(".");
   int exp = value.indexOf("E");
```

This private method isn't part of the public interface of `FormattedWriter`. It takes as input a string representation of a floating point value—possibly including an exponent, as in `1.23456E-20`—and returns a string with the number of digits to the right of the decimal point limited as specified by `decimalPlaces`. If `decimalPlaces` is `-1`, the string is left unchanged. The method next locates the position of the decimal point and exponent, if they exist.

■
```
if (exp == -1)
   places = value.length() - pos - 1;
else
   places = exp - pos - 1;
if (places < decimalPlaces)
   return value;
```

Here we compute the number of decimal places to the right of the decimal point in the current representation of the floating point value. This number is the rest of the string if there is no exponent; otherwise, it is the string from the decimal point to the position of the exponent. If `places` is less than `decimalPlaces`, there is nothing to trim and the current representation is simply returned.

■
```
String needsRounding = value.substring(0, exp);
if (exp == -1)
   return round(needsRounding);
else
   return round(needsRounding) + value.substring(exp);
```

Here we extract the mantissa, that is, the part without the exponent. This value is then rounded to the correct number of decimal places. This rounded result is then recombined with the exponent if there is one.

■
```
private String round(String s) {
   double temp = Double.parseDouble(s);
   System.out.println(temp);
   // form is a java.text.NumberFormat object
   return form.format(Double.parseDouble(s));
}
```

The standard Java class `java.text.NumberFormat` provides support for specifying the format of decimal numbers that don't contain an exponent. We use that class to do the work of rounding the mantissa to the desired number of digits. The `format()` method of `NumberFormat` operates only on floating point values, not strings. We therefore convert the string representation of the mantissa to a `double` and then use `form.format()` to get the desired rounded string. The variable `form` is set to refer to a `NumberFormat` object when it is declared as described shortly. The number of decimal places used by `form` is set by calling `form.setMaximum-DecimalDigits()` from `setDigits()`, as shown earlier.

- ```java
  private static String buildPadding(int width, char pad) {
      StringBuffer sbuf = new StringBuffer(width);
      for (int i = 0; i < width; i++)
        sbuf.append(pad);
      return sbuf.toString();
  }
  ```

This private method creates the strings of padding characters used to fill for left or right justification. Once we have filled the `StringBuffer` variable `sbuf` with the desired number of pad characters, we convert it to a string.

- ```java
  private static int MAX_WIDTH = 40;
  private static final String spaces =
      buildPadding(MAX_WIDTH, ' ');
  private static final String zeros =
      buildPadding(MAX_WIDTH, '0');
  private String padding = spaces;
  private int width = 0;
  private int justify = LEFT;
  ```

Here we create the default padding strings and set the default padding to be spaces. We also set the default justification to be left-justified and set the field width to 0 which means no limitation.

- ```java
  private int decimalPlaces = -1;
  private NumberFormat form = NumberFormat.getInstance();
  ```

The default value of `-1` for `decimalPlaces` means that no trimming is to be done. Here we create the `java.text.NumberFormat` object used in trimming the decimal digits. As an abstract class, `NumberFormat` can't be instantiated. However, it contains the method `getInstance()`, which returns an object that is an instance of a class derived from `NumberFormat`. The actual type of the object is location dependent because the standard format for numbers varies in different parts of the world.

The following short example demonstrates the use of `FormattedWriter`. It prints three numbers in three columns with headings.

```java
//FormattedOutput.java - demo of formatted text output
import tio.*;
class FormattedOutput {
  public static void main(String[] args)
        throws java.io.IOException
  {
    int x = 1, y = 22;
```
```

```
        double z = 4.5678E-20;
        FormattedWriter out = new FormattedWriter(System.out);
        out.setWidth(10);
        out.setDigits(2);
        out.printf("col1");
        out.printf("col2");
        out.println("col3");
        out.printf(x);
        out.printf(y);
        out.println(z);
    }
}
```

The output of this program is

```
col1      col2       col3
1         22         4.57E-20
```


10.5   PROBLEM SOLVING: ENCRYPTING TEXT FILES

An important technique for providing security for files is encryption. In ordinary text, called *clear text*, the text is written in words that are part of the reader's vocabulary. In this book, that vocabulary is English. With encryption, the text is transformed to apparently meaningless characters. Typically, encryption is done with an algorithm called a *cipher*. For example, a simple cipher is the *Caesar cipher*. Here the algorithm replaces each clear text letter by a letter chosen to be n places later in the alphabet. The number of places, n, is called the *cipher key*. For example, if the key is 1, the clear text "I came, I saw, I conquered." becomes "J dbnf, J tbx, J dporvfsfe."

The characters in Java are encoded as Unicode, and these codes are 2-byte integers. For example, the character `'A'` is the number 65 and the character `'a'` is the number 97. The blank character `' '` is the integer 32. We restrict our discussion here to encoding the uppercase alphabetic characters. The set of characters `'A'`, `'B'`, ..., `'Z'` correspond to the integers 65–90.

The Caesar cipher can be implemented as a Java method that transforms the character value by the value of the key.

```
//Caesar Cipher method
static char caesarCipher(char c, int key) {
    return (c - 'A' + key) % 26 + 'A';
}
```

This code is easy to break because it relies on a very simple substitution. If we have a long message in this cipher, we can use frequency tables to decrypt this cipher (see Exercise 15 on page 368). Or we can write a program that runs through the keys 1–26 and see if they yield clear text.

A slight generalization of the Caesar cipher is the *Vignere cipher*. Here we use a repeated series of displacements such as 1 3 5 to produce the text.

Clear text	I AM GOING TO UCSC
Offset	1 35 13513 51 3513
Vignere cipher	J DR HRNOJ YP XHTF

One immediate improvement is that different occurrences of a particular letter are mapped to different cipher letters. For example, the first I in the example above is mapped to J but the I in GOING is mapped to N. The longer the Vignere key, the better the cipher. Such an encryption method can be coded in the following form.

```
//Vignere Cipher method
static char vignereCipher(char c, int[] key) {
   //left as an exercise
}
```

This code is more difficult to break. Indeed, the longer the sequence of keys, the harder it is to break the cipher. If the key is as long as the clear text, we have the Vernam cipher, better known as a *one-time pad*. Such a system is provably unbreakable. If the one-time pad involves a randomly generated set of displacements, the cipher is random and only someone with the key can decrypt it.

We can simulate such a scheme by using a pseudorandom number generator to produce the one-time pad. Our scheme first involves taking the uppercase alphabet and mapping it onto 0–25. Next, we add in randomLetter—a value between 0 and 25, inclusive. We now have values between 0 and 50 that are pseudorandom, and we map them back onto the values 0–25 and add 'A' to get Unicode character values for the characters in the cipher text. Thus our total encryption formula is

```
((c - 'A' + randomLetter) % 26 + 'A')
```

and the corresponding decryption formula is

```
((c - 'A' + 26 - randomLetter) % 26 + 'A')
```

We must start encryption and decryption at the same point in our pseudorandom sequence. What happens if we forget to do so? (See Exercise 16, on page 369.)

Let's use our random number simulation of the one-time pad to encrypt the characters of clear text. In our code we use the class Random to obtain appropriate random numbers. It is found in java.util.Random. The method nextDouble() acting on a Random object returns a random value between 0 and 1. Extending this to decryption is left for you to do as Exercise 17 on page 369.

```
//VernamCipher.java - cipher based on random pad
import java.io.*;
import java.util.*;    //random number methods
import tio.*;

class VernamCipher{
```

```
    public static void main(String[] args)
       throws IOException
    {
       if (args.length < 2) {
         System.out.println("Usage: " +
             "java VernamCipher clearFile codeFile");
         System.exit(1);
       }
       ReadInput in = new ReadInput(args[0]);
       PrintWriter out = new PrintWriter(new FileWriter(args[1]));
       Random r = new Random(7);

       while (in.hasMoreElements()){
         out.println(encrypt(in.readLine(), r));
       }
       out.close();
    }
    public static String encrypt(String message, Random r) {
       System.out.println(message);
       char c;
       StringBuffer cipher = new StringBuffer(message.length());
       for (int i = 0; i < message.length(); i++){
         c = message.charAt(i);
         if (Character.isLetter(c))
           cipher.append( (char) ((Character.toUpperCase(c) - 'A' +
               (int)(r.nextDouble() * 26)) % 26 + 'A'));
         else
           cipher.append(c);
       }
       System.out.println(cipher.toString());
       return cipher.toString();
    }
}
```

10.6 READING AND WRITING BINARY FILES

For development purposes, you should use text files whenever possible. When that isn't possible or desirable, you can use the two classes DataInputStream and DataOutputStream to read and write binary files. The methods in DataInput-Stream include

```
readBoolean()
readByte()
readChar()
readDouble()
```

```
readFloat()
readInt()
readLong()
readShort()
readUTF()
```

Each method has a counterpart in `DataOutputStream` that begins with `write` instead of `read`. In each case the method reads or writes the specified primitive type, or in the case of UTF, it reads or writes string values. The strings are encoded with a modified UTF-8 format; hence the name of the method. This format allows Unicode strings composed entirely of characters from the ASCII set to be encoded with 1 byte per character instead of the 2 bytes required for Unicode characters without any encoding.

There is no type information stored in a binary file other than information that is explicitly written by the program creating the binary file. Therefore it is essential that the sequence of reads when reading a file must exactly match the sequence of writes used to generate the file.

In the following program, 1 `int` and 10 `double` values are written to a file and then are read back in from the file. Note that nothing is written to the file to separate the values. The binary format knows to read 4 bytes for an `int` and 8 bytes for a `double`. If you try to view the output file *test.bin* with an editor, you will see garbage. Again, we need two classes to read (or write) a file. The class `DataInputStream` has the desired methods `readInt()` and so on, and the class `FileInputStream` creates a byte stream from a file.

```java
//BinIOTest.java
import java.io.*;

class BinIOTest {
  public static void main(String[] args) throws IOException {
    DataOutputStream out = new DataOutputStream(
                    new FileOutputStream("test.bin"));
    double x = 1.0;
    int count = 10;
    out.writeInt(count);
    for (int i = 0; i < count; i++) {
      out.writeDouble(x);
      x = x / 3.0;
    }
    out.close();
    DataInputStream in = new DataInputStream(
                    new FileInputStream("test.bin"));
    count = in.readInt();
    for (int i = 0; i < count; i++) {
      System.out.println(in.readDouble());
    }
  }
}
```

Compare the preceding example with the following example, which does the same thing but with a text file. Here we use `println()` to place a newline character between each consecutive pair of values in the file. Without these newline characters, all the characters would run together, and we wouldn't know where one number ends and the next begins. The file *test.txt* can be viewed with any standard text editor. If this were a real application that was storing millions of values instead of 10 values, the execution time and size difference of the two resulting files, *test.bin* and *test.txt*, would be substantial.

```
//TextIOTest.java
import java.io.*;
import tio.*;

class TextIOTest {
  public static void main(String[] args) throws IOException {
    PrintWriter out = new PrintWriter(
                      new FileWriter("test.txt"));

    double x = 1.0;
    int count = 10;
    out.println(count);
    for (int i = 0; i < count; i++) {
      out.println(x);
      x = x / 3.0;
    }
    out.close();
    ReadInput in = new ReadInput("test.txt");
    count = in.readInt();
    for (int i = 0; i < count; i++) {
      System.out.println(in.readDouble());
    }
  }
}
```

Trying to use a `DataInputStream` object to read from `System.in` is tempting. Although the following program will compile and execute, it won't give the expected results. As we explained in Section 10.1, the `DataInputStream` is interpreting each byte as 1 byte of a 4-byte integer. However, the bytes produced by the keyboard are the ASCII representations of each digit.

```
//MisuseDataInputStream.java - doesn't read correctly
import java.io.*;
import tio.*;

class MisuseDataInputStream {
  public static void main(String[] args) throws IOException {
    DataInputStream input = new DataInputStream(System.in);
    System.out.println("Enter 4 integers.");
    for (int i = 0; i < 4; i++){
      int value = input.readInt();
      System.out.println("You entered " + value);
    }
  }
}
```

COMMON PROGRAMMING ERROR

Care must be taken when you're writing files. Depending on the operating system you're using and the file protections that are set, it may be possible to accidentally overwrite an existing file. In general, Java systems allow you to open an existing file for output. Using the methods previously described, any existing data are replaced with the new data. For example, if you execute the program `Hello-File` while in a directory that already contains a file named *hello.txt*, any data previously in the file are lost and no warning will be given.

To append data to an existing file you can use the class `RandomAccess-File`. This class is intended for use with binary files and provides methods similar to those in the classes `DataInputStream` and `DataOutputStream`. In addition, it allows you to skip to the end of the file before beginning to write.

Another way to append data to a file is to create an output stream and copy the existing file to a temporary file. Then using the same output stream, you can append new data. When finished, you can close the output stream and rename the temporary file using the method `renameTo()` in the class `java.io.File`. If you take this approach, be sure to select a long meaningless file name for the temporary file. A good solution is to name the file something like *temp123456*, where the digits are chosen randomly by calling `Math.random()`. An even better solution is to use the method `File.createTempFile()`, which creates a temporary file in the operating system's default temporary directory.

The class `File` also has methods that allow you to determine whether a file already exists and, if so, whether the file can be read or written.

10.7 DETECTING THE END OF AN INPUT STREAM

Because streams are most often, at least historically, associated with files, the end of a stream is referred to as *end-of-file* (EOF). Detecting the end of a stream varies from class to class. The EOF is a sentinel, or guard, value that is important for most file-reading programming idioms. Its detection is often used to terminate processing on that file.

If you're using the class `ReadInput`, you can test whether more text remains to be read by calling `hasMoreElements()`. If you fail to check for EOF by calling `hasMoreElements()` and try to read beyond the end of a stream using any method except `readLine()` or `readChar()`, the read operation will throw an exception.

The method `readLine()` returns `null` if there is no more input, and `readChar()` returns -1.

The dichotomy between `readLine()` and `readChar()`, and the other methods arises because there is no special value that a method such as `readInt()` can return to signify it has reached the end of the file. For methods such as `readLine()` that return a value of type `String`, the value `null` is a legal return value that doesn't correspond to any string value that could be read in. Note that `null` isn't the same as the empty string, `""`. An empty string occurs if a line containing nothing but a newline character is read, which is quite different from encountering the EOF.

If you're using the class `DataInputStream`, a similar dichotomy arises. The methods for reading specific primitive values discussed in this chapter throw an `EOFException` when you try to read beyond the end of a stream. However, `DataInputStream` also includes methods for reading individual bytes that don't throw `EOFExceptions`. For example, the method `read()` returns the next byte as an `int` value between 0 and 255, inclusive. If the end of the stream has been reached, the method returns -1. The class `DataInputStream` also contains a method `readLine()` that tries to interpret bytes as a string in much the same way as `readLine()` in `ReadInput`. The version in `DataInputStream` doesn't always work correctly, shouldn't be used, and is being phased out. If you try to use it, you'll get a warning message that the method has been *deprecated*. This message means that the method may not be available in future versions of Java. For reading complete lines of text, the method `readLine()` in the standard Java class `BufferedReader` can be used.

If you're using `BufferedReader` to input text, you won't get an `EOFException`. All the methods in `BufferedReader` signal EOF by returning some kind of special value. The method `readLine()` returns `null` if the end of the stream has been reached. Unlike the version in `DataInputStream`, this method always works correctly.

We summarize this information in the following table.

Class	Method	EOF detected by
tio.ReadInput	all	hasMoreElements(); returns false
	readLine()	returns null
	readChar()	returns -1
java.io.DataInputStream	read*Primitive*()	EOFException
	readLine()	returns null
	read()	returns -1
java.io.BufferedReader	readLine()	returns null
	read()	returns -1

In the following example we demonstrate detecting EOF with the standard Java class `BufferedReader`. The program simply opens the file specified on the command line and echoes its contents to the console.

```
// Echo.java - echo file contents to the screen
import java.io.*;

class Echo {
  public static void main(String[] args) throws IOException {
    if (args.length < 1){
      System.out.println("Usage: java Echo filename");
      System.exit(0);
    }
    BufferedReader input =
        new BufferedReader(new FileReader(args[0]));
    String line = input.readLine();
    while (line != null) {
      System.out.println(line);
      line = input.readLine();
    }
  }
}
```

10.8 PROGRAMMING STYLE

Although GUI-based programs currently dominate much of computing, many programs are still invoked from a command line such as a Windows or Unix command line interpreter, also called a *shell*. These programs typically have one or more parameters that are specified on the command line. Remembering the exact sequence or names of some parameters is often difficult. GUI-based programs often have a help button or menu item that can be helpful to a user. Command line-based programs can also provide online help. A standard way of providing minimal help is a default help message that's printed when no command line arguments are specified. By convention this message takes the form

```
Usage:programName arg1 arg2 ...
```

This message may be followed by a detailed explanation of the arguments or entry into an online help facility. For any Java programs that use command line arguments, you should follow this convention. Very early in the program, the size of the `args` array passed to `main()` should be checked. If the array isn't the right length, the usage message should be printed.

Also by convention, command line arguments beginning with a dash are optional arguments. Combining several of these optional arguments is often possible. A common type of online help is to have a command line argument `-help` or `-h`, indicating that an extended help message should be printed out—or, if available, an interactive online help facility should be invoked. You can easily check for arguments that begin with a dash by using

```
if (args[i].charAt(0) == '-') ...
```

Building online help facilities into your command line–based programs can make them much more user friendly.

Summary

- A file is a sequence of text or binary data that is typically accessed sequentially. A Java stream is a sequence of bytes. An input stream may be coming from a file, from keystrokes at the console, or from a network. Likewise, an output stream may be going into a file, to the console screen, or out over a network.
- You can use the class `FileWriter` from the package `java.io` to write a stream of text characters in a file. You can use the class `PrintWriter` from the same package to generate a stream of text characters from any value. The primary methods in the class `PrintWriter` are the familiar `print()` and `println()`.
- You can use the class `BufferedReader` from the package `java.io` to read a line of text at a time with the method `readLine()`. To read from a file, construct a `BufferedReader` object that passes a `FileReader` object to the constructor.
- The class `ReadInput` from the package `tio` provides a simple way to read primitive types. The method `Console.in` actually refers to an instance of `ReadInput` that is reading from the standard input stream `System.in`. To read from a file using `ReadInput`, you can construct a `ReadInput` object and pass the name of the file as a `String` to the constructor.
- Simple formatting of output can be accomplished with the class `Formatted-Writer` from the package `tio`. This class supports left and right justification of values within a field of a specified width. It also allows for specifying the number of digits to the right of the decimal point in floating point values. Standard Java provides support for text formatting in the package `java.text`. The details of using that package are beyond the scope of this book.
- There are two primary approaches to detecting the end of file (EOF) when reading data. If a distinguished value is available, such as `null` for `readLine()`, then EOF is signaled by having the method return the distinguished value. If no distinguished value is available—that is, all values are legal values—then EOF is signaled by throwing an `EOFException`.
- An important source of security for files is encryption. In encryption, ordinary text, called clear text, is transformed to apparently meaningless characters. Typically, encryption involves the use of an algorithm called a cipher.
- The two classes `DataInputStream` and `DataOutputStream` can be used to read and write binary files. These classes provide methods for reading and writing strings and all primitive types.

Review Questions

1. What two major file divisions were discussed in this chapter? Give an example of each.
2. To what type of object does `Console.in` refer?
3. What is a Caesar cipher? How can a Caesar cipher be broken?
4. What is a Vignere cipher? Why is a Vignere cipher harder to break than a Caesar cipher?
5. A Vernam cipher is better known as a _____.
6. What cipher discussed in this chapter is provably unbreakable?
7. What method can be used to capitalize alphabetic characters?
8. How is EOF detected when numbers are being read with the class `ReadInput`?
9. How is EOF detected when numbers are being read with the class `DataInputStream`?
10. In general, which results in a more compact representation of numeric data: a text file or a binary file?
11. True or false? The method `readInt()` from the class `DataInputStream` can be used to read integers from the keyboard if you construct a `DataInputStream` from `System.in`.
12. Give a Java expression, without using method calls, that converts an uppercase letter to its lowercase equivalent.
13. When you use `writeInt()` from `DataOutputStream`, how many bytes are written for the value 123456789? How many bytes are written for the same value if you use `println()` from `PrintWriter`?
14. What method from which class can be used to read strings from a binary file?
15. If the file *someData* already exists and you open the file for writing with `new PrintWriter(new FileWriter("someData"))`, what happens? Are the data in the file overwritten? Or are new data added to the end of the file?

Exercises

1. Write an array of strings to a file named *strings.txt*. Initialize the array with the four strings `"I am"`, `"a text"`, `"file written"`, and `"to strings.txt"`.
2. Create an array of strings that receive their input from the `tio` input package method `readLine()`. Write the array to *save.txt*. Specify the number of strings by asking the user to enter the number of lines to be read.
3. Redo Exercise 2 to end when the input is a special sentinel character. For example, you may use an empty string as the sentinel. You need not save all the input as an array of strings. You can use a single `String` variable to receive each line in turn.
4. Write a program that prints 1000 random numbers to a file.
5. Write a program to read 1000 random numbers from a file (see Exercise 4) and plot their distribution. That is, divide the interval 0–1 into tenths and count the numbers that fall into each tenth.

6. Modify Exercises 4 and 5 to allow the user to specify the number of random numbers and the name of the file on the command line. Store the number of numbers as the first item in the output file.

7. Redo Exercise 6 without storing the number of numbers as the first entry in the file. Use `hasMoreElements()` in the class `ReadInput` to detect the end of the input file.

8. Redo Exercise 6, using `writeDouble()` and `readDouble()` from `DataOutputStream` and `DataInputStream`, respectively.

9. Read a text file and write it to a target text file, changing all lowercase to uppercase and double spacing the output text. Use `String` and `StringBuffer` variables for internal manipulations.

10. Write a program that reads the bytes of a file one at a time with `read()`, which is a method in every input stream inherited from `InputStream`. You can open an input stream from a file with the expression `new FileInputStream("filename")`. Use `System.out.println()` to print the bytes, placing 4 bytes on each output line. Print the bytes in hexadecimal, padding with zeros so that each byte is represented by two digits. The hexadecmal digits are 0–9 and a–f. You can get the hexadecimal string representation of an `int` value x by using `Integer.toHexString(x)`. Try running this program on a text file and then on a binary file. Try it on several class files created by compiling some Java source files. Do you notice anything about the first 2 bytes of those files?

11. Modify the program in the previous exercise to also print the character value of any bytes in the range 32 to 126, inclusive. Print the characters on the same line separated by a few spaces—for example,

```
4578616d     Exam
706c6521     ple!
```

12. Create a class `Table` that represents a table of floating point values. A table is specified by a two-dimensional array of `double` values, a one-dimensional array of strings that label the rows, and a one-dimensional array of strings that label the columns. The class contains a constructor and one method, `print()`. The `print()` method should take one parameter, an `OutputStream`. The method `print()` should print the table, nicely formatted to the specified `OutputStream`. Use the class `FormattedWriter` to format the output. Print at most two digits to the right of the decimal point for the values in the table.

13. Locate and read the documentation for `java.text.NumberFormat`. Construct a `NumberFormat` object with a pattern for monetary amounts. For example, in the United States, 12345.67 should be formatted as $12,345.67. Use `NumberFormat` to modify the table in the previous exercise so that the values in the table are formatted as monetary values.

14. Make up a Vignere code based on the word "APPROXIMATE" as a key. Use it to encrypt a clear text file and write it out to the end of the clear text in the same file.

15. Write a program that reads a text file and computes the relative frequency of each of the letters of the alphabet. You can use an array of length 26 to store the number of occurrences of each letter. You can use `Character.isLetter()` to test for letters and then `Character.toLowerCase()` to convert all letters to lowercase. Subtracting `'a'` will then give you a value in the range 0 to 25, inclusive, which you can use to index into the array of counts.

16. Run the program from the previous exercise on several large text files and compare the results. How can you use this information to break a Caesar cipher?

17. Modify the class `VernamCipher` in Section 10.5, on page 359, to allow the user to specify the key as a third, optional command line argument. If none is specified on the command line, prompt the user to enter the seed at the terminal. This seed is the key needed to decode the encrypted file.

18. Write a program to decode the results of encoding a file using the `VernamCipher` program in Section 10.5, on page 359. You will need to use the same seed for encoding and decoding. What happens if you insert one extra character or drop one character from the encrypted file?

19. Write a program that tests whether a file exists. It should read the file name from the console and then print "exists" or "doesn't exist." The class `File` in the standard package `java.io` contains a method `exists()`.

20. Write a program with a GUI that reads text one line at a time from a designated file and displays the line in a `JTextField`. The file name should be placed in a text window and a button event used to open it. There should be a button for signaling that you want the next line.

21. Alter the program in the previous exercise to include a designated named output file. The text line should be modifiable and the modified text should be sent to the output file. Note how this is the beginning of an editor program.

22. A `JTextArea` component is like a `JTextField`, but it can display multiple lines. In Appendix D.6 we show how to use a `JTextArea`. Use a `JTextArea` component to create a simple editor. Allow the user to enter and edit text, save the text to a file, and specify a file for editing.

11

Exceptions

In programming, an *exception* is an error or unexpected action that occurs during computation. Until now, we have viewed an exception as an error that resulted in the program being terminated. However, there are many kinds of exceptions; sometimes the program doesn't need to be terminated. Some exceptions that we have discussed in previous chapters are

- `IndexOutOfBounds`—when an array index is less than zero or too big;
- `NullPointerException`—when an attempt is made to call a method or access a field of an object using a reference that is null; and
- `ArithmeticException`—results from attempting to divide by zero.

In this chapter we show how to catch an exception. When you catch an exception, you prevent the program from terminating immediately. That allows you to correct the problem and continue with normal execution or to provide additional diagnostic information. We also show you how to generate your own exceptions when the code you write encounters some unexpected value.

11.1 EXCEPTION HANDLING WITH `try` AND `catch`

A *robust program* deals gracefully with unexpected input. For example, when asking a user to enter numeric data in a certain range, a robust program determines whether the data are numeric and within range. If the data aren't numeric or are out of range, some appropriate action, such as asking the user to reenter the data, should be taken. In general, this type of run-time error checking can be done with the basic control flow constructs from Chapter 3; however, doing so can be cumbersome.

Suppose that we want to prompt the user for an integer, read it in, and do the checking suggested. Here is how we currently read in an integer.

```
int myData = Console.in.readInt();
```

In order to make this procedure robust, we need some mechanism for indicating that the next sequence of characters in the input stream doesn't constitute a valid integer. One option would be to modify the method `readInt()` to take a status parameter. Because the parameter would need to be modified by `readInt()`, we need to pass a reference to an object that contains a `boolean`. We can do so by using the following trivial class.

```
class Status {
  boolean flag;
}
```

By using `true` to indicate success and `false` to indicate failure, we could check the value of the status parameter with

```
//readInt() isn't defined to work this way
Status status = new Status();
int myData = Console.in.readInt(status); //hypothetical
if (!status.flag) {
  // put error handling code here
}
```

However, there are some problems with this approach. We needed to add an extra parameter to the method `readInt()`, declare the `status` variable in our code, and then test `status`. More important, we needed to test the value, even though we expect that `status` will always be `true`. So, under normal conditions, the time needed to set and test the status variable is wasted time. To add to the complexity of this approach, the preceding code may be inside another method that doesn't know how to handle the error case. In this situation, we also have to add a status parameter to the enclosing method. Then the error handling code simply sets the status parameter passed to it to be `false` and returns as shown in the following code.

```
int processInput(..., Status status) {
    ...
  //readInt() isn't defined to work this way
  int myData = Console.in.readInt(status);
  if (!status.flag) {
              // have to return something
    return 0; // assume return value will be ignored
  }
  // go on with normal processing
  ...
}
```

Programming language designers recognized this pattern of returning status values that are then tested. They realized that they could clean up such programs by providing a special mechanism for this procedure. The mechanism is called *exception handling*.

An exception is a condition in a program that is expected to occur only rarely if ever. In the preceding example, if the user follows instructions and enters the proper type of data, no exception (think of it as an error) will occur. In the exceptional case, when the user fails to follow instructions and types something that isn't an integer, the method trying to read the integer will throw an exception.

The word *throw* describes the action of an exception occurring. It may be useful to think of throw as in "to throw a special value to the operating system." Unless the program explicitly does something to recover from the exception, the program aborts and displays an error message.

The word *catch* describes the construction used to specify what to do when an exception occurs. The program specifies some code that is to be executed if an exception occurs, in which case the error is caught and prevented from aborting the program.

A `catch` includes a block of code for handling the exception type, specified as a parameter, after the keyword `catch`. It occurs immediately after a `try` block. Syntactically, a `try` block is a block of code that has the keyword `try` as a prefix. The basic layout for catching an exception is

```
try {
  // some code here that might throw an exception
}
catch (ExceptionType Identifier) {
  // some code here to handle the exception
}
```

If any statement in the block following `try` throws an exception of type *ExceptionType*, control is *immediately* transferred to the code in the block following `catch`. The rest of the statements in the block with the statement throwing the exception are skipped. When the catch block is executed, the variable *Identifier* refers to a type *ExceptionType* object that describes the exception.

The first example discussed in this section, when written using exceptions, becomes

```
int myData;
try {
  myData = Console.in.readInt();
}
catch (NumberFormatException e) {
  // put error handling code here
}
```

The statement `Console.in.readInt()` throws a `NumberFormatException` if the next set of characters in the input stream doesn't constitute a legal integer. If the exception is thrown, no characters from the input stream are consumed and `myData` remains unchanged—the assignment won't happen.

If instead the error is going to be handled at a higher level, then we don't need to do anything at the point of the call to `readInt()`. The method `processInput()` becomes

```
int processInput(...) {
  ...
  int myData = Console.in.readInt();
  // go on with normal processing
  ...
}
```

In this case, when the exception occurs in `readInt()`—because there is no `try` block—the exception is immediately passed up to the next higher level. That is, as before, the assignment to `myData` doesn't occur. In addition, the method `process-Input()` returns immediately, throwing the same exception thrown by `readInt()`. There is no return value because any assignment involving the value returned from `processInput()` also doesn't happen.

Presumably, in this situation, the exception is caught at a higher level—for example, at the point that `processInput()` is called. So let's try this approach, which seems to work better.

```
...
inputReadOK = false; // allow loop to execute once
while (!inputReadOK)
  try {
    x = processInput(...);
  }
  catch (NumberFormatException e) {
    System.out.println(e);
    Console.in.readLine(); //Consume entire line
    System.out.println("Please try again...");
  }
  inputReadOK = true; // successful input
}
// go on with normal processing
```

The following code robustly reads one integer from the console. If the user doesn't type an integer, he or she is prompted to try again.

```
// ExceptionExample.java - catch an exception
import tio.*;

public class ExceptionExample {
  public static void main(String[] args) {
    int aNumber = 0;
    boolean success = false;
    String inputString = "";
```

```
        System.out.println("Type an integer.");
        while (!success) {
          try {
            aNumber = Console.in.readInt();
            success = true;
          }
          catch (NumberFormatException) {
            inputString = Console.in.readWord();
            System.out.println(inputString +
                    " is not an integer. Try again!");
          }
        }
        System.out.println("You typed " + aNumber);
        // continue with code to process aNumber
      }
    }
```

DISSECTION OF THE CLASS ExceptionExample

- ■ `while (!success) {`

  This loop continues until the assignment `success = true` is executed.

- ■
  ```
  try {
    aNumber = Console.in.readInt();
    success = true;
  }
  ```

  If a `NumberFormatException` occurs while any statement in the `try` block is being executed, control is immediately transferred to the first statement in the `catch` block. In this case, the call to `readInt()` may throw a `NumberFormatException`, in which case `aNumber` remains unchanged and the subsequent assignment `success = true` won't execute; hence the `while` loop repeats.

- ■
  ```
  catch (NumberFormatException) {
    inputString = Console.in.readWord();
    System.out.println(inputString +
            " is not an integer. Try again!");
  }
  ```

  In this example we ignore the parameter. Having arrived at this `catch` block tells us all we need to know—a `NumberFormatException` occurred in the previous `try` block. Because `readInt()` is defined not to consume any nonwhite input characters if it fails, we use `readWord()` to read the offending white-space delimited string of characters. We print an appropriate message and then continue with the statement following the `try-catch` statement. The exception has been handled and normal execution resumes.

- ■
  ```
  while (!success) {
    ...
    success = true;
    ...
  }
  System.out.println("You typed " + aNumber);
  // continue with code to process aNumber
  ```

Eventually the user will type a legal integer. At that time the assignment to `success` is reached, the end of the `try` block is reached, the `catch` block is skipped, and the loop exits.

COMMON PROGRAMMING ERROR

Incorrectly entered input is a common programming error. In robust programs input should be tested to determine whether it is both syntactically and semantically correct. Frequently, good practice is to ask the user to confirm the value entered. The following loop does just that.

```
while (confirm = 'N') {
   //...ask for data  in dollars
   System.out.println("Did you mean " + dollars);
   System.out.println("Please Enter Y or N:");
   confirm = Console.in.readChar();
}
```

This technique can be combined with the exception handling methodology of the preceding example.

11.2   CATCHING AN `EOFException`

As discussed in the Chapter 10, sometimes an exception is used to detect the end of a file. For the standard Java class `java.io.DataInputStream`, when primitive values are being read, no special value can be returned to indicate the end of the file has been reached. Instead, an exception is thrown.

Java methods have *throws clauses* that indicate any exceptions that can happen while executing the method. Such exceptions are known as *checked exceptions*. There are also run-time exceptions, such as divide-by-zero, which are *unchecked*. A checked exception must have a corresponding `catch` to handle it or be declared in a `throws` clause; otherwise, you have a syntax error.

The following program reads integers from a binary file and prints them to the screen. Recall that a binary file doesn't store the individual characters that make up the number. Instead, the file stores the bytes that correspond to the binary representation of the number. Storage of each integer value uses 4 bytes. You can't view the files read by this program with a normal text editor.

```java
// BinaryInput.java - read some integers from
//      a binary file
import java.io.*;

class BinaryInput {
  public static void main(String[] args)
        throws IOException
  {
    DataInputStream input = null;
    if (args.length != 1) {
      System.out.println("Usage: " +
          "java BinaryInput filename");
      System.exit(1);
    }
    try {
      input = new DataInputStream(
                new FileInputStream(args[0]));
    }
    catch (IOException e) {
      System.out.println("Could not open " + args[0]);
      System.out.println(e);
      System.exit(1);
    }

    // count is used to print 4 values per line
    int count = 0;
    try {
      while (true) {
        int myData = input.readInt();
        count++;
        System.out.print(myData + " ");
        // print a newline every 4th value
        if (count % 4 == 0)
          System.out.println();
      }
    }
    catch (EOFException e)
    {
      // just catch the exception and
      // discard it
    }
    // add a newline after the last partial line
    // if necessary
    if (count % 4 != 0)
      System.out.println();
  }
}
```

DISSECTION OF THE CLASS `BinaryInput`

▪
```java
import java.io.*;

class BinaryInput {
  public static void main(String[] args)
      throws IOException
  {
    DataInputStream input = null;
    if (args.length != 1) {
      System.out.println("Usage: " +
          "java BinaryInput filename");
      System.exit(1);
    }
}
```

The user is expected to supply the name of the input file on the command line. If no file name is provided, a message is printed to remind the user how to utilize this program. The `throws` clause indicates that `IOException` is a checked exception that needs to be caught.

▪
```java
try {
  input = new DataInputStream(
            new FileInputStream(args[0]));
}
catch (IOException e) {
  System.out.println("Could not open " + args[0]);
  System.out.println(e);
  System.exit(1);
}
```

We don't need to catch this exception, but by catching it, we can print a clear message to the user. For instructional purposes we also print out the actual exception. In a real program we probably wouldn't include the second `println()`.

▪
```java
int count = 0;
try {
  while (true) {
    int myData = input.readInt();
    count++;
    System.out.print(myData + " ");
    // print a newline every 4th value
    if (count % 4 == 0)
      System.out.println();
  }
}
catch (EOFException e) {
  // just catch the exception and
  // discard it
}
```

The reading is done inside a `try-catch` statement. Note that, at first glance, the loop appears to loop forever. However, the loop is exited when the `input.readInt()` call throws an `EOFException`. At that point, control is passed to the `catch` block. In this case there is nothing to do: There is no error, and we don't want to print anything. We just continue with normal processing.

▪
```
if (count % 4 != 0)
   System.out.println();
```

After execution of the `try` block has been completed, execution continues with this statement. It is used to add a newline in case the last line contains less than four numbers.

To test the preceding program we need a sample input binary file. We can use the following program to generate a sample input file for `BinaryInput`. It writes 10 integers using a `DataOutputStream`. You won't be able to view the contents of the file generated by the following program with a normal text editor.

```java
// BinaryOutput.java - create a sample binary file
import java.io.*;

class BinaryOutput {
  public static void main(String[] args) throws IOException {
    DataOutputStream output = null;
    if (args.length != 1) {
      System.out.println("Usage: " +
          "java BinaryOutput filename");
      System.exit(1);
    }
    try {
      output = new DataOutputStream(
                  new FileOutputStream(args[0]));
    }
    catch (IOException e) {
      System.out.println("Could not open " + args[0]);
      System.out.println(e);
      System.exit(1);
    }
    for (int i = 1; i <= 10; i++)
      output.writeInt(i * 100);
  }
}
```

The output of `BinaryInput` when executed with the file created by `Binary-Output` is

```
100   200   300   400
500   600   700   800
900   1000
```

11.3 ABRUPT RETURN FROM METHODS THAT THROW EXCEPTIONS

As indicated in Section 11.2, when an exception occurs in a method without a `try` block, the method returns immediately. There is no return value, and the rest of the statements in the method are ignored, as shown in the following program.

```
// ExceptionExampleTwo.java - show control flow when
//    an exception occurs during nested method calls
import tio.*;

class ExceptionExampleTwo {
  public static void main(String[] args) {
    int x = 0;
    System.out.println("main starting");
    try {
      x = callOne();
      System.out.println("callOne OK x = " + x);
    }
    catch (ArithmeticException e) {
      System.out.println("callOne not OK: " + e);
      x = -1;
    }
    System.out.println("main exiting x = " + x);
  }

  static int callOne() {
    System.out.println("callOne starting");
    int result = callTwo();
    System.out.println("callOne returning result = " + result);
    return result;
  }

  static int callTwo() {
    int num = 0;
    System.out.println("type a number");
    int input = Console.in.readInt();
    num = 1000 / input;
    System.out.println("callTwo returning num = " + num);
    return num;
  }
}
```

If we run the program and use the input value of 10, we get the "normal" execution output shown.

```
os-prompt>java ExceptionExampleTwo
main starting
callOne starting
type a number
10
callTwo returning num = 100
callOne returning result = 100
callOne OK x = 100
main exiting x = 100
os-prompt>
```

If we run the program and use the input value 0, we get the "exceptional" execution output shown.

```
os-prompt>java ExceptionExampleTwo
main starting
callOne starting
type a number
0
callOne not OK: java.lang.ArithmeticException: /
by zero
main exiting x = -1
os-prompt>
```

The string `java.lang.ArithmeticException: / by zero` results from the method `toString()` of the exception object referred to by `e`, the parameter passed to the `catch` block. Note that the last `println()` calls in both `callOne()` and `callTwo()` weren't executed. Those methods both terminated abruptly. Because the exception wasn't caught in `callTwo()`, the method terminated abruptly, throwing the same exception thrown by the attempt to divide by zero. Likewise, `callOne()` doesn't catch the exception consequently thrown by the call to `callTwo()`, so `callOne()` also terminates abruptly, again throwing the same exception. Finally, the exception is caught in `main()`.

11.4 CATCHING SEVERAL DIFFERENT EXCEPTIONS

We can have several different `catch` blocks in a single `try-catch` statement. For example, suppose that we wanted to let the program `ExceptionExample` in Section 11.1, on page 374, continue with the default value of 0 for the variable `aNumber` if there is no more input. The method `readInt()` throws a `ReadException` if it encounters the end-of-file before reading a number. On most systems we can signal the end of input from the keyboard by typing either Ctrl+D or Ctrl+Z. We add this capability to `ExceptionExample` as follows.

```
// TwoCatchExample.java - use two catch clauses
import tio.*;

public class TwoCatchExample {
  public static void main(String[] args) {
    int aNumber = 0;
    boolean success = false;
    String inputString = "";
```

```
      System.out.println("Type an integer.");
      while (!success) {
        try {
          aNumber = Console.in.readInt();
          success = true;
          System.out.println("You typed " + aNumber);
        }
        catch (NumberFormatException exception) {
          inputString = Console.in.readWord();
          System.out.println(inputString +
                  " is not an integer. Try again!");
        }
        catch (ReadException exception) {
          System.out.println(
                  "Continuing with default value 0.");
          aNumber = 0;
          success = true;
        }
      }
      // continue with code to process a_number
    }
}
```

Note that we added a second `catch` block. If no exceptions occur during the `try` block, then both `catch` blocks are skipped and execution proceeds normally, following the last `catch` block. If an exception does occur, the first `catch` block that specifies an exception type that either matches the exception or is a super class of the exception type that was thrown, will be executed. When the `catch` block is finished, execution continues normally with the statement following the last `catch` block. At most, one of the `catch` blocks will be executed.

If one of the exception types that you're trying to catch is a superclass of another that you're also trying to catch, the one that is a superclass must be listed last. Otherwise, the more specific `catch` block is never executed.

Suppose that `ExceptionSuper` and `ExceptionSub` are two exception classes, where `ExceptionSub` is a subclass of `ExceptionSuper`. The following `try` block would be incorrect.

```
try {
  ...
}
catch(ExceptionSuper e) {
  ...
}
catch(ExceptionSub e) {
  ...
}
```

Luckily, the Java compiler will detect this error and report it with a message something like

```
Filename.java:100: catch not reached.
    catch(ExceptionSub e) {
    }
```

Putting the `catch` blocks in the other order in the previous example would be fine.

11.5 THE finally CLAUSE

Java provides a `finally` clause of a `try` block as code that is always executed whether or not an exception is thrown. This code is sometimes referred to as *cleanup code*. It is most often used to release special resources, such as open files, back to the system.

The following class, `BinaryInput2`, is a redesigned version of the class `BinaryInput`. It provides a class method, `readBinaryInput()`, that reads integers from a binary file and prints them to the screen. This method is very similar to the method `main()` in the class `BinaryInput`. The most significant change is the addition of a `finally` clause that does some last bit of cleanup. Namely, it makes sure that a final newline is written and that the appropriate open file is closed. Presumably, some other class would make a call to `BinaryInput2.readBinaryInput()`, passing it the name of the binary file from which to read and the number of integers to read from the file.

```java
// BinaryInput2.java - read some integers from
//       a binary file
import java.io.*;

class BinaryInput2 {
  public static int readBinaryInput(String filename,
                                    int howMany)
       throws IOException
  {
    DataInputStream input = null;
    try {
      input = new DataInputStream(
              new FileInputStream(filename));
    }
    catch (IOException e) {
      System.out.println("Could not open " +filename);
      System.out.println(e);
      throw e;
    }

    int count = 0;
    try {
      while (count < howMany) {
        int myData = input.readInt();
        count++;
        System.out.print(myData + " ");
        // print a newline every 4th value
        if (count % 4 == 0)
          System.out.println();
      }
    }
    catch (EOFException e) {
      // just catch the exception and discard it
    }
```

```
        finally {
          if (count % 4 != 0)
            System.out.println();
          if (input != null)
            input.close();
        }
        return count;
      }
    }
```

DISSECTION OF THE CLASS BinaryInput2

■
```
    class BinaryInput2 {
      public static int readBinaryInput(String filename,
                                             int howMany)

          throws IOException
```

This class contains the single method readBinaryInput(). In addition to the file name, we pass in the number of integers to read. The method reads howMany integers or until the end-of-file is reached. The method returns the number of integers actually read and printed.

■
```
    DataInputStream input = null;
    try {
      input = new DataInputStream(
                  new FileInputStream(filename));
    }
    catch (IOException e) {
      System.out.println("Could not open " +filename);
      System.out.println(e);
      throw e;
    }
```

In BinaryInput.main(), we called System.exit() after catching an exception while trying to open the file. In this version, we print the error message as before, but instead of aborting the entire program, we pass the exception to the calling environment by rethrowing the exception we just caught. The method calling BinaryInput2.readBinaryInput() can either catch the exception or let the program abort.

■
```
    int count = 0;
    try {
      while (count < howMany) {
        int myData = input.readInt();
        count++;
        System.out.print(myData + " ");
        // print a newline every 4th value
        if (count % 4 == 0)
          System.out.println();
      }
    }
    catch (EOFException e) {
      // just catch the exception and discard it
    }
```

We changed the loop so that it reads at most howMany integers. Unlike the earlier version, this loop can either exit normally or exit as the result of an EOFException.

-
```
finally {
    if (count % 4 != 0)
        System.out.println();
    if (input != null)
        input.close();
}
```

The code in this finally block will be executed *no matter how* the try block exits. If the try block exits because of an EOFException, then the finally clause executes after the catch, which is empty in this example. If the try block exits normally because the while loop terminates, the finally clause executes before continuing and executing the final return statement. If the try block exits because of some uncaught exception, the finally clause still executes before the method is terminated abruptly and the exception is thrown to the calling method. Note that this last case makes the code behave differently than it would if we simply placed the statements in the finally block, immediately after the try-catch statement, without using finally.

-
```
return count;
```

This statement is executed after the code in the finally clause. This statement is executed if the loop terminates normally or if an EOFException is thrown. This statement won't be executed if some other exception happens during execution of the previous try-catch statement.

11.6 PROGRAM CORRECTNESS: THROWING AN EXCEPTION

In the constructor for the class Counter in Section 6.5, we used the modulus operator to guarantee that the value field of the constructor was initialized to a value consistent with the description of the class. This approach could lead to an error in a program that would be hard to detect. Suppose that we had forgotten that the class Counter was defined to wrap around at 100 and instead thought it would wrap around at 1000—or not wrap at all. We might then decide to construct a Counter value starting at 200, as in

```
Counter bigCounter = new Counter(200);
```

Depending on how we used this Counter object, our misunderstanding might go undetected until the program containing this code was in use, possibly in a crucial situation.

An alternative definition of the constructor for Counter could notify the caller when an invalid parameter is passed to the constructor. The technique used in Java to send such a notification is to throw an exception. In the preceding sections we introduced exception handling, which is how the caller detects and attempts to handle an exceptional condition. The following modified constructor for the class `Counter` throws an exception when an attempt is made to initialize the `Counter` with an invalid value.

```
public class Counter {
  //constructors
  public Counter() {}

  public Counter(int v) {
    if (v < 0 || v >= 100)
      throw new Exception("Invalid initial value.");
    else
      value = v % 100;
  }
.....
}
```

Using this modified version of the class `Counter`, our attempt to construct a `Counter` using 200 would fail the first time it was executed. In this way, any test of the program that executes the assignment to `bigCounter` would generate an exception, allowing for the error to be detected early in the development process.

The test `if (v < 0 || v >= 100)` is called a *precondition* because it determines whether the input is suitable, that is, allows the constructor or method to work correctly. Similarly, tests can be added at the end of a method or constructor to determine whether certain conditions have been established. Such a test is called a *postcondition* because it tests a relationship that must hold if the method did its work correctly.

To illustrate the use of a postcondition we can add a test at the end of the `neighbors()` method in the class `GameOfLife` in Section 5.10.3, on page 169. The test would determine whether the computed number of neighbors was between 0 and 8, inclusive.

```
static int neighbors(int row, int column, boolean[][] w)
{
  int neighborCount = 0;

  for (int i = -1; i <= 1; i++)
    for (int j = -1; j <= 1; j++)
      if (w[row + i][column + j] == ALIVE)
        neighborCount = neighborCount + 1;
      if (w[row][column] == ALIVE)
        neighborCount--;
      if (neighborCount < 0 || neighborCount > 8)
        throw new Exception("Bad neighbor count = " +
                            neighborCount);
  return neighborCount;
}
```

As methods become longer and more complicated, the use of preconditions and postconditions—also called *assertions*—becomes even more important. They are easy to write, add robustness to code, and help other readers of the code understand its intent. They also help guarantee that methods behave as expected. Moreover, assertions help you think about correctness. This discipline is beneficial in and of itself. The placement of assertions isn't restricted to the beginning and ending statements of a method, but such placement is natural. The use of assertions is considered to be good programming style.

11.7 RuntimeExceptions AND THE throws CLAUSE

You may have noted that sometimes we used a `throws` clause when defining methods that might throw an exception. For example, in Section 10.2, on page 347, we added the clause

```
throws java.io.IOException
```

to the declaration of the method `main()` because opening a file for writing might encounter some kind of problem. At the same time, other methods that might throw exceptions didn't require a `throws` clause. For example, any time an array is indexed, an `IndexOutOfBoundsException` can occur, yet we never included the clause

```
throws IndexOutOfBoundsException
```

The designers of Java decided that certain exceptions that might occur "during the normal operation" of Java programs didn't need to be declared. In general, these are exceptions that might occur almost anywhere, such as trying to use a reference variable that isn't referencing any object (`NullPointerException`) or indexing an array with an index out of range. These are known as *unchecked exceptions*. From a practical point of view, requiring all such exceptions to be declared with a `throws` clause would have defeated any advantage of its use. All but the most trivial methods would have needed a `throws` clause with many exceptions in it. More than 20 subclasses of `Exception` are defined in the package `java.lang`.

The designers knew that they couldn't identify in advance all exceptions that shouldn't be declared with a `throws` clause. Hence they created an exception class `java.lang.RuntimeException` from which all such exceptions must be derived. Any exception class that is a subclass of `RuntimeException` doesn't need to be declared with a `throws` clause. Any exception class that isn't a subclass of `Runtime-Exception` must be handled in the method where it can occur, or the method must declare it, using a `throws` clause. These are the checked exceptions. All exceptions defined in the package `java.lang` are subclasses of `RuntimeException`.

The standard Java input methods throw a `java.io.EOFException` when they encounter the end-of-file. In `tio` we turned end-of-file exceptions, and all other `java.io.IOExceptions`, into `ReadExceptions`. The class `tio.ReadException` is a subclass of `java.lang.RuntimeException`, which is why we didn't need to include a `throws` clause in the program examples in the early chapters of this book.

As a general rule you shouldn't create new exception classes that are subclasses of `RuntimeException`. Creating such exception classes defeats the compile-time checks normally used to notify you that an exception might occur. This notification allows you to add exception handling code, making your program more robust. As you gain programming experience, you will become increasingly aware of the standard Java exceptions derived from `RuntimeException` and can decide whether you want to add code to handle any of these exceptions.

To create a new type of exception, extend an existing exception class. The *reference* in a `throw` statement such as

`throw` *reference*

must be a subclass of the class `java.lang.Throwable`. The base of all such throwable classes that represent exceptions that a reasonable program might be expected to try and handle is the class `java.lang.Exception`. The class `Exception` is a subclass of `Throwable`. The class `java.lang.Error` is a separate subclass of `Throwable` that represents throwable conditions that a reasonable program isn't expected to be able to handle. Like subclasses of `RuntimeException`, subclasses of `Error` don't need to be declared with a `throws` clause. The following diagram illustrates a partial inheritance hierarchy, showing some of the core throwable classes.

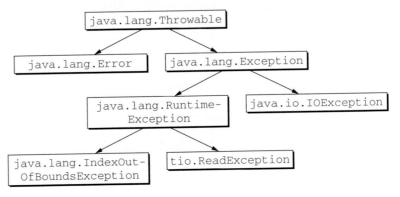

The definition of the class `ReadException` from the package `tio` is as follows.

```
public class ReadException extends RuntimeException{
  public ReadException() { super();
  }
  public ReadException(String message) { super(message);
  }
}
```

This class doesn't actually do anything. We created it so that we can use Java's dynamic typing system to create statements such as

```
try {
  ...
}
catch (ReadException exception) {
  ...
}
```

In `tio`, we turn `java.io.IOException` errors, which aren't a subclass of `RuntimeException`, into `RuntimeExceptions` with

```
public int readInt() {
  try {
    // code here might cause IOException
    ...
  }
  catch (java.io.IOException e) {
      throw new ReadException(e.toString());
  }
}
```

We catch the IOException, which would have required any method that uses read-Int() to include throws java.io.IOException. We turn right around and throw a ReadException, using the string form of the IOException as the text of the newly created ReadException. The object created by a throw statement, such as the preceding one, is passed to the exception parameter in a catch block as in

```
try {
  x = Console.in.readInt()
}
catch (ReadException exception) {
  ...
}
```

11.8 PROGRAMMING STYLE

Exception handling shouldn't be used to transfer flow of control for what otherwise can be treated with normal statement types. It should be retained for error and unanticipated conditions. The following code is a mistaken use of exceptions.

```
//Not good style
try {
  while ( v == Console.in.readInt()) {
    System.out.println(" v = " + v);
    if (v = -1) //use as a guard value
      throw new MyException();
    sum += v;
  }
}
catch(MyException e) {
  System.out.println("Sum = " + v);
}
```

What should have been done was

```
    ...
    if (v = -1)
      break;  //leave while statement
    sum += v;
}//end of while
System.out.println("Sum = " + v);
```

Exceptions should be used to test assertions about the code, particularly preconditions and postconditions as we discussed in Section 11.6. A main use of exceptions is to detect improper input behavior, such as incorrect values, EOF signals, or an inability to open files.

Summary

- An exception is generally used to describe something unexpected that happens in a program, such as an array index out of bounds error or some problem with reading from a file.
- A `try` block can be used to catch or "handle" an exception. If an exception of the specified type is thrown during execution of the `try` block, control is transferred immediately to the `catch` block.
- Some exceptions, such as `IndexOutOfBoundsException`, are generated automatically by the Java virtual machine. Exceptions can also be generated explicitly by a program, which is called throwing an exception. A `throw` statement is used to throw an exception.
- Programs can throw an instance of a predefined exception type or you can create your own exception types by subclassing one of the existing exception classes.
- All exceptions are derived from the class `java.lang.Throwable`. Those exceptions that are also derived from `java.lang.RuntimeException` or `java.lang.Error` don't need to be declared with a `throws` clause at the beginning of a method. These are unchecked exceptions. New exception classes that are a subclass of `java.lang.Exception` but not a subclass of `java.lang.RuntimeException` must be declared with a `throws` clause. In general, user-defined exceptions shouldn't be derived from `RuntimeException` or `Error`. Doing so defeats some of the type-checking safeguards that can help detect errors at compile time.

Review Questions

1. True or false? Exceptions happen only when a run-time error is discovered.
2. What types of exceptions don't have to be declared with a `throws` clause at the beginning of a method definition? What are such exceptions called?
3. If an exception isn't handled by a method, what happens to it?
4. Give an example of a standard Java exception that must be declared with a `throws` clause and one that doesn't have to be declared with a `throws` clause.
5. What happens if you use an array index that is out of range?
6. True or false? Every user-defined exception is a checked exception.
7. What is wrong with the following code fragment?

```
try {
    ...
}
catch (Exception e) {
    ...
}
catch (IndexOutOfBoundsException e) {
    ...
}
```

8. What is printed by the following program?

```
class ExceptionReview {

  public static void main(String[] args) {
    int x;
    try {
      x = foo(10);
    }
    catch (MyException e) {
      System.out.println("Caught an exception: " + e);
      x = 99;
    }
    System.out.println(x);
  }

  static int foo(int x) {
    System.out.println("foo started with " + x);
    int temp = bar(x);
    System.out.println("foo returning " + temp);
    return temp;
  }

  static int bar(int y) {
    System.out.println("bar started with " + y);
    if (y > 0)
      throw new MyException("just a test");
    System.out.println("when is this executed?");
    return y;
  }
}

class MyException extends RuntimeException  {
  public MyException(String message) {
    super(message);
  }
}
```

9. What happens if you divide by zero? Be sure to test it.
10. Is a `finally` clause executed if no exception is thrown inside its `try` block?

Exercises

1. Write a robust method for reading in integers. If the user fails to type in a valid integer, print a message, skip over the offending line of input, and try again. To skip over the rest

of a line of input you can use `Console.in.readLine()`, which reads everything up to and including the next newline character. You can use `Console.in.readInt()`, but you'll need to catch any `NumberFormatExceptions` thrown.

2. Redo Exercise 1 to fail if the user types in an integer outside the range 0 to 100 inclusive. This technique is important in data entry programs where valid data is known to be in a given range.

3. Redo Exercise 1 to include user confirmation of the entered value.

4. If you attempt to open a file for reading using

   ```
   new FileReader(filename)
   ```

   and the file doesn't exist, a `java.io.FileNotFoundException` will be thrown. Use a `try` block to create a robust program to read a file and echo its contents to the screen. The program should prompt for the name of the file. If the file can't be opened, the program should print a suitable message and ask for a new file name to be entered.

5. Repeat the previous exercise using `tio.ReadInput`. The constructor call `new ReadInput(filename)` throws a `tio.ReadException` if the file can't be opened. Recall that, in the package `tio`, all `java.io.IOExceptions` have been converted into `tio.ReadExceptions` which are a subclass of `java.lang.RuntimeException`. This conversion was made to avoid the use of a `throws` clause in the early programs.

6. Use a `try` block in the method `computeNeighbors()` in class `Living` for the Predator-Prey simulation in Section 7.8, on page 249. Using `try-catch`, you can lift the restriction that `computeNeighbors()` is never called with a border cell. If an attempt is made to go beyond the array bounds, the exception should be caught and treated as an empty cell. Modify `Living` and `PredatorPrey` to allow updates of the border cells.

7. Using a `DataOutputStream`, create a program that writes some random numbers to a file. Have the user specify on the command line the number of random values to write. Using a `DataInputStream`, create another program to read in those random values. The program that reads the random numbers shouldn't be told how many numbers are in the file. Instead the end-of-file should be detected by using a `try` block to contain the read statement. Print the distribution of random values using 10 intervals.

8. Write a program to print out the real roots of the quadratic expression $ax^2 + bx + c$. Recall that, for there to be two real roots, the discriminant $b^2 - 4ac$ must be greater than 0. If this condition fails, use an exception to generate a message that the quadratic expression doesn't have two real roots. Compare this methodology to one that avoids throwing an exception when handling this case.

9. Write a factorial method that throws an exception if the integer n would lead `int factorial(int n)` to compute an incorrect value because of integer overflow. Recall that `int` values go only to approximately 2 billion. Test the method by printing a table of values for n! until this exception occurs.

10. Repeat the previous exercise for `long factorial(long n)`.

11. The method `Math.sqrt()` when given a negative argument returns `Double.NaN` (not a number). Write and test your own version `mySqrt()` that throws an exception when given a negative number.

12

Dynamic Data Structures

Dynamic data structures can expand and contract during computation, for example, as in a list of things to do, from which you can add or delete items. Computers are frequently used to store and manipulate lists of data, which can be represented many ways in a computer. In this chapter we show how to implement a dynamic list and similar data structures.

The choice of how best to represent a list is based on how the list is to be manipulated. Will items be added at the top of the list, at the bottom, or somewhere in the middle? Will the items in the list be in some particular order, such as alphabetical? Which will be more common: searching for an item in the list or inserting a new item in the list? Many more such questions have to be considered in deciding how to implement a list. For the most part these are questions for an advanced text on data structures.

A data structure that we've already used to store lots of information is the array. The single most important difference between arrays and the list implementations that we describe in this chapter is that the capacity of an array can't change. If you need to change the size of a list implemented as an array, you have to create a new array, larger or smaller, and then copy the items from the old array to the new, resized array.

The list data structures we describe in this chapter are called dynamic data structures because they can be readily resized. A second important characteristic of such data structures is that at least part of the data structure will be implemented by a class that contains, as a member, a reference variable of the same type as the class itself. For this reason, these data structures are frequently called *self-referential*, or *recursive, data structures.*

12.1 SELF-REFERENTIAL STRUCTURES

The simplest type of self-referential list structure is a sequence of elements. Each element contains some data and a reference, often called a *pointer*, to the next element in the list. We can use this aproach in Java, as shown in the following example, allowing us to create an arbitrarily long list of integer values.

```
//IntListElement.java - a self-referential class
class IntListElement {
  IntListElement(int value) { data = value; }
  IntListElement next; //self-referential
  int data;
}
```

The declaration of `IntListElement` has two fields. The field `data` stores the data member for this element. The reference variable `next` is called a *link*. Each element is linked to a succeeding element by way of the member `next`. For convenience, we also include a constructor that fills in the data field. A list implemented with this structure can be conveniently displayed pictorially with links shown as arrows. In the following figure the field `data` contains the value 2. The field `next` is pointing to some other, unspecified element.

If there is no succeeding element because we are at the end of the list, the field `next` contains the special value `null`. We can create two elements with

```
IntListElement first = new IntListElement(1);
IntListElement second = new IntListElement(2);
```

The `next` field defaults to `null`. Pictorially, the result of this code is

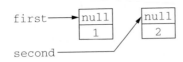

To make these two elements into a list, with `first` as the first element in the list, we link them.

```
first.next = second;
```

The diagram now looks like this.

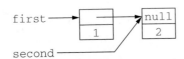

The links allow us to retrieve data from successive elements, beginning with the first element. Thus

```
first.next.data
```

has the value 2.

COMMON PROGRAMMING ERROR

A common mistake is to attempt to access a field or method for an object with a reference value that is `null`. Doing so generates a `NullPointerException`. For example, given the short list that we just created, attempting to reference `first.next.next.data` would generate a `NullPointerException`. The expression `first.next.next` refers to the reference value stored in the field `next` of the second element in the list. This field is `null`, so `first.next.next.data` is asking for the field `data` of the `null` value.

In some cases letting the program abort with the exception is acceptable. In other cases using the mechanism for handling exceptions may be appropriate—to catch the exception and take some corrective action. Yet another approach is to test for a null reference before accessing any fields. Better still is to design the program so that such null references can never occur.

12.2 A LINKED LIST IMPLEMENTATION OF A STACK

We've already discussed arrays, which are a type of container. That is, an array contains a sequence of values of the same type. Another common container used in computers is a stack. A *stack*, like an array, stores a sequence of similar objects. The difference between stacks and arrays lies in how you put values in the container. In an array, you create the container with a fixed size and then store and retrieve values at any index in the array. In constrast, a stack is like a stack of plates. You can add a plate to the top of the stack, you can look at the plate on the top of the stack, and you can remove a plate from the top of the stack. You can't look at, add, or remove plates from the middle.

A stack class for storing integers should have the following methods.

```
class IntStack {
  int top() { ... };
  void push(int value) { ... };
  int pop() { ... }
  boolean empty() { ... }
}
```

The method `top()` returns the value of the integer on the top of the stack without changing the stack's contents. If the stack is empty, it returns a 0. The method `push()` pushes an integer value onto the top of the stack, increasing the number of integers contained in the stack. The method `pop()` returns the same thing as `top()`, but it also removes the top value from the stack, reducing the number of integers contained in the stack by 1. If the stack is empty, `pop()` returns 0 and the stack is unchanged. The method `empty()` returns `true` if the stack is empty and `false` otherwise. The following figure shows the integers 1, 2, and 3 being pushed onto a stack and then popped back off.

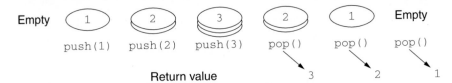

There are many ways to implement the operations of the class `IntStack`. An important aspect of Java (and other object-oriented languages) is the language syntax that allows you to hide and change the implementation without affecting other parts of a program that use the class. Here we implement the class `IntStack`, using the class `IntListElement` introduced at the beginning of the chapter.

```java
//IntStack.java - a stack implemented with a list
class IntStack {
  int top() {
    if (top != null)
      return top.data;
    else
      return 0;
  }

  void push(int value) {
      if (top == null) {
        top = new IntListElement(value);
      }
      else {
        IntListElement temp = new IntListElement(value);
        temp.next = top;
        top = temp;
      }
  }

  int pop() {
    int result = top();;
    if (top != null)
      top = top.next;
    return result;
  }

  boolean empty() { return top == null; }
  private IntListElement top = null;
}
```

DISSECTION OF THE CLASS `IntStack`

- ```
  int top() {
     if (top != null)
        return top.data;
     else
        return 0;
  }
  ```

  The private instance variable `top` is a reference to the `IntListElement` at the top of the stack. If the stack is empty, `top` equals `null` and the result of `top()` is 0. Otherwise, the result of `top()` is the `data` field for the element referred to by `top`. Note again that Java allows a variable and a method to have the same name.

- ```
  void push(int value) {
     if (top == null) {
        top = new IntListElement(value);
     }
     else {
        IntListElement temp = new IntListElement(value);
        temp.next = top;
        top = temp;
     }
  }
  ```

  We must check for the special case of pushing onto an empty list, in which case we simply set `top` to be a new element. If the stack isn't empty, we create a new element, set its link to point to the current top of the stack, and then move `top` to point to the new element. In both cases, we then store the new `value` in the `data` field of the new top element. The next figure shows the sequence of inserting an element into a nonempty stack. Here, 1 and 2 were previously pushed onto the stack, and we are now executing `push(3)`.

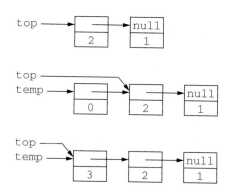

```
■   int pop() {
      int result = top();
      if (top != null)
        top = top.next;
      return result;
    }
```

We reuse the method `top()` to find the value that should be returned from `pop()`. By reusing our code in this way, we reduce the chances of making a mistake. If the stack isn't already empty, we move `top` to point to the next element in the list, thus removing what was the top element from the stack. We need to save the result before moving `top`; otherwise, we wouldn't be able to find the value to return.

```
■   boolean empty() { return top == null; }
    private IntListElement top = null;
```

The method `empty()` is straightforward, returning `true` if the stack is empty. The only instance variable is the pointer to the top element. Note the absence of any specification of how large the stack will be.

12.3 A SINGLY LINKED LIST

A stack is a specialized list because it permits insertion and removal of elements from only one end of the list, the top. In this section we consider a more general list class that implements a singly linked list. This class allows for insertion, removal, and examination of elements at any point in the list. We could just use the class `IntListElement` in each program that uses lists. Doing so, however, would require us to recode repeatedly the error prone operations of connecting and disconnecting links. Instead, we create a class that does all of the work for us.

With a stack, we always know where an insertion or removal is going to take place, namely, at the top. With a general linked list, we need some way to specify where the insertion or removal should be performed. We specify the location by having a variable called `current` that refers to an arbitrary element in the list. We can then move `current` from one element to the next. Here is a specification of our class, without any method bodies.

```
class IntList {

  void insert(int value)
  /* Insert after the element referred to by current
   * and move current to the new element.
   * If current doesn't refer to any element,
   * then insert at the head and move current to the
   * new element.
   */
```

```
int next()
/* Advance current to the next element and return
 * that element. If there is no next element or the
 * list is empty, throw an exception. If current
 * doesn't refer to any element on entry to this
 * method, then the first element in the list is
 * returned and current is set to the first element.
 */

int current()
/* Return the current element. If the list is empty
 * or there is no current element, throw an
 * exception. Initially current doesn't refer to
 * any element.
 */

void remove()
/* Remove the current element advancing current to
 * the next element. If there is no next element,
 * which happens when removing the last element,
 * set current to not refer to any element. This
 * is equivalent to moveToHead().
 * If current doesn't refer to any element on
 * entry, remove() does nothing.
 */

void moveToHead()
/* Set current to not refer to any element, which is
 * interpreted to mean before the first element.
 * A subsequent call to next() will return the
 * first element.
 */

boolean hasNext()
/* Returns true if current isn't the last element
 * in the list. This is intended to be used in
 * conjunction with next() to loop through a
 * list, examining each element.
 * Note that this isn't telling us if the list is
 * empty, but rather whether a subsequent call to
 * next() will succeed without causing an
 * exception.
 */
}
```

Before looking at an implementation of this class, let's look at some code involving the use of the class.

```
//IntListTest.java
class IntListTest {
  public static void main(String[] args) {
    IntList list = new IntList();
```

```
    // insert the integers 1 through 10 in the list
    for (int i=1; i<=10; i++)
      list.insert(i);
    // print the list
    list.moveToHead();
    while (list.hasNext())
      System.out.println(list.next());

    // try an insertion and a deletion
    list.moveToHead();
    list.next();        // current is 1
    list.next();        // current is 2
    list.insert(25);    // insert 25 between 2 and 3
    list.next();        // current is 3
    list.remove();      // remove 3
    // print the list again
    list.moveToHead();
    while (list.hasNext())
      System.out.println(list.next());
  }
}
```

This program prints 1 through 10 and then prints 1 through 10 with 3 replaced by 25. We use `next()` both to retrieve a particular element and to advance `current`. If we aren't concerned about the current element, we can simply ignore the value returned by `next()`. Note that the `IntListTest` program doesn't refer to `IntListElement`. Thus the code is independent of how `IntList` is implemented. It could be implemented with an array (see Exercise 8, on page 428), with a list built of `IntListElements`, as we do shortly, or with some other class.

Owing to the length of `IntList`, we present only the dissection, without first presenting the complete class.

DISSECTION OF THE CLASS `IntList`

▪
```
class IntList {
  private IntListElement head, current, previous;
```

There are three instance variables. The variable `head` always refers to the first element in the list or is `null` if the list is empty. The variable `current` can refer to any element in the list. If `current` is `null`, it is assumed to be pointing before the first element. In this way, `insert()` always inserts an element after `current`. The variable `previous` always points to the element before `current`. It is needed to simplify removal of elements. If `current` is pointing to the first element, `previous` will be `null`.

```
■   void insert(int value) {
      previous = current;
      if (current != null) {
        IntListElement next = current.next;        //step 1
        current.next = new IntListElement(value);//step 2
        current = current.next;                    //step 3
        current.next = next;                       //step 4
      }
      else if (head != null) {
        current = new IntListElement(value);
        current.next = head;
        head = current;
      }
      else /* list is empty */
        head = current = new IntListElement(value);
    }
```

Note that inserting in a list is much more complicated than pushing onto a stack. The variable previous is always set to current because current moves forward to the new element. There are three cases: current is pointing to some element in the list, current isn't pointing to any element but the list isn't empty, and the list is empty. The last case is easy: Point head and current at the new element. The middle case causes a new element to be inserted before the current first element. The following diagram shows an example of the middle case. Part (a) shows the initial list of 10 elements created by the first loop in IntListTest just after the first list.moveToHead(). Part (b) shows the result of subsequently executing listInsert(99).

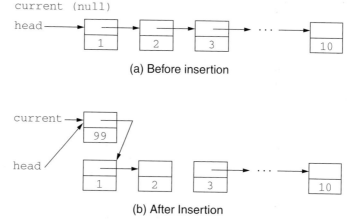

(a) Before insertion

(b) After Insertion

The remaining case is the general case when an element is inserted after an existing element. The following diagram shows the insertion of 25 between 2 and 3, as done with IntListTest. The comments //step 1 and so on in the code correspond to the similar labels on the arrows in the diagram.

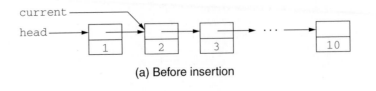

(a) Before insertion

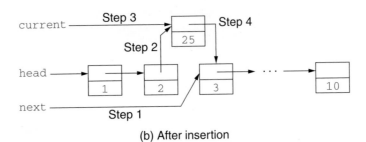

(b) After insertion

```
■   int next() {
      previous = current;
      if (current == null)
        current = head;
      else
        current = current.next;
      return current.data;
    }
```

If current is null, the "next" element is the first element in the list. If current is null at the return statement, a NullPointerException is thrown automatically. A better solution is to test for this situation and throw a NoSuchElementException. (See Exercise 5 on page 427.)

```
■   int current() {
      return current.data;
    }
```

This statement simply returns the value of the field data for the element pointed to by current. If current is null, this statement throws a NullPointerException automatically. As with next(), a better solution is to throw a NoSuchElementException.

```
■   void remove() {
      if (head == null) return;
      if (current == null) return;
      if (current == head)
        head = current = current.next;
      else
        current = previous.next = current.next;
    }
```

There are four cases for removal: The list is empty, no element is selected, the first element is selected, and some element other than the first is selected. Only the last two actually remove an element. Removing the first element is special because we also need to adjust `head` to point to whatever followed the first element. Removing an element other than the first element requires the use of `previous` to link the element prior to the removed element to the element that followed the removed element.

```
▪    void moveToHead() {
       previous = current = null;
     }

     boolean hasNext() {
       if (current != null)
         return current.next != null;
       else
         return head != null;
     }
```

These two short methods complete our implementation of `IntList`. There are two cases for `hasNext()`. First, if `current` is `null`, the next element is the first element if there is one. We therefore test whether the list is empty. Second, if `current` isn't `null`, the next element is whatever comes after `current`. In this case we test whether the `next` field of `current` isn't `null`.

12.4   MORE OPERATIONS ON LISTS

In the previous section, we introduced and described a class `IntList` that supported arbitrary insertion and removal but implemented only a minimal set of operations. Many more common operations can be used on lists, and implementing them once in our list class allows us to use them in other programs. The following is a list of typical operations; for completeness we included those already implemented.

LINEAR LIST OPERATIONS

- Create an empty list.
- Insert after the current position.
- Insert before the current position.
- Insert at position *n* in the list. Zero means insert before the first element.
- Remove the element at the current position.
- Find an element in the list.
- Append the elements of one list to the elements of another list.
- Count the elements in a list.
- Retrieve the current element.
- Move the current position forward.
- Move the current position backward.
- Move to the head of the list.

■ Move to the end of the list.

■ Print a list.

12.4.1 IMPLEMENTING THE METHOD toString() FOR THE CLASS IntList

Some list operations are easier to implement than others. A simple but useful operation is printing a list, which we did in our examples. However, by creating a method to print the list, our programming task becomes simpler. The preferred approach in Java is to create a method toString(), which returns a String representation that can then be printed. Here is a simple implementation of toString().

```
//excerpt from IntList.java
public String toString() {
  IntListElement cursor = head;
  StringBuffer result = new StringBuffer();
  while (cursor != null) {

    result.append(cursor.data + "\n");
    cursor = cursor.next;
  }
  //Convert the final StringBuffer to a String using
  //method toString() from class StringBuffer.
  return result.toString();
}
```

The class String is implicitly derived from the class Object, as are all classes except the class Object itself. Because the method toString() is defined as a public method in Object, the method, when redefined in other classes, must also be public—hence the keyword public in the definition. (See the discussion in Chapter 7.)

Often, a convenient way of working with lists is to write recursive methods. We can easily write a method that recursively calls itself to generate a string representation of a list when given a reference to the first element in the list.

```
static String toStringRecursive(IntListElement first) {
  if (first == null)
    return "";
  else
    return (first.data + "\n") + toStringRecursive(first.next);
}
```

Using this method, toString() in the class IntList can be implemented as

```
public String toString() {
  return toStringRecursive( head );
}
```

Note that there are no local variables in either of these last two methods. The result is built in the stack of method calls. Suppose that the list contains the elements 10, 20, and 30, in that order. Then a call to toString() would result in the following sequence of calls.

```
toString()
  toStringRecursive(first.data is 10)
    toStringRecursive(first.data is 20)
      toStringRecursive(first.data is 30)
        return "30\n"
      return "20\n30\n"
    return "10\n20\n30\n"
return "10\n20\n30\n"
```

Note how the result is built in reverse order as the method calls return.

12.4.2   DOUBLY LINKED LISTS

Implementing the "move current position backward" operation would be rather difficult if we used our classes `IntList` and `IntListElement`. In order to move backward, we would have to move back to the beginning and then move forward again, stopping when `current` reached what used to be the preceding element. To solve this problem, we can create a new list element class that contains two links—one pointing to the next element and one pointing to the preceding element. Such a list is called a *doubly linked list*. Here is our new list element.

```
//IntDListElement - for doubly linked lists
class IntDListElement {
  IntDListElement(int value) { data = value; }
  IntDListElement next;
  IntDListElement previous;
  int data;
}
```

We can create a list of three elements with the following code.

```
IntDListElement first = new IntDListElement(1);
IntDListElement second = new IntDListElement(2);
IntDListElement third = new IntDListElement(3);
first.next = second;
second.previous = first;
second.next = third;
third.previous = second;
```

Pictorially, this approach would result in the following structure.

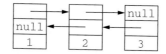

We leave it for you to do as an exercise to utilize this doubly linked element in a doubly linked list class that supports moving both backward and forward through the list.

12.5   A GENERIC STACK

The list and stack classes that we implemented in the preceding sections work only with integers. What if we wanted to store strings or other objects on a stack? One solution would be to create different classes for each type, which is cumbersome and unnecessary. Recall that Java supports polymorphism, which means that we can create one class to handle many different types. The changes to our previous classes are minor. Let's start with a generic list element.

```
//ListElement.java - a generic list element
class ListElement {
  ListElement(Object value) {
    data = value;
  }

  ListElement next;
  Object data;
}
```

We replaced `int` with `Object`. The class `Object` is a standard Java class, and a reference of type `Object` can refer to any nonprimitive type. In order to store primitive type values in our generic `ListElement`, we need to use the standard Java classes that turn primitive types into reference types (see Section 7.6). Recall that there is one such class for each primitive type. For example, the class `Integer` corresponds to the primitive type `int`, and `new Integer(3)` is a nonprimitive value that corresponds to the primitive value 3. To create a `ListElement` storing the value 3, we can use

```
ListElement elem1 = new ListElement(new Integer(3));
```

Similarly, we could create a `ListElement` containing the `float` value 1.25 with

```
ListElement elem2 = new ListElement(new Float(1.25f));
```

Strings don't require any special handling because they are already reference types. Here is a `ListElement` containing a `String`.

```
ListElement elem3 = new ListElement("element 3");
```

To retrieve the data from the elements, the program using the data has to know what type of value is really there. Provided that we know the true type, we can use a cast to convert from `Object` back to the true type (see Section 7.12). For example, if the list contains only `Float` values, we can use the following expression to retrieve a value.

```
Float x = (Float)elem2.data;
```

To recover a primitive `float` value from its `Float` class counterpart we use

```
float value = x.floatValue();
```

The other primitive types are similar; we make the obvious substitution for `float` in
`floatValue()`. If you don't know what type of value is stored in a `ListElement`,
Java provides the operator `instanceof` that you can use to test the type. (Recall our
discussion of `instanceof` in Section 7.12.)

Now that we have a generic list element, we can use it to create a generic list or
a generic stack. Here, we make the change for the stack and leave the changes for
the list for you to do as an exercise. In the following code, the changes are shown in
boldface. We replaced all occurrences of `int` with `Object` and all occurrences of
`IntListElement` with `ListElement`. The only other change was the name of the
class—from `IntStack` to `Stack`.

```
//Stack.java
class Stack {
  Object top() {
    if (top != null)
      return top.data;
    else
      return null;
  }
  void push(Object value) {
      if (top == null) {
        top = new ListElement(value);
      }
      else {
        ListElement temp = new ListElement(value);
        temp.next = top;
        top = temp;
      }
  }
  Object pop() {
    Object result = top();
    if (top != null)
      top = top.next;
    return result;
  }
  boolean empty() { return top == null; }
  private ListElement top = null;
}
```

In the following program we use the new stack to store `double` floating point
values.

```
//GenericStackTest.java
class GenericStackTest {
  public static void main(String[] args) {
    Stack stack = new Stack();
```

```
            stack.push(new Double(1.111));
            stack.push(new Double(2.222));
            stack.push(new Double(3.333));
            while (!stack.empty()) {
              double temp = ((Double)stack.pop()).doubleValue();
              System.out.println(temp);
            }
          }
        }
      }
```

We didn't have to first store the popped value in `temp`. We did so merely to show how to convert the popped value to a primitive value of type `double`. The same output would be obtained if the body of the loop was simply

```
System.out.println(stack.pop());
```

The output of this program is

```
3.333
2.222
1.111
```

COMMON PROGRAMMING ERROR

When implementing linked list data structures, you must take great care to ensure that you always create proper linked lists. For example, you could create a circularly linked list that has no beginning or end. That's fine, if that's what you intended; but if your intent was a linear linked list, operations such as `has-Next()` may never return `false`. Then an innocent loop such as

```
while (list.hasNext()) {
    ... = list.next();
    ...
}
```

becomes an infinite loop.

One good defense against such errors is the use of assertions, either formal or informal. A *formal assertion* is one that you actually place in the code to be checked. If the assertion fails, an exception can be thrown. An *informal assertion* can be in the form of a comment that should be checked by the implementer of the method.

An example of an assertion on the insert method for a list might be "The next field for the last element in the list is null." As discussed in Section 11.6, just the process of thinking about the assertions you might write can result in better code. For example, consider writing the assertion that the last element in the list is null. You should realize that you need to be sure that the first element inserted in an empty list and an element inserted at the end of a list must have their next fields set to null.

Another way to avoid problems resulting from errors in implementing your own list class is to use an existing list class that has been thoroughly debugged. Java includes an extensive collection of classes for handling lists, stacks, and related structures. These classes are included in the package `java.util`. For example, there is a class `java.util.LinkedList`. In addition, there is a widely used library called the Java Generic Library from Objectspace. The package is officially called `com.objectspace.jgl`. It is included in several Java development environments and can be obtained free from the Internet at *http://www.objectspace.com/jgl/*.

The class `Vector` from the package `java.util` is a useful and easy-to-use container. Although probably not implemented as a linked list, the class `Vector` supports essentially the same methods as those in the list classes discussed previously. For example, you can insert an element at an arbitrary point or remove an arbitrary element. A `Vector` is like an array that can be expanded as necessary to accommodate new elements. The following example shows a `Vector` being created and then one element being inserted in the middle and another removed. This program essentially mimics the operations of the class `IntListTest` in Section 12.3, on page 399. A `Vector` can only hold references, not primitive types. Therefore we use the wrapper class `Integer` that lets integers be treated as objects.

```
// VectorTest.java - using Vector as a list
import java.util.*;

class VectorTest {
  public static void main(String[] args) {
    Vector list = new Vector();

    for (int i = 1; i <= 10; i++)
      list.addElement(new Integer(i));
    System.out.println(list);
    // insert 25 between 2 and 3
    list.insertElementAt(new Integer(25), 2);
    list.removeElementAt(3);
    System.out.println(list);
  }
}
```

12.6 AN EXAMPLE: POLISH NOTATION AND STACK EVALUATION

Ordinary notation for writing expressions is called *infix*, wherein operators separate arguments. Another notation for expressions, which is very useful for stack-oriented evaluation, is called *Polish*, or parenthesis-free, *notation*. In Polish notation the operator comes after the arguments. Thus, for example,

`3, 7, +`   is equivalent to the infix notation   `3 + 7`

In Polish notation, going from left to right, the operator is executed as soon as it is encountered. Thus

`17, 5, 2, *, +`   is equivalent to   `17 + (5 * 2)`

A Polish expression can be evaluated by an algorithm using two stacks. The Polish stack contains the Polish expression, and the evaluation stack stores the intermediate values during execution. The following two-stack algorithm evaluates Polish expressions wherein all operators are binary.

A TWO-STACK ALGORITHM TO EVALUATE POLISH EXPRESSIONS

1. If the Polish stack is empty, halt with the top of the evaluation stack as the answer.
2. If the Polish stack isn't empty, pop the Polish stack into a variable called `opval`.
3. If `opval` contains a value, push the contents of `opval` onto the evaluation stack.
4. If `opval` contains an operator, pop the evaluation stack twice, first into `b` and then into `a`. Compute (a `opval` b) and push the result onto the evaluation stack. Go to step 1.

We illustrate the use of this algorithm in the following table, where we evaluate the expression

13, 4, -, 2, 3, *, +

opval	Polish Stack	Evaluation Stack	Comment
	13, 4, -, 2, 3, *, +	Empty	Initial configuration
13	4, -, 2, 3, *, +	Empty	Step 2
	4, -, 2, 3, *, +	13	Step 3
4	-, 2, 3, *, +	13	Step 2
	-, 2, 3, *, +	4, 13	Step 3
-	2, 3, *, +	4, 13	Step 2
	2, 3, *, +	9	Step 4
2	3, *, +	9	Step 2
	3, *, +	2, 9	Step 3
3	*, +	2, 9	Step 2
	*, +	3, 2, 9	Step 3
*	+	3, 2, 9	Step 2
	+	6, 9	Step 4
+	Empty	6, 9	Step 2
	Empty	15	Step 4

Next, we write a program that implements this two-stack algorithm and test it with an evaluation of the Polish expression 16, 9, *, 3, 7, +, +. We represent each element of the expression as a string.

```java
//Polish.java - two stack Polish evaluation algorithm
class Polish {

  public static void main(String[] args) {
    String[] expression =
            {"13", "4", "-", "2", "3", "*", "+"};
    Stack stack = new Stack();
    Stack intArguments = new Stack();
    String opval;

    for (int i = expression.length - 1; i >= 0; i--)
      stack.push(expression[i]);
    while (!stack.empty()) {
      opval = (String)stack.pop();
      if (!isOperator(opval))
        intArguments.push(opval);
      else
        intArguments.push(eval(opval, intArguments));
    }
    System.out.println(" = " + intArguments.top());
  }

  static boolean isOperator(String s) {
    return  s.equals("+") || s.equals("*") || s.equals("-");
  }

  // apply a binary operator to the top two operands
  // on the stack
  static String eval(String operator, Stack stack) {
    String a, b;
    b = (String)stack.pop();
    a = (String)stack.pop();
    if (operator.equals("+"))
      return  String.valueOf(Integer.parseInt(a) +
                            Integer.parseInt(b));
    else if (operator.equals("-"))
      return  String.valueOf(Integer.parseInt(a) -
                            Integer.parseInt(b));
    else
      return  String.valueOf(Integer.parseInt(a) *
                            Integer.parseInt(b));
  }
}
```

By using code that has already been written and tested, such as `Stack` in the preceding example, you have less work to do in implementing a program to evaluate a Polish expression.

12.7 QUEUES

A *queue* is a representation of a list of values for which the normal mode of operation is to insert objects at one end and remove them from the other. In the United States, people stand in lines to get into a theater or check out at a store. In England these lines are called queues. People enter at the tail and leave from the head. A queue is a *first-in-first-out* (FIFO) data structure. In contrast, the stack we discussed earlier is a *last-in-first-out* (LIFO) data structure—the last value pushed in is the first value popped out.

As with a stack, a queue can be implemented with an array or as a linked list of elements. Here we present a generic queue based on our generic class `ListElement`, which is similar to the class `Stack`. However, instead of `push()`, `top()`, and `pop()`, we have `add()`, which adds an element at the front, `front()`, which returns the element at the front of the queue, and `pop()`, which removes the element from the front of the queue and returns it. Also the class maintains two pointers—one to the head, or first element, and one to the tail, or last element. Recall that the stack had only one pointer, which referred to the top element.

```java
//Queue.java
class Queue {
  Object front() {
    if (head != null)
      return head.data;
    else
      return null;
  }

  void add(Object value) {
    if (head == null) {
      head = tail = new ListElement(value);
    }
    else {
      tail.next = new ListElement(value);
      tail = tail.next;
    }
  }

  Object pop() {
    Object result = front();
    if (head != null)
      head = head.next;
    return result;
  }

  boolean empty() { return head == null; }

  private ListElement head = null;
  private ListElement tail = null;
}
```

Our program to demonstrate the use of `Queue` is almost identical to the one we used for `Stack`. The main difference is in the output. This program prints the values in the order they are added to the queue. The output is

```
1.111
2.222
3.333
```

```
//QueueTest.java
class QueueTest {
  public static void main(String[] args) {
    Queue queue = new Queue();

    queue.add(new Double(1.111));
    queue.add(new Double(2.222));
    queue.add(new Double(3.333));
    while (!queue.empty()) {
      double temp = ((Double)queue.pop()).doubleValue();
      System.out.println(temp);
    }
  }
}
```

12.8 ITERATORS

An *iterator* is a construct that allows you to iterate over a collection of objects such as a list or an array. Any integer variable can be used as an iterator for an array. It is often useful to be able to maintain more than one iterator simultaneously for a single collection of objects. For example, using one forward iterator and one backward iterator you can reverse the elements in a list, implemented as an array, as shown in the following example.

```
int foward = 0, backward = list.length - 1;
while (forward < backward) {
  int temp = list[forward];
  list[forward] = list[backward];
  list[backward] = temp;
  forward++;
  backward--;
}
```

There are two iterators in this example: `forward` and `backward`. Because arrays are a fundamental type in Java and many other programming languages, there is a built-in syntax for iterators that iterate over arrays.

Two things are required of an iterator. You need some way to advance the iterator and fetch the next value. You also need some way to determine when you've iterated over the entire collection. For an array, increment or decrement the index variable and then test it to determine whether you've reached the end or the beginning of the array.

What about an iterator for classes such as `List` or `Stack` described in this chapter? The classes that implement singly linked lists have one implicit iterator built into the class. You can use the method `next()` to iterate over all the elements of such a list and the method `hasNext()` to detect when the entire list has been scanned. The following example involves the use of this implicit iterator to iterate over the entire list.

```
IntList list;
// code to fill the list would go here
list.moveToHead();
while (list.hasNext()) {
  int value = list.next();
  // do something with value
}
```

Using this implicit iterator, you can't maintain two simultaneous iterators moving at different times or in different directions. However, you can create a separate class to implement an iterator for a class such as List. The simplest iterators have only the two methods next() and hasNext().

In general, an iterator class will be aware of some details about how a collection is implemented. For the class IntList, the iterator class needs to know that the list is stored as a linked list of IntListElement objects. The standard way to create an iterator is to ask the class over which the iteration will occur to create one. This method is typically called iterator() in Java. Here is the new iterator() method for the class IntList.

```
IntListIterator iterator() {
  return new IntListIterator(this);
}
```

All this method does is create an IntListIterator object passing it a reference to the list. The following implementation of the iterator class requires that the field head in the class IntList be changed from private to package access (see Section 12.11.1) and that IntListIterator and IntList be in the same package.

```
// IntListIterator.java - simple forward iterator
class IntListIterator {
  // Create an iterator positioned before the first
  // element of the list.
  IntListIterator(IntList list) {
    current = null;
    this.list = list;
  }

  // Create an iterator positioned at element pos.
  IntListIterator(IntList list, IntListElement pos) {
    // pos must refer to an element in list
    current = pos;
    this.list = list;
  }

  //Same as next() in IntList.
  int next() {
    if (current == null)
      current = list.head;
    else
      current = current.next;
    return current.data;
  }
```

```
//Same as hasNext() in IntList.
boolean hasNext() {
  if (current != null)
    return current.next != null;
  else
    return list.head != null;
}

int current() {
  return current.data;
}

IntListIterator copy() {
  return new IntListIterator(list,current);
}

IntListElement current;
IntList list;
}
```

Using this class you can now have as many forward iterators at the same time for a list as you want. Suppose that you want to determine whether a list is in fact composed of two identical shorter lists concatenated together. The following method checks for this condition.

```
//IteratorExample.java
class IteratorExample {
  static boolean checkDuplicate(IntList list) {
    // count the number of elements in the list
    int numElements=0;
    IntListIterator iterator = list.iterator();
    while (iterator.hasNext()) {
      iterator.next();
      numElements++;
    }

    // check for an even number of elements
    if (numElements % 2 != 0)
      return false;
    // now compare the first half with the second half
    IntListIterator first = list.iterator();
    IntListIterator second = list.iterator();
    // advance second to the start of the second half
    for (int i = 1; i <= numElements / 2; i++)
      second.next();
    while (second.hasNext())
      if (first.next() != second.next())
        return false;
    return true;
  }
}
```

In the next example, involving two methods, we show how you can use iterators to process a list recursively. You can add these two methods to the class `IntList`. The first method simply creates an empty list and calls a private helper method to do the copy.

```
static IntList copy(IntListIterator iter) {
  return new IntList().copyHelper(iter);
}
```

The second method is the recursive helper method.

```
private IntList copyHelper(IntListIterator iter) {
  if (iter.hasNext()) {
    insert(iter.next());
    return copyHelper(iter);
  }
  else
    return this;
}
```

DISSECTION OF THE METHOD `copyHelper()`

- `if (iter.hasNext()) {`

This test is for the base case of the recursion, which occurs when the iterator has been advanced over all elements and there are no more elements to process.

- `insert(iter.next());`
  `return copyHelper(iter);`

If there are more elements to be copied, we insert the next element from the list being copied into this `IntList` object, which is the copy. Recall that the static method `copy()` created a new `IntList` object, which is the copy. The method `copyHelper()` operates on this new `IntList` object. After inserting the next element in the copy, we recursively call `copyHelper()`, which eventually returns a reference to `this`, after all the elements have been copied.

- `else`
  `return this;`

When all the elements have been inserted in the copy, which is the object referred to by `this`, the `IntList` object being operated on by `copyHelper()` simply returns a reference to the copy. This action causes all the recursive calls made in the repeated executions of the statement

```
return copyHelper(iter);
```

to return also.

12.8.1 USING ITERATORS TO IMPLEMENT THE METHOD append()

Let's implement the method append() for the class IntList. This method appends all the elements of one list to the end of another list. We present three different versions. Our first solution doesn't take advantage of any iterator methods. Our second solution uses the existing built-in iterator in IntList. The third solution shows how iterators can be used to create a simple implementation of append().

In the first solution, which doesn't use the other methods in IntList, the built-in iterators for the two lists aren't repositioned.

```
void append(IntList list) {
  IntListElement thisList = head;
  IntListElement otherList = list.head;
  IntListElement previous = null;

  // Position thisList on the last element by
  // advancing it off the end and then backing up one.
  // After the loop, previous will point to the last
  // element or be null if the list is empty.
  while (thisList != null) {
    previous = thisList;
    thisList = thisList.next;
  }
  thisList = previous;
  // Loop over the other list and insert each element
  // onto the end (pointed to by thisList).
  while (otherList != null) {
    // do the insert
    thisList.next = new IntListElement(otherList.data);
    thisList = thisList.next;
    // move to the next element of other list
    otherList = otherList.next;
  }
}
```

Use of the higher-level operations provided by a class is preferable, even when we're adding additional methods to a class. Their use minimizes the number of methods that must change in response to some low-level implementation detail change. The following code is a first attempt at the second solution, which uses the existing routines from the class IntList.

```
void append(IntList list) {
  // Position first lists built-in iterator on its
  // last element.
  while (hasNext())
    next();

  // Position the second lists built-in iterator on
  // its first element.
  list.moveToHead();

  // Add each element from the second onto the end
  // of the first.
  while (list.hasNext())
    insert(list.next());
}
```

The problem with this code is that it changes the value of the field `current` for both lists. Such a change is probably unexpected by the programmer using `append()`, particularly the change in `current` for the explicit parameter `list`. To resolve this problem, we can save both `current` and `previous` for both lists and then restore them before the method returns, as in

```
void append(IntList list) {
  // Save positions of built-in iterators.
  IntListElement saveCurrent = current;
  IntListElement savePrevious = previous;
  IntListElement listCurrent = list.current;
  IntListElement listPrevious = list.previous;

  // Position first lists built-in iterator on its
  // last element.
  current = head;
  while (hasNext())
    next();

  // Position the second lists built-in iterator on
  // its first element.
  list.moveToHead();

  // Add each element from the second onto the end
  // of the first.
  while (list.hasNext())
    insert(list.next());

  // Restore the built-in iterators.
  current = saveCurrent;
  previous = savePrevious;
  list.current = listCurrent;
  list.previous = listPrevious;
}
```

An even more robust solution is to use iterators. We first need to add a new method, `insert()`, that allows us to insert an element after the position indicated by an iterator. This method is similar to our current `insert()`, but instead of allowing insertion only after the single implicit iterator, we allow insertion after an arbitrary iterator. We leave the implementation of this new `insert()` for you to do as an exercise. Once we've added the new method `insert()` to the class `IntList`, we can implement `append()` as follows.

```
void append(IntList list) {
  IntListIterator thisList = this.iterator();
  IntListIterator otherList = list.iterator();
  // Move iterator for first list to its last element.
  while (thisList.hasNext())
    thisList.next();
  // Add each element from the second onto the end
  // of the first.
  while (otherList.hasNext())
    thisList = insert(thisList, otherList.next());
}
```

This last solution completely isolates the implementation of `append()` from the implementation details of the class `IntList`. This version of `append()` works for any list implementation that has iterators and a method `insert()` that takes an iterator and a value to insert.

12.8.2 SORTING A LINKED LIST

A simple sorting algorithm for linked lists is the *insertion sort*, which is similar to sorting a hand of playing cards by picking the cards up one at a time and placing each in its proper position. This isn't an "in place" sort, meaning that we don't modify the original list. Instead, we create a new list that is a copy of the original elements but in the proper order. In the following method to sort an `IntList` list, we use our original class `IntList` with the addition of a method to insert an element at a position specified by an iterator, as just discussed.

```java
//IntListSort.java
class IntListSort {
  static IntList sort(IntList list) {
    IntList sorted = new IntList();
    IntListIterator listIter = list.iterator();

    while (listIter.hasNext()) {
      // select the next item to be inserted
      int newItem = listIter.next();
      IntListIterator sortedIter = sorted.iterator();
      IntListIterator previous = null;

      // loop until a bigger item is found in sorted
      while (sortedIter.hasNext() &&
              newItem > sortedIter.next())
      {
        previous = sortedIter.copy();
      }
      // insert before the bigger item which we do
      // by inserting after the element before it
      if (previous == null) // insert at head
        previous = sorted.iterator();
      sorted.insert(previous, newItem);
    }
    return sorted;
  }
}
```

DISSECTION OF THE CLASS IntListSort

- `IntList sorted = new IntList();`

We create a new empty list that will eventually contain the elements from `list`, but in order, with the smallest elements first.

```
IntListIterator listIter = list.iterator();
while (listIter.hasNext()) {
```

We create an iterator and then examine each of the elements in list, using a while statement. The body of the loop inserts the elements from list in the list sorted so that elements in sorted are always in nondecreasing order.

```
int newItem = listIter.next();
IntListIterator sortedIter = sorted.iterator();
IntListIterator previous = null;

// loop until a bigger item is found in sorted
while (sortedIter.hasNext() &&
            newItem > sortedIter.next())
{
   previous = sortedIter.copy();
}
```

We use two iterators to find the insertion point. The iterator previous is null until the loop body has been executed at least once. From then on, previous points to the element before the element pointed to by sortedIter. When the loop exits, previous points to the element preceding the insertion point or is null, in which case insertion should be done at the head of sorted.

```
if (previous == null) // insert at head
   previous = sorted.iterator();
sorted.insert(previous, newItem);
```

We check for the special case of insertion at the head. To insert an element at the head we create a new iterator, positioned before the first element. Once previous has been set properly, we do the insertion.

12.9 ITERATORS AND THE INTERFACE Iterator

As we have shown, iterators need two methods: hasNext() and next(). The standard Java interface Iterator in the package java.util requires these two methods and a method remove().

Early versions of Java used an interface java.util.Enumeration, which was logically equivalent to Iterator, but without the method remove(). The method names were slightly different: hasMoreElements() and nextElement().

A class that implements the interface Iterator must include a method remove(), but the method isn't required to actually remove the item indicated by the iterator. If the method remove() doesn't remove the item, it should throw an UnsupportedOperationException.

The use of this interface simplifies code that includes iterators: All loops that have iterators now become more alike. When combined with the stylistic use of the method `iterator()` to return an iterator for a container, many loops now take on the form

```
Iterator i = container.iterator();
while (i.hasNext()) {
  SomeType localVariable = (SomeType)i.next();
  // do something with localVariable
}
```

We used `Iterator` instead of some type-specific iterator class. Its use means one less class for the reader of the code to understand. The only disadvantage is that we may need to cast the result of `next()` to the appropriate type. The specification of `next()` in the interface `Iterator` returns a value of type `Object`. As we have shown, this operation is safe in the sense that, if we attempt an illegal cast, an exception is thrown.

The interface `Iterator` is useful only for iterators that iterate over containers of nonprimitive values. The added overhead of wrapping a primitive type into a wrapper class and then unwrapping it is probably not worth it for containers such as our `IntList` from Section 12.3. The interface `Iterator` is useful when we're working with generic containers. For example, the standard Java class `LinkedList` has a method `iterator()` that returns an `Iterator` object that can be used to iterate over the elements in the `LinkedList`.

12.10 DELETING OBJECTS

We have shown how to create objects by using the keyword `new`. Each new object occupies some space in the computer's memory. So what happens to objects that are no longer needed? In some programming languages, notably C and C++, we have to explicitly tell the computer when certain data structures are no longer needed. In Java, the computer automatically figures out when an object is no longer needed and removes it. This procedure is called *garbage collection*. Using 1990s terminology, it would be better named *memory recycling*, but garbage collection was used to refer to this activity before the recycling of garbage became popular.

How does the computer know when an object is no longer needed? It doesn't, but it does know when the object can no longer be referenced by the program. If there are no legal references to an object, the memory allocated to the object can be recycled. Consider the following example.

```
String word = Console.in.readWord();
while (!word.equals("quit")) {
  // do some processing with the word
  word = Console.in.readWord();
}
```

Each call to `readWord()` returns a reference to a new `String` object. At the end of each loop iteration, `word` refers to a new `String` object, losing the reference to the previous object. If the rest of the loop doesn't create any additional references to the object referred to by `word`, the memory for all but the last `String` object can be recycled.

We don't have space for an extensive discussion of garbage collection algorithms. But to give you some idea of how they work, we describe simplified approximations of two approaches.

One way to determine if there are any legal references to an object is to locate all the variables in the active methods. A method is active if it has been called and hasn't yet returned. For each of these variables that is a reference type, mark the object it refers to as live. Then examine each live object and find the reference type variables in those objects and mark the objects they refer to as live. Continue this process until no new objects are marked as live. Any object not marked is garbage and can be recycled. This process, called *mark and sweep garbage collection*, is typically done when the computer begins to run low on memory. It can be time-consuming—possibly taking several seconds—which can be annoying to people using the system.

Another approach is to count the references to a particular object as they are created. When a reference is overwritten, the count of references to the object is decremented. When an assignment results in a new reference to the object, the count is incremented. When the count goes to zero, the object can be collected. This process is appropriately called *reference counting*, which doesn't cause the delays of mark and sweep. Instead, it slows the entire system a bit all the time because all operations that can affect references must deal with adjusting the counts.

12.11 PACKAGES

Even the simplest Java program uses classes that were written by others. This ability to reuse parts of programs is essential for building complex software systems. Collections of functions, procedures, or classes are often called *libraries*. Essentially all programming languages or their development systems provide some mechanism for a program to use these routines or classes.

In Java, groups of related classes can be placed in a *package*. There are two primary reasons for organizing classes into packages. First, a field or method that is defined without any of the access modifiers—`public`, `protected`, or `private`—can be accessed only from a method in a class from the same package. Thus classes can expose some implementation details to other classes in the same package but not to classes outside the package.

The second reason for using packages is to provide separate name spaces. This provision allows two different programmers or organizations to have classes with the same name and still use these classes in one program. For example, a software company that would like to define some of the standard mathematics functions slightly differently could create its own class `Math`. It should be placed in a package with a name derived from the company's name because part of the Java specification is a naming scheme for packages. This scheme is somewhat like Internet addresses in reverse, with the most general part of the name first. So a company with the Internet address *www.coolsoft.com* might name its package containing the class `Math com.coolsoft.general`. If the CoolSoft Corporation had a collection of classes that it used for handling standard container data structures, it might put them in a different package called `com.coolsoft.containers`. This package might have classes with some of the same names as those in the standard Java package `java.util`. For example, finding a better name than `Stack` for a class that implements a stack is difficult. There is already a class named `Stack` in `java.util`. Without packages to provide different name spaces, you couldn't write a program using `com.coolsoft.containers.Stack` in one place and `java.util.Stack` somewhere else.

12.11.1 PACKAGE ACCESS

As mentioned, a primary reason for using packages is to allow a group of classes to share methods and fields but not allow those methods or fields to be accessed from outside the package. In addition, a package can contain entire classes that aren't visible outside the package. We've already shown how the modifier `private` can be used to hide implementation details inside a class. In the same way, package access hides implementation details inside a package. Package access is the default obtained by not specifying any access modifier. Another access level that we've used is `public`, the access modifier that must be used for any classes, methods, or fields that are to be made visible or *exported* from the package. In the following example we modified `IntListElement`, `IntStack`, and `IntList` to create a package `intContainers` that exports the two classes `IntStack` and `IntList`. Only the parts that we changed are shown. The missing portions can be filled in from the earlier examples in this chapter.

```
// IntListElement.java
package intContainers;

class IntListElement {
  // omitted
}

// IntStack.java
package intContainers;

public class IntStack {
  public int top()                  // body omitted
  public void push(int value)       // body omitted
  public int pop()                  // body omitted
  public boolean empty()            // body omitted
}

// IntList.java
package intContainers;

public class IntList {
  public void insert(int value)     // body omitted
  public int next()                 // body omitted
```

```
    public void remove()            // body omitted
    public void moveToHead()        // body omitted
    public boolean hasNext()        // body omitted
    private IntListElement head, current, previous;
}
```

We added the keyword `public` to all the methods in `IntList` and `IntStack`. We also added it to the class definitions for those two classes. Note that the class `IntListElement` isn't public. It has package access, specified by the absence of either `private` or `public`. Package access prevents `IntListElement` from being used outside the package. The class `IntListElement` is an implementation detail that shouldn't be visible outside the package.

12.11.2　USING PACKAGES

Let's review how to use packages. Whenever you want to use a class from an existing package, you need to use an `import` statement to `import` the class. For simplicity, you should usually import all the classes from a package with `import` statements such as

```
import tio.*;
```

This statement imports all the classes in the package `tio`. The "`*`" is called a wild-card, meaning "give me all the classes." You can also import specific classes. For example, in most of our examples we could have used

```
import tio.Console;
```

Most of the time, the only class that we used directly was the class `Console`. Another alternative is not to use an `import` statement but instead always spell out the full name of the class. It is called the *qualified name* and includes the package name. This option can be rather awkward and isn't recommended if you intend to use the name of the package more than once. For example, you could use the following to read integers from the console.

```
int x = tio.Console.in.readInt();
```

The `import` statement told the compiler that if it encountered a class name it didn't recognize, it should try looking for it in the imported package. Import statements can save a lot of typing.

This explicit naming mechanism makes the use of two different `Math` classes possible. Here is how you could use the class `Math` from CoolSoft.

```
double x = Math.sqrt(y); // from java.lang
double y = com.coolsoft.Math.sqrt(y);
```

You don't have to import the package `java.lang`. It is imported by default into every Java class. That's why we could write `Math.sqrt()`, which uses the class `Math` from package `java.lang`, without having to use an `import` statement. The package `java.lang` is the only package that is automatically imported.

12.11.3 CREATING PACKAGES

Every Java program can use classes from one unnamed package. Any classes in a single directory on your computer's disk that don't specify a package name are part of the same unnamed package. To place the classes in a named package, you need to do two things: add a `package` statement to the top of each class in the package as shown in the preceding example, and place the classes in an appropriately named location on your computer's disk. For the `intContainers` package that we introduced, you need to place the source files in a subdirectory with the same name as the package, *intContainers*. If you're using a Unix or Windows command line to compile your Java programs, then with your current directory set to the one *containing* the subdirectory *intContainers*, execute the command

```
javac intContainers/*.java
```

Note that the current directory is *not intContainers* but the one *containing* the subdirectory *intContainers*. This command compiles all the Java source files in the subdirectory. The command shown is for Unix. On Windows you would use a "\" instead of a "/" to separate the subdirectory from the wildcard file name. If you're using an integrated development environment, you'll probably have to create a project that includes the files from the package and then compile them. A *project* is the term used by most integrated development environments for a group of related files.

By default, Java looks for packages in the directory where Java was installed and then looks for packages in the current working directory. You can change this procedure by changing the `CLASSPATH` environment variable. Check with your instructor or read the documentation for your system to determine the appropriate way to make this change. For small projects this change usually isn't necessary.

12.12 PROGRAMMING STYLE

Code reuse is the practice of reusing existing code in new programs. It has been an important part of programming from the beginning, but the amount of reuse is increasing. The complexity of current applications requires code reuse because it reduces development time and improves reliability. Increased reliability, in general, is the result of thorough testing of the reused components.

There are two aspects of code reuse: creation of reusable components and use of those components. One of the strengths of Java is the large and growing collection of reusable components called classes and collected as packages. In this chapter we introduced some basic data structures. You need to know how these data structures are created. When building real applications, you should, in general, not reimplement these basic data structures. Instead, you should select some appropriate reusable class or package that provides the functionality that your application needs.

If you determine that the performance of a class from a preexisting package is inadequate for your application, you should be able to replace that package easily with an implementation of your own.

The standard Java classes include several useful containers, such as `LinkedList`, and `Stack`, in the package `java.util`.

Another option, the Java Generic Library (JGL) from Objectspace, contains several packages. Although not standard Java packages, they are supported in many Java development systems and are freely available via the Internet. The JGL includes implementations of singly linked lists, doubly linked lists, stacks, and queues. The package provides forward and backward iterators for all container classes. It also includes several other important data structures that we haven't discussed. The JGL includes several algorithms, including the ability to sort any JGL container.

Summary

- Self-referential structures use references or pointers to link items of the same type.
- The simplest self-referential structure is the linear or singly linked list. Each element points to the next element, with the last element having a link value of `null`.
- Many list processing algorithms are naturally implemented recursively. Frequently, the base case is when the end of the list is reached. The general case recurs by moving to the "next" element.
- The abstract data type (ADT) stack is implementable as a linked list, with access restricted to its first element, called the top. The stack has a last-in-first-out (LIFO) discipline implemented by the routines `push()` and `pop()`.
- The ADT queue is also implementable as a linked list, with access restricted to its front and rear ends. The queue has a first-in-first-out (FIFO) discipline implemented by the routines `add()` and `pop()`.
- A doubly linked list has a link to the next and preceding elements. Having both forward and backward links facilitates some list operations.
- Generic list structures can be created by having the list elements store a reference to an `Object`. Any nonprimitive type can be stored directly in such an element. The wrapper classes from `java.lang` must be used to store primitive values in such a list.
- Iterators are used to iteratively process all the elements in a container, such as a list. An iterator at the very least needs the two methods `next()` and `hasNext()`.
- A group of related classes can be placed in a package. By doing so, you can expose some implementation details to other classes in the same package without making them generally accessible. Packages also provide for distinguishing between two classes with the same name—but from different packages. This provision allows both classes to be used if desired in a single program.

Review Questions

1. What causes a `NullPointerException`?
2. What is the default value for reference fields?
3. Draw a picture of a singly linked list containing the values 10, 20, and 30, in that order.

4. Draw a picture of a doubly linked list containing the values 10, 20, and 30, in that order.

5. A stack is used to process data in what order, LIFO or FIFO?

6. A queue is used to process data in what order, LIFO or FIFO?

7. What standard Java type is used to turn a primitive `int` value into an object? Why would you want to do that?

8. Why would you need an iterator for `IntList` when it already has methods `hasNext()` and `next()`?

9. `IntList` could have been implemented without the field `previous`. What operation would have been slowed down significantly if `previous` weren't used?

10. Name one operation that would be much faster on a doubly linked list than a singly linked list.

11. How is package access specified? What does it mean?

12. What was wrong with using the implicit iterator in `IntList` to implement `append()` as shown in Section 12.8.1, on page 417?

13. Each time a method is called, some context such as the value of local variables and the address of the last statement executed must be saved. When the called method returns, the context of the method that did the call is restored. What data structure is used to store these contexts? (*Hint*: Think about `methodA()` calling `methodB()` calling `methodC()` and then each returning in turn.)

14. If you wanted to write a computer program to simulate a bank teller, what data structure would you use to store the objects representing each simulated customer as he or she arrives at the bank?

Exercises

1. Write an insertion method that inserts an element before the first element of an `IntList` list.

2. Write an insertion method that inserts an element after the last element of an `IntList` list.

3. Write an insertion method that inserts an element at the first position in an `IntList` list following an element storing a particular `data` value. If there is no such element, insert the element after the last element.

4. Generalize the previous three exercises. Write an insertion function that inserts an element in the *n*th position in a list, where 0 means that the element is placed at the head of the list. If *n* is larger than the length of the list, insert the element at the tail of the list.

5. Modify the method `next()` in the class `IntList` to throw a `NoSuchElementException` if there is no next element. The syntax for throwing the exception is

```
throw new NoSuchElementException();
```

6. Add a constructor to the class `IntList` that takes an array of integers and uses the array to build an initial list. The elements in the list should be in the same order as the elements in the array.

7. Add a method `toIntArray()` to the class `IntList` that returns a new array of integers containing the same elements as the list, in the same order.

8. Write a class that implements the same methods as `IntList` but represent the list as an array of integers. Add a constructor that allows the programmer to specify the maximum size of the list. Use this constructor to set the size of the internal array.

9. Write a class `List` that can store a list of any nonprimitive type values. Start with `IntList` and make the same changes that were made to create the generic class `Stack`.

10. Create a class `Data` that contains two integer fields—one for age and one for weight—and one string field for a name. Build a list of `Data` objects, using `List` from the previous exercise. Then write a method to count the number of objects in the list that have age and weight fields above a given value.

11. Write a class `IntDList` that uses the `IntDListElement` defined in Section 12.4.2. Include methods for insertion and deletion and a method `toString()`.

12. Add a method `removeDups()` to your class `IntDList` in the previous exercise. The method removes from the list elements having duplicate values.

13. Write a class `DListElement` that is a generic list element, similar to `ListElement`, but doubly linked.

14. Use the `DListElement` of the previous exercise to implement a class `DList` with methods that function like those in `IntList`.

15. Add the method `previousElement()` to the class `DListElement` in the previous exercise.

16. Write a program that uses the class `Stack` to reverse the words in a sentence. The sentence to be reversed should be read with `Console.in.readWord()`. Use `Console.in.hasMoreElements()` to check for the end of the input. Use `lastIndexOf()` and `subString()` from the class `String` to remove the period at the end of the last word of the sentence.

17. Add a method `concatenate(IntList list)` to the class `IntList`. This method doesn't copy the elements of `list`, as does `append()`; instead, it simply sets the field `next` of the last element in the list referred to by `this` to point to the first element of the list referred to by `list`. Draw a diagram of the list that would result from `listOne.concatenate(listOne)`, where `listOne` refers to a list of two elements. What happens if the resulting list `listOne` is printed, using the method `toString()` from Section 12.4.1, on page 404?

18. In the previous exercise you constructed a cycle. A *cycle* is a pointer chain that points back to itself. Cycles are particularly nasty run-time bugs that can be hard to recognize. Add a method `iscycle()` to the class `IntList` that returns `true` if a cycle is detected and `false` otherwise. (*Hint*: Save a reference to the initial element of the list and follow the links until either `null` is reached or the initial element is encountered.)

19. Modify `concatenate()` in Exercise 17 to throw an `IllegalArgumentException` if the result of the operation would create a cycle. Don't do the concatenation in that situation. The exception `IllegalArgumentException` is defined in the package `java.lang`.

20. Add a static method `copyCat(IntList a, IntList b)` to the class `IntList` that returns a concatenated copy of the lists `a` and `b`. The original lists `a` and `b` should remain undisturbed. This method should work fine if called with both arguments referencing the same list.

21. Add a method `insert(IntListIterator iter, int value)` to class `IntList`. The method inserts a new element with the field `data` set to `value`,

following the element referred to by the iterator `iter`. The method should return a new `IntListIterator`, positioned at the element just inserted. Note that an iterator not pointing to any element (`current == null`) should be interpreted as positioned before the first element. This interpretation allows for insertion at any point. The iterator can't be positioned after the last element.

22. Using the iterator class `IntListIterator`, add a method with the signature

```
static IntList concatenate(IntListIterator index1,
                           IntListIterator index2)
```

to the class `IntList`. This method should return a new list that is the result of concatenating copies of the elements starting from `index2` to a list made from copies of the elements starting from `index1`. Write an iterative solution.

23. Use recursion to redo the previous excercise.

24. Starting with a linked list of objects as specified in Exercise 10, write a routine `sortAge()` to sort the list according to its age values. Write a function `sortName()` to sort the list in lexicographic order according to the name values.

25. Evaluate the following Polish expressions by hand.

```
7, 6, -, 3, *
9, 2, 3, *, 4, -, +
1, 2, +, 3, 4, +, *
```

26. Write corresponding Polish expressions for

```
(7 + 8 + 9) * 4
(6 - 2) * (5 + 15 * 2
6 - 2 * 5 + 15 * 2
```

27. Use the `Polish` program that we wrote in Section 12.6, on page 411, to evaluate the six Polish expressions given or derived in the previous two exercises.

28. The following lines occur in the `evaluate()` function in the class `Polish`:

```
b = (String)stack.pop();
a = (String)stack.pop();
```

What happens if you write

```
a = (String)s.pop();
b = (String)s.pop();
```

instead? The program should work properly on some Polish expressions but not on others. Explain why.

29. Write a routine that allows you to interactively initialize the contents of a Polish stack. Write a program to test your routine.

30. Add a constructor to the class `Queue` that builds a queue from an array of objects.

31. Add a method `toArray()` to the class `Queue` that returns an array containing the same elements as the `Queue`. Did you copy the elements into the new array or just the references to the elements? Discuss the two alternatives.

32. Use a general linked list structure to program sparse matrix addition. In a *sparse matrix* most of the values are zero. A nonzero element of a sparse matrix is represented by the triple (*i, j, value*). For each row *i*, the triples will be linked as a linear list. There will be an array with as many entries as there are rows in the matrix. Each

array entry will be the list for the corresponding row. To add matrix **A** to matrix **B,** we take each row in the two matrices and merge them into a matrix **C**. For each row index, if only one matrix contains elements for that row, that row is duplicated in **C**. If both matrices contain elements for a given row, the rows are merged. If both rows have a triple with the same column value, in the output row $c_{i,j}$ is the sum $a_{i,j} + b_{i,j}$. Otherwise, the element with smallest column number becomes the next element of the output row.

33. Although sparse matrix addition can be performed with just row linked lists, for multiplication both row- and column-linked lists are required. You won't be able to use the list classes developed in this chapter. Each element can potentially have both a row successor and a column successor. If the elements are implemented by the class `SMElement`, there will be two `SMElement` arrays—one for the rows and one for the columns. Each nonnull array entry in the row array will be a link to the first nonzero row entry. The columns are handled similarly. Program sparse matrix multiplication.

34. Implement a sparse polynomial class. Use a linked list of elements to represent the nonzero terms of the polynomial. A *term* is a real coefficient and a power. Write a complete polynomial manipulation package. Your package should be able to input and output polynomials, and it should be able to add, subtract, multiply, and copy polynomials.

13

Concurrent Programming with Java Threads

Some programming problems can most naturally be represented as a collection of distinct tasks to be performed concurrently. In some cases, the concurrency is obvious and unavoidable, as when two computers communicate over a network. For example, fetching a file over the Internet involves the task of reading the file from the network on one computer and the task of writing the file to the network from a different computer. In other cases, all the tasks may execute on one computer, in which case concurrent execution may only be desirable, not required. For example, suppose that you were asked to design and implement a new Internet browser. Among other things, you might want the browser to be able to load large graphics files in one window while you simultaneously followed several other links in another window. The computer is essentially being asked to do two things at once. Most operating systems today provide some support for doing several things at once, but support in popular languages was limited or nonexistent prior to Java.

Many different terms are applied to a unit of sequential program execution that is executing within a computer system that is executing many such units simultaneously. The largest unit is usually called a process. A *process* is the term for a program when it is executing. Most operating systems support concurrent execution of multiple processes. To grasp the difference between a process and a program, consider that you could have two different processes, each executing the same program.

The other terms most commonly used for units of sequential execution are *tasks* and *threads*, both of which generally refer to the execution of less than an entire program. This is in contrast to process, which usually refers to the execution of an entire program. Java provides language support for concurrent execution of parts of programs called threads. Three fundamental capabilities must be provided to support concurrent programs or threads.

1. Concurrency—There must be some way to create multiple execution threads.
2. Synchronization—There must be some way for two threads to synchronize in order to avoid interfering with each other.
3. Communication—There must be some way for two threads to exchange information.

In this chapter we describe how each of these capabilities is handled in Java.

13.1 IMPLICIT THREADS FROM AWT

Programs that use AWT or Swing to create graphical user interfaces implicitly create a concurrent thread to respond to input events and call the appropriate event listeners. We can get a clear sense of the two threads by having our method `main()` do something after creating the components of a GUI. The following program increments a count once a second, while at the same time responding to simple button clicks in a GUI. The program has three classes. The class `AwtThread` contains `main()`, which starts the GUI and then loops, printing `count` once per second. The class `ClickCounter` is a simple `ActionListener` that counts the number of times the button it is listening to is clicked. The class `GoodBye` is a simple `ActionListener` that exits when the button it is listening to is clicked. We discussed `GoodBye` in Section 8.2 and don't repeat it here.

```
//AwtThread.java - doing two things at once
import java.awt.*;
import javax.swing.*;
import tio.*;

class AwtThread {
  public static void main(String[] args)
      throws InterruptedException
  {
    createGUI();
    int count = 0;
    while (true) {
      count++;
      // go to sleep for 1 second = 1000 milliseconds
      Thread.currentThread().sleep(1000);
      System.out.println("count is now " + count);
      System.out.flush(); // force output to print now
    }
  }

  static void createGUI() {
    JFrame frame = new JFrame("AwtThread");
    Container pane = frame.getContentPane();
    JButton quit = new JButton("Quit");
```

```
      quit.addActionListener(new GoodBye());
      pane.add(quit, BorderLayout.NORTH);
      JButton counter = new JButton("Click to count");
      counter.addActionListener(new ClickCounter());
      pane.add(counter, BorderLayout.SOUTH);
      frame.pack();
      frame.show();
   }
}

//ClickCounter.java - count button clicks
import java.awt.event.*;

class ClickCounter implements ActionListener {
   public void actionPerformed(ActionEvent e) {
      count++;
      System.out.println("Total clicks is " + count);
   }
   int count = 0;
}
```

Earlier when we discussed GUIs we never did any processing in `main()` after building a GUI. All computation was driven by events. If you run the preceding example, you'll see that a window appears with the two buttons `Quit` and `Click to count`. When you click the counter button, the number of clicks is printed. No matter what you do, about once a second the variable `count` in `main()` is incremented and its value printed. You can go back and forth as much as you like. Actually, two threads are running. One is waiting for GUI events, and the other is executing `main()` with its `while` statement. The thread reading the GUI events is created by part of the AWT code, but it uses the mechanisms we describe shortly. We discuss the method `sleep()` used in this example in Section 13.7.1.

13.2 CREATING THREADS

A Java thread is represented by an instance of a class. The simplest way to create a thread that actually does something is to extend the class `Thread` from the package `java.lang`. The following example creates two simple threads. Each prints a message periodically, using the method `sleep()` to control the speed at which it prints its messages.

```
//TwoThreads.java - create two simple threads
class TwoThreads{
   public static void main(String[] args) {
      SimpleThread t1 = new SimpleThread(1, 1000);
      SimpleThread t2 = new SimpleThread(2, 1300);
      t1.start();
      t2.start();
   }
}
```

The class `SimpleThread` implements the threads. The constructor for `SimpleThread` takes two parameters: an integer used to distinguish the threads and the number of milliseconds to delay between each message. The delays are chosen so that the threads progress at different rates. In much the same way that calling the `show()` method for a `JFrame` starts a thread inside AWT to listen for events, calling `start()` in this example starts a thread that is executing the instructions specified by the class `SimpleThread`.

```java
//SimpleThread.java - periodically print a message
class SimpleThread extends Thread {

  SimpleThread(int threadId, int threadDelay) {
    id = threadId;
    delay = threadDelay; // in milliseconds
  }

  public void run() {
    System.out.println("Thread" + id + " started.");
    System.out.flush(); //needed to see the effect
    for (int i = 0; i < 10; i++) {
      try {
        sleep(delay); // sleep delay milliseconds
      }
      catch (InterruptedException e) {
        System.out.println("sleep interrupted: "+e);
      }
      System.out.println("Thread" + id + ": i = " +i);
    }
    System.out.println("Thread" + id + " finished.");
  }

  private int id;
  private int delay;
}
```

DISSECTION OF THE CLASS SimpleThread

- `class SimpleThread extends Thread {`

The class `Thread` is from the package `java.lang`. The class `Thread` implements most of the functionality required to have a separate thread. All we need to do is override the method `run()`. This is a powerful use of inheritance.

- ```java
  SimpleThread(int threadId, int threadDelay) {
    id = threadId;
    delay = threadDelay; // in milliseconds
  }
  ```

We use the constructor to initialize a simple `id` variable used to distinguish the messages in the output. The variable `delay` controls the rate at which messages are printed.
  ```

```
∎   public void run() {
        ...
    }
```

The method `run()` must be overridden to define the actions for this thread. This method is analogous to `main()` for the simple programs that we've been writing. The Java virtual machine eventually calls the method `run()` in response to a call to `start()` for an object that extends the class `Thread`. We don't call `run()` directly because the Java virtual machine needs to create some internal data structures to handle the new execution thread.

```
∎   System.out.println("Thread" + id + " started.");
    System.out.flush(); //needed to see the effect
    for (int i = 0; i < 10; i++) {
      try {
        sleep(delay); // sleep delay milliseconds
      }
      catch (InterruptedException e) {
        System.out.println("sleep interrupted: " + e);
      }
      System.out.println("Thread" + id + ": i = " +i);
    }
    System.out.println("Thread" + id + " finished.");
```

When the thread starts, we print an appropriate message. The method `flush()` forces the output to come to the screen. Without this method, the system might buffer the output for later display. We then loop 10 times, printing a message each time around the loop. To control the rate of execution, we use the method `sleep()`, which is inherited from the class `Thread`. The parameter for `sleep()` is the number of milliseconds that the thread should be put to sleep. At the end of the delay, the thread will be awakened and continue executing. This technique is the same used to control the displaying of images in an animation. In that case, the delay would be more like 100 milliseconds or less. The method `sleep()` can be interrupted, throwing an `InterruptedException` which must be caught. The specification of `run()` in `Thread` doesn't allow us to simply throw the exception up the line with a `throws` clause.

13.3 COMMUNICATION BETWEEN TWO THREADS

There are many ways for threads to communicate. The three most common forms are via shared objects, messages, or remote method invocation (RMI). In this section we discuss communication via shared objects. Later we show how to send messages over a network connection called a socket. We don't discuss RMI in this book because of space limitations.

In order for two threads to communicate via a shared object, both must have a reference to the same object. Once that has been established, any modifications made to the object by one thread are also observed by the other thread. One way to think of this is like a bulletin board on which anyone having access to it can write messages to be read by others with similar access.

One way to create a shared object is to pass it to the threads when we create them. In the following program, we modify our two-threads example, passing a reference to a shared `Counter` object when constructing a `Racer` object. Each `Racer` object clicks the shared counter 1,000,000 times and then prints the value. We set the modulus of the counter at 10 million because we are interested in counting the total number of clicks.

```java
//TwoThreads2.java - two threads sharing a counter
class TwoThreads2 {
  public static void main(String[] args) {
    Counter counter = new Counter(0, 10000000);
    Racer t1 = new Racer(1, counter);
    Racer t2 = new Racer(2, counter);

    t1.start();
    t2.start();
  }
}
//Racer.java - click the counter 1,000,000 times
class Racer extends Thread {
  Racer(int id, Counter counter) {
    this.id = id;
    this.counter = counter;
  }

  public void run() {
    System.out.println("Thread" + id + " started.");
    for (int i = 0; i < 1000000; i++)
      counter.click();

    System.out.println("Thread" + id +
            " finished counter is " + counter.get());
  }

  private int id;
  private Counter counter;
}
```

In the preceding example one `Counter` object is being shared by two threads. Both call exactly same `click()` method and increment the same instance variable `value` inside a single `Counter` object. The threads more or less take turns. This is the same kind of sharing, called *timesharing*, that lets many different people simultaneously use one computer or lets one person do several things at once on a computer. For example, most systems allow a user to do something else while downloading large files with an Internet browser.

The example also demonstrates the need for synchronization, which we discuss next. If you run the example using the `Counter` class described in Chapter 6, Exercise 6, on page 306, the total number of clicks reported by the thread that finishes last varies from run to run, and will almost always be less than 2,000,000, the expected answer. When both threads try to click the counter at "exactly the same time," some of the clicks are missed. We explain how they get missed in the next section.

13.4 SYNCHRONIZING TWO THREADS

Two types of synchronization occur between two threads. The first, *mutual exclusion synchronization*, is used to protect certain *critical sections* of code from being executed simultaneously by two threads, such as the method `click()` in the class `Counter`. This protection is often necessary to maintain the correctness of the code. The second, *signal–wait synchronization*, is used when one thread needs to wait until another thread has completed some action before continuing. Java has mechanisms for both.

All synchronization in Java is built around a relatively simple mechanism called a *lock*, and every Java object has an associated lock. Using appropriate syntax, we can specify that the lock for an object be locked when a method is called. Any further attempts to call a method for the locked object by other threads cause the thread to be suspended until the lock is unlocked. To make a method lockable, we simply specify that the method is synchronized by adding `synchronized` to the method header along with any access modifiers.

Note that a lock only locks out *other* threads. The thread that locked a lock is said to be *holding the lock*. The thread holding a lock won't be blocked if it calls another method for the same object. When a thread unlocks a lock, the thread is said to *release the lock*. The terms holding and releasing of a lock reflect the use of locks in operating systems to control access to resources that can't be used by two programs at the same time, such as a printer. A program that is using a particular resource such as a file is said to be *holding the resource*. When the program has finished with the resource it *releases the resource* for other programs to use.

13.4.1 MUTUAL EXCLUSION USING `synchronized`

How did clicks get missed in the program `TwoThreads2`? Recall that a statement such as

```
value = (value + 1) % modulus;
```

is compiled as a sequence of primitive bytecodes. First, some bytecodes will compute `(value + 1) % modulus`, leaving the result on the Java virtual machine's stack. Then the result on the top of the stack is stored in the variable `value`. We summarize this process with the following pseudocode.

```
load value
load 1
add
load modulus
mod
store value
```

Each Java thread has its own stack that it uses for executing bytecodes. When the Java virtual machine switches from running one thread to running another, it switches to a different stack. This switch is called a *context switch*. Think of it as each thread having its own calculator. Operations on one calculator don't affect the operations on the other calculator until the result is stored in memory. Because the threads share the same memory, once a result has been stored any future loads, even in other threads, encounter the modified result.

When two threads are executing simultaneously, except as discussed shortly, the Java virtual machine can decide to switch from one thread to the other at any time. Suppose that thread `t1` is somewhere after the `load value` bytecode but before the `store value` bytecode when the Java virtual machine decides to let thread `t2` execute for awhile. When thread `t1` finally resumes, it stores whatever is on the top of its stack in `value`. In the meantime, if thread `t2` has clicked the counter several times, all those clicks will be lost. The integer in the field `value` computed by thread `t2` is overwritten by the older, incorrect integer from `t1`'s stack. This type of error is called a *race condition*—hence the name of the class `Racer`. The following illustration shows a context switch while `t1` is attempting to click the counter. The bytecodes load value and store value are abbreviated lv and sv, respectively.

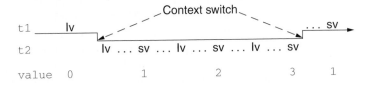

The solution in this case is to turn the method `click()` into a critical section. We don't want to allow both threads to be executing the bytecodes for `click()` at the same time on the same `Counter` object. All we need to do is declare that the method is synchronized by adding the keyword `synchronized` to the declaration, as in

```
//in class Counter
public synchronized void click() {
  value = (value + 1) % modulus;
}
```

So why not just make all methods synchronized? The reason is that synchronization of a method adds extra work for the computer. Each time a synchronized method is called, the computer must check to be sure that no other thread is already executing in the method. More important, in some cases two threads must be allowed to execute simultaneously to achieve a desired result.

13.4.2   SIGNAL–WAIT SYNCHRONIZATION

Suppose that you have two threads, one called the producer and the other called the consumer. The *producer* computes some value, that is, "produces it," and then places it in a shared object. The *consumer* reads the produced value and does something with it, that is, "consumes it." We want this activity to repeat until some terminating condition is reached, and we want the producer and consumer, whenever possible, to execute simultaneously. How do we make sure that the consumer doesn't consume the value until it has been produced? The answer is that the producer *signals* when there is a new value to consume and that the consumer *waits* until signaled by the producer. Furthermore, the producer has to wait until the consumer has read the preceding value before writing in a new one. Thus the producer has to wait for the consumer to signal that it has read the new value. This problem is called the *producer–consumer problem*, and it models many real-world computer applications.

Signal–wait synchronization is accomplished with two methods inherited from `Object`: `wait()` and `notify()`. Although not shown in the preceding example, when a thread is executing inside a synchronized method for some object, call it `obj`, any other thread that attempts to call *any* synchronized method for `obj` is blocked. It doesn't need to be the *same* method for blocking to occur. Note that synchronization actually takes place at the object, not the thread. As it executes, a thread of execution "moves" from object to object by calling methods in different objects.

When `wait()` is called from within a synchronized method, the thread is suspended and the lock for the object is released. That is, other threads are now allowed to make calls to synchronized methods for the object.

When `notify()` is called from within a synchronized method, one thread, if there is one, that is suspended as a result of a `wait()` call while executing in the same object, resumes. This thread won't actually begin execution until the thread calling `notify()` has returned from its synchronized method and released the lock. The following diagram shows the states that a thread can be in as a result of synchronization. Note that a thread can be in one of three states: It can be waiting for the lock; it can be waiting for a `notify()` from another thread; or it can be running, in which case it is holding the lock.

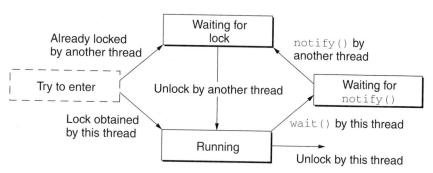

Thus there can be two or more threads "inside" synchronized methods for the same object. However, all but one are either suspended, or just awakened, waiting for the executing thread to release the lock. The methods `wait()` and `notify()` combined with synchronized methods turn any object into a synchronization construct, which is known as a *monitor*.

Our producer–consumer program looks very much like our previous examples at the top level. Let's create the two threads and start them running.

```
//ProducerConsumer.java - signal/wait synchronization
class ProducerConsumer {
  public static void main(String[] args) {
    Buffer buffer = new Buffer();
    Producer prod = new Producer(buffer);
    Consumer cons = new Consumer(buffer);

    prod.start();
    cons.start();
  }
}
```

Each thread is passed a reference to a shared buffer used to communicate the produced value from the producer to the consumer. The producer and the consumer are very similar and repeatedly try to put/get a value in/from the buffer.

```
//Producer.java - "produce" the integers 0-9
class Producer extends Thread {
  Producer(Buffer buf) {
    buffer = buf;
  }
  public void run() {
    System.out.println("Producer started.");
    for (int i = 0; i <  10; i++) {
      // code to produce a value here
      System.out.println("Producer produced " + i);
      buffer.put(i); // let i be the produced value
    }
    System.out.println("Producer is finished.");
  }
  private Buffer buffer;
}

//Consumer.java - consume first 10 integers from buffer
class Consumer extends Thread {
  Consumer(Buffer buf) {
    buffer = buf;
  }

  public void run() {
    System.out.println("Consumer started.");
    for (int i = 0; i < 10; i++) {
      int value = buffer.get();
      System.out.println("Consumer received " + value);
      // code to "consume" the value here
    }
    System.out.println("Consumer is finished.");
  }

  private Buffer buffer;
}
```

All synchronization is done in the `Buffer` object. If the buffer wasn't synchronized, the producer and consumer would just execute as fast as they could. The consumer might get the same value several times from the buffer, or the producer might try to put a new value in the buffer before the consumer read the old one.

```java
//Buffer.java - a synchronized shared buffer
class Buffer {
  synchronized void put(int newValue) {
    while (!empty)
      try {
        //wait for previous value to be consumed
        wait();
      }
      catch(InterruptedException e) {
        System.out.println("wait interrupted: " + e);
      }
    value = newValue;
    empty = false;
    notify();
  }

  synchronized int get() {
    while (empty)
      try {
        wait(); // wait for buffer to fill
      }
      catch(InterruptedException e) {
        System.out.println("wait interrupted: "+e);
      }
    empty = true;
    notify();
    return value;
  }

  private boolean empty = true;
  private int value;
}
```

DISSECTION OF THE CLASS Buffer

- `synchronized void put(int newValue)`

Both `put()` and `get()` are synchronized. Thus, if one thread is executing `put()`, the other thread will be blocked if it tries to execute `put()` or `get()` for the same object. The mutual exclusion implied by `synchronized` applies to all methods for a single object, not just simultaneous calls to the same method.

- ```java
  while (!empty)
    try {
      wait(); // wait previous value to be consumed
    }
    catch(InterruptedException e) {
      System.out.println("wait interrupted: " + e);
    }
  value = newValue;
  empty = false;
  notify();
  ```
  ```

We use the boolean field `empty` to keep track of whether the buffer contains a produced item that hasn't yet been consumed or whether the buffer is empty. The buffer is initially empty, with `empty` set to `true`. We repeatedly check whether the buffer is empty. If it is, the loop terminates and we proceed to put the new value in `value`, set `empty` to `false`, and call `notify()`. The call to `notify()` wakes up the consumer if it is waiting inside `get()`. If the buffer isn't empty, we call `wait()` to suspend the producer. This thread remains blocked until some other thread—the consumer in this case—calls `notify()` from within a synchronized method of the same `Buffer` object. The `wait()` call, like the `sleep()` call, can throw an exception that we need to catch.

- ```
  while (empty)
      //omitted
  empty = true;
  notify();
  return value;
  ```

The body of `get()` is almost the same as `put()`. We loop until the buffer isn't empty in this case, setting `empty` to `true` once the loop exits. The call to `notify()` awakens the producer if it is waiting inside the method `put()`.

13.4.3 CONDITION VARIABLES VERSUS SEMAPHORES

Many different synchronization techniques have been developed. The synchronization technique that Java implements is called *monitor sychronization*. Each object with synchronized methods is called a monitor, and only one thread is allowed "into" the monitor at a time; that is, the entrance to synchronized methods is "monitored."

To allow for more sophisticated sychronization, monitors were extended in various ways to allow controlled suspension and resumption of several threads inside a monitor. In some versions of monitors, a thread can wait for a *condition variable* to become true and other threads can signal that a condition variable has become true. These waits and signals correspond to Java's `wait()` and `notify()`. An important aspect of condition variables is that if no thread is waiting, a signal has no effect. Also, just because a condition was signaled as being true doesn't mean that it will still be true when the signaled thread finally resumes.

This is the reason that we used the loop `while (!empty)...` instead of `if (!empty)...` in our producer–consumer example. In this particular example, which one we use won't make any difference. For example, if the consumer is awakened, `empty` is guaranteed to be false. When using this type of synchronization, you should always check the condition that must be satisfied in order to continue before you actually continue. In other circumstances—for example, if there were two consumers—one consumer might wake up and find that some other consumer had already consumed the value. In that case, the consumer should just go back to waiting.

Another fundamental sychronization method is *semaphore synchronization*. At first glance, semaphores look much like monitors with `wait()` and `signal()`.
  ```

Conceptually, a semaphore is an object with two methods, `signal()` and `wait()`, and an internal counter. The method `wait()` decrements the internal counter and blocks if the counter is less than zero. The method `signal()` increments the internal counter and, if the value is less than or equal to zero, awakens one of the threads blocked in `wait()`.

There is an important difference between semaphores and the monitor style of synchronization in Java. The Java monitors don't have an internal counter. In Java, if you call `notify()` and no thread is blocked, nothing happens. A subsequent `wait()` will always wait. With semaphores, if you call `signal()`, a thread that comes along later will read the effect of that signal via the internal counter and possibly pass right through a call to `wait()` without blocking.

13.5 PASSING MESSAGES TO ANOTHER COMPUTER

All threads created as part of a single Java program run on the same computer and can share objects, as we've discussed. What about communicating with a Java program on another computer, connected with a network? In this situation several options are available. Two approaches supported in standard Java are message passing, using a network connection called a socket, or remote method invocation called RMI. As mentioned earlier, here we discuss only message passing.

A *socket* is a connection to another computer via a TCP/IP network, the dominant protocol for communicating over the Internet. Associated with every socket in Java is an input stream and an output stream. Once connected, the programs on the two ends of the connection communicate by reading and writing over these streams. When one program writes to its output stream, the same bytes appear on the input stream of the other program.

To create a socket that is connected to another computer, you need to know two things: the network name of the computer, or host name, and which port to connect to. Of the thousands of ports, most preallocated system ports lie in the range 0–1000, so unless you're connecting to an existing system server, you should choose a port number greater than 1000. For example, port 80 is the http port for connecting to web servers, and port 25 is the standard port for connecting to e-mail servers. On Unix systems you can find the assigned ports by examining the file */etc/services*. You're free to pick any number that isn't reserved—it just needs to be agreed upon at both ends of the connection. Think of the port number as being somewhat like a telephone extension.

The first step in creating a socket connection is having one of the programs begin listening for connections. This program is traditionally called the *server*. It is waiting for a request to do something. The server first begins listening for connections on a specific port. When another computer, or another program on the same computer, tries to connect to the same port, a socket connection is established. The following program listens for connections and then simply prints out the characters it receives from a socket; it also sends the same characters back over the socket.

```java
//MiniServer.java - server that echos what it receives
import java.io.*;
import java.net.*;

class MiniServer{
  public static void main (String args[])
       throws java.io.IOException
  {
    if (args.length != 1) {
      System.out.println("Usage: " +
          "java MiniServer portnumber");
      System.exit(1);
    }
    int portnum = Integer.parseInt(args[0]);

    ServerSocket sock = null;
    try {
      sock = new ServerSocket(portnum);
    }
    catch (IOException e) {
      System.out.println("Could not listen on port: "
                            + portnum + ", " + e);
      System.exit(1);
    }
    System.out.println("Now listening at port " + portnum);

    Socket clientSocket = null;
    try {
      clientSocket = sock.accept();
    }
    catch (IOException e) {
      System.out.println("Accept failed: " +
                                portnum + ", " + e);
      System.exit(1);
    }
    BufferedReader input = new BufferedReader(
        new InputStreamReader(clientSocket.getInputStream()));
    PrintWriter output =
      new PrintWriter(clientSocket.getOutputStream());
    System.out.println("Connection established.");

    int i = 0;
    String line = input.readLine();
    while (line!=null) {
      System.out.println(line);
      i++;
      output.println("line " + i + ":" + line);
      output.flush();
      line = input.readLine();
    }
  }
}
```

DISSECTION OF THE CLASS MiniServer

- ```java
  import java.io.*;
  import java.net.*;
  ```

We need classes from both packages. The socket classes are in `java.net`, and the stream classes are in `java.io`.

- ```java
  if (args.length != 1) {
    System.out.println("Usage: " +
      "java MiniServer portnumber");
    System.exit(1);
  }
  int portnum = Integer.parseInt(args[0]);
  ```

The program expects the port number to be specified on the command line.

- ```java
  ServerSocket sock = null;
  try {
    sock = new ServerSocket(portnum);
  }
  catch (IOException e) {
    System.out.println("Could not listen on port: " +
                        portnum + ", " + e);
    System.exit(1);
  }
  ```

A `ServerSocket` is used to listen for incoming connections. It doesn't create a connection. Rather, it simply creates the local connection to the port so that the server can listen for connections as shown below.

- ```java
  Socket clientSocket = null;
  try {
    clientSocket = sock.accept();
  }
  catch (IOException e) {
    System.out.println("Accept failed: " +
                        portnum + ", " + e);
    System.exit(1);
  }
  ```

The call to `accept()` for the `ServerSocket` object actually begins listening. The call won't return until an incoming request to connect is received. The call returns the actual `Socket` object to be used to communicate with the other program.

- ```java
  BufferedReader input = new BufferedReader(
      new InputStreamReader(clientSocket.getInputStream()));
  PrintWriter output =
    new PrintWriter(clientSocket.getOutputStream());
  System.out.println("Connection established.");
  ```

Associated with each socket is an `InputStream` object and an `OutputStream` object. These are what the program actually uses to send and receive data over the
  ```

socket. The same techniques used for reading and writing files in Chapter 10 can be used to read and write data over a socket. Here we chose to read and write text streams. As discussed in Section 10.3.1, a `BufferedReader` object can be used to read lines of text. To construct a `BufferedReader` object from the `InputStream` object returned by `getInputStream()`, we must first turn the `InputStream` into an `InputStreamReader`. Similarly, we can construct a `PrintWriter` object from the `OutputStream` object returned by `getOutputStream()`. We could have used the more primitive `InputStream` and `OutputStream` objects to read and write bytes, but using the classes shown allows us to easily transfer text strings over the socket.

```
int i = 0;
String line = input.readLine();
while (line != null) {
  System.out.println(line);
  i++;
  output.println("line "+ i + ":" + line);
  output.flush();
  line = input.readLine();
}
```

With the appropriate streams established, we can now loop: reading one line in from the socket, printing it to the screen, and then echoing the line back out over the same socket. The method `readLine()` returns `null` if there is nothing more to read from the input stream, at which point the loop exits and the program terminates. We added a line number on the echoed result to make clear that the data being read by our test client is in fact the line from the `MiniServer` server. The call to `flush()` is required to force the data to move over the socket to the other end without delay.

A program that connects to an established server is called a *client*. The following class is a trivial client for our `MiniServer`.

```
//MiniClient.java - simple client for MiniServer
import java.io.*;
import java.net.*;
import tio.*;

class MiniClient{
  public static void main (String args[])
        throws java.io.IOException
  {
    if (args.length != 2) {
      System.out.println("Usage: " +
          "java MiniClient hostname portnumber");
      System.exit(0);
    }
    int portnum = Integer.valueOf(args[1]).intValue();
    Socket sock = new Socket(args[0], portnum);
    BufferedReader input = new BufferedReader(
      new InputStreamReader(sock.getInputStream()));
```

```
PrintWriter output =
   new PrintWriter(sock.getOutputStream());
System.out.println("Connection established.");
System.out.println("type some characters then" +
     " return:");
String line = Console.in.readLine();
while (line != null) {
   output.println(line);
   output.flush();
   line = input.readLine();
   System.out.println("got back:" + line);
   System.out.println("type some characters " +
       "then return:");
   line = Console.in.readLine();
}
}
}
```

DISSECTION OF THE CLASS MiniClient

- ```
  Socket sock = new Socket(args[0], portnum);
  ```

The name of the server is the first command line argument. The server name and the port number are used to open the socket. The constructor won't complete its task until the socket is established. The client end is simpler than the server end. Here we simply attempt to connect to a port. If there's no server listening on the port, the constructor generates an IOException.

- ```
  BufferedReader input = new BufferedReader(
     new InputStreamReader(sock.getInputStream()));
  PrintWriter output =
     new PrintWriter(sock.getOutputStream());
  System.out.println("Connection established.");
  ```

These statements are essentially identical to those in MiniServer after the socket is established. At this point both ends of the socket look the same.

- ```
  System.out.println("type some characters then" +
       " return:");
  String line = Console.in.readLine();
  while (line != null) {
     output.println(line);
     output.flush();
     line = input.readLine();
     System.out.println("got back:" + line);
     System.out.println("type some characters " +
         "then return:");
     line = Console.in.readLine();
  }
  ```

Here we prompt the user to type something at the console. Whatever is typed at the console of the client machine is printed on the console of the server machine.
  ```

In addition, the `MiniServer` sends back whatever it receives after prepending the word `line` followed by the line number. We print out the line that is bounced back. As in `MiniServer`, the program ends when `Console.in.readLine()` returns `null`. On most Unix computers the user signals EOF at the console by typing Ctrl+D. On Windows machines the user signals EOF at the console by typing Ctrl+Z.

13.6 A MULTITHREADED SERVER

In the client–server example in Section 13.5, we didn't actually create any explicit threads. Each program running on a different computer, or at least in a different Java virtual machine, had only one main thread. However, a typical server, such as a Web server, should be capable of handling many simultaneous connections. To build in this capability we create new threads in the `MiniServer` to handle each incoming connection.

The multithreaded server is similar to the earlier, single-threaded version. There is now a loop around the call to `accept()`. The `Socket` that is returned from `accept()` is used to initialize a `WorkerThread`. The `WorkerThread` object handles all communication over the socket that it is passed. This new server works with the same client, `MiniClient`.

The class `MultiServer` is the same as the class `MiniServer` to the point at which the message "Now listening at port xxx" is printed. The revised code follows.

```
//MultiServer.java - a multithreaded server
import java.io.*;
import java.net.*;
class MultiServer {
    //omitted - same as MiniServer
    System.out.println("Now listening at port " + portnum);
    Socket clientSocket = null;
    while (true) {
      try {
        clientSocket = sock.accept();
      }
      catch (IOException e) {
        System.out.println("Accept failed: "
                            + portnum + ", " + e);
        System.exit(1);
      }
      WorkerThread worker = new WorkerThread(clientSocket);
      worker.start();
    }
  }
}
```

The loop that actually reads from a socket is now in the class `WorkerThread`. The `run()` method for the `WorkerThread` contains the code that opens the input and output streams for the socket and then loops, reading from the input and echoing the result back out over the output. The method `run()` isn't allowed to throw an `IOException`, so the entire body is wrapped in a `try-catch` statement that reports the error and exits. An `IOException` is thrown when the client breaks the connection. We also added class and instance variables that are used to distinguish the different worker threads.

```java
//WorkerThread.java - handle one connection
import java.io.*;
import java.net.*;

class WorkerThread extends Thread {
  WorkerThread(Socket socket) {
    clientSocket = socket;
    workerNumber++;
    number = workerNumber;
  }

  public void run() {
    try {
      BufferedReader input = new BufferedReader(
          new InputStreamReader(
                  clientSocket.getInputStream()));
      PrintWriter output = new PrintWriter(
                  clientSocket.getOutputStream());
      System.out.println("Connection " +
                          number + " established.");

      String line = input.readLine();
      while (line != null) {
        System.out.println(line);
        output.println("worker " + number + ":"+line);
        output.flush();
        line = input.readLine();
      }
    }
    catch (IOException e) {
      System.out.println( e );
    }
    System.out.println("worker " + number + " exiting");
  }

  private Socket clientSocket;
  private static int workerNumber = 0;
  private int number;
}
```

13.7 MORE ABOUT THE METHODS sleep(), wait(), AND notify()

We have presented some examples of how to use the three methods sleep(), wait(), and notify(). In this section we look closer at each of them.

13.7.1 CALLING sleep() FROM ANYWHERE

All execution of a Java program is associated with a Thread object. As we showed earlier in this chapter, a single Java program can have many threads. The Java virtual machine runs them so that they appear to be running at the same time. In fact, the Java virtual machine is using timesharing to run first one and then another, switching periodically from one to the next.

Hence one Thread object is always associated with the method that is currently being executed. We demonstrated in the SimpleThread example in Section 13.2, on page 434, that the method sleep() is defined in the class Thread and as such can be called directly from within the method run() of a class that extends Thread. In fact, as we showed in the first example in this chapter, AwtThread, we can call sleep() in any method; all we need to do is get a reference to the current Thread object. We do that by calling the static method Thread.currentThread() at any time. This method returns a reference to the thread currently running. Thus we called Thread.currrentThread().sleep() in the method main() of AwtThread.

Recall that sleep() can throw an InterruptedException and that in run() we were forced to catch the exception. The method run() was inherited from Thread. Because run() wasn't defined in Thread to throw an Interrupted-Exception—or any exception class that is a superclass of InterruptedExcep-tion—we can't throw such an exception in our definition of run(). In AwtThread, main() isn't inherited, so we can define it to throw any exception. We could have used a try-catch statement to catch the exception had we so desired.

13.7.2 CALLING wait() AND notify() OUTSIDE A SYNCHRONIZED METHOD

The methods wait() and notify() are inherited from class Object. Thus we might consider calling wait() for any object. For example, what happens if we call wait() for some arbitrary String object?

```
String s = "Wait for this?";
s.wait();
```

This code is syntactically correct; that is, it will compile with no errors. However, the thread that executes this statement must hold the lock for the object s, or an IllegalMonitorStateException will be thrown. Until now, the only way we have been able to obtain the lock is by calling a synchronized method.

However, we can also obtain the lock for an object by using a synchronized statement. The general form for a synchronized statement is

synchronized (*Expression*) *Block*

The *Expression* must evaluate to a reference. If we let *Expression* refer to the object *obj*, the execution of *Block* is controlled by the lock for *obj*. That is, the thread is suspended if any other thread is executing inside a synchronized method for *obj* or is executing another synchronized statement for *obj*. As with synchronized methods, calls to `wait()` and `notify()` can be placed inside *Block*. They can also be in methods that are called from inside *Block*.

The following is an example of waiting with a synchronized statement.

```
String s = "Wait for this?";
...
synchronized(s) {
  s.wait();
}
```

This code can be placed in any method. The thread that executes it blocks until some other thread executes a `notify()` call on the same object. The ellipses indicate the use of statements to pass a reference to `s` to some other thread so that the current thread can eventually be awakened.

Suppose that you were writing a program and wanted to share an object for a class written by someone else. Suppose also that it isn't possible for you to modify the class to change the methods into synchronized methods as we did for the class `Counter`. This situation is perfect for use of the synchronized statement. In the following program we modified the class `Racer` to work with `Counter`, as it was before we changed the method `click()` into a synchronized method.

```
//Racer2.java - assume click() is not synchronized
class Racer2 extends Thread {
  Racer2(int id, Counter counter) {
    this.id = id;
    this.counter = counter;
  }

  public void run() {
    System.out.println("Thread" + id + " started.");
    for (int i = 0; i <  1000000; i++) {
      synchronized(counter) {  // change from Racer
        counter.click();
      }                               // change from Racer
    }
    System.out.println("Thread" + id +
            " finished counter is " + counter.get());
  }

  private int id;
  private Counter counter;
}
```

13.7.3 THE METHOD notifyAll()

A call to the method notify() for an object wakes up one thread if any threads are waiting as a result of calls to wait() for the object. If there is more than one thread, one thread is chosen arbitrarily. A call to the method notifyAll() for an object wakes up all the threads waiting for the object. These threads, although "awakened," still need to wait to obtain the lock for the object before they proceed. Only one thread can hold the lock at any one time. The lock is passed from one thread to the next as the running thread leaves its synchronized method or block. Presumably each thread checks to determine whether it should proceed with its processing or go back to waiting.

You should use the method notify() when you know that there is at most one thread waiting or when any of the waiting threads can do the job. For example, in the producer–consumer problem, the producer can use notify() because only the consumer can be waiting.

You should use the method notifyAll() when you know that only a particular subset, including possibly none, of the waiting threads are the ones that need to be awakened. Consider a variation of the producer–consumer problem, with specialized consumers for different values. The producer would use notifyAll() to awaken all waiting consumers. Each consumer would check and determine whether the newly produced value was for it; if so, it would consume the value. If the value wasn't for that consumer, it would just go back to waiting. An apparent alternative would be to use notify() and have the awakened consumer, if it didn't want the value, call notify() to awaken the next consumer. The problem with this approach is that the specification of notify() doesn't guarantee the notification of all consumers. The choice of which waiting process to awaken is arbitrary. Two consumers could keep waking up each other without ever awakening a third consumer, which was the one that was needing the value.

COMMON PROGRAMMING ERROR

Multithreaded programs can exhibit two types of errors that never occur in sequential programs. The first type is a race condition. We showed earlier how two threads with references to a shared object can interfere with each other. Errors caused by race conditions are notoriously difficult to detect. The error may not appear, even with extensive testing, because the context switch never happens to occur in the right place to exhibit the error. Moreover, once the error has been observed, it may be difficult to reproduce the condition, making locating the problem in the code difficult. For this reason, you must take extreme care when writing programs with multiple threads that share objects.

The second type of error unique to multithreaded programs is called *deadlock*. It occurs when each thread in a group of threads is holding one lock and waiting for another lock that is currently held by another thread in the group. The potential for deadlock is one of the reasons that you can't simply add `synchronized` to all your methods in the hope of eliminating all race conditions. Suppose that you have a class with two methods—call them `methodOne()` and `methodTwo()`. If `methodOne()` calls `methodTwo()` for a different object of the same class, synchronizing the methods can lead to deadlock. If one thread is executing `methodOne()` for the first object and another thread is executing `methodOne()` for the second object, each thread will be holding the lock for one of the objects and waiting for the lock for the other object as shown in the following diagram.

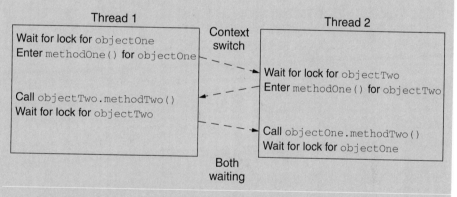

A complete discussion of avoiding deadlock is beyond the scope of this book. Briefly however, one technique for avoiding deadlock is to use *resource ordering*. With *resource ordering*, each lockable object (resource) is given a number. A thread is always required to obtain the locks for lower numbered resources before obtaining locks for higher numbered resources. This procedure isn't provided by the language; it is something that must be done by careful programming.

In this example there are two resources, `objectOne` and `objectTwo`. For resource ordering, their numbers correspond to their names. Thread 1 locks the resources in the proper order: `objectOne` and then `objectTwo`. However, thread 2 locks the resources in the wrong order, locking the higher numbered object, `objectTwo`, before the lower numbered object, `objectOne`.

The solution to this problem depends on what is actually being done by the two threads. One solution would be to have each of the two threads explicitly obtain the locks for both `objectOne` and `objectTwo` in the proper order before proceeding to call `methodOne()` for either object. We can do so by using a synchronized statement. Suppose that the actual call to `methodOne()` looked like the following in the code executed by both threads:

```
objectA.methodOne(objectB);
```

where, for thread 1, `objectA` is actually a reference to `objectOne` and `objectB` is actually a reference to `objectTwo`. Instead of relying on synchronized methods, we can obtain both locks as follows.

```
synchronized(objectA) {
  synchronized(objectB) {
    objectA.methodOne(objectB);
  }
}
```

However, this solution would still get the locks in the wrong order for thread 2, because in thread 2 `objectA` is a reference to `objectTwo`. To allow each thread to obtain the locks in a different order, we could add a resource number field to the objects. If we did that, the code might look like the following.

```
Resource resOne, resTwo;
if (objectA.getResNumber() < objectB.getResNumber()) {
  resOne = objectA;
  resTwo = objectB;
}
else {
  resOne = objectB;
  resTwo = objectA;
}
synchronized(resOne) {
  synchronized(resTwo) {
    objectA.methodOne(objectB);
  }
}
```

With this code, the earlier deadlock would be avoided because both threads would lock the locks in the same order. Thus it would be impossible for one thread to be holding one of the locks while waiting for the other lock.

Obviously, avoiding deadlock can be rather complicated. The simplest solution is to design your program, whenever possible, to never lock more than one lock at a time. Deadlock can never occur if a thread holds only one lock at a time. You can read more about deadlock in any book about operating system principles.

13.8 PROGRAMMING STYLE

Although synchronized methods are easy to create, as illustrated earlier, using them correctly isn't always so easy. One of the advantages of the data abstraction provided by the class construct is the ability to insulate the implementation details of a class from its uses. However, use of synchronized methods can unnecessarily expose implementation details of a class to the users of the class.

As discussed earlier, a synchronized method must first obtain the lock for the object used to call the method. For example, if `critical()` is a synchronized method in the class `SomeClass`, and `someObj` is an instance of `SomeClass`, then

```
someObj.critical();
```

must first obtain the lock for `someObj` before executing. However, there is no way to prevent a programmer from using `someObj` in a synchronized statement such as

```
synchronized(someObj) {
  // make calls, possibly obtaining other locks
}
```

When the program contains statements such as this one, reasoning about the correctness of `SomeClass` with respect to whether or not it will deadlock becomes much more difficult. In any part of the program we can lock the lock needed by the call to `critical()`.

An alternative that doesn't expose this synchronization aspect of `SomeClass` is to use an internal private lock object and synchronized statements instead of sychronized methods. The following example shows how to do this.

```
class SomeClass {
  void critical() {
    synchronized(lock) {
        // method body here
    }
  }
  private Lock lock = new Lock();
}
```

The class `Lock` can be a trivial empty class or any existing class, such as `Boolean`. We never use the `lock` object except for its implicit built-in lock, which is part of every object in Java.

In the preceding example, note that we need only to examine the code for the class `SomeClass` and the class called by the methods in `SomeClass`, to determine whether the code might deadlock. Users of `SomeClass` can't accidentally cause the method `critical()` to be locked out by inappropriate use of synchronized statements that synchronize on instances of `SomeClass`.

Summary

- A thread is a sequence of instructions executed by a program. In Java programs, many threads can be executing simultaneously.
- Programs that use AWT are implicitly multithreaded. They contain a main thread specified by `main()`, and a second thread that responds to events and drives the AWT-based part of the program.
- Threads are created in Java by extending and instantiating the class `Thread`. The top level, or main, instructions for the thread are specified in the method `run()`. To

start the thread, call the method `start()`. You shouldn't call the method `run()` directly.

- The easiest way for two threads to communicate is for them to share an object. Any modifications made to the object by one of the threads is observed by the other.

- When you use shared objects, you should synchronize the threads' actions. Without synchronization, race conditions can cause errors. Race conditions can be hard to track down because the behavior of a program may not be consistent from one execution to the next.

- The keyword `synchronized` on a method prevents multiple threads from simultaneously accessing that method or other synchronized methods in the same object.

- A thread executing inside a synchronized method can explicitly yield control to another thread by calling `wait()`. The thread remains suspended until it resumes as the result of a call to `notify()` or `notifyAll()`.

- A call to `notify()` for an object results in at most one thread, suspended by a call to `wait()` for the same object being resumed. The resumed thread isn't actually allowed to continue until the thread calling `notify()` has released the lock. If several threads are waiting, an arbitrary thread is selected to be resumed. If no threads are waiting, this call has no effect.

- The method `notifyAll()` is similar to `notify()`, except that all threads suspended by calls to `wait()` for the same object resume. These threads still need to wait and take turns obtaining the lock for the synchronized object.

- A thread that has resumed after a `wait()` should verify that the condition that it was waiting for has actually been satisfied. In our example, the consumer needs to verify that the buffer is full before proceeding.

- The style of synchronization used in Java involving synchronized methods (also known as critical sections), along with methods `wait()` and `notify()`, is called monitor synchronization. Although similar in appearance, semaphores behave somewhat differently. Specifically, a monitor `wait()` always waits, at least briefly, but a semaphore may continue without waiting, as a result of previous `signal()` operations.

- A socket can be used to connect two programs running on different computers. In Java, data are read and written over a socket by first obtaining an input stream and an output stream associated with the socket. These streams can then be used like any other stream, such as the stream to the console or to a file.

- Creating a socket connection is asymmetrical, although once established, the connection is symmetrical. The server must first begin listening for connection requests, using the `accept()` method from class `ServerSocket`. The client can then connect by creating a client socket implemented by the class `Socket`. The `accept()` call returns the server end of the client socket to the server.

- By combining sockets and threads, you can create a multithreaded server to handle simultaneously many client connections with a single Java program.

Review Questions

1. What three capabilities are needed to support multiple threads?
2. What is the implicit thread created inside AWT used for?
3. What are the units of time for the method `sleep()`?

4. What method do you call to run a thread?
5. What method in a thread is similar to `main()` for the entire program?
6. Failing to synchronize a shared object can result in a _____ condition.
7. A lock is associated with what? A thread, an object, a method, or a variable?
8. What is the difference between a Java monitor `wait()` and a semaphore `wait()`?
9. State why you should generally use

```
while ( condition ) {
  wait();
}
```

instead of

```
if ( condition ) {
  wait();
}
```

10. Once a socket connection has been established, reading and writing data over the socket are just like _____ .
11. What class defines the method `sleep()`? `wait()`? `notify()`?
12. Even after being awakened via `notify()`, a thread must wait for what before continuing?

Exercises

1. Add a menu or other GUI component to class `AwtThread` from Section 13.1, on page 432, that allows you to control the speed of counting. For example, the menu could have faster and slower selections that affect the time argument for the method `sleep()`.
2. Write and test the class `ThreeThreads`, which is similar to `TwoThreads` from Section 13.2, on page 433, but with three threads. Use `sleep()` to make thread 1 run twice as fast as thread 2 and thread 2 run twice as fast as thread 3.
3. Modify the classes `Racer` and `TwoThreads2` to prompt the user for the number of times to click the counter. Using an unsynchronized counter, run the program with different values. Approximately how large does the input value need to be for the race condition to show up? Start with 10 and increase by a factor of 10 for each run.
4. Modify the class `ProducerConsumer` to create two producers and two consumers. Does the program still work?
5. Modify the `Buffer` used in the class `ProducerConsumer` to use a ring buffer. A ring buffer can store as many as n items simultaneously. It behaves like a queue with producers inserting items at one end and consumers removing items from the other end. Use an array of size n. The buffer must maintain two indices for the array: one for the insertion point and the other for the removal point. If all array cells are empty, any consumers will block. If all cells are full, any producers will block. What problem might arise if you used a queue with unbounded capacity instead of a fixed size array?
6. Write a program to implement a simple countdown timer. The program should prompt the user for the number of minutes and seconds. After you enter the seconds

the timer starts automatically. Have it print out the time remaining every 5 seconds. You can cause your terminal to beep when the time has expired by printing out a string that includes \007, which is the escape sequence for the character to ring the bell on your terminal.

7. Create a version of the program in the preceding exercise that uses a graphical user interface. Include a `Start` button and a text field for entering the time setting. As the time ticks down, display the time remaining in the text field. You may notice that using `sleep()` to control the progress of the timer doesn't always give accurate results.

8. If you used `sleep(5000)` to count off 5 seconds in the previous two exercises, you have failed to account for the actual time required to execute the parts of the program. You can use the method `Date.getTime()` to get the current time in milliseconds since midnight January 1, 1970, GMT. Use this method to create a more accurate timer.

9. Another classic program for studying concurrent programming issues is called the *dining philosophers problem*. In this problem, five philosophers are seated around a table. In the center of the table is a bowl of spaghetti. In front of each philosopher is a plate and between each plate is a fork, as shown in the diagram.

Each philosopher needs two forks to eat the spaghetti. Each philosopher repeatedly thinks then eats. In order to eat, the philosopher must pick up the fork on the right and the fork on the left. If either fork is busy, the philosopher simply waits for his or her colleague to put the fork down. The problem is to make sure that none of the philosophers starve. One solution is to have some start with their left fork and others start with their right fork. Implement the dining philosophers problem in Java. Each philosopher should be represented by a separate thread. The forks are to be objects with synchronized methods `pickup()` and `putDown()`.

10. Modify the `MiniServer` and `MiniClient` programs to implement a simple Internet talk program. With this program, two users on different computers can each type at their consoles, and anything that they type will be echoed on the other person's console. Be sure to use some prefix on each line to separate what the local user is typing from what the remote user is sending. You'll need two threads: one to accept input from the console and send it out over the socket and the other to accept input from the socket and echo it to the console.

11. Write a version of the talk program in the previous exercise that uses a graphical user interface. You can use two `JTextArea` objects: one for the local user to type in and another to echo the text from the remote user.

12. The HTTP protocol used for Web servers is text based. In other words, control messages exchanged between client and server are text. Web browsers normally connect to port 80, but they can be directed to any port by appending :*nnn* to the URL, giving the port number *nnn*. Create a Web server that responds to all requests by send-

ing a simple message in HTML. The server should listen for connections on port 80 if your computer allows it; if not, use another port. When a connection is made, ignore the input stream and use the following code to send a message over the output stream, `output`.

```
String message = "<HTML>\n" +
    "<center><H1>Hello from, Your Name Here</H1>" + "</html>\n";

output.println("HTTP/1.0 200 OK\n" +
                "Date: <gone> \n" +
                "Server: 1.0 \n" +
                "Content-type: text/html \n" +
                "Content-length: " +
                message.length() + "\n\n" +
                message);
output.flush();
```

Modify the message any way you like. For example you could include the count of how many times this "Web server" had been visited. The lines before the message comprise a header, which tells the client what's coming. When your server is running, point a Web browser at it by entering the url *http://yourComputersName:nnn*, where *nnn* is the port number. You can leave off the *nnn* if you use port 80. To learn more, find some HTTP documentation and make your server actually interpret the incoming requests.

13. Write a class `Semaphore` that implements semaphore synchronization. The class should have two methods: `signal()` and `wait()`. Use your class `Semaphore` to synchronize access to the shared buffer in the producer–consumer problem. Compare this solution to the one based on monitor synchronization in Section 13.4, on page 440.

14. Use the method `sleep()` and a `JApplet` to create a simple animation. The applet should include an instance of a class—call it `Animation`—that extends `JCompo-nent`, similar to `Star` in Section 8.5. Override the method `paint()` in class `Ani-mation` to draw a simple object—it could be as simple as a circle representing a ball. In a separate thread, created and started from the method `init()` of the `JAp-plet`, repeatedly modify the position of the object and call `repaint()` for the `Animation` object. You will need to pass a reference to the `Animation` object to the thread so that it can call the `Animation`'s `repaint()` and also call some method in the `Animation` to adjust the image, for example changing the position of the ball. You may also want to override the `update()` method of the `Anima-tion` to just call `paint()`. The default `update()` method, inherited from `JCom-ponent`, redraws the component in the background color and then calls `paint()`. This drawing of the background can cause a flicker.

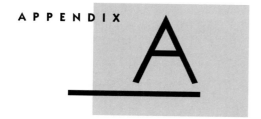

APPENDIX

Getting Down to the Bits

In this appendix we take a closer look at how numeric primitive types are represented and how some operations can be used to manipulate individual bits of memory. All data are represented using strings of 1s and 0s. We show how those strings of 1s and 0s are combined to represent more familiar numeric symbols.

A.1 INTEGER BINARY REPRESENTATION

Integers are stored as binary numbers. Binary numbers are represented using only 2 digits, compared to the more familiar decimal numbers, which are represented using 10 digits. The number of distinct digits used in representing numbers determines the base. For example, decimal numbers are called base 10 numbers. Likewise, binary numbers are base 2 numbers. In this appendix, when we switch to a different number base, we use the notation (*sequence of digits*)$_{\text{base}}$, where base is the selected number base. Any numbers not written this way or otherwise indicated are decimal, or base 10, numbers.

A.1.1 TWO'S COMPLEMENT BINARY ARITHMETIC

Recall that decimal notation of numbers uses a positional notation to combine powers of 10 multiplied by one of the 10 digits 0 through 9. Therefore 123 equals

$$1 \times 10^2 + 2 \times 10^1 + 3 \times 10^0$$

461

Because computers use only two digits, 0 and 1, integers are stored in binary notation, which combines powers of 2 multiplied by one of the two digits 0 or 1. The
binary notation for the decimal notation value $(123)_{10}$ is $(1111011)_2$, which is the
same as

$$1 \times 2^6 + 1 \times 2^5 + 1 \times 2^4 + 1 \times 2^3 + 0 \times 2^2 + 1 \times 2^1 + 1 \times 2^0$$

or, after doing the multiplications, $64 + 32 + 16 + 8 + 0 + 2 + 1$.

The magnitude of the largest number respresentable in binary notation depends
on the number of bits available, that is, the number of binary digits that can be
stored. The number of bits for the integral types is given in the table in Section 2.9.1,
on page 43.

From that table, we see that type `byte` uses 8 bits and the range of values is
from -128 to 127, inclusive. How are negative numbers represented, and why is 127
the largest value when the binary notation number $(11111111)_2$ fits in 8 bits and
equals 255? The answers are related.

In some early computers, negative numbers were represented by allocating the
left-most bit as a sign bit—0 for positive and 1 for negative—called *signed magnitude*. For the 8-bit integer type, that would mean $(00000010)_2$ is +2 and $(10000010)_2$
is -2. This notation isn't very convenient for doing binary arithmetic.

A more convenient form is called *one's complement*. In it we negate a number
by simply changing all 1s to 0s and all 0s to 1s. Therefore -2 would be represented
as $(11111101)_2$. Note that all negative numbers have a left-most bit of 1, as in the
earlier form, but now we can perform normal binary arithmetic on any two numbers,
with the modification that any carry out of the left-most position must be added back
into the right-most bit. For example,

```
 11111101       -2            11111101       -2
+00000001       +1           +00000011       +3
---------       --            ---------       --
 11111110       -1           100000000
                               +      ▶ 1
                             ---------
                              00000001       +1
```

This representation does have a drawback: There are two forms of 0, +0 and –0,
represented by all 0s and all 1s, respectively. To avoid this problem, most computers
today use what is known as *two's complement* binary representation for negative
numbers. The positive numbers and 0 appear the same way in all three representations. To obtain the *n*-bit two's complement representation for a negative number,
we add 2^n and treat the result as an *n*-bit unsigned number. For example, -2 as an 8-
bit two's complement binary number would be $2^8 + (-2)$ which is $256 - 2 = 254$ or
$(11111110)_2$ in binary. As with one's complement, arithmetic is straightforward; in

fact we simply throw away any carry out of the last position. Using our same example we now get

```
 11111110      -2             11111110      -2
+00000001      +1            +00000011      +3
---------      --            ---------      --
 11111111      -1           100000001      +1
```
discard

There is an even easier way to negate a number in two's complement; that is, we can compute the one's complement by toggling all the bits and then add 1. One peculiarity of two's complement is that there is a slight asymmetry in the negative and postive numbers. Because zero uses one of the bit combinations with a left-most 0, the magnitude of the most negative number is 1 greater than the magnitude of the most positive number as shown in Section 2.9.1.

A.2 FLOATING POINT REPRESENTATIONS

The floating point numbers are represented using the IEEE 754-1985 standard. It is based on *scientific notation* for numbers. In scientific notation, numbers are represented by a sign, some significant digits called the *mantissa*, and some power of 10, called the *exponent*. For example, in -2.56×10^{-53}, the sign is negative, the mantissa is 2.56 and the exponent is -53.

Floating point numbers are represented by allocating 1 bit for the sign, some bits for the mantissa (stored as an integer), and some bits for the exponent. Specifically, Java uses the IEEE standard, which allocates the bits as shown for the single precision floating point type `float`.

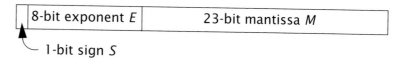

The bits are interpreted as follows.

- If S is 0, then the number is positive; otherwise it is negative.
- E is the exponent as a power of 2, not of 10. The exponent is interpreted as an excess-127 code integer. That is, the actual value of the exponent is $E - 127$, treating E as an unsigned binary integer. The result is that the exponent ranges from -127 to 128.
- M is the mantissa. Normal scientific notation places one decmial digit before the decimal point, for example, 1.27×10^{-15}. Similarly, M represents the mantissa with the binary point to the right of the first significant binary digit. Since the first significant digit is 1 unless the entire value is 0, the leading 1 isn't

stored. Therefore the actual value of the mantissa is $(1.M)_2$. The only exception is when the exponent, E, is 0, in which case the actual value of the mantissa is $(0.M)_2$.

For example, suppose that the 32 bits of a floating point value are

```
0 01001101 01101110000011010111011
```

Thesign is 0, so the number is positive. The exponent is $(01001101)_2 - 127$, which is $77 - 127$, or -50. The mantissa is $(1.01101110000011010111011)_2$, which is approximately 1.4298929. So the complete number is 1.4298929×2^{-50}, or approximately 1.27×10^{-15}.

Unlike some programming languages, floating point arithmetic operations in Java never generate an exception. Instead, three special values can result: *positive infinity*, *negative infinity*, and *Not a Number*. The way that these three special values arise is shown in the following table.

Name	Prints as	Results from	Example
Positive infinity	+Inf	Overflow	1.0e31f*1.0e8f
Negative infinity	-Inf	Overflow	-1.0e31f*1.0e8f
Positive 0	+0	Underflow	1.0e-44f*0.0001
Negative 0	-0	Underflow	-1.0e-44f*0.0001f
Not a Number	NaN	Undefined	0.0/0.0

Excess-127 is used for the exponent to facilitate comparison of two floating point values. If x_b and y_b are the binary representations of two positive floating point values x and y, then $x_b < y_b$ if and only if $x < y$. That is, the same hardware used to compare integers can be used to compare floating point values. That wouldn't be true if one's complement or two's complement representations were used for the exponent. At the same time, addition and subtraction of exponents is more difficult. For most programs, this cost is outweighed by the easier comparison.

COMMON PROGRAMMING ERROR

The computer, using floating point numbers, can't exactly represent all numbers. Hence, when doing arithmetic with floating point numbers, the computer can't produce precise results. This inability leads to both representational and roundoff errors. Roundoff errors result when, in performing a mathematical computation (e.g., adding two numbers), the result is inexact. On a computer, $1.0 + e$ can end up being 1.0, with e, some very small number, getting lost.

As an exercise, run the following program and explain the result. The simplest solution to roundoff errors is to modify the program to avoid combining numbers having widely differing magnitudes.

```
//TestFloat.java - Compute with doubles
class TestFloat {
  public static void main(String argv[]) {
    double sum = 0.0;
    double d = 1000000.0;
    double e = 1.0 / 100000;

    for (int i = 1; i <= 1000; i++)
      sum = sum + d + e;
      System.out.println(sum);
    }
}
```

A.3   MANIPULATING BITS

Java has seven operators that allow you to manipulate directly the bits used to represent the integral types. An `int` value can be viewed as an ordered collection of 32 boolean values, where 1 means true and 0 means false. These are not actual Java primitive type `boolean` values; they can just be viewed in a similar way. For example, you can't use them in the test expression for an `if` statement. You can, however, perform boolean operations on them.

A.3.1   BITWISE OPERATORS

There are four bitwise operators: `&` (and), `|` (or), `^` (exclusive-or), and `~` (complement). The first three operators are binary operators. When these binary operators are applied to two integer values, the specified boolean operation is applied between each pair of bits in the two operands. For example `3 & 5` is equal to `1`, as shown below:

```
3 is represented as 00000000000000000000000000000011
5 is represented as 00000000000000000000000000000101

3 & 5 is then       00000000000000000000000000000001
```

Only the right-most bit position contains `1` (true) in both operands, so all bits of the result are `0` (false) except the right-most.

Similarly, the result of `(3 | 5)` is `7`, which has the binary representation $(111)_2$. The boolean operation exclusive-or results in true if and only if exactly one of the operands is true. Java doesn't provide this operator for the primitive boolean type. As a bitwise operator, the result bit is 1 if exactly one of the operand bits is `1`.

The value of the expression (3 ^ 5) is 6, which has the binary representation $(110)_2$. The unary complement operator ~ changes all 0s to 1s and 1s to 0s.

These operations are summarized in the following table, where x and y are each one bit:

x	y	x & y	x | y	x ^ y	~x
0	0	0	0	0	1
0	1	0	1	1	1
1	0	0	1	1	0
1	1	1	1	0	0

When these operators are applied to integral types, binary numeric promotion is first applied, as with the arithmetic operators (see Section 2.10). That is, both operands are converted to either type `int` or type `long`.

These operators make possible the compact storage of many 1-bit data values. For example, *pixels* are the dots that are displayed to create a computer-generated image. For black and white images, each pixel is represented by a single bit. If the bit is 1, the pixel is black, and if the bit is 0, the pixel is white. Using the bitwise operators we can store 8 pixel values in a variable of type `byte`. For example, a graphical representation of the letter A might be encoded by the 10 bytes 24, 60, 36, 102, 102, 126, 126, -61, -61, -61. We can illustrate this result by taking their binary representations and stacking them as follows.

```
24      00011000              **
60      00111100            ****
36      00100100            *    *
102     01100110          **    **
102     01100110          **    **
126     01111110          ******
126     01111110          ******
-61     11000011        **        **
-61     11000011        **        **
-61     11000011        **        **
```

In addition to its being a compact representation of the graphical A, we can convert it to a reverse video version by applying the complement operator ~ to each of the 10 values.

These operators have many other applications. The & operator is typically used to *mask out* certain bits. For example, the expression (x & mask) retains the bit values from x in each position where mask has a 1 and all other bits are set to 0, or *masked out*. Likewise, we can force certain bits to be "on" by using the | operator. In the expression (x | flagBits), the result retains all the 1s in x and, in addition, turns on (i.e., sets to 1) any bits that are 1 in flagBits.

Be careful of expressions like (x & y < 13), which is equivalent to ((x & y) < 13). This is not an expression that is true whenever x and y are both less than 13 and false otherwise. See the Common Programming Error box at the end of this appendix.

A.3.2   SHIFT OPERATORS

In addition to turning bits on and off with the bitwise operators, integers, viewed as a sequence of bits, can be shifted right or left. Shifting bits to the left s bits is the same as multiplying by 2^s. This action is equivalent to always shifting in 0s to fill any vacated bits. The following sequence shows the initial value 3, represented using 8 binary digits, being shifted left, 1 bit at a time.

```
00000011  equals  3
00000110  equals  6
00001100  equals  12
```

Shifting a positive value s bits to the right is equivalent to integer division by 2^s. Shifting negative values to the right can be done by either shifting in 0s, called *zero extension*, or shifting in duplicates of the sign bit, called *sign extension*. The next sequence shows shifting to the right with sign extension of an 8-bit value two's complement negative number. Java operates only on 32-bit and 64-bit values, but we use 8 for simplicity. For this example, simply note how the bits move to the right and that the left-most bit retains it original value.

```
11110100  equals  -12
11111010  equals  -6
11111101  equals  -3
```

The next sequence shows 0 extension of the same starting value. Note that, after the first shift, the value becomes positive. The second shift shows that shifting to the right is like division by 2 for positive values.

```
11110100  equals  -12
01111010  equals  +250
00111101  equals  +125
```

Recall that `0x01020408` is Java notation for an `int` literal in hexadecimal notation, which is useful when dealing with bits. Converting a hexadecimal number to binary is easy. Hexadecimal numbers can be converted to binary one digit at a time, as illustrated here.

```
   0    1    0    2    0    4    0    8  (hex)
0000 0001 0000 0010 0000 0100 0000 1000  (binary)
```

Hexadecimal notation is used in the examples for the shift operators, summarized in this table.

Operator	Operation	Example
<<	Shift left	`0x01020408` << 4 equals `0x10204080`
>>	Shift right, sign extend	`0x80402010` >> 4 equals `0xf8040201`
>>>	Shift right, 0 fill	`0x80402010` >>> 4 equals `0x08040201`

For example, shift operators can be used to assemble `int` and `long` values from bytes read from a network. If a 32-bit integer was read from some low-level device or network connection as 4 bytes—call them `byte0`, `byte1`, `byte2`, and `byte3`—these four bytes might be assembled into an `int` with the expression

```
int x = byte0 | (byte1 << 8) | (byte2 << 16) | (byte3 << 24)
```

COMMON PROGRAMMING ERROR

The symbol `&` is both the bitwise operator, as just discussed, and a form of logical operator. If `x` and `y` are `boolean` valued expressions, then `(x & y)` has the same value as `(x && y)`. The only difference is that, in the former case, both expressions `x` and `y` will be evaluated no matter what. In the latter case, which is the most commonly used, `y` will be evaluated only if `x` is true. The common form, `&&`, is called the *conditional-and* or *short-circuit-and* operator because the second operand isn't always evaluated.

Similarly, the common form of logical-or, `||`, is actually the *conditional-or* operator. It evaluates its right operand only if the left evaluates to false. The symbol `|` is the logical-or operator that always evaluates both of its operands.

These double meanings for `&` and `|` can result in a very insidious mistake when we try to code statements such as "If *x* and *y* are both less than 13 do ... .". It is tempting to code this statement as

```
if (x & y < 13) ...
```

The correct Java expression is

```
if (x < 13 & y < 13) ...
```

or better still, use the conditional-and operator

```
if (x < 13 && y < 13) ...
```

The bad part about this error is that the first statement is syntactically correct – it will compile. The result of `(x & y)` is a number that *can* be compared against 13, although it won't necessarily yield the desired result in this case.

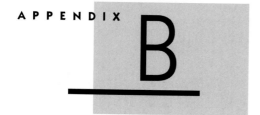

A P P E N D I X

B

Reference Tables

For reference, here we include a complete operator precedence table and the standard Java math functions.

B.1   OPERATOR PRECEDENCE TABLE

The precedence and associativity of all Java operators is given in the following table. The operators in the same row have the same precedence. The rows are ordered with the operators having the highest precedence at the top.

Precedence						Associativity
Highest	( )	[ ]	.expr++	expr--	.	Left to right
	unary +	unary -	++expr	--expr	~	!	*Right to left*
	new	cast				*Right to left*
	*	/	%			Left to right
	+	-				Left to right
	>>	>>>	<<			Left to right
	>	>=	<	<=	instanceof	Left to right
	==	!=				Left to right
	&					Left to right

Precedence			Associativity
	^		Left to right
	|		Left to right
	&&		Left to right
	||		Left to right
	?:		*Right to left*
Lowest	=	op=	*Right to left*

Keep this table handy when you begin using Java. Some useful generalizations can help you learn this table for the most commonly used operators. Unary operators have high precedence; then come multiplicative operators, followed by additive operators. In the middle of the precedence table are the relational operators, followed by the equality operators, followed by logical operators. Lowest on the list are assignment and operator–assignment.

B.2 THE STANDARD JAVA MATH FUNCTIONS

Java provides a standard library of mathematics functions in the class `java.lang.Math`. Because the package `java.lang` is part of every program by default, you can access the functions in the `Math` class by specifying the name of the class, `Math`, followed by a dot and the name of the method implementing the function. The functions in the class `Math` are listed in the following table:.

`return_type name(argument list)`	Comments
`double sin(double a)`	Return the sine of `a`, where `a` is in radians. The argument `a` is automatically converted, using a widening primitive conversion if necessary. To store the result in anything other than a `double` requires an explicit cast such as `float x = (float)sin(y);`
`double cos(double a)`	Return the cosine of `a`.
`double tan(double a)`	Return the tangent of `a`.
`double asin(double a)`	Return the arcsine of `a`. The result is in radians.
`double acos(double a)`	Return the arccosine of `a`. The result is in radians.
`double atan(double a)`	Return the arctangent of `a`. The result is in radians.

`return_type name(argument list)`	Comments
`double atan2(double a, double b)`	Return the arctangent of `b/a`. This argument can be used to convert from rectangular coordinates to polar coordinates. The result is in radians.
`double exp(double a)`	Return e^a, where e is the base of the natural logarithms.
`double log(double a)`	Return the natural logarithm of `a`.
`double sqrt(double a)`	Return the square root of `a`.
`double pow(double a, double b)`	Return a^b.
`double ceil(double a)`	Return the ceiling of `a`, that is, the smallest integer not less than `a`. The result, although mathematically an integer, isn't a Java integral type.
`double IEEEremainder(double a, double b)`	Return `a-b`n, where n is the integer value nearest to `a/b`.
`double floor(double a)`	Return the floor of `a`, that is, the largest integer not greater than `a`—see comment for `ceil`.
`double rint(double a)`	Return the result of rounding to the nearest mathematical integer—see comment for `ceil`.
`int round(float a)`	Return the result of adding 0.5 then casting to an `int`.
`long round(double a)`	Return the result of adding 0.5 then casting to a `long`.
`double random()`	Return a uniform pseudorandom value greater than or equal to 0.0 but less than 1.0—see Section 4.6.
`T abs(T a)`	Return the absolute value of `a`; T can be any of `int`, `long`, `float`, or `double`. The return type will be the same as the argument type.
`T min(T a, T b)`	Return the smaller of `a` and `b`; T can be any of `int`, `long`, `float` or `double`. If both arguments aren't of the same type, then a widening primitive conversion will be applied to make them the same.
`T max(T a, T b)`	Return the larger of `a` and `b`—see comment above for min.

For a complete specification of the behavior of these functions in the vicinity of extreme values, refer to the documentation for the class `java.lang.Math` that came with your Java system. Surprisingly, for example, taking the `abs()` of the most negative `int` value returns that same negative value. This situation is an overflow, and Java doesn't signal integer overflow via an exception. The most negative `int` value has no corresponding positive `int` value.

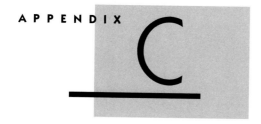
The Text I/O Package `tio`

Here we present the source for the text input–output package that we used. The package contains five classes. The main class is `ReadInput`, which we present first. The second important class is `FormattedWriter`, which we discussed in Section 10.4. The class `ReadException` is a type of exception thrown by some methods in class `ReadInput`. The remaining two classes are both convenience classes. The class `Console` creates a `ReadInput` object that can be used to read the standard input stream, as in `Console.in.readInt()`. It also creates a `FormattedWriter` object that can be used to write to the standard output stream using `Console.out.printf(...)`. The class `PrintFileWriter` allows for simpler declaration of output text streams to a file. The code is available on the Web at `ftp://ftp.awl.com/cseng/authors/pohl-mcdowell/`.

C.1 THE CLASS `tio.ReadInput`

```java
package tio;

import java.io.*;

/**
 * The class <code>ReadInput</code> contains methods that
 * allow for simple input of numbers, strings and
 * characters from a text stream.
 *
 * @author C. E. McDowell
 * @version 1.1, release for Java By Dissection
 */
public class ReadInput {
```

```java
/**
 * Constructs a ReadInput object for reading from any
 * Reader object.
 *
 * @param input the Reader text stream to read from.
 */
public ReadInput(Reader input) {
    // can look ahead over 1024 white space characters
    // when checking for the end of file mark
    this.input = new PushbackReader(input, 1024);
}

/**
 * Constructs a ReadInput object for reading from a
 * file.
 *
 * @param filename the name of the file from which
 *      to read.
 * @exception FileNotFoundException if the file can't
 *      be opened.
 */
public ReadInput(String filename) {
    try {
        FileReader fin = new FileReader(filename);
        this.input = new PushbackReader(fin, 1024);
    }
    catch (java.io.IOException e) {
        throw new ReadException(e.toString());
    }
}

/**
 * Constructs a ReadInput object for reading from any
 * InputStream.
 *
 * @param input the InputStream to read from.
 */
public ReadInput(InputStream input) {
    this(new InputStreamReader(input));
}
```

```java
/**
 * Check to see if there are any non-white space
 * characters left in the input. If used to terminate
 * reading with readLine(), any trailing blank lines
 * will be ignored. To read trailing blank lines, do
 * not use hasMoreElements() and instead read with
 * readLine() until an EOFException is thrown.
 *
 * @return true if the input contains more non-white
 *         space characters and false otherwise.
 */
public boolean hasMoreElements() {
  try {
    if (atEof)
      return false;
    else if (whiteSpaceBuffered)
      return true;//something followed the white space
    // look ahead to see if any non-white remain
    int nextChar = input.read();
    if (Character.isWhitespace((char)nextChar)) {
      // save white space in case readLine() comes next
      whiteSpaceBuffered = true;
      buffer[0] = (char)nextChar;
      for (bufferCount = 1; bufferCount < 1024;
           bufferCount++)
      {
        nextChar = input.read();
        if (nextChar == -1) {
          atEof = true;
          break;
        }
        else if (!Character.isWhitespace((char)nextChar))
        {
          input.unread(nextChar);
          break;
        }
        buffer[bufferCount] = (char)nextChar;
      }//end for
    }
    else if (nextChar == -1) {
      atEof = true;
      input.unread(nextChar);
    }
    else
      input.unread(nextChar);
    return !atEof;
  }
  catch(java.io.IOException e) {
    throw new ReadException(e.toString());
  }
}
```

```
/**
 * Read the next character. White space is not skipped.
 * readChar() cannot be used to reread input characters
 * that resulted in a NumberFormatException trying
 * to read a number. readLine() will return the
 * characters of a failed number read.
 *
 * @return the int value of the next character.
 */
public int readChar() {
  try {
    int result;
    // tokenRead will be true if a token was read
    // but couldn't be parsed. readChar() cannot
    // be used to reread such a token, discard it.
    tokenRead = false;
    if (whiteSpaceBuffered) {
      input.unread(buffer, 0, bufferCount);
      whiteSpaceBuffered = false;
    }
    result = input.read();
    if (result == -1)
      atEof = true;
    return result;
  }
  catch (java.io.IOException e) {
    throw new ReadException(e.toString());
  }
}

/**
 * Attempt to interpret the next white-space delimited
 * input characters as a double.
 *
 * @return the double value of the next white-space
 *     delimited input string.
 * @exception NumberFormatException if the next input
 *     string does not contain a parsable double.
 */
public double readDouble() {
  try {
    readToken();
    double result = Double.parseDouble(token);
    tokenRead = false; // this token has been used up
    return result;
  }
  catch (java.io.IOException e) {
    throw new ReadException(e.toString());
  }
}
```

```java
/**
 * Attempt to interpret the next white-space delimited
 * input characters as a float.
 *
 * @return the float value of the next white-space
 *      delimited input string.
 * @exception NumberFormatException if the next input
 *      string does not contain a parsable float.
 */
public float readFloat() {
  try {
    readToken();
    float result = Float.parseFloat(token);
    tokenRead = false; // this token has been used up
    return result;
  }
  catch (java.io.IOException e) {
    throw new ReadException(e.toString());
  }
}

/**
 * Attempt to interpret the next white-space delimited
 * input characters as an int.
 *
 * @return the int value of the next white-space
 *      delimited input string.
 * @exception NumberFormatException if the next input
 *      string does not contain a parsable int.
 */
public int readInt() {
  try {
    readToken();
    int result = Integer.parseInt(token);
    tokenRead = false; // this token has been used up
    return result;
  }
  catch (java.io.IOException e) {
    throw new ReadException(e.toString());
  }
}
```

```
/**
 * Read the next complete input line up to the newline
 * character. The terminating newline character is read
 * and discarded. It is not part of the return string.
 * If the previous read was an attempt to read a number
 * that generated a NumberFormatException, readLine()
 * will return the input line including the input
 * characters that caused the exception. This can be
 * used to try and recover from failure to read numeric
 * input.
 *
 * @return the next input line as a String.
 */
public String readLine() {
  try {
    if (tokenRead) {
      tokenRead = false;
      return token + readLine(input);
    }
    else {
      return readLine(input);
    }
  }
  catch (java.io.IOException e) {
    throw new ReadException(e.toString());
  }
}

/**
 * Attempt to interpret the next white-space delimited
 * input characters as a long.
 *
 * @return the long value of the next white-space
 *     delimited input string.
 * @exception NumberFormatException if the next input
 *     string does not contain a parsable long.
 */
public long readLong() {
  try {
    readToken();
    long result = Long.parseLong(token);
    tokenRead = false; // this token has been used up
    return result;
  }
  catch (java.io.IOException e) {
    throw new ReadException(e.toString());
  }
}
```

```java
/**
 * Read the next white-space delimited string.
 *
 * @return the next white-space delimited input string.
 */
public String readWord() {
  try {
    readToken();
    tokenRead = false; // this token has been used up
    return token;
  }
  catch (java.io.IOException e) {
    throw new ReadException(e.toString());
  }
}

/**
 * Do the work of reading a line of text.
 * White space may have been buffered up from a
 * call to hasMoreElements(). If so, unread the
 * buffered white space then read one line.
 */
private String readLine(PushbackReader in)
        throws IOException
{
  StringBuffer result = new StringBuffer(80);
  if (whiteSpaceBuffered) {
    in.unread(buffer, 0, bufferCount);
    whiteSpaceBuffered = false;
  }
  int nextChar = in.read();
  while (nextChar != -1 && nextChar != '\n' &&
         nextChar != '\r') {
    result.append((char)nextChar);
    nextChar = in.read();
  }
  if (nextChar == -1) {
    atEof = true;
    in.unread(nextChar);
  }
  else if (nextChar == '\r') {
    nextChar = in.read();// check for cr/newline
    if (nextChar != '\n')
      in.unread(nextChar);
  }
  if (atEof && result.length() == 0)
    return null;
  else
    return result.toString();
}
```

```java
/**
 * Read the next white-space delimited string.
 * This will then be parsed by the appropriate
 * routine to return one of the desired types.
 */
private void readToken() throws IOException {
  if (atEof)
    throw new EOFException(
      "Attempt to read beyond the end of the stream.");
  if (!tokenRead) {
    //discard any buffered white space
    whiteSpaceBuffered = false;
    StringBuffer result = new StringBuffer(80);
    int nextChar = input.read();
    while (Character.isWhitespace((char)nextChar))
      nextChar = input.read();
    while (nextChar != -1 && nextChar != '\n' &&
           nextChar != '\r' &&
           !Character.isWhitespace((char)nextChar))
    {
      result.append((char)nextChar);
      nextChar = input.read();
    }
    token = result.toString();
    if (nextChar == -1)
      if (token.length() == 0)
        throw new EOFException(
      "Attempt to read beyond the end of the stream.");
      else
        atEof = true;
    input.unread(nextChar);
    tokenRead = true;
  }
}
private String token;
private boolean tokenRead = false;
private PushbackReader input;
private boolean atEof = false;
private boolean whiteSpaceBuffered = false;
private char[] buffer = new char[1024];
private int bufferCount;
}
```

C.2 THE CLASS tio.FormattedWriter

```java
package tio;

import java.io.*;
import java.text.*;

/**
 * The class <code>FormattedWriter</code> contains
 * methods that allow for formatted printing.
 * It includes support for setting the width of the
 * output field, using left or right justification in
 * the output field, using an arbitrary fill
 * character, and setting the number of digits to the
 * right of the decimal point in floating point values.
 *
 * @author C. E. McDowell
 * @version 1.1 released for Java by Dissection
 */
public class FormattedWriter extends PrintWriter {
  // constants for specifying justification
  public static final int LEFT = 1;
  public static final int RIGHT = 2;

  /**
   * Constructs a FormattedWriter object for an OutputStream.
   *
   * @param os the OutputStream to write to
   */
  public FormattedWriter(OutputStream os) {
    super(os, true); // make default auto-flushing
  }

  /**
   * Constructs a FormattedWriter object for a FileWriter.
   *
   * @param writer the FileWriter to write to
   */
  public FormattedWriter(FileWriter writer) {
    super(writer, true);
  }

  /**
   * Constructs a FormattedWriter object for writing
   * to a file.
   *
   * @param filename the name of the file to write to
   */
  public FormattedWriter(String filename)
    throws java.io.IOException
  {
    this(new FileWriter(filename));
  }
```

```
/**
 * Set the output field width. If the value being
 * printed is less than the width of the field, then
 * the field will be padded with the pad character
 * (see setPadChar()). The field can be either left
 * or right justified (see setJustify()).
 *
 * @param width the width of the output field
 */
public void setWidth(int width) {
  if (width < 0)
    this.width = 0;
  else if (width > MAX_WIDTH)
    this.width = MAX_WIDTH;
  else
    this.width = width;
}

/**
 * Set the number of digits to be printed to the
 * right of the decimal point in floating point
 * values.
 *
 * @param places the number of places to the right
 *     of the decimal point
 */
public void setDigits(int places) {
  decimalPlaces = places;
  form.setMaximumFractionDigits(decimalPlaces);
}

/**
 * Set the justification to be LEFT or RIGHT.
 *
 * @param leftOrRight use FormattedWriter.LEFT
 *     or FormattedWriter.RIGHT
 * @exception IllegalArgumentException if not LEFT
 *     or RIGHT
 */
public void setJustify(int leftOrRight) {
  if (leftOrRight != LEFT && leftOrRight != RIGHT)
    throw new IllegalArgumentException(
      "use FormattedWriter.LEFT or" +
      " FormattedWriter.RIGHT");
  justify = leftOrRight;
}
```

```java
/**
 * Set the character to be used in padding.
 * The default padding character is a blank.
 *
 * @param pad the character to use in padding
 */
public void setPadChar(char pad) {
  if (pad == ' ')
    padding = spaces;
  else if (pad == '0')
    padding = zeros;
  else
    padding = buildPadding(MAX_WIDTH, pad);
}

/**
 * Print a String in a field of the current
 * width using the current padding character
 * and justification.
 *
 * @param s the String to print
 */
public void printf(String s) {
  if (s.length() >= width)
    super.print(s);
  else if (justify == LEFT)
    super.print(s +
        padding.substring(0, width - s.length()));
  else
    super.print(
        padding.substring(0, width - s.length()) + s);
}
/*
 * The next set of methods convert their parameter
 * to a string and then pass that to
 * printf(String) above.
 */
public void printf(boolean value) {
  printf(String.valueOf(value));
}
public void printf(char value) {
  printf(String.valueOf(value));
}
public void printf(char[] value) {
  printf(String.valueOf(value));
}
public void printf(int value) {
  printf(String.valueOf(value));
}
public void printf(long value) {
  printf(String.valueOf(value));
}
public void printf(Object value) {
  printf(value.toString());
}
```

```java
/**
 * Print a double in a field of the current
 * width, with the current number of digits to the
 * right of the decimal point and using the current
 * padding character and justification.
 *
 * @param value the value to print
 */
public void printf(double value) {
  printf(trimDigits(String.valueOf(value)));
}

/**
 * Print a float in a field of the current
 * width, with the current number of digits to the
 * right of the decimal point and using the current
 * padding character and justification.
 *
 * @param value the value to print
 */
public void printf(float value) {
  printf(trimDigits(String.valueOf(value)));
}
/*
 * The next set of methods use printf() followed
 * by a call to println() to add the newline to
 * the formatted output from printf().
 */
public void printfln(String s) {
  printf(s);
  println();
}
public void printfln(boolean value) {
  printf(value);
  println();
}
public void printfln(char value) {
  printf(value);
  println();
}
public void printfln(char[] value) {
  printf(value);
  println();
}
public void printfln(int value) {
  printf(value);
  println();
}
public void printfln(long value) {
  printf(value);
  println();
}
```

```java
public void printfln(Object value) {
  printf(value);
  println();
}
public void printfln(double value) {
  printf(value);
  println();
}
public void printfln(float value) {
  printf(value);
  println();
}

/*
 * Trim the number of digits to the right of the
 * decimal point if there is one.
 */
private String trimDigits(String value) {
  int places;

  if (decimalPlaces == -1)
    return value;
  int pos = value.indexOf(".");
  int exp = value.indexOf("E");
  if (exp == -1)
    places = value.length() - pos - 1;
  else
    places = exp - pos - 1;
  if (places <= decimalPlaces)
    return value;
  String needsRounding =
    value.substring(0, exp);
  if (exp == -1)
    return round(needsRounding);
  else
    return round(needsRounding) +
      value.substring(exp);
}

/*
 * Round the last digit of s. E.g. 1.2345 would be
 * returned as 1.235 and 1.234 would be returned as
 * 1.23.
 * This is done using a java.text.NumberFormat
 * object that had its decimal places set in
 * setDigits() above.
 */
private String round(String s) {
  // form is a java.text.NumberFormat object
  return form.format(Double.parseDouble(s));
}
```

```
/*
 * Create an array of pad characters used for
 * quickly building strings of pad characters
 * by a call to substring (see println(String s))
 */
private static String buildPadding(int width,
                                   char pad)
{
  StringBuffer sbuf = new StringBuffer(width);
  for (int i = 0; i < width; i++)
    sbuf.append(pad);
  return sbuf.toString();
}

private static int MAX_WIDTH = 40;
private static final String spaces =
    buildPadding(MAX_WIDTH, ' ');
private static final String zeros =
    buildPadding(MAX_WIDTH, '0');
private String padding = spaces;
private int width = 0;
private int justify = LEFT;

// -1 means use max precision
private int decimalPlaces = -1;
// used in trimming decimal digits
private NumberFormat form =
    NumberFormat.getInstance();
}
```

C.3   THE CLASS `tio.ReadException`

```
package tio;

import java.io.*;

/**
 * The class <code>ReadException</code> is used to convert
 * java.io.IOExceptions into a subtype of
 * RuntimeException. By doing this, users of ReadInput
 * methods do not need to use throws declarations,
 * simplifying beginning programs. Subtypes of
 * RuntimeException do not need to be declared using
 * a throws clause.
 *
 * @author C. E. McDowell
 * @version 1.1, Released for Java By Dissection
 *
 */
public class ReadException extends RuntimeException {
```

```
  /**
   * Constructs a ReadException object with no
   * specific message.
   */
  public ReadException() {
    super();
  }

  /**
   * Constructs a ReadException object with the
   * specified message.
   *
   * @param message the error message
   */
  public ReadException(String message) {
    super(message);
  }
}
```

C.4   THE CLASS `tio.Console`

```
package tio;

import java.io.*;

/**
 * The class <code>Console</code> is a convenience class.
 * It contains a static variable <code>in</code> that is
 * initialized to refer to a ReadInput object, reading
 * from the standard input stream System.in.
 * It also contains a static variable <code>out</code>
 * that is initialized to refer to a FormattedWriter,
 * writing to the output stream System.out.
 */
public class Console {
  public final static ReadInput in =
        new ReadInput(new InputStreamReader(System.in));
  public final static FormattedWriter out =
        new FormattedWriter(System.out);
}
```

C.5 THE CLASS tio.PrintFileWriter

```java
package tio;

import java.io.*;

/**
 * The class <code>PrintFileWriter</code> is a
 * convenience class. It adds one constructor to its
 * parent class, PrintWriter. This new constructor
 * takes the name of a file.
 * <p>
 * <code>new PrintFileWriter(fileName)</code> is the
 * same as <code>
 * new PrintWriter(new FileWriter(fileName))
 * </code>.
 */
public class PrintFileWriter extends PrintWriter {
  public PrintFileWriter(String filename)
     throws IOException
  {
    super(new FileWriter(filename));
  }
}
```

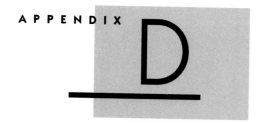

Summary of Selected Swing Components

Early versions of Java provided the GUI building package AWT. Later, the more comprehensive and flexible GUI package Swing was added. In this appendix we provide a summary of selected Swing components. The components covered are those that correspond to the GUI building components in the original AWT package. We selected this subset of Swing because it includes the components most commonly used.

All the components described have additional features that we don't discuss here. For a complete description of the methods available with any component, check the documentation that came with your Java development system. This information is also freely available from JavaSoft on the World Wide Web at *www.javasoft.com*.

Although already covered, for ease of reference we include the classes `JButton`, `JLabel`, and `JTextField` in this section. Included in the descriptions are the names of the primary listeners that can be added to the various components. We described these listeners in Section 9.7.

D.1 THE CLASS `JButton`

This book contains several examples of the use of the class `JButton`. You construct a `JButton` by passing it a string that is used as the label for the button. To have some action performed when a button is pressed, you add an instance of `ActionListener` to the `JButton` object, using `addActionListener()`. A second string, called the *action command*, is associated with a button. This command is passed to the `action-Performed()` method of any `ActionListener` as part of the `ActionEvent`. By changing the action command, you can change the behavior of a button as the program executes.

A `JComboBox` component creates a pull-down list of options from which to choose. You create an empty `JComboBox` object and then add items. In its simplest form, the items are strings. The item currently selected is displayed when the list isn't pulled down. To have some action performed when a new item is chosen, you add an `ItemListener` to the `JComboBox` object.

The following example shows what a `JComboBox` object looks like.

```
//JComboBoxTest.java - a pull-down menu
import javax.swing.*;
import java.awt.*;

class JComboBoxTest {
  public static void main(String[] args) {
    JFrame frame = new JFrame("JComboBoxTest");
    Container display = frame.getContentPane();
    JComboBox list = new JComboBox();

    list.addItem("Java");
    list.addItem("C++");
    list.addItem("Pascal");
    list.addItem("Ada");
    display.add(list, BorderLayout.NORTH);
    frame.pack();
    frame.show();
  }
}
```

The screen shot in part (a) is the normal view, showing `Java` selected. The screen shot in part (b) is what happens when you press the mouse button while pointing at the `JComboBox` object and then drag down to select `C++`.

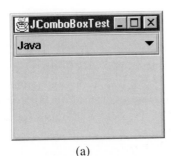

(a)

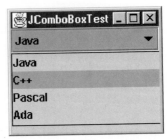

(b)

D.3   THE CLASS JList

A JList component creates a list of options from which to choose. It is similar to a JComboBox, except that the list is always displayed instead of being hidden and then displayed only when selected. The currently selected item is highlighted, and more than one item can be selected simultaneously. To have some action performed when a new item is selected, you add an ItemListener, as for JComboBox. The list items can be something other than simple strings. A JList can be made scrollable by placing it inside a JScrollPane (discussed in Section D.8).

```
//JListTest.java - a simple list of items
import javax.swing.*;
import java.awt.*;

class JListTest {
  public static void main(String[] args) {
    JFrame frame = new JFrame("JListTest");
    Container display = frame.getContentPane();
    String[] items = {"Java", "C++", "Pascal", "Ada", "Fortran"};
    JList list = new JList(items);

    display.add(list);
    frame.pack();
    frame.show();
  }
}
```

Here is the output. We selected the first item, Java.

D.4   THE CLASS JLabel

A JLabel is a very simple component. It displays static text or an image. No events are particular to the class JLabel. Because a JLabel is also a Component, you could add a ComponentListener to it. You can change the text by calling set-Text(), but the user can't edit the text.

The `JLabel` constructor accepts an optional second parameter that can be used to set the alignment of the text. The possible values for the alignment parameter are `JLabel.LEFT_ALIGNMENT`, `JLabel.RIGHT_ALIGNMENT`, `JLabel.CENTER_ALIGNMENT`, `JLabel.TOP_ALIGNMENT`, and `JLabel.BOTTOM_ALIGNMENT`. We used labels in `MiniCalc` in Section 8.4

D.5 THE CLASS `JTextField`

A `JTextField` is like a `JLabel`, but the user can edit it. `JTextField` is the standard component for getting simple keyboard input such as numbers or strings from the user. It can be constructed with a default string to display, or it can be constructed to have space for a fixed number of characters.

To have an action performed when the text is changed, you have two options. In our earlier examples we added an `ActionListener`. The `ActionListener`'s `actionPerformed()` method is called when the user hits Return in the `JTextField`. For finer control over text changes, you can add a `TextListener` to the `JTextField` object. The `textValueChanged()` method in `TextListener` is called whenever any change is made to the text, which includes adding or deleting a single character. As shown in the `MiniCalc` example in Section 8.4, you can call the `getText()` method of the `JTextField` to identify the new contents of the field.

Whether a `JTextField` is editable by the user can be controlled with the method `setEditable()`. The default is for the text to be editable. Calling `setEditable()` with `false` changes it to be not editable.

D.6 THE CLASS `JTextArea`

A `JTextArea` is like a `JTextField`, except that it can display mutliple lines. When you place the `JTextArea` in a `JScrollPane`, the text area can be scrolled. In a scrollable container, you can specify the number of lines to display and the number of characters per line when constructing the `JTextArea`. In addition to replacing the entire text string associated with a `JTextArea`, you can replace portions of the text. You can also respond to changes in the text by using a `TextListener`, as with `JTextField`.

Using a `JTextArea`, adding simple text editing capability to any application is trivial. The `JTextArea` is a simple editor that supports insertion and deletion of text. In the following example you can edit the text in the window with the usual editing operations. The mouse and arrow keys can be used to move the insertion point or highlight a section to replace or delete with the Delete or Backspace key.

This example creates a small text area to display four lines of at least 20 characters each. Any text that goes beyond this can be viewed by using the scroll bars.

```
//TextAreaTest.java
import javax.swing.*;
import java.awt.*;

class JTextAreaTest {
  public static void main(String[] args) {
    JFrame frame = new JFrame("TextAreaTest");
    Container display = frame.getContentPane();
    JTextArea area = new JTextArea(4, 20);
    JScrollPane pane = new JScrollPane(area);

    area.append("This is a scrollable text area.\n");
    area.append("It was constructed to display 4 lines");
    area.append(" of 20 characters.\n");
    area.append("The scrollbars can be used to view");
    area.append(" text that doesn't ");
    area.append("fit into the window.\n");
    area.append("This is the fourth line.\n");
    area.append("This is the fifth line.\n");
    display.add(pane);
    frame.pack();
    frame.show();
  }
}
```

The following are four views of the output. The screen shot in part (a) shows the one that comes up first. Part (b) shows the window after the user has scrolled to the right. Part (c) shows how the mouse can be used to drag and select text. If Delete were hit at the point shown in part (c), the highlighted text would be deleted, resulting in the text shown in part (d).

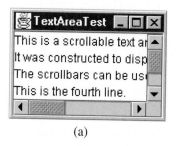

(a)

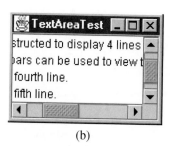

(b)

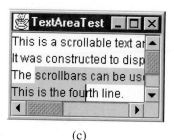

(c)

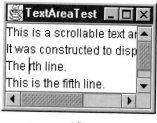

(d)

D.7 THE CLASS JPanel

A JPanel has no appearance of its own. A JPanel is a Container used to group several components. For example, a JFrame's content pane, using a BorderLayout manager, can display only five components. However, because any one of those five components could be a JPanel, you can actually display any number of components. You can of course put JPanels inside JPanels.

The following example places a JPanel on the north and south borders of the main content pane and then places two labels in each of the JPanel objects. To fill out the display, additional labels are placed in the remaining BorderLayout positions.

```
//JPanelTest.java - a simple container
import javax.swing.*;
import java.awt.*;

class JPanelTest {
  public static void main(String[] args) {
    JFrame frame = new JFrame("JPanelTest");
    Container display = frame.getContentPane();
    JPanel top = new JPanel(new BorderLayout());
    JPanel bottom = new JPanel(new BorderLayout());

    top.add(new JLabel("one west"),BorderLayout.WEST);
    top.add(new JLabel("one east"),BorderLayout.EAST);
    bottom.add(new JLabel("two north"), BorderLayout.NORTH);
    bottom.add(new JLabel("two south"), BorderLayout.SOUTH);
    display.add(top, BorderLayout.NORTH);
    display.add(bottom, BorderLayout.SOUTH);
    display.add(new JLabel("  display center  "),
                BorderLayout.CENTER);
    display.add(new JLabel("display west"),BorderLayout.WEST);
    display.add(new JLabel("display east"),BorderLayout.EAST);
    frame.pack();
    frame.show();
  }
}
```

In the output the labels "two north" and "two south" are flush left because the default alignment for labels is left-aligned.

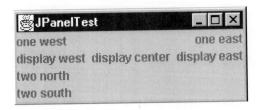

D.8 THE CLASS JScrollPane

A JScrollPane is like a JPanel that can be scrolled. A JScrollPane can contain only a single component, but because that Component can be a JPanel, the JScrollPane can effectively scroll any collection of components.

We showed a simple example of a JScrollPane in the preceding JTextArea example. In the following example we included several of the components described earlier in this appendix.

```java
//JScrollPaneTest.java
import javax.swing.*;
import java.awt.*;

class JScrollPaneTest {
  public static void main(String[] args) {
    JFrame frame = new JFrame("JScrollPaneTest");
    Container display = frame.getContentPane();
    JPanel panel = new JPanel(new BorderLayout());
    JScrollPane pane = new JScrollPane(panel);

    panel.add(new JButton("North"), BorderLayout.NORTH);
    panel.add(new JTextField("South"), BorderLayout.SOUTH);
    panel.add(new JLabel("Center"), BorderLayout.CENTER);
    String[] listItems = {"West1", "West2", "West3"};
    JList list = new JList(listItems);
    panel.add(list, BorderLayout.WEST);
    JComboBox choice = new JComboBox();
    choice.addItem("East1");
    choice.addItem("East2");
    choice.addItem("East3");
    panel.add(choice, BorderLayout.EAST);
    display.add(pane);
    frame.pack();
    frame.show();
  }
}
```

In part (a) the screen shot shows the display when the program starts. By default the JFrame makes itself large enough to show the entire JScrollPane. We used the desktop resize facility to reduce the size of the window, as shown in part (b). Note that scrollbars have been added automatically.

(a)   (b)

Index